The
DISCOVERY
of DEDUCTION

An INTRODUCTION *to* FORMAL LOGIC

by Joelle Hodge;
Aaron Larsen, DA;
and Shelly Johnson, PhD

CLASSICAL
SUBJECTS
CREATIVELY
TAUGHT™

The Discovery of Deduction:
An Introduction to Formal Logic
© Classical Academic Press®, 2009
Version 2.2

ISBN: 978-1-60051-033-5

Cover art and interior design by Lenora Riley
Illustrations by Jason Rayner

Classical Academic Press
515 S. 32nd St.
Camp Hill, PA 17011

www.ClassicalAcademicPress.com

VP.05.22

TABLE OF CONTENTS

Unit III: Categorical Syllogisms

Unit IV: Terms and Definitions

Appendices

Note: Throughout this book, you will see URLs that look like this: <http://capress.link/dd1006>. All you have to do is type that URL (without the angle brackets <>) into the address field of your browser and it will take you directly to the correct website. We have also provided a complete list of these links on ClassicalAcademicPress.com under the Support tab on *The Discovery of Deduction* product page.

LESSON 1.1
Formal vs. Informal Logic

POINTS TO REMEMBER

Formal Logic
- Reasoning in the abstract
- Mostly **deductive**
- Concentrates on understanding the **form** of an argument
- Can be analyzed using **symbols**

Informal Logic
- Evaluating the end product of reasoning
- Mostly **inductive**
- Concentrates on evaluating the **content** of an argument
- Deals with **ordinary-language arguments** in the interchange of ideas between people

> PERHAPS SOMEONE WILL SAY, 'WHY CANNOT YOU WITHDRAW FROM ATHENS, SOCRATES, AND HOLD YOUR PEACE?' . . . I TELL YOU THAT NO GREATER GOOD CAN HAPPEN TO A MAN THAN TO DISCUSS HUMAN EXCELLENCE EVERY DAY . . . AND THAT THE UNEXAMINED LIFE IS NOT WORTH LIVING.[1]
> —SOCRATES

Logic, the art and science of reasoning, is commonly divided into two main sections: **formal** and **informal logic**. (You may already have studied informal logic, particularly **fallacies**, in *The Art of Argument*.) Formal logic looks at reasoning in the abstract and focuses primarily on **deductive reasoning**, which deals with types of arguments in which the conclusion must be true if the premises used to support it are true. Formal logic studies how an argument is put together—the form, or structure, of arguments—rather than what the argument is about—the content, or substance, of arguments.

For example, consider the following argument: "All men are mortal. Socrates is a man. Therefore, Socrates is mortal." Formal logic is less concerned with the *content* of an argument—if "Socrates is mortal" is true or false—but very much concerned with the *form* of the argument—if the logical steps taken to get from "All men are mortal" to "Socrates is mortal" are **valid** or **invalid**. It is not that the content of deductive arguments is not important—it certainly is. However, when people argue deductively, they often begin with **statements**, which are called **propositions** in **deductive logic**. Most, if not all, people accept these propositions as true. They then use the process of deduction to discover new truths and ideas based on those accepted truths.

For instance, in the previous argument about Socrates, the first two propositions of the argument are a given. That is, no one would doubt those propositions. So, the focus of this argument would not be on whether or not the facts of the argument are true, because everyone knows they are, but rather on whether or not the argument is structured correctly. This is typically true of deductive arguments. Because the propositions in the argument are often considered to be true, the analysis of the argument focuses on the form of the argument to see if the reasoning process is correct. This concentration on form means that the content of a formal argument is more or less interchangeable, which is why the ordinary language of such arguments is often replaced with symbols. Using symbols to replace the ordinary language in an argument, and then evaluating the relationships between those symbols, will help you to learn how to analyze the form of arguments more easily.

Let's look at another example of this:

All readers of excellent literature are people who think deeply.

All habitual readers of Shakespeare are people who read excellent literature.

Therefore, all habitual readers of Shakespeare are people who think deeply.

As you can see from the argument above, most, if not all, people would agree with both the first and second propositions. Therefore, the focus of this argument is not so much on the content of the propositions as it is on whether or not the argument is structured correctly so that we can know that the person making this argument is reasoning properly from **truth** to truth.

The most fundamental difference between formal and informal logic is that formal logic focuses on the structure of an argument, whereas informal logic focuses on evaluating the weight and relevance of the evidence. That is, informal logic focuses on evaluating the *content* of ordinary-language arguments, while deductive logic focuses on evaluating the structure of an argument. The ordinary-language arguments found in informal logic are usually inductive in nature, arguing from certain particular evidence or observations to a more general conclusion

that is probable but not certain. One historian of logic described informal logic as "**dialectical** logic" because it is the language of debate and the interchange of ideas between people.[2] While it is true that people can use both types of logic individually or in conversation, people often use deductive logic, whether they realize it or not, to make sense of the world around them. In some ways, it is the simplest type of logic because people use single truths they already possess or believe in order to arrive at new truths.

As a matter of fact, even though you may not be aware of it, you use formal logic regularly. Every day, in order to discover new truths or new knowledge, you use propositions or truths that you believe to be true. Sometimes you use this process in order to discover simple truths, such as making observations about things you see every day. For instance, you might notice a child in a certain school uniform and reason, "All children I have seen who wear that uniform go to Seton Preparatory School, so I bet that child goes to Seton Preparatory School." Other times, you use formal logic to discover complex truths, such as when you make choices regarding ethics. For example, you might reason, "If I want to contribute to society, I should start by being a good neighbor. I think I will help my new neighbors move into their house today." (Of course, you are assuming in this argument that helping your new neighbors move into their house is the way to be a good neighbor.)

In order to help you understand how you can use formal logic to discover both complex and simple truths, consider the following examples. You have probably heard the famous Latin saying *Cogito ergo sum*, which, translated into English, means "I think; therefore I am." A French philosopher named René Descartes originally coined this famous statement.[3] Descartes was interested in the source of our knowledge and how we can know whether or not what we believe is accurate. In other words, because Descartes was aware of how easily human beings can be deceived by their thought processes, he wondered how humans could know whether or not any of their beliefs were actually true. Therefore, he decided he would question everything he believed in order to determine if he could find any truth that was undeniable or self-evident. As he did this, he soon realized that his doubts were evidence of his own thought processes. After all, a person must think in order to doubt, and there cannot be thought unless there is a sentient—

EVERY DAY, IN ORDER TO DISCOVER NEW TRUTHS OR NEW KNOWLEDGE, YOU USE PROPOSITIONS OR TRUTHS THAT YOU BELIEVE TO BE TRUE.

thinking—being generating those thoughts. Therefore, Descartes reasoned that the one undeniable truth was that his thoughts were evidence of his existence.[4]

If you were to translate this argument into formal logic, you would write something like this:

> All beings that think are (i.e., they exist).
>
> I think.
>
> Therefore, I am (i.e., I exist).[5]

Some people might argue that this is a waste of a deductive argument. After all, who really questions whether or not he exists? Although many people do not ponder questions such as this, philosophers certainly do, and deductive logic is one tool that allows them to reach conclusions and therefore learn more about reality, knowledge, or values.

But let's look at a more practical example of deductive logic, something about which ordinary people might think. Imagine that two different people are considering whether or not to vote for a particular political candidate whom we will call Candidate X. This candidate believes in increasing taxes to fund social programs. One person might argue the following:

> All candidates who wish to provide social programs care for the citizens of a nation.
>
> Candidate X wishes to provide social programs.
>
> Therefore, Candidate X cares for the citizens of the nation.

The other person might argue the following:

> All candidates who believe in increasing taxes will hurt the economy.
>
> Candidate X desires to increase taxes.
>
> Therefore, Candidate X will hurt the economy.

Notice that although these two people arrived at very different views of the candidate, they both used deductive logic to arrive at those views. That is, they used propositions that they believed to be true—the first two propositions in both of the arguments—to discover a third and new proposition. One person believes that Candidate X will care for the citizens of the nation. The other believes the candidate will hurt the economy. Both conclusions, or new beliefs, come from previous propositions the two people already believed to be true.

Did you know that this same deductive process often occurs in your mind when you buy a new product as a result of advertising? Let's say, for example, that you see an advertisement about a toothpaste that is guaranteed to whiten teeth. As a result of that commercial, you purchase the toothpaste and start using it. Your reasoning for purchasing the toothpaste might look something like this:

> People who want to have whiter teeth use toothpaste A.
>
> I want to have whiter teeth.
>
> I will use toothpaste A.

As you can see, people use formal deductive arguments to arrive at conclusions about things as simple as toothpaste and as complex as theories of their own existence. However, you should be aware that it is possible to misuse deductive arguments, whether you are reasoning about simple or complex things. Therefore, as we proceed through the rest of this book, you will learn both how to structure your own proper formal arguments and how to critique others' formal arguments. In this way, you will become proficient in the two key aspects of formal deductive logic: construction and analysis.

DEFINE

1. Logic:

_____

_____

_____

2. Formal Logic:

_____

_____

_____

3. Informal Logic:

_____

_____

_____

_____

4. Dialectical Logic:

_____

_____

_____

ANSWER

1. What is the most important, or fundamental, difference between formal and informal logic?

_____

_____

_____

2. Why aren't very many symbols used in informal logic?

_____

_____

_____

_____

DEDUCTION IN ACTION

Logic and Socratic Dialogue

Some of the most interesting examples of logic are the dialogues of an ancient Greek philosopher named Socrates. Socrates was devoted to helping people examine their thoughts, search for wisdom, and overcome error and illogical thinking. Socrates was so dedicated to this goal, in fact, that it eventually led to his death. Don't worry, those results are not typical to the study of logic. It is not likely you will suffer any negative results from pursuing logic (other than occasionally encountering your own illogical thoughts); it is more likely that you will gain a great deal of benefit from it. However, if you would like to learn more about the story of Socrates and his pursuit of wisdom, you can find it in a dialogue called the *Apology.*

You can find this dialogue, as well as the others mentioned in this book, at the following link: <http://capress.link/dd0101>.

You can also download a copy of the *Apology* from this link: <http://capress.link/dd0102>.

Read the Apology *and then answer the following questions:*

1. What did the Delphic oracle reveal to Socrates?

2. How did Socrates go about trying to prove the Delphic oracle wrong?

3. Why did Socrates' attempt to prove the oracle wrong anger some of his fellow citizens?

4. What were the two charges brought against him?

5. When Socrates was found guilty, he made a joke about what his sentence should be. What did he say his sentence should be, and why did he say it should be that?

6. Why, according to Socrates himself, could he not stop himself from doing what he was doing?

LESSON 1.2
Deductive vs. Inductive Reasoning

POINTS TO REMEMBER

Deductive Logic
- Starts with **given propositions** or **axioms**
- Evaluated as either valid or invalid
- Deals with certainty (given the premises)

Inductive Logic
- Starts with observations (used as **evidence**)
- Evaluated as either strong or weak
- Deals with probability

> LOGIC IS THE ANATOMY OF THOUGHT.
> —JOHN LOCKE[1]

The Art of Argument emphasized that informal logic tends to be more inductive and formal logic tends to be more deductive. First, let's quickly review the differences between inductive and deductive reasoning. **Inductive reasoning** tends to start with evidence that we can observe and compile. For example, if someone were studying the characteristics of excellent schools, he would carefully examine several examples of schools that are considered to be excellent in order to discover common characteristics between those schools. Those common characteristics become the evidence upon which his inductive argument will be based.

Inductive logic often works toward **generalizations** that are reasonably accurate with more or less **probability**. This means that inductive reasoning does not lend itself to absolute certainty, which is why inductive arguments are evaluated as "strong" or "weak." In our example of the study about the characteristics of excellent schools, the researcher might discover that all of the schools he examined had high expectations for their students. Therefore, he might claim that one characteristic of an excellent school is that it has high expectations for its students. It would be difficult to prove absolutely that this characteristic is a cause of a school's excellence, but the more careful and thorough the work of the researcher, and the more schools he examines in his study, the more probable his conclusions become.

Deductive reasoning, on the other hand, does not start with observations of evidence so exclusively, but rather with a proposition (a statement that can be proven true or false) that is used as a given to start an argument. Examples of propositions that could be used in such an argument are: "All men are mortal" or "Thoughts indicate a thinking being" (do you remember Descartes' argument from the last chapter?). These propositions are generally assumed as a starting point, or as givens (things that are accepted as self-evident), and are often called axioms or **postulates**. Deductive reasoning focuses on things that are either "black" or "white," which is why deductive arguments are evaluated in the more

certain terms of "valid" or "invalid." In contrast, inductive reasoning tends to focus on "shades of gray." For example, if you consider the postulate "All men are mortal," you will note that men are either mortal or they are not. This is a black-or-white issue, so you know this postulate is based on deductive reasoning. On the other hand, if you consider the characteristics that create an excellent school, you will note that they are more difficult to determine absolutely, which places them in the "shades of gray" area of inductive reasoning.

Since we can analyze inductive reasoning, just as we can deductive reasoning, there are approaches to induction that could be classified as "formal logic."[2] After all, inductive arguments can be analyzed in ways that focus only on the form or structure of the argument and in ways that don't involve the back-and-forth, interpersonal dimension of debate between people. But remember, we are discussing inductive reasoning in this chapter for the sake of review. The primary focus of the rest of this book will be on deductive reasoning, with only an occasional mention of inductive logic as a basis for comparison.

REVIEW
DEFINE

1. Inductive Reasoning:

_____

_____

_____

_____

2. Deductive Reasoning:

_____

_____

_____

_____

3. Evidence:

_____

_____

_____

_____

FILL IN THE BLANK

1. Inductive reasoning tends to start with _____ that we can _____ and compile. It often works toward _____ that are reasonably accurate with more or less _____. This means that inductive reasoning does not lend itself to absolute _____.

2. Deductive arguments are evaluated as either _____ or _____, and inductive arguments are evaluated as either _____ or _____.

DEDUCTION IN ACTION
A Look at Philosophy

Throughout this book, you will notice that we include all sorts of different arguments to help you understand how deductive logic works. A person can actually use deductive reasoning in any type of argument concerning any subject. However, there are some fields of study or areas of life in which people may more commonly rely on deductive logic, and therefore, in those situations, you may see more of those types of arguments than others.

For example, deductive logic is integral to the work, study, and thought processes of philosophy. The word "philosopher" derives from the Greek words *philos*, meaning "love," and *sophia*, which means "wisdom." Philosophers, therefore, are lovers of wisdom, and they attempt to discover wisdom and truth about the underlying concepts and beliefs held by mankind. As you can imagine, since beliefs and concepts aren't things that are easily measured, philosophers cannot do scientific experiments to test whether they are correct or incorrect. Therefore, they often use *a priori* truths in order to discover new truths, which, of course, is deductive logic. In fact, Peter Kreeft, a modern philosopher, said, "Logic is to philosophy what a telescope is to astronomy or a cookbook to a meal. It is an instrument. It is no substitute for the real thing, but it makes the 'real thing' work much better."[3] Philosophers generally prefer to use deductive rather than inductive arguments because deductive arguments are certain, whereas inductive arguments are only probable.

You can see this reliance on deductive philosophy in the works of the earliest philosophers. For example, the following quote is by early Greek philosopher Anaximander concerning his beliefs about the origin of men. Because Anaximander could not directly observe the origin of man, he attempted to figure out the truth using logic. Notice his argument:

> [Anaximander said] that in the beginning man was born from animals of a different sort, arguing from the fact that whereas animals are soon able to fend for themselves, the young of humans are dependent for a long period of time. Hence, if man had been in the beginning as he is now, he would never have been able to survive.
>
> He held that there arose from warm water and earth creatures which were either fish or fish-like. Inside these humans were formed, remaining like fetuses until the time of puberty. At this time the creatures broke open, and men and women already capable of getting food for themselves emerged.[4]

Put Anaximander's argument into your own words. Then answer the following question: What a priori *truth does Anaximander use to reach his new truth?*

LESSON 1.3
Categorical vs. Propositional Logic

POINTS TO REMEMBER

Categorical Logic
- Basic building block is a category of things called a **term**
- Building blocks are connected by the "being" verb[1]

Propositional Logic
- Basic building block is a statement, called a proposition
- Building blocks are connected by **logical operators**

> HE THAT CANNOT REASON IS A FOOL.
> HE THAT WILL NOT IS A BIGOT.
> HE THAT DARE NOT IS A SLAVE.
> —ANDREW CARNEGIE[2]

As you have probably realized by this point, there are several different types of formal logic. You may wonder, as you learn more about them, why it is necessary for them to exist. You may also wonder how to move between the different types of logic and how to use them properly in conjunction with one another.

To understand the *purpose* of the different types of logic, it may help you to consider that they are like the different magnification settings of a microscope. These different levels of magnification allow you to go from a broad view of something to a very close, detailed view. Similarly, the different types of logic allow you to look at human thought from broad or detailed perspectives.

Let's look at this analogy using the two most widely studied types of formal logic: **categorical logic** and **propositional logic**. Keep in mind that the differences between these two types of formal logic are similar to the differences between the levels of a microscope's magnification. The basic component of categorical logic is an individual noun (or noun phrase) called a term, which represents a **category** of things. When we use categorical logic, it is like we are examining human thought very closely and in great detail, as though we are using a very high magnification on a microscope. On the other hand, the basic building block of *propositional* logic is an entire sentence called a proposition. When we use propositional logic, it is like we are looking at thought processes from a distance in order to get a better view of more comprehensive, complex thinking operations. It is as though we are looking at them using a very low magnification on a microscope.

Let's look at a few examples to illustrate this point more clearly. In the first argument that follows, there is a **categorical syllogism**, which is the key argument type in categorical logic. You will notice that it deals with three single, specific categories: people, compassionate beings, and me (I). Through connecting these three categories, a specific point is made: I should be compassionate.

All people should be compassionate beings.

I am a person.

Therefore, I should be a compassionate being.

Now look at the following example of propositional logic:

If I want to improve the world, I should help my neighbor.

I want to improve the world.

Therefore, I will help my neighbor.

This second type of argument is called a **hypothetical syllogism**, and it is one of the argument types of propositional logic. You will notice that it is a more complex argument because it is dealing with a hypothetical, possible scenario—the possibility that I might want to improve the world and what I should do based on that desire. Although I do discuss some other things—the world, my neighbor, and me—I do so in the context of this broad, hypothetical look at the world.

It is accurate to say that categorical logic, while it can deal with abstract concepts, is primarily used to reason about a few *actual* things, while propositional logic reasons with complex reasoning situations, such as **hypotheticals**, **either-or scenarios**, or **dilemmas**. To return to our microscope analogy, categorical logic helps us examine specific things up close, as if under high magnification. Propositional logic helps us examine things from a distance to get the big picture and general outline of a thing or idea, as if under low magnification.

For another example, consider the following situation. The other day, I went to meet my friend at the school at which she works in order to help her set up her classroom. Unfortunately, on the way there, I got lost and ended up being forty minutes late to meet her. When I got there, my friend said, "I'm glad you're OK. I thought that either you had forgotten about our meeting or that something had happened to you on the way over. Since I didn't think you would forget the meeting, I was worried something had happened." In this situation, my friend was using propositional logic. She used entire propositions, or complete thoughts, to reason about why I was late. You will notice that her use of propositional logic allowed her to reason about

the whole scenario in general, and it also allowed her to hypothesize different reasons why I might be late.

In contrast, if my friend had used categorical logic, she might have reasoned like this:

All people who are late have forgotten their appointments.

My friend is late.

Therefore, my friend has forgotten her appointment.

Or, she could have reasoned:

All people who are late have been in accidents.

My friend is late.

Therefore, she has been in an accident.

You will notice that some similar thought processes occur in both the propositional and the categorical arguments. However, the categorical argument deals with one concrete idea at a time, as if looking at the situation up close, detail by detail. The propositional argument examines complex, possible scenarios all at once, as if looking at the entire situation from a distance.

Now let's switch to a different analogy that will help you understand how to *move between* the different types of logic. We could say that the different types of logic are like different cultures. If you traveled to another country, you would most likely find that its culture was different from yours. Even though you would notice some things that were similar to your own culture, such as the presence of stores, holidays being celebrated, and some sort of transportation system being in place, there would be enough differences that you would probably have to adapt to the new culture quite a bit. Different cultures tend to have unique laws, procedures, customs, and symbols to which newcomers must adjust. You might experience a bit of culture shock at first, but soon you would adjust and be able to appreciate the uniqueness and adventure of the new place.

Just as different cultures contain unique procedures, rules, languages, and practices, so do the different types of logic. Another similarity is that all types of logic have some things in common with one another, as do cultures. For

instance, you will find that the different types of formal logic use some similar terms, and that all of the different types of arguments have rules for constructing good arguments and avoiding bad ones. Such comparisons will help you to move between the different types of logic because you will be able to follow the common concepts between them. However, you will also find, just as with understanding a different culture, that you must learn the different aspects of each individual logic system in order to understand and appreciate it properly. Although this may frustrate you at first when you encounter a new type of logic, realize that soon you will adapt and be able to appreciate it for its own sake.[3]

At this point, you may be wondering why we are starting with categorical logic. After all, there are a number of other logic textbooks that begin with propositional logic (or a branch of it sometimes called truth-functional logic).[4] There are several reasons for our decision to start with categorical logic, and if you are like many students, it may help you to study this book more thoroughly if you understand the logic behind the way it is set up.

First, categorical logic is the more traditional logic. It was seen as essential for understanding the thinking processes of many foundational thinkers, such as **Plato**, **Aristotle**, **Augustine**, and **Aquinas**. When you read the works of these philosophers, you will find that their writing mirrors the categorical thought processes that you will learn in this book. By studying categorical logic, you will be able to better understand their writing. Furthermore, categorical logic was developed first historically, and unless there's a good reason not to, why not teach first things first? Lastly, our experience has been that students generally find categorical logic easier to understand because it deals with fewer forms. Therefore, when students study categorical logic first, they move from simpler to more complex forms of logic in a systematic manner, much like how students studying math move from simple calculations to more complex operations as they gain more advanced math skills.

As you begin the study of categorical logic, realize that you will learn to analyze the basic units of thought in a clear, systematic manner so that you can more easily proceed to examining complex arguments. In addition, you will follow the learning trajectory of many of history's great thinkers and philosophers.

REVIEW
DEFINE

1. Categorical Logic:

_____

_____

_____

_____

DEFINE (CONTINUED)

2. Propositional Logic:

_____

_____

_____

_____

_____

_____

FILL IN THE BLANK

1. While the basic building block in categorical logic is an individual word called a
   _____, which represents a basic category of things, the basic building block of
   propositional logic is an entire sentence, called a _____.

2. You could say that categorical logic is like the _____ magnification setting on
   a microscope because it allows you to examine things in _____. On the other
   hand, you could say that propositional logic is like the _____ magnification
   setting on a microscope because it allows you to examine things from _____.

EXPLAIN

1. In your own words, explain why it is important to examine issues from a close, detailed
   perspective, as well as from a broad, more comprehensive perspective. Provide an example of
   a subject in which you are currently interested or that is important in our culture right now.
   Explain at least two different things you could learn from examining this topic up close and
   in detail, as well as from a distance in a more general manner.

_____

_____

_____

_____

_____

_____

_____

_____

EXPLAIN (CONTINUED)

2. In your own words, explain why it might be helpful to consider the different types of logic as different cultures. Provide at least two reasons.

_____

_____

_____

_____

_____

_____

_____

_____

_____

DEDUCTION IN ACTION

Logic and the Movies

As mentioned before, people can use deductive logic to argue about any topic in any field of study. Having said that, sometimes deductive logic shows up in the oddest places and in the oddest ways. Take the movies, for instance. One of the most famous British comedies is a movie called *Monty Python and the Holy Grail*. In one very famous scene in this movie, some townspeople try to prove that a local woman is a witch. A "wise" man in the crowd, Sir Bedevere (along with a little help from a visiting King Arthur), helps them with their logic, and the result is memorable, to say the least. Read the following dialogue and then answer the questions at the end.

Various Peasants: Witch! A witch! We've got a witch!

First Peasant: We have found a witch. May we burn her?

[Various calls to burn her.]

Sir Bedevere: How do you know she is a witch?

Peasants: She looks like one. [Various calls to burn her.]

Sir Bedevere: Bring her forward.

Accused Girl: I'm not a witch! I'm not a witch!

Sir Bedevere: But you are dressed as one.

DEDUCTION IN ACTION (CONTINUED)

Accused Girl: *They* dressed me up like this. And this isn't my nose; it's a false one.

Sir Bedevere: Well?

First Peasant: Well, we did do the nose.

Sir Bedevere: The nose?

First Peasant: And the hat, but she's a witch.

[Yeah, burn her!]

Sir Bedevere: Did you dress her up like this?

Peasants: No. No. No. No. No. Yes. Yes, a bit. A bit. A bit. A bit. She has got a wart.

Sir Bedevere: What makes you think she's a witch?

Second Peasant: Oh, she turned me into a newt.

Sir Bedevere: A newt?

Second Peasant: I got better.

Third Peasant: Burn her anyway! Burn her!

Sir Bedevere: Quiet! Quiet! Quiet! Quiet! There are ways of telling whether she is a witch.

Peasants: Are there? What are they? Tell us!

Sir Bedevere: Tell me, what do you do with witches?

Peasants: Burn them!

Sir Bedevere: And what do you burn apart from witches?

First Peasant: More witches!

Third Peasant: Wood!

Sir Bedevere: So, why do witches burn?

First Peasant: 'cause they're made of . . . wood?

Sir Bedevere: Good!

Peasants: Oh, yeah.

Sir Bedevere: So how do we tell whether she is made of wood?

First Peasant: Build a bridge out of her!

Sir Bedevere: Ah, but can you not also make bridges out of stone?

First Peasant: Oh, yeah.

Sir Bedevere: Does wood sink in water?

First Peasant: No, no.

Third Peasant: It floats. It floats!

First Peasant: Throw her into the pond!

Peasants: Yeah! Yeah! The pond!

DEDUCTION IN ACTION (CONTINUED)

Sir Bedevere: What also floats in water?

Peasants: Bread! Apples! Very small rocks! Cider! Gravy! Cherries! Rum! Churches! Lead!

King Arthur: A duck.

Sir Bedevere: Exactly. So logically. . . ?

Peasants: If she weighs the same as a duck . . . she's made of wood.

Sir Bedevere: And therefore. . . ?

Peasants: A witch? A witch! She's a witch! Burn her!

Sir Bedevere: We shall use my largest scales!

[Various cries.]

Sir Bedevere: Remove the supports.

[Various cries.]

Peasants: A witch! A witch!

Accused Girl: It's a fair cop.*

Sir Bedevere: Who are you who are so wise in the ways of science?

Arthur: I am Arthur, king of the Britons.

Sir Bedevere: My liege.[5]

*"Cop" is a slang term meaning "catch, capture, or purchase."

From what you know about deductive logic so far, see if you can write the aforementioned argument in some semblance of a deductive argument (mind you, it's certainly a silly deductive argument). The "argument" begins when Sir Bedevere claims that there are ways of telling whether or not the woman is a witch.

LESSON 2.1
Part I: Aristotle Gets the Ball Rolling
Classical Origins and Medieval Recovery

POINTS TO REMEMBER

1. The Greek philosophers, particularly Aristotle, developed formal logic.
2. The rediscovery of logic was central to the rebirth of higher learning and the advancement of philosophy and science.

> IT IS THE MARK OF AN EDUCATED MIND TO BE ABLE
> TO ENTERTAIN A THOUGHT WITHOUT ACCEPTING IT.
> —ARISTOTLE[1]

It may help you to think more clearly about logic in general and the different types of logic specifically if you think about it as a discipline that aids people in the search for truth. Since the beginning of time, people have been interested in finding truth or in being certain about what they know, or what they think they know. As people began to think about this process and the search for truth, they began to consider rules by which they might be able to determine if their reasoning was good or bad or their beliefs true or false. In determining this, they believed it would aid them in analyzing their beliefs effectively.

The Egyptians and other ancient people first began experimenting with these concepts when they began using geometric concepts to build amazing buildings, such as the pyramids in Egypt and some of the temples in Central and South America. The basis of geometry is the postulate, or axiom, which is a truth that is accepted as a given. For instance, it is accepted as a given that the three angles of a triangle always equal 180 degrees. Everything from geometry flows from these axioms, or postulates. Therefore, geometry would work like this: Since axiom A is true and axiom B is true, then C must follow. Since the Egyptians and ancient peoples in the Americas used laws like this, they were familiar with the concept of logic, although they may not have had a formal program of study centered on it.

However, as the ancient Greek civilization developed, people became interested in identifying and codifying the logic they found in geometry and other reasoning processes they were using to discover the truth of the world around them. In fact, the ancient Greek philosopher Aristotle, who lived from 384 to 322 BC, wrote the first logic "textbook" that has survived the passage of time. This collection of his writings is called the *Organon*, which means "instrument." This title was used because logic was seen as an instrument, or tool, of science and philosophy.[2] Aristotle addresses various topics in the *Organon*, including informal fallacies, but its primary focus is categorical logic.[3] Aristotle was fascinated by all sorts of subjects, including philosophy, politics, science, and medical studies. He believed that our senses were the main vehicle through which we discovered the truth. Therefore, he believed people should determine those things which could not be denied by the senses and then derive

everything deductively from those *a priori* (self-evident) truths. Because of Aristotle's influence, categorical logic dominated the field of logic in the ancient world. Even today, categorical logic is sometimes called Aristotelian logic.[4]

It may seem as though a great philosopher such as Aristotle would have easily been able to analyze and categorize all of the rules of logic in his lifetime. However, logicians and philosophers over the years have realized that our thought processes and reasoning systems are so complex that they take a great deal of consideration and analysis from multiple angles. For instance, a school of philosophers called the **Stoics**, founded in the third century BC,[5] loved to study arguments, propositions, and paradoxes that did not fit Aristotle's system of logic.[6] For example, the Stoics liked to study problems in logic such as the liar's paradox. This paradox occurs when someone who has claimed that he always lies utters the phrase, "I am lying." As you can see, this presents a problem. Do we simply accept his assertion that he is, indeed, lying? Or, do we assume that he is lying when he says he is lying and, therefore, he is not lying? The Stoics dealt with propositions and arguments that were more complex than those with which Aristotle's logic dealt.

Although Aristotle's studies in logic did not exhaust the study of human thought, his studies were so significant, useful, and profound that the study of Aristotelian logic dominated the field of logic even into the Middle Ages (AD 456-1400). At first, much of the learning of the classical world was lost in the wake of the fall of Rome and the confusion during the transition to the medieval era. Medieval scholars, therefore, had a considerable amount of rebuilding to do in retrieving and translating past writing in the area of logic.[7] However, once Aristotle's works had been recovered and translated, along with several other key logic texts, medieval scholars were convinced of logic's importance. As William of Ockham (1285-1347), a famous medieval logician, wrote, "Logic is the most useful tool of all the arts."[8]

During the Middle Ages, logicians, scholars, and philosophers recognized that logic was a necessary tool for the progress of philosophy and science. In addition, people desired to understand the world in an orderly way after experiencing so much chaos and confusion in the early Middle Ages, during which time there had been little time for contemplation of how the world worked. Consequently, scholars in the later Middle Ages were particularly attracted to the orderly categories of Aristotle.[9] In fact, many medieval scholars used Aristotelian logic to prove Christian doctrine.[10] For instance, Thomas Aquinas (1225-1274) used Aristotle's logic to develop arguments for the existence of God. The emphasis on Aristotelian logic, at the expense of other approaches, continued throughout the Middle Ages and into the Renaissance. At that time, logic took a firm place, along with grammar and rhetoric, as a member of the "trivium," the three liberal arts considered foundational to education. As people began to rediscover the learning and knowledge that had been lost in the collapse of the Roman Empire, Aristotle's organized system of thinking and classification helped them to begin to make sense of a seemingly chaotic world.

REVIEW
ANSWER

1. Who wrote the first known textbook on logic? What was its title and what did that title mean?

_____

_____

ANSWER (CONTINUED)

2. Summarize the contribution to the field of logic made by the three philosophers (or group of philosophers) listed below.

a. Stoics:

_____

_____

b. Thomas Aquinas:

_____

_____

c. William of Ockham:

_____

_____

3. Explain why Aristotle's categorical logic might have especially appealed to people during the Middle Ages.

_____

_____

_____

4. For another interesting look at the complexities of logic, go to the link listed below and study Zeno's most famous paradox, which is the riddle about Achilles and the Tortoise: <http://capress.link/dd0201>.

In the space provided below, explain Zeno's paradox and why it presents a challenge to logicians even today.

_____

_____

_____

_____

_____

_____

_____

_____

_____

ANSWER (CONTINUED)

5. William of Ockham, a medieval logician mentioned in this chapter, is known for his famous principle called Ockham's razor. Do some research about this principle and then explain its basic idea in the space provided below. You can find information about this principle at the following link: <http://capress.link/dd0202>.

_____

_____

_____

_____

_____

_____

_____

_____

DEDUCTION IN ACTION

Think About It

We want to get you warmed up to thinking about evidence, reasons, and arguments. Look at the quote at the beginning of the chapter and provide an answer for these two questions:

1. Why is it important to be able to entertain an idea without accepting it?

2. Why is entertaining an idea without accepting it especially hard to do?

LESSON 2.2
Part II: Aristotle Is Lost and Then Found
The Growth and Divergence of Modern Logic

POINTS TO REMEMBER

1. During the Renaissance and Reformation, people began to question the prominent status of Aristotelian logic.
2. People like Francis Bacon, John Stuart Mill, and George Boole attempted to address some of the weaknesses and limitations of Aristotelian logic.

> THE LOGIC OF WORDS SHOULD YIELD
> TO THE LOGIC OF REALITIES.
> —LOUIS BRANDEIS[1]

During the Renaissance and Reformation, which took place between the fourteenth and seventeenth centuries, people began to question the prominent status of Aristotelian logic in the curriculum. There were several reasons why this occurred. First, new avenues of thought and new research tools emerged. People became increasingly interested in experience and the information acquired through the senses as a basis for knowledge. For example, the English scholar Francis Bacon (1561-1626) wrote a highly influential work entitled *Novum Organum*, which means "new instrument." Bacon insisted that more attention needed to be paid to inductive logic and less to the deductive logic stressed by Aristotle. Bacon believed that rather than reasoning deductively from *a priori* assumptions, we should collect observations and examples from the world and form theories based on these observations.[2] This new emphasis on induction formed the basis of the scientific method and was largely responsible for the advances in the empirical sciences achieved during the Scientific Revolution. (See *The Argument Builder* for a more in-depth discussion of Francis Bacon and some of his contributions to inductive logic.)

The second reason later scholars did not continue to hold Aristotelian logic in high esteem was the abuse and limitations of Aristotle's logic. One limitation of Aristotle's logic was that he often accepted truths that appeared obvious from common sense that, in actuality, were false. For example, Aristotle had proposed the idea that heavier objects would fall faster than lighter objects based on "common sense" observation. As later scientists, such as Galileo, proved, this was not true. Suddenly, Aristotle's process of arriving at new truths through deduction from *a priori* beliefs appeared to be, at least occasionally, unreliable. Therefore, later scholars, especially in the University of Paris, began to doubt that Aristotelian logic was the "last word" in the field of logic. They began to react to the view that Aristotelian logic was like a gospel truth that could not be questioned. They realized that regarding Aristotelian logic as the best form of logic could prevent scholars from adding new perspectives and fashioning new logical tools, thus limiting advances in science and philosophy. As a result,

Aristotelian logic continued to be taught as a required subject in European universities well into the nineteenth century, but it had lost its status as *the* primary tool of serious scholarship.[3]

As the nineteenth century continued, philosophers and especially mathematicians took a second look at deductive logic and began to develop it in various ways, particularly in the area of propositional logic. For instance, George Boole (1815-1864) developed a system of symbolic logic known as Boolean logic. One of the strengths of Boolean logic was that it provided a logical framework for dealing with arguments or propositions about categories of things that didn't actually exist or that were hypothetical possibilities, such as unicorns or ghosts.[4] This was in contrast to Aristotle's logic, which had focused on propositions about things that *did* exist. Boole also developed a logical system that applied to math, which became known as Boolean algebra, and he and other logicians increasingly applied logic to math. Later scholars began to apply logic to computer systems.[5] Another influential philosopher, John Stuart Mill, explored rules that could help scientists determine cause-and-effect relationships. Cause-and-effect relationships are especially important in many scientific, medical, social, and psychological sciences. For instance, when doctors attempt to discover the catalysts (causes) for diseases like cancer and diabetes, they are studying cause-and-effect relationships. Mill's methods are still studied in modern college logic textbooks, especially in deductive reasoning texts.

These new topics of study in logic were certainly helpful. However, logic increasingly became an isolated, abstract, and specialized "science," rather than an "art" to be studied and used as a tool by all educated people. Perhaps this was partially responsible for logic's slow disappearance from the list of required courses in universities over the next century. It just didn't seem practical for the everyday person anymore. Logic either became an arcane subject that few students ever encountered, or it was repackaged as "critical thinking," which tended to focus more on lists of types of bad arguments. Although the study of critical thinking and the study of bad arguments (also called fallacies) is extremely helpful, people can gain an overly narrow view of logic if they only study fallacies and neglect the useful aspects of a traditional study of deductive logic.

This approach lasted until the 1970s when, partially as a result of the emergence of classical schools and classical curricula, there was a revival of the idea that all thinking people needed to understand the basics of logic as a tool for life.[6] Today, this movement continues and is expanding. As the movement grows, many people are rediscovering the benefits of Aristotelian logic, in conjunction with other types of logic, for clarifying and strengthening thinking.

As you continue your study of logic, it is important to realize that although categorical logic has some limitations, just as all types of logic do, it has helped people in the past to discover and formulate some of the most profound philosophical and scientific truths of our world. Furthermore, this logic still forms the foundation of many fields of study today, such as philosophy and ethics. Learning to use logic well will allow you to strengthen your own thinking and become an effective seeker of truth.

ANSWER

1. What were the two reasons why Aristotelian logic gradually became less dominant after the Middle Ages?

_____

_____

_____

_____

2. Name two of the modern thinkers (people who lived after the Middle Ages) mentioned in this lesson and summarize their contributions to the field of logic.

a. _____

_____

_____

_____

b. _____

_____

_____

_____

DEDUCTION IN ACTION
Thinking About Logic

Throughout this book, as you encounter more Deduction in Action exercises, you will notice that some of them will help you to understand how logic is used in different areas of life, while others will aid you in analyzing other people's arguments. Still other times, the Deduction in Action exercises will ask you to develop your own arguments. Especially at the beginning of the book, don't be too concerned about how good your argument is or if it is structured properly. After all, you have just started learning about logic. At the beginning, focus primarily on putting your thoughts into words. Later, we will help you make sure that your argument is thoroughly developed and properly structured.

Consider this question: Why is it important for you to learn logic? As you will soon learn, all arguments have two main parts: a **conclusion**, which is the point you are proving, and a **premise**, which is the reasoning behind the conclusion. On a separate piece of paper, write a short argument with a premise and conclusion explaining why it is important for you to learn logic. Your conclusion will be this: "It is important for me to learn logic." Your premise should be a specific reason that supports this conclusion. Make sure that your premise is specific and different from the conclusion. For example, you want to avoid arguments like this: "It is important for me to learn logic because logic is a good skill to have." This supporting premise is weak, vague, and unhelpful. The more specific your premise is, the more helpful it will be.

CHAPTER
3
*Formal Logic
and the Three Acts
of the Mind*

DIALOGUE 3.1

Thinking About Thinking
The Nature of Formal Logic

Nate is going for a walk in the wooded outskirts of a college campus when he runs across his friend, Socrates, sitting under a tree.

Nate: Good morning! What are you up to today?

Socrates: Well, I was thinking.

Nate: I might have guessed. What were you thinking about?

Socrates: Actually, I was thinking about thinking.

Nate: *(as he sits down)* Now you're just being evasive. In what way were you thinking about thinking?

Socrates: Actually, I was musing on the subject of formal logic. Remember how I taught you and Tiffany some informal logic? Do you know what the difference is between formal and informal logic?

Nate: Hmm. . . . I guess if you just go by the terminology, you might come to the conclusion that formal logic is where you evaluate the *form* of an argument, and informal logic is where you judge it by other criteria.

Socrates: If you were to draw such a conclusion from the terminology, then you would be on the right track. Let's think a little bit more about what I taught you in our discussions about informal logic. What standards did we use to evaluate recommendations?

Nate: We used the standards of **relevance**, **presumption**, and **clarity**.

Socrates: Absolutely. What were we doing with those standards?

Nate: We were judging arguments.

Socrates: That is what we were doing, for the most part, but remember that the same standards can be used for evaluating explanations and rhetorical tricks.

Nate: Refresh my memory. What is the difference between an **argument** and an **explanation**?

Socrates: While I admit that we philosopher types tend to use those two words in a very specific way, it's not really so far removed from how most people use them. Think about it. If I said that a friend of yours was trying to "argue for" something, what would you assume he was trying to do?

Nate: I would guess that he was trying to convince others to agree with him.

Socrates: You would be guessing correctly. How would he go about trying to convince them?

Nate: He would give them reasons to believe whatever it is.

Socrates: Exactly. He would be making an argument by supporting his **thesis**, or main point, with logical evidence. Now, what if your friend did something that you didn't agree was right, and you were trying to explain his actions? What would you be doing then? Would you be trying to convince yourself that what he did was right, even though you didn't agree with what he did?

Nate: No, not necessarily. You have to make a distinction between *explaining* something and *justifying* it.

Socrates: Why?

Nate: Well, if you were not able to try to understand something without justifying it, it would be hard to make much sense out of anything. For example, if you couldn't keep straight in your mind the difference between an explanation and a justification, you couldn't seek to understand the Mongol invasions without becoming a big fan of Genghis Khan. I guess that's the big difference between an argument and an explanation: An argument is trying to get you to agree with something, whereas an explanation is just trying to help you to understand it.

Socrates: Quite so. Remember also that an argument goes from premise to conclusion, whereas an explanation usually goes from **cause** to **effect**.

Nate: Ah, yes, I remember. Now that we've reviewed, let's get back to this formal logic stuff. In our discussions of informal logic, we mentioned that it is about evaluating arguments, explanations, and rhetorical tricks, and that you do so through the three guidelines of relevance, presumption, and clarity. So how is formal logic different?

Socrates: Well, I mentioned that formal logic is basically thinking about thinking. You could say that informal logic is about weighing, evaluating, and critiquing specific arguments and explanations. Formal logic, on the other hand, tries to break down and understand the process of thinking that people use when they create any argument or explanation. To put it in a nutshell, informal logic is "dialectical" in nature, whereas formal logic is "**structural**."

Nate: Whoa! That's a pretty large nutshell you're using. Please explain what you mean by that.

Socrates: By "dialectical" I mean that informal logic is about the back-and-forth, the ebb-and-flow of argument between people. By "structural" I mean that formal logic is about the process that an individual goes through as he begins to reason from one statement or proposition to another.

Nate: So, informal logic is about evaluating other people's arguments, and formal logic is about your own arguments?

Socrates: Well, that might often be true, but you can also be dialectical with yourself and your own arguments.

Nate: Huh? How can there be a "back-and-forth" or an "ebb-and-flow" when you're the only person in the room?

Socrates: Oh, come, now. Haven't you ever conversed with yourself?

Nate: Well, I don't like to admit it, but yes, sometimes I do. I'd hate to have people think I'm crazy or something, though!

Socrates: There's no need to be ashamed of it. After all, being able to dialogue with oneself, to weigh and critique one's own reasoning as you go along, is a part of what it means to be a person. While the dialectical aspect of informal logic usually involves other people, the important thing to remember is that it is all about weighing, evaluating, and critiquing the results of that reasoning. Formal logic is "structural" because it is more about how the process of good thinking works.

Nate: So then, informal logic is all about making arguments about the results of reasoning, whereas formal logic is more concerned with making explanations about how the process of good reasoning works.

Socrates: Ah, I like how your mind works. That's the basic idea. Informal logic is all about deciding whether or not you should accept or reject the

arguments made by others. It can also be about having that conversation with yourself as you attempt to determine whether the arguments and explanations are fair and make good sense. What we do in formal logic is quite different. In studying formal logic, we break the process of reasoning apart and make sense of the process itself. Informal logic is all about "real-world application," whereas formal logic is about understanding the theory behind reasoning. It's thinking about thinking!

Nate: So what are you thinking about thinking right now?

Socrates: Well, I was just musing over the system of formal logic created by the student of a student of mine.

Nate: You mean Aristotle?

Socrates: Yes, very good. Aristotle was the founder of formal logic. He created a very useful way to understand how the process of thought works

based on three **acts of the mind**, which are **simple apprehension**, **judgment**, and **inference**.

Nate: That sounds kind of interesting. How does this system work?

Socrates: Well, let's take the three acts of the mind one at a time. Let's start with simple apprehension. When you say you "apprehend" something, what is going on in your mind?

Nate: Well, to be honest, I don't use that word too often. But, if I were to say such a thing, I suppose that would mean that I "sense" it.

Socrates: Yes, but there's more to it than that. After you sense that thing, you put it into some sort of category. For example, if you were to see a dog, you would see a four-legged, furry creature with (most likely) big, floppy ears. Then you would mentally put it into a category of things that you identify as dogs. That is a process we call **abstraction**. First you see something, then you pull out a category that seems to fit it, and finally, you mentally put that thing that you see into a category. Do you follow?

Nate: I think so. Hey, is that why deductive logic is called categorical logic? Is it because it works by putting things into categories?

Socrates: That's one reason. There are other categories in this type of logic as well, but that is a conversation for another day. Let's see how the process continues once we have put things into categories. Once you apprehend something, it can become the first building block for logic: a term. You then put together terms to form propositions. That process is called judgment. Then you move from propositions that you do know to ones that you don't know. That process is called inference.

Nate: Whoa! Slow down!

Socrates: OK. I guess the best way for me to explain this is for me to give you an argument and then break it down into those three layers for you.

Let's start with a very commonly used argument.

> All men are mortal.
> Socrates is a man.
> Therefore, Socrates is mortal.

Nate: That argument sounds kind of familiar.

Socrates: I'm not surprised. It seems like every logic textbook and every logic teacher starts right off with an argument about my being mortal. It's a bit unsettling to constantly be reminded of my mortality. Anyway, that argument fits into a pattern that we refer to as a **syllogism**, a special kind of three-statement deductive argument. Each of those statements is what we call a proposition. Each of those propositions takes two terms and shows how they relate to each other.

Nate: So, you would first apprehend the two terms "men" and "mortal" and then show how they relate to each other by saying that "all men are mortal"?

Socrates: Exactly. When you show how two terms relate to each other, that act of the mind is called judgment. As we noted, the result of that act is called a statement or a proposition. Now, when you then move on from the statements "All men are mortal" and "Socrates is a man" and decide on the basis of those two statements that, therefore, "Socrates is mortal," then what have you done?

Nate: Well, you have figured out something that you didn't know on the basis of something that you already did know.

Socrates: In theory. I'm sure that you were not at all ignorant of my mortality beforehand. What you certainly have done, though, is show that if you were to accept the first two propositions, then the last one must follow. The mental act of drawing conclusions on the basis of what you already know (or at least assume) is referred to as the **process of inference**. In this case, it is what we refer to as a **deductive inference** because this is a deductive argument.

Nate: So, you could also do something similar to make an inference from an inductive argument, and it would be called an **inductive inference**?

Socrates: Exactly. You could also use a process of inductive inference to make inductive explanations. However, inductive inference works very differently from deductive inference. In inductive inference, we take propositions that we gather from our observations of the world around us and use them to make "educated guesses" about things we haven't observed yet.

Nate: Educated guesses? That sounds kind of chancy.

Socrates: It is, actually, but some inductive arguments and explanations are very reliable. It all has to do with just how much evidence you can bring to bear on the problem. Unlike deductive arguments, however, the premises of an inductive argument will never make the conclusion absolutely necessary. They will only make it more likely. A deductive argument, if properly formed, is said to be valid. In a valid deductive argument, if you accept the truth of the premises, the conclusion absolutely must be true as well. Inductive arguments aren't like that. Instead, they are said to be either strong or weak.

Nate: It sounds like it would be better to use a deductive argument, since it gives you more certainty.

Socrates: Perhaps so, but there are situations in which we don't really have a choice. There are many times in life when you simply need to draw a conclusion from the information that you have, and you may not be absolutely sure that it is the right conclusion. Such is the human condition, I guess. In any case, most logic teachers like to teach deductive inference before they tackle the complexities and "gray areas" of inductive reasoning. After all, the study of deductive inference was begun earlier—by Aristotle, if you recall—and it is a good foundation for all kinds of formal logic.

Nate: This is very interesting, but I must be getting to class now. I want to hear more about this stuff, and I do hope to see you again soon.

Socrates: You can count on it, my friend!

1. Explain the differences between formal and informal logic or reasoning.

EXPLAIN

_____

_____

_____

_____

_____

2. Explain the differences between a logical argument and an explanation.

_____

_____

_____

_____

3. Explain how people use the three acts of the mind when they make arguments.

_____

_____

_____

_____

_____

_____

_____

_____

_____

_____

_____

_____

_____

EXPLAIN (CONTINUED)

4. Explain why deductive arguments are referred to as valid or invalid, whereas inductive arguments are referred to as strong or weak.

_____

_____

_____

_____

_____

_____

_____

_____

_____

_____

DEFINE

1. Three Acts of the Mind:

a. Simple Apprehension: _____

_____

b. Judgment: _____

_____

c. Inference: _____

_____

2. Syllogism:

_____

_____

_____

3. Inductive Inference:

_____

_____

_____

CHAPTER
3
*Formal Logic
and the Three Acts
of the Mind*

LESSON 3.2
The Three Acts of the Mind

POINTS TO REMEMBER

1. The three basic building blocks of categorical logic are: 1) the term; 2) the proposition; and 3) the argument.
2. The three acts of the mind are: 1) simple apprehension; 2) judgments; and 3) inferences.
3. Simple apprehension occurs when we put things into groups, classes, or categories in our minds.
4. When we think about a relationship between two terms, we make a judgment.
5. We make an inference when, after making one or more judgment propositions, we conclude that yet another proposition necessarily follows from the first ones.

> NEVER BE AFRAID TO SIT AWHILE AND THINK.
> —LORRAINE HANSBERRY[1]

Aristotle, who first organized traditional categorical logic, looked at the subject as you would if you were using blocks to build a structure. He distinguished three basic building blocks in categorical logic and called them terms, propositions, and arguments. They were based on his philosophy of how we reason. He believed that people reason using three acts of the mind, which he named simple apprehension, judgments, and inferences. Through simple apprehension we produce terms, through judgments we produce propositions, and through inferences we produce arguments.

Simple Apprehension

Simple apprehension occurs when we put things into groups, classes, or categories in our minds. We usually do this automatically, without really thinking about it when we are doing it. In other words, simple apprehension seems to come naturally to us as thinking human beings. So, for example, when we see a motorized vehicle with four wheels coming down the road, we automatically think "car." Or, when we see a flying bird land on a pond and swim, we think "duck." We mentally place these things into a group or class of similar things with which we are familiar. Only when we see new things with which we are unfamiliar do we actually think about how they should be categorized. Notice that we always have the impulse to categorize things whether or not we are familiar or unfamiliar with them. When we engage in simple apprehension, it results in our naming the category or class to which something we have apprehended belongs. In categorical logic, the mental category in which we place something is called a term, which is a word or phrase that represents a class of related things.

Judgment

When we think about a relationship between two terms, we make a judgment. For example, if we think about the relationship between the terms "frogs" and "animals," we might think that all frogs are animals. In the world of categorical logic, the relationships we are usually interested in are ones of **class inclusion**. That is, one class, or some members of that class, are included within another class. Subsequently, we think the "frogs" class is included in the "animals" class, but not the opposite, because not all animals are frogs, right? Let's look at another example. When we say, "Socrates is a man," we are really saying that the class of things known as "Socrates" (and he's in a class all by himself) is included within the class of things we refer to as "men."

There are some other types of relationships between terms that we apprehend through the act of judgment, which we will examine a little later. Notice that when we think or speak of the relationship between two terms, we do so in the form of a proposition, such as "All frogs are animals" or "Socrates is a man."

Inference

We make an inference when, after making one or more judgment propositions, we conclude that yet another proposition necessarily follows from the first ones. The syllogism given in the dialogue between Nate and Socrates entitled "Thinking About Thinking: The Nature of Formal Logic" is a good example of this process:

All men are mortal.

Socrates is a man.

Therefore, Socrates is mortal.

Here we first stated a relationship between the terms "men" and "mortal." The term "mortal" is defined as a class of things that must die. Then we stated the relationship between the terms "Socrates" and "men." After doing so, we can see that a third proposition about the relationship between the terms "Socrates" and

"mortal" necessarily follows from the first two. In other words, if the first two propositions are true, the third proposition also has to be true.

In the next couple of chapters, we will look more closely at each step of the thought process in order to be able to accomplish the end step, which is building arguments more effectively.

1. Simple Apprehension:

_____

_____

2. Judgment:

_____

_____

3. Inference:

_____

_____

Now that you have read about the three mental acts, it's time that you saw an example of them in real life. Read the story below and then complete the following activity.

Elena was walking through the woods one day, when she noticed a beautiful plant with small red globes on it. She was very hungry, so she stepped forward eagerly, hoping she might be able to eat part of the plant. However, as she stepped forward, she recognized the globes on the bush as berries. She thought to herself, "These globes are the poisonous berries I've read about in my botany book." Then she thought, "Poisonous berries can make people extremely sick or even kill them. Obviously, I don't want that to happen, so I don't care how hungry I am, I'm not eating the berries."

In the space below, explain at which point Elena makes a simple apprehension, a judgment, and then an inference. Remember, these three items should all be related in that they are part of an argument she is making to herself.

1. Simple Apprehension:

_____

_____

2. Judgment:

_____

_____

3. Deductive Inference:

_____

_____

IDENTIFY

Here is a second story. Read the story and then identify at which part in the story simple apprehension, judgment, and inference occur.

Andrew Pachek, who had recently read an article on bike safety, was riding his bike home from school one day, when he recognized a driveway up ahead with a car about to back out of it. He thought to himself, "Driveways with drivers backing out of them are dangerous to bikers because drivers don't always watch where they are going." Then he thought, "This could be dangerous. I'm going to watch carefully."

1. Simple Apprehension:

_____

_____

_____

2. Judgment:

_____

_____

3. Inference:

_____

_____

_____

MATCH

Match the act of the mind with that which results from it by drawing a line between them.

1. Simple Apprehension   a. Proposition

2. Judgment: b. Argument

3. Inference: c. Term

DEDUCTION IN ACTION

Logic and Personal Thoughts

If you use logic, one of its greatest personal benefits is the ability it gives you to examine and clarify your own personal thoughts, or your own mental acts. You might remember that part of Socrates' quote at the beginning of the first chapter was "The unexamined life is not worth living." One of the reasons it is so important to examine our own thoughts, or mental acts, is because doing so can save us from a lot of worry.

Let me illustrate this with an example that may be familiar to many of you. When I was in high school, I would often get extremely nervous after a test when I thought I had missed some of the problems or questions on it. My stomach would be in knots. This was usually because I was making some of the following judgments and inferences: "I didn't know some of the answers on the test. I must have failed the test. I will fail other tests. I'm going to fail school. I'm not going to be able to go to college. I'll never get a job. I'll be living on the streets!"

Now, of course, these thoughts look ridiculous when written out, but that's the point. When these thoughts were swimming around unidentified in my brain, they could cause a lot of unnecessary worry and anxiety. To combat this tendency of mine, my mom used to play the "What's the worst that could happen?" game with me. This was actually a way for me to confront my exaggerated judgments and inferences. For example, she would ask me, "What's the worst thing that can happen if you missed some items on the test?" Of course, I might have wanted to respond, "I'll fail school and become a homeless person," but I knew, as I was thinking it, that it was silly. So, I would usually say something like, "Well, I might fail the test, but more likely I might get a B or C."

Suddenly, things became much less dramatic and anxiety-producing. Then my mother would say, "What is the worst that could happen if you failed the test?" I would answer, avoiding unnecessary drama, "Well, I wouldn't like it, but I could ask the teacher for help, and if I had made some honest mistakes, he might let me take it over." With each "What's the worst . . ." question my mom asked me, she would force me to state my judgments and inferences (although she did not ever call them by those names and probably did not know that was what she was doing).

It's very hard for overly dramatic thoughts to hide in the plain light of day. This is one reason, I think, that Socrates continually urged people to examine their thoughts. Unexamined thoughts can hide in our brains, causing unnecessary drama or resulting in wrong beliefs or actions. Later on in this book, you will have a chance to read a dialogue in which Socrates tries to help a guy examine some of his seriously misguided thinking. For now, just pay a little more attention to your mental acts and see if you can make your life a little easier.

Stop the Drama

Try the "What's the worst thing that could happen?" game with your own thoughts. Take something that is really bothering you and ask yourself, "What's the worst thing that could happen?" for each of your fears. Make note below of any incorrect or overly dramatic judgments or inferences that you are making. If you have problems doing this with your own thoughts, ask someone to do it for you and to challenge you on your incorrect or overly dramatic judgments.

DIALOGUE 4.1
Introduction to Argument Translation

Socrates is walking through campus and sees Nate sitting beneath a big maple tree looking perplexed.

Socrates: You seem to be lost in deep thought today, Nate. Is something troubling you?

Nate: Yeah, . . . no . . . well, sort of.

Socrates: Perhaps I can help.

Nate: Yes, maybe you can. I've been thinking a lot about what we talked about last time, especially about syllogisms and how we use them to make deductive inferences.

Socrates: I see, and this is what is troubling you—syllogisms and deductive inference?

Nate: Well, no, not syllogisms and inference, per se. After all, it seems pretty clear how they work.

Socrates: What seems to be troubling you, then?

Nate: It's just that I've been trying to analyze arguments so that I could practice making deductive inferences.

Socrates: And how did it go?

Nate: That's the problem. No one seems to use syllogisms. I've been listening closely, and I've heard some arguments that sound close to syllogisms, but I haven't heard anyone use a clear syllogism all week—not even me.

Socrates: Ah, now I understand the problem. You are not sure how to use formal logic with everyday arguments because they don't seem to be structured formally.

Nate: Exactly!

Socrates: Very good. You are asking all the right questions.

Nate: I guess I didn't realize I was asking any questions.

Socrates: Perhaps you did not consciously form your thoughts into questions, but I believe what you are asking is "How do I tell when arguments are formal arguments, and how do I analyze them properly?"

Nate: I guess you're right. That's definitely what I want to know. So, how do I do it? How do I figure out which arguments are formal and which ones are right and wrong?

Socrates: Those are actually two separate questions: one pertains to the arrangement of the argument and one pertains to the validity of the argument.

Nate: That word sounds familiar. What's validity?

Socrates: Validity refers to whether or not a deductive argument is structured properly.

Nate: Well, aren't structure and arrangement the same thing?

Socrates: They certainly have some things in common, but when we want to analyze arguments for their deductive validity, we must first make sure that they are arranged, or **translated**, properly.

Nate: What do you mean by "translate"?

Socrates: I mean that you boil down everyday language so that you can write it into basic syllogistic form and analyze what is going on in the argument.

Nate: I see. It's kind of like a math story problem, then.

Socrates: How so?

Nate: With story problems, you have to figure out what mathematical operations are called for by the problem. Then you have to toss out the unimportant information and translate the words into a mathematical formula.

Socrates: I see. Yes, I believe the two processes do have some similarities.

Nate: That makes a lot more sense, then. So how do I translate ordinary language into syllogistic form?

Socrates: There are various rules that can guide you in the process, but perhaps it would help if we started with an example.

Nate: That would be great.

Socrates: OK, let's use your own argument as an example.

Nate: My argument?

Socrates: Certainly. When we began this conversation today, you were confused about how to use formal logic with everyday conversation, correct?

Nate: Yes, but I don't understand how that is an argument.

Socrates: Well, you probably thought something like this: "In order to use formal logic, I must have a syllogism. But nobody speaks in syllogisms in everyday life. Therefore, I cannot use formal logic in everyday life."

Nate: Hmm. I didn't think about it that way, but I guess you're right. I *was* thinking something like that.

Socrates: You also may not have realized it, but as you thought through these various beliefs, you were, indeed, using a syllogism to reach your conclusion. If we reword your argument, your thoughts would look something like this:

> All arguments I can analyze with formal logic are arguments arranged in a syllogism.
>
> No everyday arguments are arguments arranged in a syllogism.
>
> Therefore, no arguments I can analyze with formal logic are everyday arguments.

Nate: It sounds kind of weird, but I think that's what I was thinking, more or less.

Socrates: It does sound a bit awkward because we have translated your thoughts into syllogistic format. However, this is a necessary step in the process of deductive analysis.

Nate: I think I'm beginning to understand. Can we try another example? For instance, I was listening to a discussion in the cafeteria the other day. Someone was arguing for better food in the cafeteria. He said, "The school should have better food in the cafeteria because I can't eat this stuff, and when I am hungry, I can't concentrate in class."

Socrates: A very interesting argument and one, if I am not mistaken, that is fairly common across the campuses of this country's universities. Let's see if you can figure out this one. In order to turn this into a syllogism, you need to formulate two propositions that naturally lead to a third proposition. Give it a try.

Nate: Let's see. It seems like there are several ways I could do this, but here goes:

> All hungry students are students who can't concentrate.
>
> I am a hungry student.
>
> Therefore, I am a student who can't concentrate.

Socrates: Superb! As you mentioned, there are several arguments or implications present in the statements of the fellow in the cafeteria. Here is another argument his ideas imply:

> All habits that improve student concentration are habits that should be adopted.
>
> Providing good cafeteria food is a habit that improves student concentration.
>
> Therefore, providing good cafeteria food is a habit that should be adopted.

Nate: I think I'm getting the hang of it now. So, how do I know whether or not these syllogisms are valid?

Socrates: That's an excellent question. However, explaining that will take quite a bit of time, so let's save that for another conversation. By the way, I've missed Tiffany. Is she still around?

Nate: Oh, yes, she's still on campus. We just don't have as many classes together this semester, so we often hang out at night or on weekends instead of during the day. Plus, she took logic class during the summer, and she already seems to have all this stuff figured out.

Socrates: She certainly is a smart one.

Nate: Yes, she is. Well, I need to think about this whole translation thing. I'll see you later, Socrates. Thanks for clearing up my confusion.

Socrates: Always a pleasure!

REVIEW
ANSWER

1. Why can using deductive logic with everyday English initially seem confusing?

_____

_____

_____

2. How can a person overcome the barrier created by the convoluted nature of everyday English?

_____

_____

_____

_____

LESSON 4.2
Categorical Form Introduced

POINTS TO REMEMBER

1. **Categorical form** is the arrangement of terms and words in a proposition so that the proposition either affirms (supports) or negates (denies) something about a specific topic.
2. Translating arguments into categorical form is a process.
3. Arranging an ordinary-language proposition into categorical form is the first step in the process of translating arguments into categorical form.

> DON'T TAKE THE WRONG SIDE OF AN ARGUMENT JUST BECAUSE YOUR OPPONENT HAS TAKEN THE RIGHT SIDE.
> —BALTASAR GRACIAN[1]

Remember that in formal categorical logic we can learn how to evaluate whether or not an argument is valid—that is, uses right reasoning form—regardless of the content of the argument. This is because although an argument's content is important, when people use deductive logic, they usually reason from *a priori* propositions. Therefore, since the content of the propositions is a given, they are focusing more on the structure of the argument. Since the content of a categorical argument is not the main focus, logicians have developed a commonly agreed-upon symbolic system to represent the building blocks of a deductive argument—terms, propositions, and arguments. This makes it easier to apply the rules of reason to see if the argument's form, or structure, is valid.

As you go through this text, you will learn how to translate ordinary-language propositions and arguments into symbolic form. Translating these arguments into symbolic form is like a building inspector taking off the siding, or skin, of a house to examine the wood or steel frame so that he can determine whether the way the wood or steel supports are put together will hold up the house. When you translate ordinary-language arguments into symbolic form, you can more easily see whether the structure of the argument is valid, regardless of the topic, clever language, or emotion of the argument. Learning this skill will also help you in the future to reason critically about all areas of study, morality, and people's worldviews.

Translating arguments into symbolic form, also called logical form, is a process. Each step of the process is a building block for future concepts. It's going to be important to master the definitions and concepts of each piece because each lesson builds upon the previous lesson. As with all branches of formal learning, logic has its own unique vocabulary, which can be a challenge to master. Some vocabulary may be familiar, while other terms may be new and different. Be prepared to exert effort to stay up-to-date with the lessons and master the new language.

There are several steps that have to be taken in sequential order so that you can successfully translate ordinary-language propositions and arguments into symbolic, or logical, form. The first step is to arrange the ordinary-language propositions into categorical form. Categorical form is the arrangement of the terms and words in a proposition so that the proposition either affirms (supports) or negates (denies) something about a specific topic. This will be our focus in the next lesson.

REVIEW
ANSWER

1. How can it be helpful to translate arguments into logical form?

_____

_____

2. In your own words, explain what it means to translate an argument into categorical form.

_____

_____

3. Explain the relationship between the terms "categorical form" and "symbolic form."

_____

_____

DEDUCTION IN ACTION

Logic and Paradoxes

You have already learned about the liar paradox in lesson 3.1 when we discussed the Stoics. You also had a chance to read about Zeno's paradox about Tortoise and Achilles. Here is another of Zeno's paradoxes that might tickle your brain (or drive you crazy). It is called the arrow paradox. Arguments like these can seem overwhelming because they are counterintuitive (i.e., they go against common sense), and yet, it is difficult to figure out if and where they are wrong in reasoning. Read the argument and think about which of the propositions you might be able to critique or which of the words in the proposition might be used in an incorrect manner (these are two common ways to critique an argument like this):

> "If everything is at rest when it is in a place equal to itself, and if the moving object is always in the present and therefore in a place equal to itself, then the moving arrow is motionless."[2]

Once you have attempted to critique this argument, take a look at the following links, which offer some critiques of Zeno's paradoxes:
<http://capress.link/dd0401>
<http://capress.link/dd0402>.

By the way, both the Tortoise and Achilles paradox and the arrow paradox could provide you with two of the most creative homework excuses ever presented in school:

Student to teacher: "I tried to do my homework last night, but, as there are an infinite amount of steps between me and my homework, I couldn't actually reach my textbook to complete the assignment."

Or student to teacher: "I wanted to do my homework, but as I could only be in the place where I was, as this place was equal to myself, and as I could not be in the place where I was not, which is where, alas! my homework was, I could not complete the assignment."

LESSON 4.3
Propositions

POINTS TO REMEMBER

When determining whether or not a sentence is a proposition, consider the following questions:

1. Does the sentence have a **truth-value**? If we can say the sentence is true or false, then it is a proposition.
2. Is the sentence a question, command, exclamation, greeting, or nonsense? If it is not any of these, and it has a truth-value, then it is a proposition.

> THERE IS NOTHING TO FEAR EXCEPT THE PERSISTENT REFUSAL TO FIND OUT THE TRUTH, THE PERSISTENT REFUSAL TO ANALYZE THE CAUSES OF HAPPENINGS.
> —DOROTHY THOMPSON[1]

To help guide you through the next couple of chapters as we discuss how to translate arguments into categorical form, we want to provide you with an overview of each step of the process. We will continue to remind you of this list so that as we move from chapter to chapter, you will understand where you have come from and where you are going. The following are the basic steps of translating an argument into categorical form:

1. Determine the three propositions of an argument (each of these propositions should have a subject and a predicate).

2. Rewrite the proposition so that it contains a being verb, along with the subject and predicate.

3. Determine the proposition's **quantity** and **quality**.

4. Supply the proper **quantifier**.

Now let's learn the first of these steps. As we noted in the previous lesson, categorical form is defined as the arrangement of words in a proposition so that it either affirms (supports) or negates (denies) something about a specific topic.

So, what is a "proposition" for logic purposes? A proposition is a single declaration or report of facts or opinions. For logic purposes, propositions always have a truth-value. That means the proposition always expresses something that is either true—a "true" truth-value—or false—a "false" truth-value. Calling something a "true proposition" is just another way of saying the proposition has a true truth-value, just as calling something a "false proposition" is just another way of saying the proposition has a false truth-value. Truth-value, then, is the truth or falsity of a proposition.[2]

For example, the proposition "Water freezes at thirty-two degrees Fahrenheit" has a true truth-value. The proposition "The sun revolves around the earth" has a false truth-value. Both of these claims are legitimate propositions in logical form, but they have different truth-values.

So, for the purposes of logic, propositions must report facts or opinions with a truth-value, meaning that a proposition in logic always either affirms or denies an idea. To put it another way, any sentence that does *not* have a truth-value is *not* a proposition for the purposes of logic. Can you think of types of sentences that would not qualify as logical propositions? If you thought of **questions**, **commands**, **exclamations**, **greetings**, **nonsense sentences**, or **self-reports**, you are correct. None of these types of sentences qualify as propositions for logic purposes because they do not have any truth-value.

Let's look at some examples of these types of sentences so that you can see the difference between them and propositions more clearly.

Questions

Questions raise issues and ideas by inquiring or asking another's perspective, but they do not report facts or opinions, so they have no truth-value—you cannot say they are either true or false.

Example Question: Did the Athenians win the battle at Marathon during the Persian Wars?

Commands

A command is a directive or an order to do, think, or say something. Commands do not report facts or opinions, either, so they can't be true or false.

Example Command: Go to your room!

Exclamations and Greetings

An exclamation is an expression delivered suddenly, and a greeting is a form of salutation. Neither exclamations nor greetings report facts or opinions, so they don't have any truth-value, either.

Example Exclamation: Watch out![3]

Example Greeting: Good morning, dear logic student.

Nonsense Sentences

We don't usually rely on nonsense sentences to communicate in everyday English. But, because logic students are crafty and like to ask lots of tricky questions, we include nonsense sentences in our list of sentences that do not qualify as propositions for logic purposes. Simply put, nonsense sentences, while superficially having the structure of a proposition, do not qualify because they make no sense. Because they make no sense, they cannot report a fact or opinion, and thus, have no truth-value.

Example Nonsense Sentence: Photo run leaf coaster on Tuesday for lobsters.

Self-Reports

Self-reports are expressions of feeling or belief. In logic, people do not argue over self-reports because we generally take people at their word. Therefore, because we take people at their word when they give self-reports of their feelings or thoughts, self-reports are generally not considered propositions.

Example Self-Report: I think that movie stinks.

Because questions, commands, exclamations, nonsense sentences, and self-reports cannot be argued or analyzed in logical form, it is important to identify the actual propositions in an argument. That way you know you are focusing on something that can be analyzed or argued. In the next chapter, we will learn how to find all of the propositions in an argument.

DEFINE

1. Propositions:

_____

_____

_____

2. Truth-Value:

_____

_____

_____

3. True:

_____

_____

_____

4. False:

_____

_____

_____

5. Questions:

_____

_____

_____

6. Commands:

_____

_____

_____

7. Greetings:

_____

_____

_____

DEFINE (CONTINUED)

8. Exclamations:

_____

_____

_____

9. Nonsense Sentences:

_____

_____

_____

10. Self-Reports:

_____

_____

_____

DETERMINE

Look at the following sentences and determine what category they fall under: proposition, question, command, greeting, exclamation, or nonsense sentence. Give reasons to support your answers.

1. *Quo Vadis*, by Henryk Sienkiewicz, is a work of historical fiction depicting the persecution of the early Christians under the rule of the violent Roman emperor, Nero.

Category: _____

Explanation: _____

2. How much longer is this class?

Category: _____

Explanation: _____

3. Those who *will not* read good books have no advantage over those who *cannot* read good books.

Category: _____

Explanation: _____

4. Attention all members of the debate club: Report to the office immediately!

Category: _____

Explanation: _____

DETERMINE (CONTINUED)

5. I tree the thing was clean the post-it clover stuff yellow paste in run.

Category: _____

Explanation: _____

6. Aristotle argues that excellence is not confined to action, but is the result of habit.

Category: _____

Explanation: _____

TRUE OR FALSE

Circle the correct answer.

1. A proposition does not necessarily have to have a truth-value.   T   F

2. A false proposition is a sentence that is not really a proposition.   T   F

3. Questions and commands are not propositions.   T   F

4. A self-report can be an exclamation and therefore a proposition.   T   F

5. Propositions have a subject, predicate, and verb.   T   F

DEDUCTION IN ACTION
Supporting Propositions

Select one of the following propositions and determine its truth-value. Then, do some research regarding the proposition you choose and write a short paragraph essay supporting your conclusion.

1. The helots were a people group enslaved by the Spartans.

2. Napoleon Bonaparte was an effective French ruler.

LESSON 4.4

Translating Arguments Step 1
Finding the Propositions

POINTS TO REMEMBER

1. Deductive arguments typically have three propositions: the conclusion, which is the point of the argument, and the two premises, which are the evidence for the conclusion.
2. **Conclusion indicators** are words or phrases such as "therefore," "thus," "so," "it follows that," and "in conclusion" that indicate that the conclusion is about to follow.
3. **Premise indicators** are words or phrases like "since," "because," "for these reasons," and "it follows from," which indicate that the premises are about to follow.
4. Propositions contain a subject, which is what the proposition is about, and a predicate, which is the word(s) that come(s) after the verb and describe(s) or rename(s) the subject.
5. To correctly identify the argument, use the natural breaks in the argument, along with premise and conclusion indicators, to locate the three propositions that contain a subject and a predicate and that have a truth-value.

> I ARGUE VERY WELL. ASK ANY OF MY REMAINING
> FRIENDS. I CAN WIN AN ARGUMENT ON ANY TOPIC,
> AGAINST ANY OPPONENT. PEOPLE KNOW THIS, AND
> STEER CLEAR OF ME AT PARTIES. OFTEN, AS A SIGN OF
> THEIR GREAT RESPECT, THEY DON'T EVEN INVITE ME.
> —DAVE BARRY[1]

Now that we know what a proposition is in logic, we want to make sure that we have identified the three propositions in an argument and that we have translated them into categorical form. It will be helpful for you to know that the deductive arguments we will be examining in this book contain three propositions: one conclusion, which is the belief or opinion that the argument is claiming, and the premises, which are the two propositions that provide the supporting evidence for the argument. The good news is that it is often easy to identify the premises and conclusion of an argument because of some helpful words called conclusion indicators and premise indicators. Conclusion indicators are words or phrases that tip you off that the conclusion is coming, such as "in conclusion," "so," "therefore," "it follows that," and "thus." If conclusion indicators are words or phrases that demonstrate that the conclusion is about to follow, you can probably guess that premise indicators are words or phrases that indicate that premises are about to follow. These are words or phrases such as "since," "because," "for the reason that," or "the reasons are." If you look for premise and conclusion indicators as you are analyzing arguments, it will make it much easier for you to find the three propositions in an argument.

There is one other thing you should know before we begin analyzing arguments to locate premises and conclusions. You should know that working with propositions in ordinary language can prove difficult when testing for validity (you'll learn about validity in chapter 8) or determining the quality and quantity of a proposition (this will be covered in lesson 4.6 and also in chapter 7). This is because arguments in English are often convoluted, filled with extra phrases and clauses, and are written in such a way that the premises and conclusions are often separated by words and expressions that are actually irrelevant to the argument. This happens because when people are making arguments in everyday life, they don't always think in a clear, organized fashion. Furthermore, they often interject emotive statements (statements of feeling) and extraneous details into an argument that, while they may be interesting, do not actually pertain to the argument.

This is one of the main reasons it is necessary to learn to categorize propositions by rewriting them in categorical form. Doing so helps us weed out the information that is irrelevant to the argument so that we can just focus on the argument itself. Therefore, in the rest of this lesson, we will practice identifying key propositions and identifying the premises and the conclusion of an argument, which will put us in a good position to translate that argument into categorical form. The easiest way to find the key propositions that are the core of an argument is to identify the **key terms** of the argument. To do this, you begin by separating the argument into its three propositions and analyzing each one individually. The first two propositions of an argument are typically referred to as the premises, or the reasons given that lead to the arguer's conclusion. Sometimes there is only one premise in an argument, and sometimes there are more than two premises, but we will generally be working with two premises in our exercises. The conclusion of the argument is the point of persuasion and is usually the third proposition in a categorical argument. There is never more than one conclusion. (We'll deal with premises and conclusions in more detail later.)

It may help you to find each proposition in an argument more easily if you know that a proposition will always contain two key terms: a **subject term** and a **predicate term**. You know from your studies of grammar that a subject is what a sentence is about. So, if you have the proposition "Sparta was a city-state," the term "Sparta" is obviously the subject, because it is what the sentence is about. As such, a subject in a logic proposition plays the same role as a subject in a regular sentence. A predicate in logic, however, is a little different from a predicate in grammar. In regular English grammar, the predicate of a sentence is the verb. However, in logic, the predicate is the word that comes *after* the verb and describes the subject. In English grammar, this word is often referred to as the predicate nominative or the predicate adjective. However, in logic, it is just the predicate. For example, in the sentence we used earlier about Sparta, the term "city-state" is the logic predicate because it comes after the verb and describes the subject.

Read the following short argument and try to find the three propositions that make up the argument. Remember, look for three propositions, each with a subject and a predicate. In addition, remember those premise and conclusion indicators that tip you off to the premises and the conclusion.

> Since all dogs are four-legged animals, and since all Labrador retrievers are dogs, it follows that all Labrador retrievers are four-legged animals.

Did you find all three propositions? Were you able to find the subjects and predicates of each proposition? Let's

examine how to go about the process, and you can see how you did. The first thing we need to do is break up the argument into its three propositions. The clue to finding the breaks between the propositions is to look for the natural breaks in grammatical structure by identifying connector words and phrases, as well as the premise and conclusion indicators. Did you notice the word "since" in the example? That's one of the common premise indicators, so we know that the part of the sentence containing that word is probably one of our premises. We can also see that it is one of our four premises because it has a subject—"dogs"—and a predicate—"four-legged animals." When we examine the next proposition, which is, "Since all Labrador retrievers are dogs," we realize it, too, is a premise since it contains a premise indicator—"since"—a subject—"Labrador retrievers"—and a predicate—"dogs." Finally, we look at the last proposition and realize that it must be the conclusion because it begins with the conclusion indicator "it follows," and it contains a subject and a predicate. Therefore, we have identified an argument with two premises and a conclusion, each of which contains a subject and a predicate. After breaking up our example argument, we come up with these three propositions:

All <u>dogs</u> are *four-legged animals*.
All <u>Labrador retrievers</u> are *dogs*.
It follows that all <u>Labrador retrievers</u> are *four-legged animals*.

You will notice that we have left out a few words in our restatement of the argument. For instance, in our first proposition, we left out the word "since." It is common to do this when you are simplifying an argument for analysis. Just make sure that you retain the most important parts of the proposition. In other words, make sure that your simplified propositions contain a subject and a predicate and that the propositions actually have a truth-value—that is, that they are either affirming or denying an idea.

When we look back at our propositions, we realize that we have, indeed, identified the propositions correctly. The first premise contains the subject "Labrador retrievers" and the predicate "four-legged animals" and has a truth-value. The second premise contains the subject "dog" and the predicate "four-legged animals." It also has a truth-value. Furthermore, the conclusion also has a truth-value, and it

contains the subject "Labrador retrievers" and the predicate "dogs." By assessing the different parts of our argument, we can see that we have met all of the necessary criteria for an argument. (Note that in the example provided, the subject in each proposition is underlined and the predicate is in italics.) Identifying the subject and predicate is the next step in the process of translating an argument into categorical form, which you will learn in the next lesson.

Now, let's try another argument, one in which it may be a little more difficult to identify the separate propositions.

Lifeguards are always watching swimmers, no matter what. So, Angela is always watching the swimmers, even when she's eating her lunch, because she is a lifeguard.

This argument is a little bit more difficult to break down into categorical form because it seems to have some extra phrases and words like "no matter what" and "even when she is eating her lunch," which are more for description than to aid in defining the argument. Remember the process of identifying propositions. You want to look for three propositions that contain a subject and a predicate, and you also want to look for premise and conclusion indicators. When you do this, you will notice the first proposition, "Lifeguards are always watching swimmers." It doesn't have any kind of indicator, but it does have a subject—"lifeguards"—and a predicate—"swimmers." Taking that into account, you know that this is one of the propositions. You can figure out which one it is exactly after you finish looking at the rest of the argument. The next proposition has a conclusion indicator—"so"—a subject—"Angela"—and a predicate—"swimmers." You have probably found the conclusion. The last proposition has a premise indicator—"because"—and it also contains a subject—"she"—and a predicate—"lifeguard." When you look over the argument, it makes sense that the following is the organization of the argument:

Lifeguards always watch swimmers.
Angela is a lifeguard.
Therefore, Angela always watches swimmers.

You will notice that we left out a couple of phrases: "no matter what" and "even when she is eating her lunch." Although these phrases add extra meaning and emphasis in the original argument, they are unnecessary to include

when we are examining the basic structure of the argument. Leaving out these extra words and phrases allowed us to concentrate on the heart of the argument. We were able to identify three propositions and that each of those propositions has a subject and a predicate.

It is important to realize that most of the time when people argue in everyday life, they do not speak in nice, neat arguments that are organized conveniently for analysis. More often, it is necessary for us to reword the propositions and terms, leaving out unnecessary words and phrases, so that we can better observe the logical structure of a person's argument. As long as your rewording contains three propositions that confirm or deny an idea, and as long as they have a subject and predicate, you are simplifying the ideas correctly.

Now that we have examined the rudimentary skills for locating arguments and propositions, we will take a closer look at propositions in the next lesson. As you might remember from our list in lesson 4.3, it takes a few more steps to get propositions into proper categorical form. That will be the focus of the next few chapters.

REVIEW
DEFINE

1. Premise Indicator:

_____

_____

2. Conclusion Indicator:

_____

_____

3. Premise:

_____

_____

4. Conclusion:

_____

_____

5. Subject Term:

_____

_____

6. Predicate Term:

_____

_____

7. Proposition:

_____

_____

In your own words, explain at least three steps a person uses to locate the three propositions of an argument.

EXPLAIN

_____

_____

_____

Find the proposition(s) in the following sentences.

FIND

1. Classically trained students study Latin and logic.

_____

_____

2. Photojournalists not only take pictures, but they also have to arrange the pictures in a way that tells a story.

_____

_____

3. President Roosevelt knew the attack on Pearl Harbor was coming, and he failed to notify the navy.

_____

_____

4. Because farmers provide our food, they are the lifelines of our country.

_____

_____

5. Wise people speak few words.

_____

_____

GOING FURTHER

1. Using any of your school textbooks, identify and list three sentences that contain propositions.

_____

_____

_____

_____

49

GOING FURTHER (CONTINUED)

2. Swap the sentences you found with those of a classmate. Write your classmate's sentences in the spaces provided below and then rewrite the propositions from those sentences separately.

Sentence 1:

_____

Separate propositions:

_____

Sentence 2:

_____

Separate propositions:

_____

Sentence 3:

_____

Separate propositions:

_____

DEDUCTION IN ACTION
Logic and Sherlock Holmes

Sherlock Holmes is one of our most beloved literary characters, and he, along with Dr. Watson, never ceases to amaze us with his amazing logic skills. It's all very elementary to him, of course. Holmes uses a blend of inductive and deductive logic as a basis for his genius sleuthing technique. It is evident, from reading the stories about Sherlock Holmes, that he has made a very careful habit of examining human beings—their customs, habits, and the meaning of their smallest, seemingly most insignificant actions. What he consistently observes becomes an *a priori* truth for him, which is induction. He then uses that truth to reason deductively. To get a feel for how Sherlock Holmes does this, read the story "A Case of Identity," which can be found at the following link: <http://capress.link/dd0403>.

Once you have read the story, answer the following questions:

1. At the beginning of the story, Sherlock makes an argument about why big crimes are the easiest to solve. See if you can put his argument into categorical form.

2. At the end of the story, as he explains how he solved the crime, Holmes lists several *a priori* beliefs he had, which led him to be able to reason out what had happened. Not all of his beliefs will be directly stated, so you may need to figure some of them out from what Holmes says about the case. List at least five *a priori* beliefs Holmes used in his reasoning process in this story. We have provided one to get you started:

    Men marrying much older women are marrying for money.

LESSON 4.5
Translating Arguments Step 2
Finding the Subject Term and the Predicate Term

POINTS TO REMEMBER

1. The subject term in a proposition is represented by the letter *S*.
2. The predicate term in a proposition is represented by the letter *P*.
3. The verb used in categorical form is usually a **verb of being** and is called a ***copula*** in logic.
4. A proposition in categorical form must be organized in a particular way: subject first—*S*—then the *copula*, or verb of being—is—and finally the predicate—*P*.
5. If a proposition is not arranged in the form *S is P*, the proposition must be rearranged to include a verb of being connecting the *S* to the *P*.

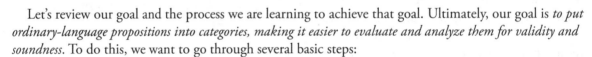

> TRUTH SPRINGS FROM ARGUMENT
> AMONGST FRIENDS.
> —DAVID HUME[1]

Let's review our goal and the process we are learning to achieve that goal. Ultimately, our goal is *to put ordinary-language propositions into categories, making it easier to evaluate and analyze them for validity and soundness*. To do this, we want to go through several basic steps:

1. Determine the three propositions of an argument (each of these propositions should have a subject and a predicate).

2. Rewrite the proposition so that it contains a being verb, along with the subject and predicate.

3. Determine the proposition's quantity and quality.

4. Supply the proper quantifier.

You will be reminded of these steps periodically as you continue to learn the steps involved in obtaining our goal. In the last chapter, we learned step 1 of this process. Now we are going to move on to the next step, which helps us tackle ordinary-language sentences more effectively.

As we have mentioned before, to write propositions in categorical form, they must be organized in a particular way. That is, they must either affirm (support) or negate (deny) something about a specific category of things. In this chapter, you will learn how to translate propositions so that they contain three important components: the subject, a being verb (the *copula*), and the predicate. In the last chapter, we discussed subjects and predicates, but we did not discuss being verbs, or *copulas*. Those being verbs are what we will address in this chapter because when we translate a sentence so that it contains a being

verb, we put it into a form in which it is either affirming or denying something about the subject. That is, the proposition will either say that the subject *is* something or that the subject *is not* something.

Let's look at our Labrador retriever example from the previous lesson:

Since all Labrador retrievers are four-legged animals, and since all dogs are four-legged animals, it follows that all Labrador retrievers are dogs.

The first proposition we find in the example is this:

Labrador retrievers are four-legged animals.

Like all propositions, this one joins two concepts, which in this case are represented by the terms "Labrador retrievers" and "four-legged animals." The first term, "Labrador retriever," is the *subject* of the proposition. It is joined to the second term—"four-legged animals"—which is the *predicate* of the proposition. What joins the subject term to the predicate term in the proposition is a verb of being (or being verb), which in this case is the word "are." You may remember from English class that there are many forms of the verb "to be." For instance, you probably memorized a list that goes something like this: am, is, are, was, were, be, being, been. These are all forms of the verb "to be." However, in logic, we primarily use the "is" and "are" forms of the verb "to be." In order to be in logical form, a proposition must contain a form of the verb "to be" as its verb, linking the subject and the predicate. In logic, we call this being verb which links the subject and the predicate of a proposition the *copula*.

To take the next step in translating our first Labrador retriever proposition into categorical form, we label "Labrador retriever," which is the subject term, *S*. We label "four-legged animals," which is the predicate term, *P*. We then connect the letter symbols with the proposition verb, which is "are." This gives us the form of the proposition, which is *S is P*. When a proposition is in categorical form, it allows us to use an *S* to stand for its subject, a *P* to stand for its predicate, and it also has a form of the word "be" as its verb, or *copula*.

The Labrador retriever example was already very close to categorical form. That is, it was very close to the *S is P* form

already, so it was easy to translate it into categorical form. However, as we alluded to before, when we have ordinary-language propositions that are *not* organized in the form *S is P*, we have to take a couple of extra steps to get them into categorical form. Sometimes when we put the propositions into categorical form, they will sound awkward, strange, and ungrammatical. That's OK, though, because we are not putting them in that form for writing or speaking purposes, but to analyze the form of the argument. By rearranging the proposition into the proper form, it will make translation of the ordinary-language argument into symbolic form easier.

Let's practice putting a couple of ordinary-language propositions into categorical form. We will rewrite the following sentences in categorical form by finding their propositions, locating *S* (subject), *P* (predicate), and the being verb. Then we will reorganize the sentence to put the *S* first and the *P* last and join the *S* and *P* with a verb of being, even if the original proposition does not use one.

Example 1

Some of our neighborhood dogs howl.

The following are two ways to put this proposition in categorical form:

- Some of our neighborhood dogs are dogs that howl.

- Some of our neighborhood dogs are howlers.

The second proposition, though it is a bit awkward, is a better example of categorical form because it is more concise and contains fewer words. Generally, when you are translating a proposition into categorical form, you want to make it as short and concise as possible. To do this, you often change a clause, such as "dogs that howl," into a word like "howlers." Even though we don't use the word "howlers" in normal English, it's a good word to use in the categorical form of the proposition because it makes the sentence shorter and more concise. Now that we have arranged the sentences in proper categorical form, we know that *S* is "dogs," *P* is "howlers" or "dogs that howl," and we have provided a being verb: "are." Therefore, we can break it down even more to: "Dogs are howlers." The sentence is now in the categorical form of *S is P*.

It can be awkward at first to supply being verbs, or *copulas*, so let's try a few more before we move on to full arguments.

PROPOSITIONS WRITTEN IN CATEGORICAL FORM MUST EITHER AFFIRM (SUPPORT) OR NEGATE (DENY) SOMETHING ABOUT A SPECIFIC CATEGORY OF THINGS.

Consider this proposition: "Some political candidates tell the truth." As you can see, this proposition is also missing a *copula*. So, how can we supply this being verb and change the proposition to be in categorical form? We would start it like this: "Some political candidates are. . . ." We have supplied the *copula*, and now we need to add a predicate that keeps the meaning of the end of the original sentence the same. We could change "tell the truth" to "truth-tellers," which is a noun that will effectively complete the proposition. Now our proposition looks like this: "Some political candidates are truth-tellers." In this sentence, we kept the original words "tell" and "truth," but we changed the form of the words to "truth-tellers" in order to make them complete the sentence. If you look at example 1, "Some of our neighborhood dogs howl," you can see that we did this same thing when we changed it to "Some dogs are howlers." We kept the word "howl" but changed it to a noun so that we could put the proposition in categorical form.

Let's try one more that is slightly different. Consider this proposition: "Some used-car salesmen sell lousy cars dishonestly." We know that in order to change this to categorical form, we must begin it like this: "Some used-car salesmen are. . . ." Now that we have written our sentence with a subject and *copula*, we need to supply a predicate. That is, somehow, we need to change "sell lousy cars dishonestly" into a predicate. We could try to include every single word and change it to something like this: "Some used-car salesmen are dishonest, lousy car salesmen." However, this is awkward and even a bit inaccurate. Therefore, a proposition like the following is probably better: "Some used-car salesmen are dishonest salesmen." Notice we left out the word "lousy" to keep the proposition as clear as possible. However, our new sentence still retains the basic and most important meaning of the original sentence. You will notice that changing a sentence into categorical form is not an exact science. However, as long as you include a subject, a predicate, and a *copula* in a proposition that retains the meaning of the original sentence, you will be on the right track.

Example 2

Now let's try putting another ordinary-language proposition in categorical form.

> The eloquently written *Julius Caesar* by William Shakespeare is a magnificent play.

Julius Caesar is the subject—*S*—"play" is the predicate—*P*—and the being verb is "is." The simplified categorical form of this proposition is "*Julius Caesar* is a play." The sentence is now in the categorical form of *S is P*. You will notice that we left out the word "eloquently." Although this adjective is helpful for expressing meaning in the original sentence, it is not necessary for us to include it when we are examining a proposition logically. You will find that when you change ordinary language into categorical form, you will tend to leave out a lot of adjectives, adverbs, modifying adverbs, and clauses. Once again, as long as your new proposition contains a subject, predicate, and a *copula*, and it retains the basic meaning of the original sentence, you have likely arranged it in proper categorical form.

Let's take a moment to see how far we have come in the process of changing everyday arguments into categorical form. We have learned that we need to locate three propositions in an argument. These are the premises and the conclusions. We locate those propositions by noticing the natural breaks in an argument, by using premise and conclusion indicators, and by making sure that each of the propositions we have identified contain a subject and a predicate and that they contain a truth-value. Furthermore, we have learned how to change a proposition so that it has a subject, predicate, and *copula*.

In the next chapter, we will examine several more concepts related to the process of changing propositions into categorical form.

DEFINE

1. Categorical Form:

_____

_____

2. Subject Term:

_____

_____

3. Predicate Term:

_____

_____

4. Verb of Being:

_____

_____

5. *Copula*:

_____

_____

REWRITE

Rewrite the following sentences in categorical form by finding S, P, and the being verb. Remember, you may need to reorganize the sentence to incorporate a verb of being if the sentence doesn't already have one.

1. Big federal governments complicate people's lives.

S: _____

P: _____

Categorical Form: _____

2. Governments that provide needed services to people fulfill their social obligation.

S: _____

P: _____

Categorical Form: _____

3. In about two weeks, Jen and Ben will be new parents.

S: _____

P: _____

Categorical Form: _____

REWRITE (CONTINUED)

4. We know about the world through our senses.

S: _____

P: _____

Categorical Form: _____

(Hint: If you are having problems figuring this one out, think of using the predicate "sensory beings" or "sensory perceivers" to rewrite the sentence into a proposition.)

5. Stephen joined us for Christmas dinner.

S: _____

P: _____

Categorical Form: _____

GOING FURTHER

The examples on the previous page are fairly easily translated, but that isn't the case with the following examples. Try to break these propositions down to their categorical form.

1. "The only purpose for which power can be rightly exercised over any member of a civilized community, against his will, is to prevent harm to others."[2]

Propositions:

S: _____

P: _____

Categorical Form: _____

_____

2. "The history of all hitherto existing society is the history of class struggles."[3]

Propositions:

S: _____

P: _____

Categorical Form: _____

_____

DEDUCTION IN ACTION
Logic and Shakespeare

It is interesting that logic often pops up in classic literature, such as Shakespeare, for example. This is not so surprising when we consider that from the time Aristotle was rediscovered in the Middle Ages until the late 1800s and early 1900s, logic, especially deductive logic, was considered an essential part of an educated person's course of study. Therefore, educated people, especially those who acquired a college education, were often familiar with the rules of logic, and when people debated things in everyday life, they adhered to the rules of logic. This is why you will occasionally see logic pop up in the writing of classic authors like Shakespeare—it was a natural part of their education. Sometimes, as in the following excerpts from some of Shakespeare's famous plays, the logic was more subtle, rather than overtly stated, and other times, as you will notice in one of the excerpts, the logic was used for comic effect.

1. *Julius Caesar*, Act II, Scene II

Read this short monologue several times to grasp the meaning. Then, see if you can translate the argument being made into two premises and a conclusion.

> Cowards die many times before their deaths:
> The valiant never taste of death but once.
> Of all the wonders that I yet have heard,
> It seems to me most strange that men should fear,
> Seeing that death, a necessary end,
> Will come, when it will come.
> —William Shakespeare[4]

2. *Hamlet*, Act IV, Scene III

After reading this excerpt, list the several premises Hamlet seems to be using in his reasoning to reach his odd conclusion (i.e., that his father is his mother). Be aware that this is a list of premises, one supposedly leading to another, rather than a normal argument with premises and a conclusion.

Hamlet: . . . Farewell, dear mother.

King: Thy loving Father, Hamlet.

Hamlet: My mother. Father and mother is man and wife. Man and wife is one flesh. Therefore, my mother.[5]

3. *A Midsummer Night's Dream*, Helena to Hermia, Act I, Scene I

Read this monologue several times and then translate it into an argument with two premises and a conclusion.

> Call you me fair? That fair again unsay.
> Demetrius loves your fair: O happy fair!
> Your eyes are lode-stars; and your tongue's sweet air
> More tuneable than lark to shepherd's ear
> When wheat is green, when hawthorn buds appear.
> Sickness is catching: O, were favour so,
> Yours would I catch, fair Hermia, ere I go;
> My ear should catch your voice, my eye your eye,
> My tongue should catch your tongue's sweet melody. . . .
> O, teach me how you look, and with what art
> You sway the motion of Demetrius' heart.[6]

LESSON 4.6
Translating Arguments Step 3
Affirmo *and* Nego

POINTS TO REMEMBER

1. The quality of a proposition pertains to whether it is positive or negative.
2. The quantity of a proposition pertains to whether a proposition is universal or particular.
3. There are four types of propositions: *A, I, E, O*.
4. The propositions *A* and *I* get their name from the Latin word ***affirmo***, which means "I affirm."
5. The propositions *E* and *O* get their name from the Latin word ***nego***, which means "I deny."
6. Quantifiers are words such as "all," "no," "some," and "some not," which help us determine the quality and quantity of a proposition.

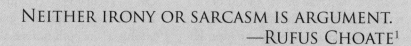

> ### NEITHER IRONY OR SARCASM IS ARGUMENT.
> ### —RUFUS CHOATE[1]

Before we explain the third step of translating arguments into categorical form, let's review our goal. Our goal is *to put ordinary-language propositions into categories, making it easier to evaluate and analyze them for validity and soundness.* We have already learned how to identify propositions in an argument and to translate them into categorical form by supplying the subject, predicate, and *copula*.

Now we need to move to the next step. In this step, we're going to focus on how we put ordinary-language propositions in categorical form so that they either affirm (support) or negate (deny) something about a specific topic. This will allow us to classify what kind of propositions they are. You've probably noticed that the word "categorical" looks and sounds a lot like the word "category." This is because the premises and conclusions of a categorical argument always fit into one of four categories. To help us understand this better, let's look at these four categories: **universal affirmative**, **universal negative**, **particular affirmative**, and **particular negative**. These may seem like highly technical names, but the meaning behind the names will quickly become clear. For right now, consider the following examples of each type of proposition.

Universal Affirmative: "All cats are four-legged creatures."

Universal Negative: "No cats are four-legged creatures."

Particular Affirmative: "Some cats are four-legged creatures."

Particular Negative: "Some cats are not four-legged creatures."

IN LATIN, *AFFIRMO* MEANS "I AFFIRM," AND *NEGO* MEANS "I DENY."

Note that the names of the four categories include a word describing the *quantity* of the proposition—whether the proposition is universal or particular—and they also include a word describing the *quality* of the proposition—whether the proposition is affirmative or negative.

Before we go on, it is important that you understand the words "quality" and "quantity" more thoroughly because doing so will help you to classify propositions more accurately. That will allow you to put them into categorical form more easily. Whenever we speak of the *quality* of a proposition, we are speaking about whether or not a proposition affirms or denies something about an idea. For instance, in the examples provided, you will notice that the propositions "All cats are four-legged creatures" and "Some cats are four-legged creatures" confirm something about an idea: that cats are four-legged creatures. On the other hand, the propositions "No cats are four-legged creatures" and "Some cats are not four-legged creatures" deny something about the same idea. Therefore, we could say that the first two propositions have an *affirmative* quality, while the second two propositions have a *negative* quality.

As another set of examples, consider these propositions: "All people who vote are participants in democracy," "Some people who vote are participants in democracy," "No people who vote are participants in democracy," and "Some people who vote are not participants in democracy." Notice, once again, that the first two propositions have a positive quality because they affirm something: that people who vote are participants in democracy. In contrast, the last two propositions have a negative quality because they deny the previously stated idea. As you can see, one important aspect of a proposition is its quality—whether it affirms or denies an idea.

As you were reading these propositions, you probably noticed that while the affirmative propositions both affirmed something, they were slightly different from each other. Also, the negative propositions both denied

something, but they were also slightly different from each other. This difference pertains to another important characteristic of propositions: quantity. The quantity of a proposition indicates whether the proposition is universal or particular. When we say that a proposition is universal, we mean that it is talking about everything in a category. When we say that a proposition is particular, we mean that it is only talking about some things in a category.

For example, consider our original propositions about cats and four-legged creatures. The propositions "All cats are four-legged creatures" and "No cats are four-legged creatures" are both **universal propositions**. One confirms that every single cat is a four-legged creature, and the other one denies that every single cat is a four-legged creature. That is, they are confirming or denying something about every single cat. Therefore, their quantity is universal. On the other hand, consider the other two propositions: "Some cats are four-legged creatures" and "Some cats are not four-legged creatures." These propositions are particular because they are talking about some of the cats. One proposition affirms that some cats are four-legged, and the other denies that some cats are four-legged. Therefore, they are **particular propositions** because they are only talking about some, rather than all, cats.

Because both affirmative and negative propositions can be either universal or particular, there are four categories, or kinds, of propositions in categorical logic. When people were further developing categorical logic in the Middle Ages, they gave a name to each of these propositions in order to help people remember them more easily. The names of the four **categorical propositions** are: *A, E, I,* and *O.* These may seem like unusual names until you learn that they come from two Latin words: *affirmo,* which means "I affirm," and *nego,* which means "I deny." Since the universal affirmative and particular affirmative propositions are affirmative, they are called *A* (universal affirmative) and *I*

(particular affirmative) because they get their names from the *a* and *i* in the word *affirmo*. The universal negative and particular negative propositions deny something about a proposition, and so they are called *E* (universal negative) and *O* (particular negative) because they get their names from the *e* and *o* in the word *nego*.

Let's look at these propositions again with their appropriate names assigned:

A: All cats are four-legged creatures.

I: Some cats are four-legged creatures.

E: No cats are four-legged creatures.

O: Some cats are not four-legged creatures.

Determining the quality and quantity of a proposition is important when you are trying to put a proposition into categorical form. This is because, as we will learn later, one of the things we look at when we are considering whether or not a deductive argument is valid is how its affirmative and negative and universal and positive propositions work together in the argument.

You have probably noticed that each proposition includes words such as "all," "no," "some," and "some . . . not," which help us determine the proposition's quantity and quality. These words are the quantifiers used in categorical logic. These are the words that help us determine whether a proposition is universal or particular. However, you have probably noticed that quantifiers, when we examine them along with the *copulas* in a proposition, also help us to determine whether or not a proposition is affirmative or negative as well. That is, quantifiers not only help us determine the quantity of a proposition, but they also help us to determine a proposition's quality.

For example, when we read the proposition "All cats are four-legged creatures," the quantifier "all" tells us that this is a universal proposition because we are talking about *all* cats. When we examine the quantifier "all" along with the *copula* "are," we also realize that this is an affirmative proposition because it is affirming something about cats. By the same reasoning, when we read the proposition "Some cats are not four-legged creatures," the quantifier "some . . . not" lets us know that this is a particular proposition because it is only talking about *some* cats. The quantifier and *copula*

together—"some are not"—also tells us that this is a negative proposition because it is denying something about cats.

Now that you understand the concepts of quality and quantity and the roles of the quantifier in determining these characteristics of a proposition, you should know that the last important step in changing a proposition into categorical form is to supply the appropriate quantifier so that we know whether the proposition is an *A*, *I*, *E*, or *O* proposition. As we mentioned before, you will discover later in this book that it is important to determine the types of propositions in an argument because certain types of proposition combinations are valid, while some are not. Before we move on to more complex arguments, however, we need to discuss how you can determine the quality and quantity of ordinary-language propositions, which will be the topic of the next lesson.

At this point, you have learned all of the major steps for translating propositions into categorical form. Once we have practiced identifying quantifiers in everyday-language propositions, you will have mastered one of the most important concepts for understanding categorical logic.

DEFINE

1. Quality:

_____

_____

2. Quantity:

_____

_____

3. Quantifier:

_____

_____

EXAMPLES

In the space below, provide one example for each of the categorical propositions: A, I, E, *and* O.

1. *A*:

_____

2. *I*:

_____

3. *E*:

_____

4. *O*:

_____

EXPLAIN

Explain from where we get the proposition names A, I, E, *and* O.

_____

_____

_____

_____

1. Identifying Quality

Please identify the quality of each of the propositions below. If a proposition is affirmative, write A in the space provided. If a proposition is negative, write N in the space provided.

1. All scientists are mathematical. _____

2. Some mirages are highly convincing. _____

3. No domestic cat with claws is truly safe. _____

4. Some pit bulls are safe. _____

5. No people believe in leprechauns. _____

6. All things on earth have a cause. _____

7. Some people know who really shot JFK. _____

8. No people know for certain if the Loch Ness Monster exists. _____

9. Some Democrats are pro–state rights. _____

10. Some Republicans are for the war in Iraq. _____

2. Identifying Quantity

Below are the same propositions about which you determined quality. Now determine whether they are universal or particular propositions. If a proposition is universal, write U in the space provided. If a proposition is particular, write P in the space provided.

1. All scientists are mathematical. _____

2. Some mirages are highly convincing. _____

3. No domestic cat with claws is truly safe. _____

4. Some pit bulls are safe. _____

5. No people believe in leprechauns. _____

6. All things on earth have a cause. _____

7. Some people know who really shot JFK. _____

8. No people know for certain if the Loch Ness Monster exists. _____

9. Some Democrats are pro–state rights. _____

10. Some Republicans are for the war in Iraq. _____

List four steps for translating arguments into categorical form.

_____

_____

_____

_____

DEDUCTION IN ACTION
Deduction and Induction Working Together

Often when you hear an argument in everyday life or when you read one in the newspaper, it will be a mixture of inductive and deductive logic. Before we look at an example of this, let's review the definition of inductive logic. Remember, when people use inductive logic, they make generalizations based on observations of everyday life. For example, someone might observe a dozen or more people who exercise a lot and who are cheerful, and he might generalize that people who exercise a lot are cheerful. As another example, a person might read the writings of several authorities who claim that people who attend religious services regularly are more hopeful in their outlook on life and, based on the observations of these authorities' opinions, she might generalize that people who regularly attend religious services tend to have a more hopeful outlook. As a final example, someone might read a list of statistics that claim that a high percentage of schools in which the principal knows every student's name are high-performing schools. From these statistics, the individual might generalize that schools in which the principal knows all the students' names tend to be higher-performing schools. So, as you can see, inductive logic is based on generalizations made from one, several, or many observations. On the other hand, you know by now that deduction is based on inference made from *a priori* assumptions or premises.

Frequently, a person will use deductive logic to construct an inductive argument effectively. It is as though the inductive argument provides the general framework for the argument, but the deductive logic helps a person move through the argument effectively. For example, on the following website, there are several arguments about gun control, which is an issue around which considerable debate flows in American culture: <http://capress.link/dd0404>.
Go to the link above and read the article "Opposing View: We're Not Done, Yet." Then, answer the following questions:

1. What deductive argument does the article contain? (Note: It is in everyday language, so you will need to translate it into a categorical argument with two premises and a conclusion.)

2. This article makes two other generalizations. One generalization is based on the opinion of people in a very specific group. The other generalization is based on the opinion of legal experts. Explain what these two generalizations are.

LESSON 4.7
Translating Arguments Step 4
Supply the Proper Quantifier

POINTS TO REMEMBER

1. You must often translate ordinary-language arguments to determine their quality and quantity and to put them into categorical form.
2. Common affirmative key words and phrases include "all," "every," "everybody," "some," "any," "anybody," "several," "many are," and "most are."
3. Some of the common affirmative key words are universal and some are particular.
4. Common negative key words and phrases include "none," "no," "no one," "nobody," "some are not," "several are not," "many are not," and "most are not."
5. Some of the common negative key words are universal and some are particular.

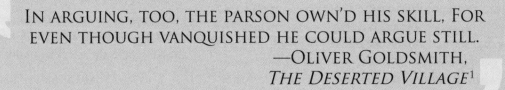

IN ARGUING, TOO, THE PARSON OWN'D HIS SKILL, FOR
EVEN THOUGH VANQUISHED HE COULD ARGUE STILL.
—OLIVER GOLDSMITH,
THE DESERTED VILLAGE[1]

Now that we have determined what quality and quantity are in categorical propositions, we need to practice determining the quality and quantity of regular English sentences. This will be important when we later examine deductive arguments because, depending on the combination of different kinds of propositions, an argument can be either valid or invalid. Therefore, determining the quality and quantity of a proposition will later help us determine the validity of a deductive argument.

If you know what you're looking for, categorizing propositions in ordinary English as affirmative or negative, universal or particular is easy. Although ordinary propositions that are affirmative won't always start with the words "all" or "some," they do tend to use one or more of the following key words or phrases to affirm an idea: "all," "every," "everybody," "some," "any," "anybody," "several," "many are," and "most are." These words and phrases are clues that the proposition is written to convey what *is*, therefore confirming that they are affirmative words and phrases. Whenever a proposition is written to convey what is, we say that the quality of the proposition is *affirming*. You can probably already tell that some of these affirmative words and phrases indicate a universal quantity, while others of them indicate a particular quantity. We will examine how to determine quantity in ordinary language in just a minute.

Just as English has common words that it uses for affirmative proposition, it also has common words for negative propositions. The English language will often use one or more of the following key words or phrases to indicate negative quality: "none," "no," "no one," "nobody," "some are not," "several are

not," "many are not," and "most are not." These words and phrases are clues that tell what something *is not*. Whenever a proposition is written to convey what is not instead of what is, we say that the quality of the proposition is *negating*. Furthermore, just as with the common affirmative words, you will notice that some of these negative words seem to indicate universal quantity, while others of them indicate particular quantity.

Let's look at a few more examples of affirmative and negative propositions in everyday English so that we can better determine the quality and quantity of these propositions. Since determining the quality of a proposition is an important step in putting propositions into categorical form, we will also review what we already know about this process.

Let's consider the proposition "Anybody who wants to get good grades should study." We notice the word "anybody" and realize that this is an affirmative proposition. We know that affirmative propositions are either *A* propositions or *I* propositions. As we think about this proposition more, we realize that it could also be translated "All people who want to get good grades should study." It is making a statement about what *all* people—not just some—should do if they want to get good grades. So it is universal and affirmative, rather than particular and negative.

Now that we have determined that it is an *A* proposition, we need to finish putting the proposition into categorical form. The proposition should begin like this: "All people who want to get good grades are. . . ." Now we need to supply an appropriate predicate by changing the phrase "should study" into a proper proposition ending. If we change that phrase to "are people who should study," the meaning of the proposition stays the same, and it provides an appropriate predicate. Therefore, our new proposition written in categorical form is this: "All people who want to get good grades are people who should study." To make it more concise, it could be shortened even further to: "All desirers of good grades are studiers."

Let's look at another affirmative example. Consider the sentence "Sometimes our perceptions are deceptive." The words "sometimes" and "are" let us know that this is an affirmative sentence. Furthermore, it is clear that "sometimes" indicates that this is a particular affirmative proposition because it is not claiming that all of our perceptions deceive us, only some of them. Therefore, the quality of the sentence is affirmative, and its quantity is particular. We could easily reword this proposition in this manner: "Some of our perceptions are deceptive."

Now that we have identified the quality of this proposition, we need to put it into categorical form. We can start the proposition like this: "Some of our perceptions are . . ." We have supplied the quality, the subject, and the *copula*. Now we need a predicate. How about the phrase "deceptive perceptions" for a predicate? Our new proposition would read like this: "Some of our perceptions are deceptive perceptions." Then, we could shorten it even further to say "Some perceptions are deceptive." Our proposition is now in categorical form. It has a clear quality and quantity. It contains a subject, a *copula*, or being verb, and a predicate, and it retains the meaning of our original sentence.

Let's look at an example of a negative proposition to see if we can translate it into categorical form: "Nobody likes a tattletale." When we see the word "nobody," we know that the proposition is denying something, so it is a negative sentence. Furthermore, we realize that nobody is denying something about every person or thing, rather than just some things or some people. Therefore, this is a universal negative proposition and will start with the word "no." If we want to translate the beginning of this proposition into categorical form, it will go something like this: "No person is. . . ." In order to use the word "no," which is proper categorical form, we need to supply a subject here. We can easily do that with the word "person" and still keep the original meaning of the proposition. Now we need to translate the phrase "likes a tattletale" into a proper predicate. There are probably several predicates that could

WHENEVER A PROPOSITION IS WRITTEN TO CONVEY WHAT IS, WE SAY THAT THE QUALITY OF THE PROPOSITION IS AFFIRMING.

work, but the phrase "tattletale admirer" certainly keeps the meaning of the original sentence. Therefore, we can now complete the new categorical form of the proposition in this way: "No person is a tattletale admirer." We now have a universal negative proposition that is in categorical form but keeps the meaning of the original proposition.

Since the last few chapters have focused on translating everyday arguments into categorical form, let's review these steps before we move on to the next chapter. To translate arguments into everyday form, follow these steps:

1. Determine the three propositions of an argument (each of these propositions should have a subject and a predicate).

2. Rewrite the proposition so that it contains a being verb, along with the subject and predicate.

3. Determine the proposition's quantity and quality.

4. Supply the proper quantifier.

You may find that in the beginning, you go through each of these steps individually, whereas later you may combine several steps in your translation process. This is OK and perfectly natural as you become more comfortable with categorical form and deductive logic.

Now that we have examined how we translate everyday propositions into categorical form, in the next lesson we will examine some propositions that can pose a particular challenge. You will find that, although they might be intimidating at first, they aren't as scary as they seem.

REVIEW
DEFINE

1. Categorical Propositions:

_____

2. Quality of a Proposition:

_____

3. Quantity of a Proposition:

_____

4. Universal Propositions:

_____

5. Particular Propositions:

_____

6. Universal Affirmative Propositions:

_____

DEFINE (CONTINUED)

7. Universal Negative Propositions:

_____

8. Particular Affirmative Propositions:

_____

9. Particular Negative Propositions:

_____

DETERMINE

Classify each proposition by determining if it is universal affirmative, universal negative, particular affirmative, or particular negative. Then label your answer with the appropriate symbol: A, E, I, or O.

	Classification	Symbol
1. Some winter days are cold days.		
2. None of her sisters are dancers.		
3. All of my pets are dogs.		
4. Some mathematicians are not math teachers.		
5. Few are able to live a righteous life.		
6. Some sense perceptions are false.		
7. Nobody accepts the geocentric theory of the universe anymore.		
8. Everybody loves Raymond.		
9. The truth is out there.		
10. Every tyrannical government abdicates its right to authority.		

DEDUCTION IN ACTION
Political and Cultural Arguments

In the last chapter, you examined an argument that was in favor of the right to bear arms. You examined this argument to determine both the deductive and inductive arguments that it contained. If you pay attention to the political and cultural arguments you hear and read, you will notice, once again, that many of them contain a mixture of induction and deduction. As an example of the argument in favor of gun control, go to the following link and read "Our View on the Second Amendment: Court Expands Gun Ruling But Allows Reasonable Limits": <http://capress.link/dd0405>. Then, answer the following questions.

1. As you can see, this article describes the way in which Supreme Court justices wrestle with different phrases of the Constitution. At the end, it describes a particular interpretation of Justice Samuel Alito. See if you can put his argument into syllogistic form with two premises and a conclusion.

2. In addition to this deductive argument, the article makes a generalization based on the opinions of several different authorities. Who are the authorities whose opinions are being considered in this article?

LESSON 4.8
Translating Arguments Step 5
Propositions Translated into Categorical Form

POINTS TO REMEMBER

1. Propositions containing names are always universal and require the quantifier "all" or "no."
2. Use context clues and research to determine the quantifiers of **indefinite** propositions.

> ONE OUGHT NOT TO ACT AND
> SPEAK LIKE PEOPLE ASLEEP.
> —HERACLITUS[1]

The previous two lessons covered the basics of determining the quality and quantity of propositions, and they also explored how to determine the quality and quantity of ordinary-language sentences. There are several other types of regular everyday sentences that may pose a particular challenge, so we want to take a look at those now.

Singular Subjects

I am a tennis player.

What's the quantity of this proposition? Is "I" referring to all of its class (in this case, me) or just part of its class? It refers to all of me, making it a universal proposition. While it may seem more natural to present this claim as an *I* (particular affirmative) proposition because one person is one member of the class of humans, note that the claim refers to only one person, so it is a class that has only one member. That makes this an *A* proposition.

We know the quantity of the proposition, so let's move on to the quality. Is this proposition stating what is or isn't the case about the subject? It's stating what is, making it an affirmative proposition. Therefore, this proposition is really saying, "All I am a tennis player." It sounds awkward, but this is a universal affirmative proposition and would be translated "all." How do we know that this proposition needs the word "all"? Remember that the last step in translating propositions into categorical form is to supply a quantifier. Furthermore, remember what we covered in the last lesson: In categorical logic, we work with four types of propositions—*A* (the universal affirmative), *I* (the particular affirmative), *E* (the universal negative), and *O* (the particular negative). Each of these propositions has a quantifier. The quantifier of the *A* proposition is "all," the quantifier for the *I* proposition is "some," the quantifier for the *E* proposition is "no," and the quantifier for the *O* proposition is "some . . . not." Therefore, once we figure out, as we did for the tennis player proposition, that a proposition is the universal affirmative, or the *A* proposition, we automatically know that the correct quantifier to supply is "all" because "all" is always the quantifier for the *A* proposition.

What if I were to say, "I am not a tennis player"? We said that the word "I" was referring to all of me, making it a universal proposition. Is this proposition stating what is or is not the case about the subject? Since it is stating what *is not* the case, it is a negative proposition. Therefore, this sentence is really saying, "No I (none of me) am a tennis player." This is a universal negative proposition and would be translated to include the word "no." You may feel a little unconfident about supplying this quantifier, especially since it makes the sentence awkward, but just take a minute to think it through. If this is a universal negative proposition, and the quantifier for the universal negative is always "no," then "no" is the correct quantifier for this proposition.

Indefinite Subjects

Dogs are dangerous.

How do we determine the quantity of this proposition? After all, it doesn't have any of the normal affirmative and negative words, and it is not talking about one person. That means that the subject is *indefinite*. So, how do we know its quality? With a proposition like this, we often have to figure out the meaning *implied* by the sentence, or the context of the sentence, in order to determine its quantity. While it may seem impossible to determine the original intent of a sentence like this if it is by itself, if you consider its context, or the sentences surrounding it, you may be able to figure it out. Consider our proposition in the context of the following argument: "If you have a large dog that is not used to being around people, you should put it on a leash when you take it out on a walk. After all, dogs are dangerous." It seems clear from the surrounding propositions that this person is talking about only some dogs—namely, large dogs that are not used to being around people. Therefore, through context, we can determine that the quantity of this proposition is particular. The proposition in categorical form would read like this: "Some dogs are dangerous." Be assured that it is very unlikely that you will encounter a single proposition in absence of a surrounding context. Therefore, one of the best ways to determine the quantifier of an indefinite subject is to examine its context.

However, some propositions are a little trickier. For instance, consider the following proposition:

Trees shed their leaves in the fall.

What's the quantity of this proposition? Is "trees" referring to all of its class or just part of it? You may or may not know from studying science that some trees, such as conifers, do not shed their leaves in the fall. Therefore, if you know this fact, you can figure out that the word "trees" in this proposition refers to some, but not all, of its class. If you knew that it referred to some, you would realize that it is a particular affirmative proposition, and the correct quantifier is "some" because "some" is always the quantifier for an *I* proposition.

However, what if you did not know this fact? That is, what if you run into a proposition whose quantity is unclear and whose context is confusing or unfamiliar to you? In these cases, you may need to do a little further research to determine the quantifier of the sentence.

For instance, consider the following proposition: "Totalitarian rulers use violence to control their people." If you are familiar with the term "totalitarian," you know that totalitarian rulers often use force and violence to maintain their power. However, you still may be uncertain as to whether or not this is a universal or particular proposition. If this proposition were a part of an argument in a book, you would likely be able to determine the author's meaning from the context of the proposition. However, if this was still unclear, you might have to do some more research in history books, encyclopedias, or on the Internet to determine if violence was a typical component of totalitarian regimes. Since it almost always, if not always, is true that totalitarian rulers use violence to control their people, it probably makes sense to use the quantifier "all."

Be assured that in the majority of cases, you will be able to determine the quantity of an argument from the propositions themselves or from the context surrounding the propositions. For those tricky ones, research further to determine the most likely quantity, and you will likely be correct, since few arguments that you will encounter will contain such obscure facts that you are unable to make an educated guess about the quantity implied in the sentence.

Putting It All Together

Now that we've looked at all of the steps involved in translating arguments into categorical form, let's review the steps we have been working on and then put all of them together.

First, in order to analyze the categorical or symbolic form of an argument, we need to identify the premises and conclusion, or the propositions, of an argument. To help us identify the three propositions, we need to look for natural breaks in arguments, use premise and conclusion indicators, and make sure that our propositions contain a subject, predicate, and *copula* and that they affirm or deny something about a topic. As we have mentioned, there will be times when ordinary-language propositions require us to change the wording of sentences in order to put them into a form that will allow us to analyze them categorically or symbolically. That is because when sentences are in true categorical form, they will have the following items: a quantifier, a subject, a *copula*, and a predicate. Few regular everyday sentences contain all of these elements, so sometimes we must change the wording of the sentences to supply those elements. As long as our translation of a sentence retains its original meaning, it is OK to do this.

Remember that we are dealing with categorical logic, so once you translate your proposition into categorical form, it should fit into one of the four categories of proposition:

All S is P. ....*A* proposition
Some S is P. ....*I* proposition
No S is P. ....*E* proposition
Some S is not P. ....*O* proposition

Now that we have reviewed the steps, let's go through a few examples together. Here's our first argument.

> No state secession from the United States is permissible by the Constitution since state secession from the United States is treason, and no treason is permissible by the Constitution.

When we look at this argument, right away we notice three propositions:

1. No state secession from the United States is permissible by the Constitution.

2. State secession from the United States is treason.

3. No treason is permissible by the Constitution.

Furthermore, we notice the word "since," which is a premise indicator. This helps us to realize that the next

proposition and probably the one after it are our premises. Therefore, the argument can be structured something like this:

> State secession from the United States is treason.
>
> No treason is permissible by the Constitution.
>
> Therefore, no state secession is permissible by the Constitution.

For the most part, these propositions are nicely laid out in categorical form for us. That is, most of them contain a quantifier, subject, *copula*, and predicate. However, the first proposition, "Secession is . . . treason," is missing a quantifier. We can easily supply this, however, when we consider that the meaning of this proposition is certainly that all state secession from the United States is treason. Since the sentence implies "all," it is a universal positive proposition, and therefore, it needs the quantifier "all." As such, here is our argument in categorical form:

> All state secession from the United States is treason.
>
> No treason is permissible by the Constitution.
>
> Therefore, no state secession is permissible by the Constitution.

Now let's look at a more difficult argument that is in ordinary language.

> Tyrannical governments don't have a right to rule the people because only governments that protect their people's rights have the authority to rule the people, and governments that become tyrannical do not protect the people's rights.

When we look at this argument, we notice several propositions:

> Tyrannical governments don't have a right to rule the people.
>
> Only governments that protect their people's rights have the authority to rule the people.
>
> Governments that become tyrannical do not protect the people's rights.

In addition, we notice the premise indicator "because" in these arguments, which lets us know that the following

propositions or two are premises. It makes sense to organize the argument in this manner:

> Only governments that protect their people's rights have the authority to rule.
>
> Governments that become tyrannical do not protect the people's rights.
>
> Tyrannical governments don't have a right to rule the people.

We have found our premises and conclusions, but these propositions are a little tricky because, as you will notice, they are not in categorical form. We need to translate them into this form before we can assign symbols to them. We know that to translate the arguments into categorical form, we need to make sure they each have a quantifier, a subject, a *copula*, and a predicate. When we look at the first proposition, "Only governments that protect their people's rights have the authority to rule," we realize that this proposition is a universal positive proposition because it is basically saying that governments that protect their people's rights have the right to rule. We could rewrite the proposition this way: "All governments that protect their people's rights have a right to rule." So far, so good. Now we need to supply a clear subject, predicate, and *copula*. We will change the subject a little bit and begin the sentence like this: "All governments protective of people's rights are. . . ." Now all we need is a predicate. We can change the phrase "right to rule" to "legitimate governments" and still preserve the original meaning of the proposition. Therefore, our new first proposition is "All governments protective of people's rights are legitimate governments."

The next premise can easily be translated to: "No tyrannical governments are protective of people's rights." The last premise can be translated: "No tyrannical governments are legitimate governments." You will notice that while we changed a few of the terms in the propositions, all of the translated propositions retain the meaning of the original propositions. Therefore, here is our new argument:

> All governments protective of people's rights are legitimate governments.
>
> No tyrannical governments are governments protective of people's rights.

> No tyrannical governments are legitimate governments.

Let's do one last one just to make sure you are getting the hang of this. We will move through the steps quickly on this one since this is our third time through the process.

> Emma will certainly succeed in college as she is responsible and intelligent, and responsibility and intelligence are indicators for success in college.

Here are our three propositions:

> Emma is responsible and intelligent.
>
> Responsibility and intelligence are indicators for success in college.
>
> Emma will certainly succeed in college.

When you look at the first proposition, you should remember that propositions that have a name for the subject are always universal; therefore, even though it looks awkward, we will reword the first proposition to read "All of Emma is a responsible and intelligent student." We want to make the next proposition somewhat compatible to the first, so we will change it to read like this: "All responsible and intelligent students are successful in college." You will notice that although this is quite a bit different than the original proposition, it still retains the basic meaning. In order to give the last proposition an appropriate quantifier and *copula*, we will word it like this: "All of Emma is a student who will be successful in college." So, with all of those translations in place, here is our new argument:

> All of Emma is a responsible and intelligent student.
>
> All responsible and intelligent students are students who are successful in college.
>
> All of Emma is a student who will be successful in college.

Now that you know how to translate propositions into categorical form, you are ready to translate them into symbolic form in order to analyze them for validity. In addition, in a later lesson, you will also learn how to construct your own valid arguments, and, of course, you will use the same skills to analyze your own arguments for validity.

TRANSLATE

Translate each of the following propositions into categorical form. Then, label each according to its quality and quantity.

1. "Ingenious men may say ingenious things."[2]

Subject: _____   **Predicate:** _____

Quality: _____   **Quantity:** _____

Categorical Form: _____

2. "You cannot conquer America."[3]

Subject: _____   **Predicate:** _____

Quality: _____   **Quantity:** _____

Categorical Form: _____

3. "We have no other alternative than independence."[4]

Subject: _____   **Predicate:** _____

Quality: _____   **Quantity:** _____

Categorical Form: _____

4. "Nature has imposed upon every being the law of self-preservation."[5]

Subject: _____   **Predicate:** _____

Quality: _____   **Quantity:** _____

Categorical Form: _____

GOING FURTHER

Read the following passages and identify the arguments. Separate the arguments into their three categorical propositions. Translate each proposition into categorical form. Then, label each proposition according to its quality and quantity.

1. Whenever it rains in our area, our son Jared's ceiling leaks. Often in July, we get heavy rains in our area. So, some times in July are times when Jared's ceiling leaks.

Argument:

_____

_____

_____

Proposition 1: _____

    Quality: _____   **Quantity:** _____

GOING FURTHER (CONTINUED)

Proposition 2: _____

    Quality: _____ **Quantity:** _____

Proposition 3: _____

    Quality: _____ **Quantity:** _____

2. According to Mortimer Adler, part of knowing how to read a book requires students to assimilate the knowledge they have learned (a process he calls "enlightenment"). Students who can assimilate knowlege in this way are among the best students. Therefore, some of the best students really know how to read a book.

Argument:

_____

_____

_____

Proposition 1: _____

    Quality: _____ **Quantity:** _____

Proposition 2: _____

    Quality: _____ **Quantity:** _____

Proposition 3: _____

    Quality: _____ **Quantity:** _____

DEDUCTION IN ACTION
Code Breaking

As you have studied already, deductive logic is based on inference. You may not realize it fully yet, but being skilled at inference can be a very helpful talent. As an example of one way in which inference can be helpful, consider code breakers. Code breakers are people who interpret codes for a variety of reasons. Usually, they break codes in order to be able to interpret enemy intelligence during times of war. Although code breakers use a number of methods to break codes, depending on the type and complexity of the code, one of their methods, called frequency analysis, uses inferences. Read about frequency analysis at the following link and then explain how inference is key to the process of frequency analysis: <http://capress.link/dd0406>.

DIALOGUE 5.1
Introduction to the Square of Opposition

Socrates sees Nate sitting under the tree again.

Socrates: Well, Nate, you look much happier than you did the last time I saw you.

Nate: I have to tell you, Socrates, I'm hooked.

Socrates: Good heavens! That sounds painful.

Nate: No, it's just a saying. It means I'm really into it.

Socrates: "Into it"? Oh, dear, I think you've lost me again.

Nate: Sorry, that was another figure of speech. What I mean is that I'm becoming fascinated by deductive logic.

Socrates: Now *that's* something I don't hear every day. What is it exactly about deductive logic that has "hooked" you, as you say?

Nate: Now that I know what I am looking for, I see it and hear it everywhere. In fact, it makes me much more aware of the meaning behind people's words.

Socrates: Has this happened to you recently?

Nate: Yes, just today, in fact. I was talking with my friend, Pete, at a coffee shop. Pete and I always argue about politics. He's what you would call a liberal, and I guess I'm a conservative.

Socrates: I see. I think I'm familiar with those terms politically.

Nate: Anyhow, we were arguing, and in the middle of our conversation, Pete said that all conservatives were resistant to change. Suddenly, a light went on in my head, and I realized that he had implied that I was resistant to change as well. The thing is, he didn't realize until I pointed it out to him that he'd made this implication.

Socrates: What happened?

Nate: I said, "Pete, if you think that all conservatives are resistant to change, that means you think that I'm resistant to change, too." Suddenly he got this perplexed look on his face, and he started backtracking, explaining that he meant that only *some* conservatives were resistant to change, and he didn't necessarily think I was one of them.

Socrates: Nate, I think you have just stumbled onto something called the **square of opposition**.

Nate: What is that?

Socrates: I'll tell you in a minute. Go on.

Nate: Well, my moment of triumph was short-lived. We kept arguing, and soon enough, I made the same mistake. I argued that no liberals are proponents of small government. All of a sudden, I realized that I had just implied that Pete was not a proponent of small government.

Socrates: Is he?

Nate: Well, his beliefs are a little complex. He believes in government aid for some important social services, but not for a lot of things for which typical liberals might desire it. In fact, in many ways, he *is* a proponent of small government.

Socrates: I see. We often find that real-life people's views are much more complex than how we stereotype them.

Nate: I think I am beginning to figure that out. Anyhow, as soon as I said that, Pete smiled at me, and we both decided that we needed to think through the implications of our propositions more carefully. Anyhow, after we left, I started thinking about other beliefs I had in order to see if they implied unexpected things. For instance, I thought about some of my conservative friends who were extremely well educated. I've generally believed that a lot of conservatives are well educated. Then I wondered if that automatically implied that *some* conservatives *were not* well educated, or if it implied, somehow, that I believed that liberals were not well educated.

Socrates: Nate, you are very curious. I like that in a person. After all, true wisdom lies in recognizing that which you do not know.

Nate: Hey, isn't that one of your famous sayings or something?

Socrates: Let's hope so. Anyhow, as I was saying earlier, you have stumbled upon something called the square of opposition.

Nate: Tell me more about that, please.

Socrates: Briefly put, the square of opposition is a tool used to determine inference. It demonstrates what each proposition implies in relationship to other propositions.

Nate: Wait, which propositions are we talking about here?

Socrates: In your studies of deductive logic, I'm certain you've run across *A*, *E*, *I*, and *O* propositions, correct?

Nate: Oh, yes. Now I understand.

Socrates: The square of opposition demonstrates how these four propositions relate to one another and what they imply about each other. For instance, let's take the proposition your friend, Pete, made about conservatives. When he said, "All conservatives are resistant to change," what kind of propositions was he using?

Nate: Let's see. That would be an *A* proposition.

Socrates: Right, and you realized immediately that this *A* proposition implied the *I* proposition. What would that be?

Nate: Oh, I get it. The *I* proposition is "Some conservatives are resistant to change." When Pete made the *A* proposition, I realized he was also talking about me—I was the "some conservatives" implied in the "all conservatives" proposition.

Socrates: Correct. You recognized a relationship called **subimplication**. That relationship states that the particular is implied in the universal. That means that if something is true about the universal proposition, it is also true about the particular proposition.

Nate: I think I'm beginning to understand. Are there more of these relationships?

Socrates: We generally speak of five: **contrariety**, **contradiction**, **subcontrariety**, subimplication and **superimplication**. Each of these relationships has certain rules of inference that can help you answer the kinds of questions you were asking earlier.

Nate: Thanks, Socrates! This is really helpful. I think I'm going to go study this square of opposition thing.

Socrates: (*smiling to himself*) One more captive freed from the cave.

1. What is the purpose of the square of opposition?

_____

_____

_____

_____

2. List each of the relationships of opposition.

a. _____

b. _____

c. _____

d. _____

e. _____

LESSON 5.2
The Square of Opposition

POINTS TO REMEMBER

1. The square of opposition is a model that helps you understand the relationships of opposition that exist between the four categorical propositions.
2. The relationships between the four categorical propositions are called **relationships of opposition** because they are the relationships that exist between propositions of opposing quality and/or quantity.

> NOWHERE AM I SO DESPERATELY NEEDED AS AMONG A SHIPLOAD OF ILLOGICAL HUMANS.
> —SPOCK[1]

You have learned that deductive logic helps you to understand the art of inference. That is, it helps you understand the implications of *a priori* truths. This is important because if we don't understand the implications of what we are saying or thinking, we can sometimes end up holding contradictory ideas simultaneously. Understanding how the propositions relate to each other will help you comprehend the ideas that naturally proceed from your ideas and those of other people as well.

Remember that in categorical logic, there are four kinds of propositions: *A*, *I*, *E*, and *O*. The relationships between these four propositions are called relationships of opposition because they deal with the relationships that exist between propositions with opposing quality and/or quantity. For example, one relationship of opposition that we will study is the relationship between *A* and *I* propositions. Although these propositions have the same quality (positive), they have opposite quantity (*A* is universal, and *I* is particular). Therefore, an examination of how these propositions relate to one another shows us how propositions of opposite quantity interact. Another relationship we will examine is the relationship between *E* and *I* propositions, which have opposite quality *and* quantity. Examining the relationship between these propositions will reveal how they are related to each other based on this opposing quality and quantity.

We will study the relationship between the four propositions by looking at something called the square of opposition, which is a diagram developed by logicians to visually illustrate the relationships between the propositions. In order to understand why the square of opposition can be such a helpful tool, it is important for you to understand the difference between the words "infer" and "imply" because they will show up frequently during our discussion. Indeed, the entire purpose of the square of opposition is to help you make valid inferences from the implications of other people's propositions as well as your own.

The words "infer" and "imply" are related, but they are also distinct from each other. When we *infer*, we derive an idea from what we already know. That is, we consider facts and propositions we know to be true, and this leads us to other truths that proceed from those facts and propositions.[2] You might recall that we have already discussed the fact that deductive logic is based on inference by using previously established truths to reach new truths. This is exactly what we are doing when we construct syllogisms.

To understand the process of inference better, let's look at one of the most common methods of forming a syllogism. Consider a syllogism with which you are very familiar by now: "All men are mortal. Socrates is a man. Therefore, Socrates is mortal." The first premise, which is a true proposition, creates a category—men—and then assigns a descriptive term—"mortal"—to that category. Next, in the second premise, which is also a true proposition, it affirms that another term—"Socrates"—belongs in the first category—men. This is where inference comes in. Because we have affirmed that the new term "Socrates" is in an old category—men—about which we already know something—men are mortal—we can infer something new about Socrates—that he is mortal, too—based on our past information. In other words, since we already know something about the category of men, we can also infer something about Socrates, once we affirm that he is also in that category.

Now let's consider a real-life scenario of inference. Let's say that you know a family named the LaDucs. Although you have not met all of the LaDucs, you know, because you have been told, that all of the LaDuc family members are concert violinists. Later, you meet Robert, another member of the LaDuc family. Since you already know that all of the LaDuc family members are concert violinists, you can automatically infer that Robert is also a concert violinist since he is in that family. This relation of new terms to old categories is the process by which we construct inference in a syllogism.

It is important to note, however, that not only can we make inferences with syllogisms, we can also infer ideas from single propositions. For instance, if the proposition "All Oregon coffee shops are eclectic" is true, we know the proposition "Some Oregon coffee shops are not eclectic" is false. That is, we can *infer* the falsity of the second proposition through the truth of the first. Now, you may be wondering, "Well, how do I know that I can infer that 'Some Oregon coffee shops are not eclectic' is false if the proposition 'All Oregon coffee shops are eclectic' is true?" This is where the square of opposition comes in. It gives us a set of rules to help us understand the proper inferences we can make from different propositions. Once you study the square of opposition in the next several chapters, you will better understand how these rules work with the four categorical propositions—*A*, *I*, *E*, and *O*—that are the foundation of categorical logic.

Now that we have looked at the word "infer," let's examine the word "imply." As mentioned before, the word "imply" is similar to infer, but is distinct from it. When we *imply*, we express or state something indirectly because what we say involves another truth as a necessary or logical consequence.[3] For instance, let us say that some children are being noisy in church, and an older woman turns around and says to them, "Children should be seen and not heard." She is implying that the children should be quiet. She knows that her proposition logically entails that the children should be quiet because if the people to whom she is talking are children, which they are, and if children should be seen and not heard, then these people who are children should be seen and not heard. In other words, they should be quiet. A person who implies uses a truth to suggest another truth, although the second truth is not directly stated. As you can imagine, in order to argue or discuss ideas effectively with people, you must be aware of what you are implying through your propositions, as well as what other people are implying through their propositions.

Inference and implication go hand in hand. When someone states a proposition, he automatically implies something else, but this implication will only be detected if people infer it properly. This is what the square of opposition helps us to do: make correct inferences by accurately recognizing the truths that different propositions imply. As we explore the square of opposition, you will learn some of the traps into which you can fall when you make bad inferences.

Now that you understand the difference between inference and implication, we will turn our attention to the five relationships of categorical propositions:

1. **Contradiction:** The relationship of contradiction examines the relationship between *A* and *O* propositions and *E* and *I* propositions, which have opposing quality and quantity.

2. **Contrariety:** The relationship of contrariety examines the relationship between *A* and *E* propositions, which have opposing quality.

3. **Subcontrariety:** The relationship of subcontrariety examines the relationship between *I* and *O* propositions, which have opposing quality.

4. **Subimplication:** Sometimes called **subalternation**, the relationship of subimplication examines the relationship between *A* and *I* propositions, which have opposing quantity. It also examines the relationship between *E* and *O* propositions, which also have opposite quantity. The relationship of subimplication examines the universal proposition first to see what it implies about the particular proposition.

5. **Superimplication:** Sometimes called **superalternation**, the relationship of superimplication examines the same propositions as the relationship of subimplication. However, it examines the particular proposition first to see what it implies about the universal proposition.

These relationships are considered the relationships of opposition because they demonstrate how the truth-values of propositions are related to one another. (In chapter 6, we will analyze how propositions are *similar* to one another as we study the **relationships of equivalence**.) Take a look at the diagram of the square of opposition so that you can start to become familiar with it:

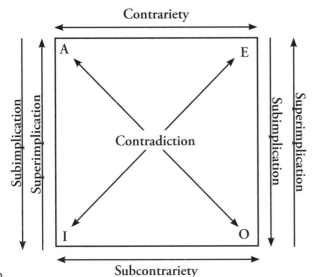

Before we examine each of these relationships more thoroughly, let's look at an example of a conversation in which someone doesn't fully recognize the implications of her beliefs. Julie and Tiffany are best friends who go to school together. In this dialogue, Tiffany is already sitting at the lunch table, when Julie joins her.

Julie: *(sitting down)* Hey, Tiffany, I just heard the juiciest piece of gossip about Leah and that guy she's been hanging around lately. I've got to tell you!

Tiffany: Come on, Julie. You know I don't like to talk about other people's business. Gossip can really hurt people.

Julie: Come on, Tif. I think some gossip is harmless. After all, it's not like I'm lying or slandering Leah's reputation. Sometimes talking about people is just entertainment or blowing off steam.

Tiffany: I have to disagree. From what I've seen, no gossip is harmless.

Julie: Really? OK, I'm curious. Convince me!

Tiffany: Well, would you agree with me that if you talk about someone and what has happened in his life rather than talking to him, there's always the possibility that you could be in error or that you could misinterpret what has actually happened?

Julie: Yeah, I guess so.

Tiffany: Would you also agree that when we believe something incorrect about someone, it could lead us to think badly of him?

Julie: Sure, it's possible. I mean, it doesn't happen all the time, but I guess you could say it's always possible.

Tiffany: Would you also agree that thinking badly of someone when that bad opinion is incorrect has the possibility of harming someone?

Julie: Sure, I guess that seems right.

Tiffany: If something has the possibility of harming someone, it's not harmless, right?

Julie: That makes sense.

Tiffany: Then it would seem that no gossip is harmless because all gossip carries the possibility of harming someone.

Julie: Boy, I never thought of it that way. It does seem that no gossip is harmless. OK, you've convinced me. I will purge my bit of juicy gossip from my mind and reform my ways. That's why I keep you around, girl—you always make me think. *(steals one of Tiffany's french fries)*

Tiffany: I think you really just keep me around for my french fries.

You may have noticed that Tiffany was playing a role in this conversation very similar to the role Socrates played in the *Apology* (you can refresh your memory of the *Apology* by checking out your answers to the exercises in the Deduction in Action section of lesson 1.1). That is, she asked Julie a series of questions and posed a series of scenarios that demonstrated a contradiction in Julie's beliefs. Notice that at the beginning of the conversation, Julie said that she believed that *some* gossip was harmless. However, by the end, she had admitted that she believed that *no* gossip was harmless. How is it that she held these contradictory beliefs and did not realize it?

It is important to note that we all hold a vast number of beliefs about both trivial and important matters. Some of these things we believe because we have carefully considered the issues involved. However, there are other things we believe just because everyone else around us believes them or because it is easy and comfortable to believe them. When we believe something merely because it is comfortable or because the people around us believe it, we often fail to think through the various implications of our belief. This was likely the case with Julie. She probably enjoyed gossiping now and then, and everyone else around her did it, too, so she truly thought she believed that some of it was harmless. However, once she actually thought through the implications of gossip, she realized that she didn't actually believe it was harmless after all. As you can see from the example of Julie and Tiffany's conversation, dialogue and personal reflection are two tools that are helpful in thinking through the implications of the many beliefs we possess.

Learning about the square of opposition, along with the other tools in this book, will help you to more effectively argue, discuss, dialogue, and reflect. So, now that we have an idea of what the square of opposition is and why it can be helpful, it is time for us to take a look at the first relationship in it: contradiction. This will be the subject of the next chapter.

REVIEW

EXPLAIN

1. Why are the relationships on the square of opposition considered relationships of opposition?

_____

_____

2. What is the purpose of the square of opposition?

_____

_____

3. What is the difference between the words "infer" and "imply"?

_____

_____

PRACTICE   Study the square of opposition on p. 78 for several moments, memorizing the placement of the different propositions on the square, as well as the different relationships illustrated on it. In the space below, replicate the square of opposition as accurately as you can. (This square is something that you will continue to practice in the next few lessons ahead).

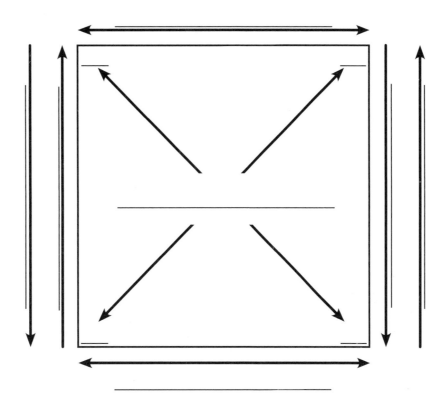

DISCUSS   1. Why do people often hold contradictory beliefs without realizing it?

_____

_____

_____

_____

_____

_____

_____

_____

DEDUCTION IN ACTION

Sherlock Holmes and Code Breaking

In the previous lesson, you read about how code breakers use logic, primarily inference, to break some types of codes with a technique called frequency analysis. In an earlier lesson, you read a Sherlock Holmes story in which you examined how the famous Sherlock Holmes used deductive logic (along with inductive logic) to solve a crime. Now we will combine inference and deductive logic to answer questions about a Sherlock Holmes story entitled "The Adventures of the Dancing Men." Sir Arthur Conan Doyle wrote a story illustrating how Holmes uses frequency analysis, just as code breakers do, to solve a crime. Read the story and then answer the questions that follow. You can download or read the story "The Adventure of the Dancing Men" at the following link: <http://capress.link/dd0501>.

1. What are some of the clues that Holmes uses to figure out that Watson does not plan to invest in South African securities?

2. Holmes tells Watson, "It is not really difficult to construct a series of inferences, each dependent upon its predecessor and each simple in itself. If, after doing so, one simply knocks out all the central inferences and presents one's audiences with the starting point and the conclusion, one may produce a startling . . . effect."[4] Think about the meaning of the word "inference" in the context of this quote. Does this sound more like inductive or deductive logic? Are the clues listed in the previous question examples of deductive logic? Explain your answer.

3. What appears to be mysterious about Elsie Cubitt's behavior toward her husband concerning her past, and what does she say about her past? What does she make her husband promise before their marriage?

4. What disturbing events had brought Hilton Cubitt to Holmes?

5. When Holmes breaks the code and travels to Riding Thorpe Manor, what tragedy does he discover has happened?

6. List at least five clues Holmes noticed at the crime scene, which he then uses to prove to the police that there was a third person who fired another shot.

7. List three inferences and hypothetical guesses Holmes made to break the code.

8. Looking back on the manner in which Holmes solved this case, do you think he used more deductive or inductive logic? Why? Do you think that this is the same kind of logic police use today to solve crimes? Give an example of how they might use inductive or deductive logic in solving a crime, such as car theft, burglary, or arson (an illegal setting of a fire).

LESSON 5.3
Contradiction

POINTS TO REMEMBER

1. Contradiction is the relationship between *A* and *O* propositions and *E* and *I* propositions.
2. Contradictory propositions cannot both be true at the same time.
3. Contradictory propositions cannot both be false at the same time.
4. If one contradictory proposition is true, the other must be false.
5. If one contradictory proposition is false, the other must be true.

> MEN WHO ARE LOVERS OF WISDOM MUST BE INQUIRERS INTO MANY THINGS INDEED.
> —HERACLITUS[1]

In this chapter, we will examine the first relationship in the square of opposition: contradiction. We often hear this term used in everyday life. For instance, my mother used to tell me I was an exercise in contradiction because I didn't like tomatoes but absolutely loved spaghetti sauce, ketchup, tomato soup, and chili. Since spaghetti sauce, ketchup, tomato soup and chili are all made with a tomato base, it seems like a contradiction to like one and not the other. The word "contradiction" comes from the Latin words *contra*, which means "against," and *dicere*, which means "to speak." Therefore, the word "contradict" literally means "to speak against" something. That is, when we contradict ourselves, we speak against something we have already said (like the child who says she doesn't like tomatoes but loves tomato products), or, when we contradict others, we speak against what they have said. As another example, consider a hypothetical classroom scenario.

Teacher: Please get your homework from last night out. We need to go over it.

Student: We didn't have homework last night. You said we didn't have to finish it until Wednesday.

Teacher: Don't contradict me. We are not grading it. We are just going over what you have done so far to see if you have any questions.

You will notice that in this scenario, the student is speaking against what the teacher has said ("Get your homework from last night out") by denying that the students had homework to do the previous night. You have probably had similar situations with your parents or teachers in which you disagreed with them, and they told you not to contradict them. We are very familiar with these uses of the word "contradiction" in everyday life. However, the logical meaning of contradiction is a little bit different from the way it is used in its everyday context. Therefore, it is necessary to define contradiction in the context of logic.

In logic, contradiction defines how *A* and *O* propositions and *E* and *I* propositions relate to each other. Turn back to the diagram of the square of opposition on page 78. Notice that the arrows of contradiction make an X in the center of the square. This shows that *A* propositions relate to *O* propositions and vice versa, and that *E* propositions relate to *I* propositions and vice versa. Take note of the arrowheads at both ends of the lines. Those arrowheads indicate that the relationship goes both ways. Remember, *A* propositions are universal affirmatives: *All S is P*. *O* propositions are particular negatives: *Some S is not P*. Consider the following proposition:

> I always lose when I play tennis with my brother-in-law, Stephen. But, I did beat him two weeks ago when we played.

When this is written in standard form, it becomes this:

> All the times I play Stephen are times I lose. (*All S is P*)

> Some of the times I play Stephen are not times I lose. (*Some S is not P*)

You can readily see that both of these two propositions cannot be true at the same time. It must be that either I always lose, or I don't always lose. We see from this example that there isn't any way for *all* of the class of *S* to be *P* and at the same time say that *some* of the class of *S* is not *P*. It's just not possible for them both to be true at the same time. Let's look at a few other examples to help us better understand this concept. Consider the following sets of propositions:

> *A*: All moons are satellites.
> *O*: Some moons aren't satellites.

> *O*: Some rooms do not have windows.
> *A*: All rooms have windows.

> *A*: All squares have four sides.
> *O*: Some squares don't have four sides.

> *O*: Some rings are not gold.
> *A*: All rings are gold.

Each of these examples demonstrates that it's not possible for an *A* proposition to be true at the same time that its corresponding *O* proposition is true. If *A* is true, then *O* is false. If *O* is true, then *A* is false.

The same relationship holds true for *E* and *I* propositions. If *E* is true, then *I* is false. If *I* is true, then *E* is false. We know that *E* propositions are universal negatives: *No S is P*, and that *I* propositions are particular affirmatives: *Some S is P*. The following examples show that it is not possible for both an *E* and an *I* proposition to be true at the same time.

> *E*: No fish are able to live out of water.
> *I*: Some fish are able to live out of water.

> *I*: Some diamonds are man-made.
> *E*: No diamonds are man-made.

> *I*: Some thieves are noble.
> *E*: No thieves are noble.

> *I*: Some television shows are worthwhile.
> *E*: No television shows are worthwhile.

Of course, it follows that since *A* and *O* and *E* and *I* propositions can't be true at the same time, it is not possible for both *A* and *O* propositions and *E* and *I* propositions to be *false* at the same time. So, if *O* is false, then *A* must be true and vice versa. And if *E* is false, then *I* must be true and vice versa. Let's look at some examples of this.

> *A*: All music is instrumental music.

Clearly, this is a false proposition since we know that it is true that *some* music is not instrumental music.

> *O*: Some ocean water is not salt water.

This is also a false proposition since we know that all ocean water is salt water.

> *E*: No men are good water-skiers.

This is obviously a false proposition as well. In fact, you may even know some men who are good water-skiers, thus proving that this is a false proposition.

To understand how logically contradictory ideas show up in everyday life, think back to the conversation between Julie and Tiffany in the previous lesson. At the beginning of the discussion, Julie stated that she believed that some gossip is harmless. However, by the end of her conversation with Tiffany, she admitted she believed that no gossip was harmless. Therefore, she realized that she had contradictory beliefs, and she either had to reject her old belief in order to accept the

new, or vice versa. Let's continue to consider contradiction by looking at this dialogue between Matthew and Nate:

Matthew: I would never vote for a political candidate who dodged the draft. All draft dodging is an act of cowardice.

Nate: Well, what about if someone is a pacifist? After all, there have been pacifists, such as Gandhi or Martin Luther King, Jr., for example, who were very brave but who also believed that killing is morally wrong. Wouldn't it be legitimate for these people to dodge the draft?

Matthew: They could go and serve in the medical or engineering units. You don't have to kill people if you are drafted into the military. There are other options for service. Everyone should be willing to serve his country in a way that doesn't conflict with his beliefs.

Nate: OK, I can see your point there, but when you say, "Everyone should be willing to serve his country," it seems as though you are assuming that the country is a just country involved in a just war. After all, do you think that everyone should be willing to serve a tyrannical government by participating in its wars? Wouldn't someone be justified in dodging the draft of an unjust war for an unjust government? Couldn't that be a brave form of protest?

Matthew: That's an interesting point. No, I don't think people should serve a tyrannical government by participating in an unjust war. But it seems to me that the bravest way someone can serve that type of government is by protesting in public, even if it means going to jail, rather than just tucking his tail and running.

Nate: That's a good point. Certainly, that may be a very brave way for someone to serve a country that is unjust. However, what if he is supporting a wife and family, and public protest against this unjust government may put the lives of his family members at risk? Might not the bravest thing be to dodge the draft and escape with his family to a safe place where he can best provide for them, even though people may slander his reputation because of it?

Matthew: That's a tricky one. I suppose there could be some instances in which that could be true.

Nate: So, you would have to say that not all draft dodging is an act of cowardice, right?

Matthew: Yes, I guess there might be some draft dodging that is not an act of cowardice.

Notice that Matthew, much like Julie in the dialogue about gossip, believed one notion at the beginning of the dialogue, but then actually admitted that the contradictory notion might be true at the end of the dialogue. That is, he realized, through considering the implications of his ideas, that he held contradictory beliefs: "All draft dodging is an act of cowardice" and "Some draft dodging is an act of cowardice." When people realize that they hold contradictory beliefs, they must reject the one and choose the other or choose the one and reject the other. For instance, Matthew must either cling to his belief that "All draft dodging is an act of cowardice" and reject the notion that "Some draft dodging is an act of cowardice," or vice versa.

Remember that we mentioned in the last lesson that it is common for people to hold contradictory beliefs without realizing it. This is because, as we mentioned, many people accept beliefs without thinking through all of the implications of those beliefs. It may seem awkward to engage in this kind of Socratic dialogue (that is, dialogue that follows the questioning model used by Socrates), but dialogues such as these can be a helpful way for you to clarify what you believe about something.

For example, let's say that you want to decide what you believe about capital punishment. Many times, when students enter high school or college, they become concerned about such beliefs because they know they already are or will be voting about these issues in the near future. If you were not clear about what you believed about capital punishment, you would start by adopting a position. For example, you could say, "Let's assume that all capital punishment is ethical," or "Let's assume that no capital punishment is ethical." (You could also adopt an *I* or *O* proposition about this topic.) Once you have adopted a stance (either because you believe it or because you are adopting it for the sake of discussion), you can explore your belief in much the same way that Socrates did

in the dialogue you read in the *Apology* or in the way Julie and Tiffany and Nate and Matthew did in the dialogues you have read in this lesson and the previous one. You can explore your idea yourself or with another person.

For instance, let's say that Julie and Tiffany are discussing capital punishment, and, for the sake of argument, Tiffany adopted the stance "All capital punishment is just." Their dialogue might play out like this:

Tiffany: OK, Julie, I tend to be in favor of capital punishment, so for the sake of argument, let's say that all capital punishment is just.

Julie: OK.

Tiffany: Now, would you agree, Julie, that when something is just, it gives someone what he deserves and does not give him what he doesn't deserve?

Julie: That seems like a good definition.

Tiffany: If someone has killed a person, then killing the murderer seems like an equal penalty. After all, if a child steals $10 from someone, his parents will make him give back at least $10, if not more, to restore justice. Isn't this right?

Julie: Certainly.

Tiffany: If someone were to wreck someone's car, we would say the just thing would be for him to restore the person's car to its original condition or replace it with an equally valuable car, right?

Julie: Sure.

Tiffany: So, justice has this notion of giving an equally valuable thing for something that has been taken, ruined, or lost.

Julie: I think that's right.

Tiffany: So, taking someone's life if that person has taken a life fulfills this kind of equal payment.

Julie: It would seem so.

Tiffany: Now, what if someone did not take someone's life, but he was punished capitally anyway? That is, the person was accused of a murder, but he did not do it. He is wrongly accused. It would be unjust for him to receive the death penalty, wouldn't it?

Julie: Of course.

Tiffany: So, capital punishment when administered to someone who has not taken a life is unjust?

Julie: It certainly is.

Tiffany: So, not all capital punishment is just—only capital punishment exacted on someone who has taken a life is just. That means that, in fact, some capital punishment is unjust, right?

Julie: You seem to be right on both accounts.

As you can see from this dialogue, Tiffany started with the notion that all capital punishment was just. But then, through her discussion with Julie, she realized that some capital punishment is unjust. These propositions are obviously contradictory. Therefore, Tiffany will likely give up her first belief that "All capital punishment is just" to accept her new belief that "Some capital punishment is unjust." On the other hand, she might decide that her discussion with Julie missed the mark in some way. For example, perhaps in thinking about their discussion, Tiffany will later decide that their definition of justice was wrong, or maybe she will decide that they overlooked some important detail. If that is the case, Tiffany may hold on to her original belief and try to look at the topic from a different angle.

The point is that contradictory beliefs cannot both be true or both be false at the same time. If one is true, the other has to be false; if one is false, the other has to be true. In addition, most of us, at some point in the course of our lives, hold contradictory beliefs because we have so many beliefs, and we don't always consider all the implications of our beliefs. Part of becoming a logical thinker is recognizing contradictory beliefs and amending them so that they are no longer contradictory. Discussion and dialogue are great ways to do this. In this lesson, we have specifically examined the ways in which our ideas can be in opposition to each other because they are contradictory. In the next lesson, we will examine how they can be in opposition to each other because they are contrary.

DEFINE

    1. Contradiction:

_____

_____

FILL IN THE BLANK

    1. Contradictory propositions cannot both be _____ at the same time.

    2. Contradictory propositions cannot both be _____ at the same time.

    3. If one contradictory proposition is _____, the other must be _____.

    4. If one contradictory proposition is _____, the other must be _____.

EXAMPLES

Create one proposition for each of the four types of categorical propositions. Then, write the contradiction of each.

    a. *All S is P.*

_____

_____

    b. *No S is P.*

_____

_____

    c. *Some S is P.*

_____

_____

    d. *Some S is not P.*

_____

_____

ASSESS

Check out the Calvin and Hobbes comic at this link: <http://capress.link/dd0502>. Then, explain what contradictions are involved.

_____

_____

_____

_____

PRACTICE

Experimenting with Socratic Dialogue: Because Socratic dialogue can be an effective way to explore and critique beliefs, you will find that you will have several opportunities throughout the rest of this book to read dialogues or create them. For your first attempt at creating a Socratic dialogue, keep it really simple. Consider the contradictory beliefs below:

A: All cats are snooty. *O*: Some cats are not snooty.

A: All homework is busy work. *E*: No homework is busy work.

E: No television programs are valuable. *I*: Some television programs are valuable.

E: No classic literature is interesting. *I*: Some classic literature is interesting.

Your goal is to choose one of the above sets of contradictory propositions about which you will write a dialogue (you may also make up your own set of propositions). To write a Socratic dialogue, we recommend that you follow these steps:

1. Make your dialogue between two people. One person believes one of the pair of contradictory propositions, and the other person believes the other.

2. Your goal is for one person to ask a series of questions, which will move the other person from affirming one of the pair of contradictory propositions to admitting the other of the pair (i.e., he changes his mind by the end of the dialogue).

3. To get your dialogue started, feel free to jump right into the conversation. You can have someone say, "Julie, I heard you say the other day that you believe *A* is true. I believe that *O* is true. I was wondering if you could explain why you believe what you do." (Of course, you will use real propositions in place of the letters).

4. To get the dialogue moving, start with several questions, the answers to which both people can agree upon. Then use other scenarios and questions to move from the *A* to the *O* proposition or the *E* to the *I* proposition.

5. When you want to make a point, ask a question that makes it. Don't just state your point. (Making your point in the form of a question helps your dialogue partner to see the validity of your point.)

DEDUCTION IN ACTION

Logic and Socratic Dialogue

You read the *Apology* by Plato in lesson 1.1, and you read some dialogues in this lesson, as well as the last, that were similar to the Socratic dialogues in the *Apology*. By now, you are somewhat familiar with Socrates' mode of questioning people and how two people might use this method to explore their own beliefs. In Plato's work entitled *Euthyphro*, Plato created a discussion between Socrates and a character named Euthyphro, in which he implemented many of Socrates' questioning practices. In this discussion, we can catch a glimpse of inference and the relationships of opposition in action.

Euthyphro takes place before the trial of Socrates. While Socrates is waiting to be called to trial, he encounters a young man, Euthyphro, who is prosecuting his father for murder. Upon questioning Euthyphro, Socrates discovers that a slave belonging to Euthyphro's father cut another slave's throat. Euthyphro's father was so angry with the slave that he bound him hand and foot and threw him into a ditch until he could discover what the law would do with him. While the father was seeking this out, however, the slave died from cold and hunger.

Therefore, Euthyphro decided that he would prosecute his own father for murder. Upon even further questioning, Socrates finds out that Euthyphro is extremely sure of himself and his own judgment. Euthyphro believes his intelligence level is quite a cut above average, especially in matters pertaining to justice and the will of the gods. As you might recall from the *Apology*, this is just the kind of person with whom Socrates enjoys discussing matters: someone who is not wise but believes he is. Through clever questioning, Socrates shows Euthyphro that he holds contradictory beliefs.

Visit the following link and read *Euthyphro*: <http://capress.link/dd0503>. Then, answer the questions that follow.

1. What contradictory belief does Euthyphro hold concerning what piety is?

2. How does Socrates show Euthyphro that the belief he holds is contradictory?

LESSON 5.4
Contrariety and Subcontrariety

POINTS TO REMEMBER

Propositions of Contrariety

1. Contrariety is the relationship between *A* and *E* propositions.
2. Propositions of contrariety cannot both be true at the same time.
3. Propositions of contrariety can both be false at the same time.
4. If one contrary proposition is true, the other must be false.
5. If one contrary proposition is false, it does not necessitate the truth or falsity of the other one.

Propositions of Subcontrariety

1. Subcontrariety is the relationship between *I* and *O* propositions.
2. Propositions of subcontrariety can both be true at the same time.
3. Propositions of subcontrariety cannot both be false at the same time.
4. If one subcontrary proposition is true, it does not necessitate the truth or falsity of the other.
5. If one subcontrary proposition is false, then the other one must be true.

> HE HOPED AND PRAYED THAT THERE WASN'T
> AN AFTERLIFE. THEN HE REALIZED THERE WAS A
> CONTRADICTION INVOLVED HERE AND MERELY HOPED
> THAT THERE WASN'T AN AFTERLIFE.
> —DOUGLAS ADAMS[1]

The next relationships in the square of opposition are the relationships of contrariety and subcontrariety. Look back to the diagram of the square of opposition on p. 78. You'll note that the relationship of contrariety is between *A* and *E* propositions, and the relationship of subcontrariety is between *I* and *O* propositions. Note that there are arrowheads on both ends of the line between each type of proposition, indicating that the relationship goes both ways. This means that the *A* proposition is contrary to the *E* proposition, and the *E* proposition is contrary to the *A* proposition. In the same way, the *I* proposition is subcontrary to the *O* proposition, and the *O* proposition is subcontrary to the *I* proposition.

Let's begin with contrariety, the relationship of *A* and *E* propositions. The law of contrariety states that contrary propositions cannot both be true at the same time, but that they can both be false at the same time. Let's look at these propositions symbolically.

A: All S is P.

E: No S is P.

Right off the bat, you'll probably note that it's impossible for all of *S* to be something at the same time that none of *S* is that same thing. So it won't come as any surprise to learn that propositions of contrariety cannot both be true at the same time. Let's look at some examples of these propositions with actual terms in them.

A: All spruce trees are conifers. True

E: No spruce trees are conifers. False

It's easy to see that if it is true that *all* of a class of things is something, then it is impossible for *none* of that class of things to be that same something. That is, if all spruce trees are conifers, it is impossible for no spruce trees to be conifers as well. The opposite notion also applies: If it is true that none of a class of things is something, then it is impossible for all of that class of things to be that same something. Therefore, if no spruce trees are conifers (hypothetically speaking), then it is impossible for all spruce trees to be conifers. It is clear that contrary propositions cannot both be true at the same time, but can they both be false at the same time? Look at the following propositions:

A: All birds are hummingbirds. False

E: No birds are hummingbirds. False

This example illustrates the fact that although propositions of contrariety cannot both be true at the same time, they *can* both be false at the same time. That is, it's neither true that all birds are hummingbirds, nor is it true that no birds are hummingbirds. Instead, what is true is that some birds are hummingbirds, and some birds are not hummingbirds. We can see that contrary propositions can both be false at the same time because not all universals are true about many topics.

To better understand this concept, consider the following brief dialogue. Tiffany and Nate decided to get some friends together to watch a movie at Tiffany's house on Friday night, but before they invited their friends, they wanted to decide what type of movie to see. Here is what they discussed:

Tiffany: I really want to see that new romantic comedy. I think it's called *My Myopic Valentine*.

Nate: *(groaning)* Come on, Tiffany. I hate romantic comedies. They're all so contrived and formulaic. I really want to watch a movie that's going to make me think, at least a little bit.

Tiffany: Romantic comedies *are* thoughtful. *You've Got Mail* highlights the destructive effects of corporate monopolies, and *Just Like Heaven* illustrates the problems surrounding end-of-life issues.

Nate: I don't buy that. I think those ethical issues were merely plot devices to move the story forward. Romantic comedies are simply emotional fast food for girls.

Tiffany: That's unfair! Just because a movie ends happily doesn't mean it isn't thoughtful.

Nate: Tiffany, just face it. Romantic comedies are dumb.

As you can probably imagine, Nate and Tiffany's conversation isn't going to get very far. You may have detected that the primary roadblock to their communication is that they are adamant about contrary propositions: "All romantic comedies are thoughtful" and "No romantic comedies are thoughtful." So, because those propositions are contrary, unless Nate and Tiffany can prove that one of their propositions is true and the other one is false, they won't be able to resolve their disagreement.

As we discussed before, it isn't possible for both an *A* and an *E* proposition to be true at the same time. However, there are certainly some cases in which one of a pair of contrary propositions is true. For example, consider two people who are having an argument about Venus flytraps. One person says, "All Venus flytraps are carnivorous." The other person says, "No Venus flytraps are carnivorous." In this argument, one person is definitely right, and one person is definitely wrong. Venus flytraps either are, or they are not, carnivorous. So, as you can see, there are certainly instances in which one position is totally right and the contrary is totally wrong. As another example, let's say that two people were arguing about whether or not playing four hours of video games every day harms a person's brain. It may be a little harder to verify the truth in this argument, but it is another argument in which the subject is either right or wrong. That is, either playing four hours of video games every day is bad for your brain, or it is not.

Although there are definitely some arguments in which the proposition is either true or false, there may be times when it is right some of the time and wrong some of the time. This is where the law of contrary propositions can be helpful. Remember that with contrary propositions there is the possibility that both of the universal propositions are wrong and, instead, the particular propositions are the accurate propositions concerning an argument. Nate and Tiffany's argument about romantic comedies is definitely one of these types of arguments. They would solve their argument so much more easily if they conceded the particular propositions in their argument, which are "Some romantic comedies are thoughtful" and "Some romantic comedies are not thoughtful." Later, after they stopped being upset with each other, they had this conversation:

Nate: OK, Tiffany. I admit I am being a bit pigheaded about all of this. Help me understand why you think romantic comedies are so great and why you think some of them are thoughtful.

Tiffany: OK, Nate. Would you generally consider Shakespeare a thoughtful writer?

Nate: Of course. Who doesn't?

Tiffany: Would you agree with me that some of his plays, such as *A Midsummer Night's Dream* and *Twelfth Night*, are comedies?

Nate: Of course. They're hilarious! I love those plays.

Tiffany: Would you also agree that they are romantic?

Nate: Sure. They have other elements in them, but they are certainly romantic comedies.

Tiffany: Do you remember that when we read Austen's *Pride and Prejudice* in English class, you hated it at the beginning, but then at the end you said it was very insightful into human nature and also very witty and ironic?

Nate: Sure. I still think that.

Tiffany: Would you agree with me that one of the main themes of that book is love and romance?

Nate: I don't think I can deny it.

Tiffany: But you also think it is very funny and thoughtful?

Nate: I do. I love Mr. Bennet's clever remarks and the absurdity of Mr. Collins.

Tiffany: Would you agree with me that these stories have been made into movies?

Nate: Of course. We watched them in class.

Tiffany: Would you agree that if romantic comedies written today contained elements similar to the elements in the romantic comedies of Shakespeare and Austen that they would be thoughtful, too?

Nate: I think I can agree with that.

Tiffany: Then, it seems, Nate, that there are at least some thoughtful romantic comedies out there.

Nate: Tiffany, Socrates would be proud of you! I think I just haven't seen any romantic comedies lately that were worth seeing.

Tiffany: Well, I guess I have to agree there. I have to admit that a lot of the more recent ones are pretty formulaic. I guess I just don't want to see anything too depressing this weekend since my week has been kind of stressful. Is there some movie we can watch that's thoughtful, a little bit hopeful, and funny, too?

Nate: I'm sure we can find something. You get the popcorn and invite our friends, and I'll get one thoughtful, yet hopeful, and possibly even funny, movie. I'm not promising any romance, though!

Tiffany: It's a deal!

As you can see, it can really hinder a conversation if two people stubbornly cling to opposing, contrary propositions when doing so is not necessary. In everyday conversation, it is important to consider the merit of other people's ideas, as well as considering the weakness of your own position. For instance, consider how many cultural debates are stymied by people saying, or implying, things like "All Democrats are . . . ," or "All Republicans are . . . ," or "All people who drive Hummers are . . . ," or "All people who drive hybrids are. . . ." As you can imagine, people usually complete these propositions with terms that often misrepresent the people in that group, which hinders a truthful flow of ideas.

In all the discussions you have in your life, there will certainly be times when you must cling to one of a pair of contrary propositions. If you believe that your proposition is true, this implies, through the law of contrary propositions, that the opposing proposition is false. However, in every argument of this kind, you should also consider whether it could be true that your proposition, as well as your opponent's proposition, is false and that the truth lies in the particular propositions. Before we move on to subcontrary propositions, let's sum up the key points of contrary propositions:

1. Contrariety is the relationship between *A* and *E* propositions.

2. Propositions of contrariety cannot both be true at the same time.

3. Propositions of contrariety can both be false at the same time.

4. If one contrary proposition is true, the other must be false.

5. If one contrary proposition is false, it does not necessitate the truth or falsity of the other one.

Now that we have the relationship of contrariety under our belts, let's examine the third type of relationship in the square of opposition: subcontrariety. As noted earlier in this lesson, subcontrariety is the relationship between *I* and *O* propositions. The law of subcontrariety states that subcontrary propositions can both be true at the same time. If one of them is false, however, the other has to be true. Let's look at subcontrary propositions in symbolic form:

Some S is P.

Some S is not P.

Take a look at the following illustration. What you see is a big circle, which represents all *S*. You can see that the circle of all *S* has been divided equally in half, with one half being *P* and the other half being *not P*. This illustrates that subcontrary propositions can both be true at the same time.

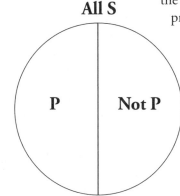

All S

P | Not P

The following are examples of contrary propositions with terms in them:

I: Some presidential candidates create good arguments to support their ideas.

O: Some presidential candidates do not create good arguments to support their ideas.

Think about these propositions. Can both of them be true at the same time? If you are thinking that they can be, you are correct. The truth of one proposition of subcontrariety does not necessitate the falsity of the other. It is entirely possible for some (or part) of a class of things to be something and for another part not to be that same thing simultaneously. Therefore, it is possible that some presidential candidates create good arguments to support their ideas, while others do not. For further examples of propositions of subcontrariety, consider the following:

I: Some men are good cooks.
O: Some men are not good cooks.

I: Some women are good athletes.
O: Some women are not good athletes.

I: Some ice storms are destructive.
O: Some ice storms are not destructive.

I: Some cupcakes are messy.
O: Some cupcakes are not messy.

These propositions all illustrate that subcontrary propositions can both be true at the same time. In fact, this relates exactly to what we were discussing when we talked about contrary propositions. You will recall that we mentioned that sometimes, with a topic, both of the universal propositions are false, but the particular propositions are true. Therefore, when Nate and Tiffany were arguing that "All romantic comedies are thoughtful" and "No romantic comedies are thoughtful," they were both wrong. The truth is that "Some romantic comedies are thoughtful" and "Some romantic comedies are not thoughtful." So, you are already familiar with this idea that particular propositions—subcontraries—can both be true at the same time. It is important to note, however, that just because subcontraries *can* both be true at the same

time, it doesn't mean that they always *are* both true. For example, consider this pair of subcontrary propositions:

> Some boys are males.

> Some boys are not males.

Notice that these are certainly subcontrary propositions, and so they can both be true at the same time. But are they? Obviously they are not. The second proposition, "Some boys are not males," is definitely false.

This brings us to another question concerning subcontrary propositions. What if one of the propositions in a pair of subcontrary propositions is false? Does the falsity of one necessitate the falsity or the truth of another? To find the answer to this question, let's look at this false proposition: "Some habitual liars are honest people." Of course, this proposition is obviously false. The question is, what does this imply about its subcontrary proposition: "Some habitual liars are not honest people"? If you think about it, you will realize that if one proposition in a pair of subcontrary propositions is false, the other proposition must be true. That is, if it is false that "Some habitual liars are honest people," then the proposition "Some habitual liars are not honest people" must be true.

But why? Well, think about it. If it is false that even *some* habitual liars are honest, then it must be true, at the least, that some habitual liars are not honest. Note that if it is false that even some habitual liars are honest, it also implies that no habitual liars are honest. However, we are only concerned with the *O* proposition here, and it is certainly safe to say that if it is false that even some habitual liars are honest, then, at the least, it is true that some habitual liars are not honest.

Let's consider this idea with the romantic comedy example. Consider the *I* proposition: "Some romantic comedies are thoughtful." Let's say that we decide that this proposition is false. If it is false that even some romantic comedies are thoughtful, it must certainly mean, at the least, that some of them are not thoughtful. Of course, if we say that it is false that even some romantic comedies are thoughtful, we are implying that no romantic comedies are thoughtful, but we are just looking at the *O* proposition right now.

As a final example, consider this *O* proposition: "Some professional boxers are not physically fit people." This proposition is false. Now consider that if it is false that some professional boxers are not fit people, it must be true, at the least, that some professional boxers are physically fit people.

Are you still having problems understanding why the falsity of one subcontrary proposition necessitates the truth of the other? There is another way that you can figure out the truth or falsity of subcontrary propositions by using the square of opposition. It's a bit of a long route to understanding the same concept, but it may be helpful to you. Look at the square below to remind yourself of the different relationships we have discussed thus far:

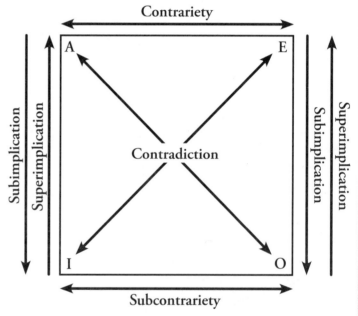

Now let's walk through what you already know about contradictory and contrary propositions, and you will soon see how this applies to subcontrary propositions. (It may help if you follow the progression in the square of opposition by pointing at each symbol with your finger as you read each of the following sentences.) If we say that an *O* proposition is false, then by *contradiction*, the *A* proposition must be true. But, if an *A* proposition is true, then by *contrariety*, the *E* proposition is false. But, if an *E* proposition is false, then by *contradiction*, the *I* proposition is true. This is kind of a long process for understanding the relationship between subcontrary propositions, but it gives

you a second way to look at it. Let's try another example using actual propositions.

Consider the following proposition: "Some triangles have six sides." This is obviously a false proposition. We know, according to the law of subcontrary propositions, that if the proposition "Some triangles have six sides" is false, then the proposition "Some triangles do not have six sides" must be true. But to gain a better understanding of why this must be so, let's trace this idea through the different relationships of the square of opposition. If the *I* proposition "Some triangles have six sides" is false, then by contradiction, the *E* proposition "No triangles have six sides" is true. But, if the *E* proposition "No triangles have six sides" is true, then by contrariety, the *A* proposition "All triangles have six sides" is false. And if the *A* proposition "All triangles have six sides" is false, then by contradiction, the *O* proposition "Some triangles do not have six sides" must be true.

As you can see, this is definitely a longer way of figuring out the relationship between the *I* and *O* propositions, but it can be helpful if you are having problems figuring out the relationship between the *I* and *O* propositions through the law of subcontrary propositions. Before we move on, let's summarize the rules of subcontrariety:

1. Subcontrariety is the relationship between *I* and *O* propositions.
2. Propositions of subcontrariety can both be true at the same time.
3. Propositions of subcontrariety cannot both be false at the same time.
4. If one subcontrary proposition is true, it does not necessitate the truth or falsity of the other.
5. If one subcontrary proposition is false, then the other one must be true.

Now that you understand the relationship of subcontrary propositions on a technical level, let's look at it on a practical level. Understanding the relationship between subcontrary propositions can prevent you from making unwarranted inferences from people's propositions. This can often happen with subcontrary propositions. When people work with "some" or "some . . . not" propositions, they often make the mistake of assuming that one implies the other. For instance, let's say that your friend is a fan of a particular book series. You are intrigued by the main idea of the series and interested in reading it, but you have heard the books are really scary, and you don't like horror books. You ask your friend if the books are really as scary as people say they are. She says, "Some are." Should you then automatically assume that some aren't? No. It may be that as you quiz your friend further, you find that, indeed, some of the books aren't scary. On the other hand, it may be that she made her initial proposition of "some are" because she couldn't really remember much about the rest of books, which actually are, indeed, horror books. Remember that although *I* and *O* propositions *can* both be true, it doesn't mean that they *are* both true. Therefore, just because it could be true that some of the books are scary and some are not, it doesn't mean that both of these ideas are true. You may think that you would not make such assumptions, and you may be right. However, we are more likely to make false assumptions when we really want to believe something. Some people actually use this human tendency to their advantage. For instance, let's say that you are interested in buying a house. You ask the realtor if there are any plumbing problems. The realtor says, "Well, the bathroom pipes are leaky, but you'll have that in an old house." The realtor has admitted that *some* of the pipes *are* leaky. From that proposition it could seem that she is implying that the rest are fine—*some are not* leaky. However, on further inspection, you discover that all of the pipes have major leakage problems. Did the realtor actually lie? No, not technically. However, she was obviously hoping that you would make an unwarranted inference.

As mentioned before, when we really want to believe something, we are more likely to make unwarranted assumptions. For instance, if you had fallen in love with the house, you might have been much more likely to make the unwarranted assumption that the rest of the pipes were fine. Unfortunately, many unscrupulous salespeople use this human tendency to want to believe something to their benefit. Remembering the laws of contrary and subcontrary propositions can help you to avoid being unnecessarily stubborn or making an unwarranted inference.

So far, we have covered three relationships on the square of opposition: contradiction, contrariety, and subcontrariety. That's three down and two to go. In the next lesson, we will cover the last two relationships of inference: subimplication and superimplication.

DEFINE

For each of the following words, provide an appropriate definition.

1. Contradiction:

_____

_____

_____

2. Contrariety:

_____

_____

_____

3. Subcontrariety:

_____

_____

_____

FILL IN THE BLANK

Below are the rules for each kind of relationship of opposition we have studied thus far. Fill in each of the blanks that complete the sentence.

Contradictory Propositions

1. Contradictory propositions cannot both be _____ at the same time.

2. Contradictory propositions cannot both be _____ at the same time.

3. If one contradictory proposition is _____, the other must be _____.

4. If one contradictory proposition is _____, the other must be _____.

Contrary Propositions

1. Contrariety is the relationship between _____ and _____ propositions.

2. Propositions of contrariety cannot both be _____ at the same time.

3. Propositions of contrariety can both be _____ at the same time.

4. If one contrary proposition is _____, the other one must be _____.

5. If one contrary proposition is false, it does not necessitate the _____ or _____ of the other.

FILL IN THE BLANK (CONTINUED)

Subcontrary Propositions

1. Subcontrariety is the relationship between _____ and _____ propositions.

2. Propositions of subcontrariety can both be _____ at the same time.

3. Propositions of subcontrariety cannot both be _____ at the same time.

4. If one subcontrary proposition is true, it does not necessitate the _____ or _____ of the other.

5. If one subcontrary proposition is false, then the other one must be _____.

EXAMPLES

Please do the following: a) Write the relationship that exists between each of the following propositions. b) Note whether each proposition is true or false, and c) explain whether or not the propositions follow the rules of the relationship of opposition that they demonstrate. You may need to do some research to provide the correct answers for some of the examples.

1. Some Egyptians are Christians. No Egyptians are Christians.

   a. _____

   b. Some Egyptians are Christians. _____

   No Egyptians are Christians. _____

   c. _____
   _____
   _____

2. Some conifers are evergreens. Some conifers are not evergreens.

   a. _____

   b. Some conifers are evergreens. _____

   Some conifers are not evergreens. _____

   c. _____
   _____
   _____

3. Some U.S. residents are U.S. citizens. Some U.S. residents are not U.S. citizens.

   a. _____

   b. Some U.S. residents are U.S. citizens. _____

   Some U.S. residents are not U.S. citizens. _____
   _____
   _____

   c. _____
   _____
   _____

EXAMPLES (CONTINUED)

4. All blueberries are berries. No blueberries are berries.

   a. _____

   b. All blueberries are berries. _____

   No blueberries are berries. _____

   c. _____
   _____
   _____

5. All humpback whales have long flippers. Some humpback whales do not have long flippers.

   a. _____

   b. All humpback whales have long flippers. _____

   Some humpback whales do not have long flippers. _____

   c. _____
   _____
   _____

6. All kiwis are flightless birds. No kiwis are flightless birds.

   a. _____

   b. All kiwis are flightless birds. _____

   No kiwis are flightless birds. _____

   c. _____
   _____
   _____

7. Some blueberries are berries. Some blueberries are not berries.

   a. _____

   b. Some blueberries are berries. _____

   Some blueberries are not berries. _____

   c. _____
   _____
   _____

8. Some pythons are not snakes. Some pythons are snakes.

   a. _____

   b. Some pythons are not snakes. _____

   Some pythons are snakes. _____

   c. _____
   _____
   _____

EXAMPLES (CONTINUED)

9. Some saxophones are not woodwind instruments. All saxophones are woodwind instruments.

a. _____

b. Some saxophones are not woodwind instruments. _____

   All saxophones are woodwind instruments. _____

c. _____
_____
_____
_____

TRANSLATE AND DESCRIBE

Please do the following: a) Translate the following propositions into categorical form, and b) describe the relationship between them. Assuming the truth-value of one of the claims, what will be the truth-value of the other claim?

1. Some logic students understand the square of opposition easily, without any trouble at all. However, that is not the case for all logic students.

a. _____
_____

b. _____
_____

2. Some humpback whales spawn in the North Pacific Ocean, while others spawn in the North Atlantic Ocean.

a. _____
_____

b. _____
_____

3. One never finds tulips living under the sea. Some tulips are dwellers on the ocean's bottom.

a. _____
_____

b. _____
_____

In the space below, recreate the square of opposition as best as you can.

Look at the quote at the beginning of this lesson and explain what is humorous about it and what contrary problem is involved.

EXPLAIN

_____

_____

_____

_____

_____

_____

_____

_____

_____

DEDUCTION IN ACTION
Practicing Socratic Dialogue

It takes a while to get the hang of Socratic dialogue, and yet it is a very helpful tool for clarifying your thoughts. Therefore, we want to give you several opportunities for practicing this useful skill. When you create this dialogue, you will illustrate the idea that contrary propositions can both be false. Remember that although contrary propositions cannot both be true at the same time, they can both be false. This is the idea that you will illustrate in this dialogue. To do this, start with two sets of contrary ideas. You may use one of the scenarios listed below, or you may come up with your own contrary ideas.

It may help you if you structure your dialogue much like the Nate and Tiffany dialogue about romantic comedies. To begin the dialogue, make both of your characters adamant about contrary ideas. Then, make one of your characters ask the other person to explain his or her viewpoint. Next, make the second person ask a series of Socratic questions that lead both of the characters to the conclusion that the particular propositions are more accurate than the universal propositions in their argument.

Scenario #1

Two people are arguing about whether or not people who drive SUVs are irresponsible. One person claims, "All people who drive SUVs are irresponsible," and the other person claims, "No people who drive SUVs are irresponsible."

Scenario #2

Two people are arguing about whether or not welfare is beneficial to American society. One person argues, "All welfare is beneficial to American society." The other person argues, "No welfare is beneficial to American society."

Scenario #3

Two people are arguing about whether or not school days should be longer. One person argues, "All proposals for a longer school day are a good idea," and the other person argues, "No proposals for a longer school day are a good idea."

Scenario #4

Two people are arguing about whether or not kids should get an allowance from their parents. One argues, "All kids should get an allowance," and the other person argues, "No kids should get an allowance."

LESSON 5.5
Subimplication and Superimplication

POINTS TO REMEMBER

Subimplication

1. Subimplication is the relationship between universal propositions and their particulars. *A* relates to *I*; *E* relates to *O*.
2. The truth of the universal implies the truth of its particular.
3. The falsity of the universal does not necessitate the truth or falsity of its particular. When a universal is false, the truth-value of the particular is unknown.

Superimplication

1. Superimplication is the relationship between particular and universal propositions. *I* relates to *A*; *O* relates to *E*.
2. The truth of the particular proposition does not necessitate the truth or falsity of the universal proposition.
3. The falsity of the particular proposition implies the falsity of the universal proposition.

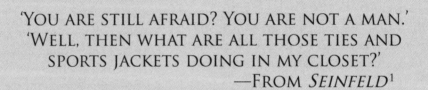

'YOU ARE STILL AFRAID? YOU ARE NOT A MAN.'
'WELL, THEN WHAT ARE ALL THOSE TIES AND
SPORTS JACKETS DOING IN MY CLOSET?'
—FROM *SEINFELD*[1]

The last relationships of opposition are the propositions of subimplication and superimplication. An example will help illustrate how these relationships work. Let's say that a geography teacher is teaching her class about latitude and longitude, and she makes the following proposition: "The entire southern hemisphere experiences winter while the northern hemisphere experiences summer and vice versa. So, while those of us in the United States celebrate Christmas just after the winter solstice when the temperatures are generally cold or cool, our friends in Australia celebrate Christmas during one of the warmest times of their year."

If you reread the first sentence from the previous paragraph, you'll notice that the teacher mentioned that the entire southern hemisphere is on a schedule opposite to that of the northern hemisphere. It is important to note, however, that while the teacher selected Australia to illustrate the point, she could have just as easily selected an Indonesian country, or even India. Why? It is because if the entire southern hemisphere is a particular way, it is implied that each individual part of the southern hemisphere, such as India or an Indonesian country, is also that way.

In other words, if the universal is true, then the particular cases are also true. This illustrates the next relationship in the square of opposition: subimplication. Subimplication is the relationship between the universal and the particular proposition. Turn back to page 78 and take another look

at the square of opposition. Notice that the arrow of subimplication goes from the universal to the particular only. Subimplication is a one-way relationship. The law of subimplication only applies if you begin with a universal proposition and carry the implication through to its particular.

The following are the laws of subimplication:

1. True *A* propositions imply the truth of *I* propositions.

2. True *E* propositions imply the truth of *O* propositions.

It is important to note that with subimplication, *truth* is implied from the universal to the particular, but falsity is not implied from the universal to the particular. That is, if the *A* or *E* proposition is false, it is not necessarily the case that the *I* or *O* proposition is false as well.

Let's look at a few examples that illustrate the relationship of subimplication. Perhaps one of the greatest examples of subimplication is found in the U.S. Declaration of Independence, which says, "We hold these truths to be self-evident, that all men are created equal, that they are endowed by their Creator with certain inalienable Rights, that among these are Life, Liberty and the Pursuit of Happiness."[2]

It's a hotly debated issue as to what Thomas Jefferson actually meant when he penned the words "all men." Equality of the individual was a revolutionary idea during the time in which Jefferson wrote the Declaration. Initially, equality was only applied to free white males, but that's not what the sentence says. It says "all men." It wasn't long before the logical implications associated with the word "all" took hold. If you define "man" as all human males, then that sentence naturally implies that men, regardless of ethnicity, station, or color, are equal. If you broaden the term "man" to include all humans, then the sentence naturally implies that all humans, regardless of gender, ethnicity, station, or color, are equal.

This example illustrates subimplication with the *A* and *I* relationship. When Americans read the Declaration of Independence, they realized that the proposition "All men are created equal" meant that each individual man was created equal (and later, they extended that definition to include women as well). This is because the particular—

each individual man—is included in the category "All men." Remember, with subimplication, the particular, which in this case is "individual men," is contained in the universal, which in this case is "all men." Now let's look at the *E* and *O* relationship using an example from the U.S. Constitution. (Remember, *E* is the universal negative, and *O* is the particular negative.) In the Bill of Rights, Amendment I, it states, "Congress shall make no law respecting an establishment of religion, or prohibiting the free exercise thereof." The first part of this sentence is referred to as the establishment clause, and the second part is called the free exercise clause. Judicial courts use this universal proposition—"Congress shall make *no* law"— whenever they examine a situation to determine if it violates the Constitution.

For instance, in the court case *Engel v. Vitale* in 1962, the courts ruled that New York public school districts could not mandate that a prayer be said at the beginning of class each day.[3] That is, they decided that because no law establishing religion was a constitutional law (universal negative proposition), this particular practice—establishing prayer in public schools—was not constitutional. This is another example of how subimplication works. In this case, because the universal was true—no law establishing a religion is a constitutional law—the particular was true. That is, the particular law that established religion by mandating prayer in public schools was unconstitutional, too. On the other hand, in 1999, a court ruled that the Newark police force could not force Muslim police officers to shave their beards because it interfered with the free expression of their religion.[4] That is, the courts ruled that because no law prohibiting the free exercise of religion was constitutional, this law, which prohibited the Muslim police officers from practicing their religion, was not constitutional. You will notice that in this example, the universal proposition placed in categorical form is "No laws prohibiting the free exercise of religion are constitutional." Because U.S. citizens and judicial courts believed that this is true, it meant that the particular case in which Muslims' free exercise of religion was being prohibited was also unconstitutional.

These previous examples have illustrated that when the universal proposition is true, it implies the truth of the particular proposition. What about when the universal proposition is false? What does that imply about the

particular proposition? Let's look at some examples of situations in which the universal is false in order to explore this idea with real propositions. Consider the proposition "No policemen are intelligent men." This is certainly a false proposition. However, just because the proposition "No policemen are intelligent men" is false, it does not mean that the particular *O* proposition of "Some policemen are not intelligent" is also false. It also doesn't mean that it is true. We actually don't know the truth-value of the *O* proposition. It might be true that some policemen are not intelligent, and it might not be true. Based on the falsity of the *E* proposition, we are unable to determine whether or not the *O* proposition is true or false. All we can say is that the proposition "No policemen are intelligent men" is false.

The point of this is that the law of subimplication states that if the universal is true, then the particular is true. But if the universal is false, the truth-value of the particular is unknown. By the same token, consider this *A* proposition: "All opera singers are high-maintenance." Let's say that this proposition is false. Does it also imply that the particular proposition "Some opera singers are high-maintenance" is false? No. We actually do not know the truth-value of the *I* proposition "Some opera singers are high maintenance" based on the falsity of the *A* proposition. Therefore, it is important to remember with the law of subimplication that, while the truth of the universal implies the truth of the particular, the falsity of the universal does not imply the falsity of the particular.

Understanding the law of subimplication can help you to avoid making accidental implications in your everyday speech that can offend other people. A scene from an episode of *Bones*, a television show aired by the FOX network, illustrates this common error well. In this show, Agent Seeley Booth is an FBI agent who works on homicide cases with his partner, Dr. Temperance Brennan, a brilliant forensic scientist who tends to make detached, scientific observations about people and events without realizing how those observations affect those around her. In this particular episode, Booth is shooting hoops in a gymnasium as he and Brennan are waiting to interview some basketball players about the recent murder of one of their teammates. The following conversation ensues:

Brennan: Sports should not have such a priority in the university.

Booth: You know what? That's just crazy.

Brennan: No, anthropologically speaking, sports are just a way for boys to practice their battle skills.

Booth: Yeah, okay. . . .

Brennan: The truth is, athletes are basically emotionally arrested in boyhood, acting out childish games as though they had adult importance. The only thing more juvenile are grown adults who watch sports.

Booth: Why do you gotta say stuff like that?

Brennan: What? You mean the truth?

Booth: All right, you know what? I'm a jock, so when you say, you know, those things, what are you saying about me?

Brennan: Nothing. You grew out of it.

Booth: No, I didn't, all right?[5]

As you can see from the example, Brennan did not mean to insult her partner. She was making what she believed was a completely logical and scientific universal observation about a group of people. However, Booth did not see it as a neutral empirical observation, and since he considered himself to be a part of the universal group Brennan was describing, he felt insulted.

Believe it or not, people make this mistake quite frequently. As we mentioned in lesson 5.4 when we were talking about contrary relationships, this mistake often occurs because when we speak about something about which we feel strongly, we tend to speak in universals (e.g., "All sports players are . . . ," "All Republicans are . . . ," "All Democrats are . . . ," "All librarians are . . . ," etc.). Sometimes we speak in universals because every person that we have met in this category does, indeed, fit our description. If a person has encountered or researched a wide variety of examples, she may actually mean "all" or "no." In such a case, it is appropriate for this person to use the universal, as long as she is open to discovering particulars that may disprove the universal. Unfortunately, however, many people use universal propositions for a much less noble reason: because noting the exceptions (telling the truth) would weaken their point.

For instance, groups of people who disagree frequently, such as Republicans and Democrats, socialists and free-

market proponents, pro-life people and non-pro-life people, tend to state universal propositions about each other because universal propositions are more emotionally persuasive. For instance, let's say that a Republican candidate is trying to persuade people to vote for him by claiming, "All Democrats are anti-religious zealots intent on removing religion from the public arena." By making such a sweeping universal proposition, he may be able to frighten and persuade people much more effectively than if he said something like, "Well, there are some Democrats who do not like religion and are trying to remove it from all public institutions. I don't like what they are doing, and I am afraid they might influence other Democrats. However, not all Democrats are like this. In fact, my neighbor is a Democrat and a committed Catholic, and my Aunt Sue sometimes votes Democrat, and she has attended her Presbyterian church every Sunday of her life."

As you can see, a more moderate proposition like this is not as scary. By the same token, a Democratic candidate who is extremely pro-environment may argue, "Republicans just want to pillage the earth to build their financial empires." This is much more emotionally inflammatory than saying something like, "Some Republicans definitely don't care enough about the environment and are only concerned about making as much money as they can. However, I do know some Republicans who really care about both the earth and preserving a free-market economy. They believe that the best balance to strike is to create policies that allow companies independence to maximize profits and stimulate the economy, while at the same time enforcing some general guidelines about the way in which these companies interact with the environment."

As you can see, using scary, emotionally charged universal propositions can be much more effective than using more restrained propositions. Therefore, some people will purposely misuse universals they know are false in an attempt to persuade others. On the other hand, some people casually misuse universals without intending any deception. For instance, let's say a woman makes this offhanded comment: "Teenagers are so disrespectful these days!" What she probably means is "I saw some teenagers the other day who were noisy and loud." If you questioned this lady further, she would probably say, "Oh, I don't mean all teenagers. After all, my niece and nephew are both in

high school and are just wonderful kids! I just mean some teenagers today just don't seem to have any manners." In this case, this woman was speaking carelessly, rather than trying to deceive.

Although some situations require strong universal propositions, it is wise to use universal propositions sparingly and cautiously because they can carry implications that you do not intend. Although many people will understand that you don't actually mean the universal, some people may feel offended and hurt because you are unintentionally insulting them by saying something universally disparaging about a category to which they belong.

Now that we have looked at the relationship between universals and their particulars, we want to look at the relationship between particulars and their universals. As you may have guessed by looking at the square of opposition, there is one final relationship that we need to discuss: superimplication. Just like subimplication, superimplication is the relationship between universal and particular propositions and is a one-way relationship. The rules of superimplication only apply if you begin with a particular proposition and carry the implication through to its universal. While subimplication is a relationship based on the truth of the universal, superimplication is a relationship based on the falsity of the particular. This means that if a particular proposition is false, it is implied that the universal is also false. However, if a particular proposition is true, it does not necessitate the truth of the universal.

Let's look at the first rule of superimplication:

1. The falsity of an *I* proposition implies the falsity of the *A* proposition.

In symbolic language, this means that if *Some S is P* (*I* proposition) is false, then it follows that *All S is P* (*A* proposition) is false as well. For example, consider the following proposition: "Some cowboys are fainthearted." Let's say that this is a false proposition. Notice that if the particular is false, then the universal must be as well. That is, if it is false that even *some* cowboys are fainthearted, it must certainly be false that *all* cowboys are fainthearted. Here is another way of looking at this. If the less all-encompassing proposition (the *I* proposition) is false, then certainly the more all-encompassing proposition (the *A* proposition) is false, too.

IT IS WISE TO USE UNIVERSAL PROPOSITIONS SPARINGLY AND CAUTIOUSLY BECAUSE THEY CAN CARRY IMPLICATIONS THAT YOU DO NOT INTEND.

Now let's look at the second rule of superimplication, which covers the relationship between the *O* and the *E* proposition:

> 2. The falsity of an *O* proposition implies the falsity of the *E* proposition.

In symbolic language, this means that if *Some S is not P* is false, then it follows that *No S is P* is also false. Let's look at an example of this with real propositions. Consider the proposition "Some boys are not males." This is obviously a false proposition. Note that if simply the particular proposition "Some boys are not males" is false, it must certainly be the case that the universal proposition "No boys are males" is also a false proposition. Once again, that is because the universal proposition is more inclusive and all encompassing than the particular proposition, which is less inclusive and all encompassing. Therefore, if the less-encompassing proposition is false, then certainly the more all-encompassing proposition must be false, too.

Just as we did with the relationship of subimplication, let's look at the relationship of superimplication from another angle. It is important to note that the relationship of superimplication only applies to the implication of *falsity* from the particular to the universal. There is no implication of *truth* from the particular to the universal. That is, just because the particular is true, it does not mean that the universal is true as well. Let's look at an example of this. Consider the proposition "Some primates are orangutans." This is a true proposition. Does this proposition also imply that the universal proposition "All primates are orangutans" is true? No, it doesn't. In fact, the proposition "All primates are orangutans" is a false proposition. Now, is the falsity of the universal proposition implied by the truth of the particular? No, it's actually not. That is, even if the particular proposition "Some primates are orangutans" is true, it does not imply the truth *or* falsity of the universal proposition.

Consider an example. Let's say that Tiffany makes this comment: "Some of my friends are not athletes." Does this imply that none of her friends are athletes? No, it doesn't. We actually don't know the truth-value of the proposition "None of my friends are athletes" based on the truth-value of the proposition "Some of my friends are athletes." It could be that some of Tiffany's friends are athletes and some of them aren't. On the other hand, it could also be the case that none of Tiffany's friends are athletes, but for some reason, she just couched this truth in the milder proposition "Some of my friends are not athletes." The point is, we don't know the truth-value based on her original proposition. This is because the truth-value of the universal cannot be inferred from the truth of the particular.

As you can imagine, recognizing the relationship of superimplication can guard you, once again, from making unwarranted assumptions or inferences. For instance, let's say that Nate asks Tiffany, "Are our friends that you invited to watch a movie tonight coming over?" and Tiffany responds, "Some are." Should Nate then assume that some of the friends are not coming or that all of them are coming? No. He shouldn't assume either of these propositions. It could be that half of the friends have accepted the invitations and the other half are not coming. Or, it could be that the rest are going to come but have not yet responded. There is no way that Nate or Tiffany can infer either of these scenarios from the fact that half of the invited friends have accepted their invitation. They will just have to wait and see.

The relationships of subimplication and superimplication examine the relationships between the universal and particular propositions. The law of subimplication states that if the universal is true, then the particular is true. The law of superimplication states that if the particular is false, then the universal is false. Now you have learned all of the relationships of opposition. Congratulations on your progress!

DEFINE

1. Square of Opposition:

_____

_____

_____

2. Contradiction:

_____

_____

_____

3. Contrariety:

_____

_____

_____

4. Subcontrariety:

_____

_____

_____

5. Subimplication:

_____

_____

_____

_____

6. Superimplication:

_____

_____

_____

_____

MATCH

For each of the following pairs of propositions, determine the relationship that is illustrated by the propositions and write it in the space provided.

1. Some primates are orangutans. Some primates are not orangutans. _____

2. All primates are orangutans. Some primates are not orangutans. _____

3. No primates are orangutans. Some primates are not orangutans. _____

4. All primates are orangutans. No primates are orangutans. _____

5. All primates are orangutans. Some primates are orangutans. _____

CREATE

Create or find an example of each of the following relationships of opposition: contradiction, contrariety, subcontrariety, subimplication, and superimplication. Remember, each of your examples should include both halves of the relationship (e.g., if you are illustrating contradiction and have an A proposition, then you would need to provide the O proposition as well to fully illustrate the relationship of contradiction). For the relationships of contradiction, subimplication, and superimplication, make sure that you include examples of all of the possible relationships. (Remember that contradiction exists between the A and the O propositions and the E and the I propositions. Subimplication exists between the A and I and the E and O propositions. Superimplication exists between the I and A and the O and E propositions.)

1. Contradiction:

_____

_____

2. Contrariety:

_____

_____

3. Subcontrariety:

_____

_____

4. Subimplication:

_____

_____

5. Superimplication:

_____

_____

EXPLAIN

Is the quote at the beginning of the chapter proper or improper inference? Explain your answer.

_____

_____

_____

_____

_____

_____

COMPLETE

Fill in the square of opposition below. Then, in the sentences that follow, see if you can complete each of the rules for each relationship of opposition. List the key points for each relationship and attempt to explain the relationships in your own words.

```
┌─────────────────────────┐
│                         │
│                         │
│                         │
│                         │
│                         │
│                         │
│                         │
└─────────────────────────┘
```

1. Contradictory Propositions:

   a. Contradictory propositions cannot both _____ .

   b. Contradictory propositions cannot both _____ .

   c. If one contradictory proposition is true, _____ .

   d. If one contradictory proposition is false, _____ .

2. Contrary Propositions:

   a. Contrariety is the relationship between _____ and _____ propositions.

   b. Propositions of contrariety *cannot* both _____ .

   c. Propositions of contrariety *can* both _____ .

   d. If one contrary proposition is true, _____ .

   e. If one contrary proposition is false, it does not necessitate _____ .

COMPLETE (CONTINUED)

3. Subcontrary Propositions:

   a. Subcontrariety is the relationship between _____ and _____ propositions.

   b. Propositions of subcontrariety can both _____ .

   c. Propositions of subcontrariety cannot _____ .

   d. If one subcontrary proposition is true, _____ .

   e. If one subcontrary proposition is false, then _____ .

4. Subimplication

   a. Subimplication is the relationship that exists between the _____ and _____ propositions. _____ relates to _____ . _____ relates to _____ .

   b. The truth of the universal implies the _____ of the particular.

   c. The falsity of the universal _____ imply the truth or falsity of the particular.

5. Superimplication:

   a. Superimplication is the relationship between _____ . _____ relates to _____ . _____ relates to _____ .

   b. The truth of the particular proposition does not necessitate _____ _____ .

   c. The falsity of the particular proposition implies _____ .

DEDUCTION IN ACTION

Scrutinizing Universals

Think of a universal belief that you know other people hold about a group of people. For example, you might hear people says things like "All Republicans are . . . ," "All Democrats are . . . ," "All teachers are . . . ," "All parents are . . . ," or some other such proposition. Sometimes universals are true, but sometimes they are just declarations we make when we don't want to think carefully. This can be dangerous because sometimes a universal proposition is not only false but also misleading and insulting as well. Therefore, take a moment to examine some common universal beliefs to see if they hold up to scrutiny.

To do this, write a common universal proposition on a separate piece of paper and then see if you can think of a particular that seems to disprove the proposition. For instance, if you hear kids say, "All teachers favor the kids that get good grades," write this proposition on a separate piece of paper and then think of a particular that disproves the universal. You might be able to think of a teacher that spends a lot of extra time with students who struggle in class. Write this counterexample, which disproves the universal proposition, next to the universal proposition. The point of this exercise is to help you to practice analyzing whether or not a universal proposition is accurate.

DEDUCTION IN ACTION
Reality vs. Fantasy

Now that you have learned about the relationships of opposition, we have a tricky question for you. What if you have the proposition, "All mermaids are women with fish tails who swim in the sea"? What is the truth-value of this proposition? Is it true or false? If you were Aristotle and attempting to develop a consistent system of logic, why might propositions about things such as mermaids, unicorns, and dragons pose a challenge? Read about how two different men—Aristotle and George Boole—dealt with this problem and answer the questions that follow.

Special Case: Boolean Conventions

George Boole was a logician, who influenced set theory in mathematics as well as the field of logic. He uncovered a possibly questionable assumption within the Aristotelian use of the square of opposition.

The relationships of subalternation (which we refer to as subimplication) and superalternation (which we know as superimplication) apply when Aristotelian conventions are assumed. In Aristotelian logic, one assumes that if a universal proposition is true, then there are actual members in that class of things. For example, if one claims that all humans are mortal, it makes perfect sense to infer that particular humans, such as Socrates, would also be mortal. However, consider odd cases in which the universal proposition addresses a class of things that has no existing members. For example, consider the following: "All unicorns are horse-like creatures having a single horn on the forehead."

This claim is a true universal claim about the concept "unicorn"; however, there are no actual existing members (i.e., unicorns aren't real). According to Aristotelian conventions, this universal claim would have to be called false because there are no members, while Boolean conventions allow this universal claim to be true. Boolean conventions assert that only particular claims have existential import, which means, simply, that the propositions themselves actually imply that there are existing members. This may seem like a foolish distinction, but keep in mind that it enables one to make claims about conceptual things as well as about empirically real things.

Let's look at another claim: "All dragons are fire-breathing beasts." This claim is true for the category of dragons, although no dragons actually exist (to our knowledge). If the subimplication relationship were assumed, then the claim that "Some dragons are fire-breathing beasts" would also be true. However, we know that this is a false *I* proposition. For this reason, the Boolean framework rejects the subimplication relationship.

1. What is existential import?

2. Describe the problem of existential import in relation to the square of opposition.

3. Explain how both Aristotle and George Boole addressed the problem of existential import.

LESSON 5.6
The Square of Opposition and Inference Analysis

POINTS TO REMEMBER

1. Analyzing the implications of your various beliefs can help you to avoid holding contradictory beliefs.
2. Holding and acting upon contradictory beliefs can cause frustration and inner conflict.

> I WILL NOT GIVE UP PHILOSOPHY AND EXHORTING YOU AND DECLARING THE TRUTH TO EVERY ONE OF YOU WHOM I MEET, SAYING, AS I AM ACCUSTOMED, 'MY GOOD FRIEND, YOU ARE A CITIZEN OF ATHENS, A CITY WHICH IS VERY GREAT AND VERY FAMOUS FOR ITS WISDOM AND POWER—ARE YOU NOT ASHAMED OF CARING SO MUCH FOR THE MAKING OF MONEY AND FOR FAME AND PRESTIGE, WHEN YOU NEITHER THINK NOR CARE ABOUT WISDOM AND TRUTH AND THE IMPROVEMENT OF YOUR SOUL?'
>
> —SOCRATES,
> THE *APOLOGY*[1]

Now that we have learned all of the various relationships in the square of opposition, it is time to examine another way in which you can practically apply this helpful tool. This is something we call inference analysis. It is a methodical way to discover what you believe about a certain scenario, value, or proposition. We will begin with the topic of lying. For instance, if you are trying to figure out what you believe about lying, such as whether it is always right or always wrong, you can start by examining all possible beliefs pertaining to lying:

A **Proposition:** All lying is wrong.   *E* **Proposition:** No lying is wrong.

I **Proposition:** Some lying is wrong.   *O* **Proposition:** Some lying is not wrong.

Let's say that you decide that you believe the *A* proposition "All lying is wrong" is true. What are you implying through this belief? Remembering what you have learned about the square of opposition, you look next at the *E* proposition and realize that the acceptance of *A* as true automatically implies the falsity of the *E* proposition "No lying is wrong." You know that if you believe the proposition "All lying is wrong" is true, that means that the proposition "No lying is wrong" is false. So far, so good. You

believe that you are on the right track. That is, you haven't violated the rule of contrary propositions because you do believe the proposition "No lying is wrong" to be false.

However, next you look at the *O* proposition "Some lying is not wrong," and you feel a little hesitant. You know that, according to the square of opposition, if you believe that the *A* proposition is true, it automatically means that the *O* proposition is false. That is, you must believe that the proposition "Some lying is not wrong" is false. This gives you pause, however, because you realize that you actually do think some lying is not wrong. For instance, if you knew a friend was suicidal, and she asked you if there was any poison in the house, you believe it would be acceptable to lie to her in order to save her life. So, based on that, you realize that you don't actually believe the *A* proposition. Instead, you believe the *O* proposition.

Then, as you look at the *I* proposition "Some lying is wrong," it makes you feel even more sure of your altered position because you can believe that the *O* proposition is true and still believe that the *I* proposition is true—the relationship of subcontrariety allows for both the *I* and the *O* propositions to be true at the same time. Therefore, you adjust your belief to reflect the *O* proposition "Some lying is not wrong," which also allows for the truth of the *I* proposition "Some lying is wrong." In fact, you realize that you can actually believe that *most* lying is bad, with only a few instances of it being OK, such as lying to save someone's life. You know it is OK to believe these two propositions simultaneously because when you change the proposition "Most lying is wrong" into logical form, it becomes "Some lying is wrong." When you translate the proposition "Only a few instances of lying are not wrong" into logical form, it becomes "Some lying is not wrong." Therefore, you know that you believe that two subcontrary propositions are true, and this follows the rule of subcontrariety.

To understand better how this process works, let's look at another example. Let's say that Thomas, a freshman in high school, is having a particularly bad day. He is at a new school, and he is a freshman, the lowest man on the totem pole. He hasn't made new friends as quickly as he would have liked to, and some upperclassmen have acted rather haughty and condescending to him. He goes home after

school, flops on the couch, and thinks to himself, "Everyone hates me." From your practice in translating propositions, you know that he is actually saying, "All people are people who hate me," but is this actually true? Let's look at all of the possible propositions containing the terms "people" and "people who hate me."

> *A* **Proposition:** All people are people who hate me.
> *I* **Proposition:** Some people are people who hate me.
> *E* **Proposition:** No people are people who hate me.
> *O* **Proposition:** Some people are not people who hate me.

As you can imagine, if Thomas takes a minute to think about his high school experience, he will likely be able to think of one person, and likely several people, who act as though they don't hate him, and, indeed, actually are very friendly. That is, he knows that "Some people are not people who hate him." Therefore, it can't be true that "All people hate him."

Now you might be thinking, "Come on! Thomas is just having a bad day. He just needs to blow off steam by talking to someone, shooting hoops, or playing a marathon video game session. We don't really need to bring this into the square of opposition, do we?" You are probably right in that Thomas probably doesn't really believe that everyone hates him. He probably just had a bad day and does need to blow off steam. However, it is important to note that all of our actions proceed from beliefs that we hold. We get up in the morning because we believe it's important to accomplish the day's tasks or at least avoid punishment for not accomplishing them. We brush our teeth because we believe it's important to avoid tooth decay. We play marathon gaming sessions because we believe that having fun is important, and it's fun to play games.

While it is certainly true that when most people say, "Everyone hates me," it is an exclamation of passing frustration, if a person thinks things like this consistently without challenging the truth of the proposition (and people certainly do this), he might start acting as though everyone really *does* hate him. And if a person acts as though everyone hates him, he will likely act in a rude, hostile, and surly or withdrawn manner, which may lead to everyone disliking him at the very least. We are not saying that a person is going to think to himself, "Using the square of opposition, I shall examine my beliefs today

in order to determine if I hold any contradictory beliefs." This is obviously absurd. Instead, a clear understanding of inference, which you are learning through the square of opposition, will allow you to recognize these contradictions and other inference problems more quickly. In other words, by understanding the laws of inference, you are developing the ability to question your own assumptions and beliefs, much like Socrates did when he questioned Euthyphro and the people at his trial.

Let's look at another example in which a person holds contradictory assumptions that are not, at first, as straightforward. Imagine a man named David who believes that his family should have first priority in his life. If we were to word this in a proposition, we could do it as an *A* proposition in the following manner: "All activities that make my family second priority are bad priorities." He knows that this proposition is true. This automatically means, according to the law of contradiction, that the *O* proposition is false: "Some activities that make my family second priority are not bad activities." David would agree with this, too.

However, as David goes along in his life, he begins to feel frustrated and restless. He feels like his life is out of kilter. In reexamining his beliefs and actions, he realizes that though he says he believes the proposition "All activities that make my family second priority are bad priorities," his work schedule actually reflects a different belief. That is, he has gotten into the habit of working so much overtime that he has actually started to neglect his family in favor of his work. This means that, though he does not realize it, he is acting like he believes this proposition: "Some activities that make my family second priority—namely, working overtime—are not bad activities." Now, David can figure this out without knowing a thing about the square of opposition. Nevertheless, however he figures it out, what he is doing is realizing that his actions are contradictory to his beliefs.

Whenever we act in a way that is contradictory to our beliefs, we feel strain and stress, especially as we become more aware of the contradiction. This is because, generally, people want to act in a way that is true to their beliefs. That is, we want to act according to what we believe is right and important. The ancient philosophers said this another way:

"All people seek the good." Therefore, when we discover that our actions and beliefs are misaligned, we realize this is not good, and it causes us stress.

Here's the point: Whether your belief is about moral values, about the thoughts of those people around you, or about your own priorities, it is never helpful and often harmful to hold false, contradictory, or absurd beliefs. Therefore, a normal part of becoming a mature, thoughtful, happy, and responsible person is the examination of beliefs and values with the goal of adopting the most logical, good, and consistent values. As we mentioned before, this is why Socrates said, "The unexamined life is not worth living."[2] The square of opposition is a tool you can use to examine your life and your thoughts because it teaches you to understand what you can infer from your beliefs and the beliefs of others. Sometimes you will do this informally and quickly, such as when you realize through intuition that you are acting in a way that contradicts your stated beliefs. Other times, it will occur when you systematically observe your beliefs and those of other people and the inferences you can make because of those beliefs.

DEDUCTION IN ACTION
Examining Your Personal Beliefs

On a separate piece of paper, write a paragraph explaining a belief or value you hold. To do this, take one of the topics listed below (or another topic of your choice) and state what you believe about the topic in the form of one of the propositions—*A*, *I*, *E*, or *O*. Then, use the square of opposition to explain at least two inferences that proceed from the truth-value of your proposition. Afterward, provide at least three examples that support your proposition or the inferences of your proposition in order to answer the following questions: Do these inferences cause you to change your mind? Why or why not? Your paragraph should contain both an introductory and a concluding sentence.

Topics:

- Adultery
- Reading
- Watching television
- Gaining knowledge
- Stealing
- Honoring your country

- Gossiping
- Lying to a friend
- Voting Democrat
- Being a good friend
- Taking care of your health
- Making money

- Voting Republican
- Flag burning
- Draft dodging
- Caring for your family
- Caring for the poor
- Visiting your grandparents

DIALOGUE 6.1
Introduction to the Relationships of Equivalence

Nate finds Socrates wandering around the quad on campus.

Nate: Socrates, I need your help again.

Socrates: Another logic dilemma?

Nate: You could say that. Every time I think I am making progress with this whole formal logic thing, I hit another roadblock.

Socrates: What is it that is confusing you now?

Nate: The English language—it's just so . . . convoluted!

Socrates: Yes, I often wish more people around here spoke Greek. I think it would simplify things greatly. Could you give me an example of what you mean by "convoluted"?

Nate: Yes. See, I have been thinking through the implications of my propositions carefully, and I have become pretty good at translating ordinary language into syllogisms.

Socrates: Go on.

Nate: Well, all of a sudden today, when I was arguing with this girl from my ethics class, I encountered a sentence that completely messed me up.

Socrates: Is this another one of your sayings?

Nate: What? Oh, yes, it is. It just means that I was totally confused.

Socrates: What was the sentence that confused you?

Nate: This girl and I were arguing about war and pacifism. She's a committed pacifist, and she said that she had met no pro-peace people who were not non-violent.

Socrates: Oh, dear.

Nate: Yeah, that's what I mean. I sort of understood what she was saying, but all of her no's, nots, and nons gave me a headache. I didn't know what to say or how to interpret her argument. In fact, she talks this way a lot. I don't know if she thinks it sounds more intelligent or if she's just confused herself. You don't happen to have some other nifty logic tool up your sleeve that would help me analyze complete nonsense, do you?

Socrates: Ah, the English language—so colorful. I think I'm getting the hang of these crazy idioms. And, yes, I do think I have something that might help.

Nate: Socrates, you're the best! You need to start a website. Instead of "Ask Jeeves," it could be "Ask Socrates."

Socrates: Who is Jeeves?

Nate: Never mind. What is this tool?

Socrates: I will tell you, but first explain to me the function of the square of opposition, which we discussed in our last conversation.

Nate: The purpose of the square of opposition is to determine how propositions are in opposition to each other or what they imply about each other.

Socrates: That's very good. Did you know that just as there are relationships of opposition, there are also relationships of equivalence?

Nate: I did not know that, but it makes sense. Equivalence—that means relationships or propositions that are equal to each other, right?

Socrates: Exactly!

Nate: I think I understand the use of the relationships of equivalence. For instance, you could use those relationships to show me to what the proposition "no pro-peace people are not non-violent" is equal, right?

Socrates: It will take a little bit of work, but, yes.

Nate: So how do these relationships of equivalence work?

Socrates: Well, it may help you to understand that better if I tell you that there are three main relationships of equivalence. They are **conversion**, **contraposition**, and **obversion**. Each of these propositions has specific rules that allow you to use it as a type of tool for changing propositions into equivalent propositions.

Nate: Hmmm . . . a tool for changing propositions. I think I understand. Do you mean that, according to certain rules, I can use the relationships of equivalence to change confusing propositions into clear propositions?

Socrates: Precisely!

Nate: Hey, that's kind of like reducing fractions.

Socrates: In what way is it similar?

Nate: Well, sometimes you have a really big and complicated fraction with which it is impossible to work, but you can actually reduce it to a smaller, simpler number so that it is easier to manipulate.

Socrates: There are certainly some similarities.

Nate: Great! Thanks, Socrates. I think I'm going to go study these. Then maybe I can finally have a clear conversation with that girl in my ethics class!

REVIEW
ANSWER

1. What is the purpose of the relationships of equivalence?

_____

_____

_____

_____

2. List each of the relationships of equivalence.

a. _____

b. _____

c. _____

LESSON 6.2
Logical Equations

POINTS TO REMEMBER

1. The relationships of equivalence help us understand which propositions are identical to each other.
2. The relationships of equivalence can help in simplifying confusing arguments or in looking at an argument from a different angle.

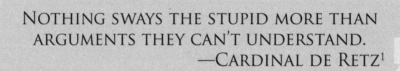

> NOTHING SWAYS THE STUPID MORE THAN ARGUMENTS THEY CAN'T UNDERSTAND.
> —CARDINAL DE RETZ[1]

Have you ever tried these brainteasers with your friends? "I didn't not go to the store yesterday," or "He wasn't not prohibited to go on that road." Throwing double or triple negatives into a sentence can make it a real puzzle to figure out. The quadruple negative is almost unheard of: "She didn't never not go without running through the puddles." That one's enough to make your head swim.

In chapter 5, you studied the relationships of opposition. As you learned, categorical propositions can be opposed to each other in a variety of ways. But categorical propositions also have characteristics of equality. Equality means that two things are the same. In mathematics, we say that two sides of an equation are equivalent if the value of one side is the same as the value on the other side. For instance, $3 \times 3 = 9$ is an equation because one side equals the other. Both sides don't, however, look identical. The values that they represent may be expressed differently, but the values remain equal. The same can be said of logically equivalent propositions. Propositions may mean the same thing but can be worded very differently.

To continue with our mathematical example, in order to determine that both sides of our example equation are equivalent, you probably did some mental math. You converted 3×3 into 9 by performing the operation of multiplication. It's that concept of converting a proposition from one form into another that will be the key to understanding relationships of equivalence, which are also known as **immediate inferences**. We'll learn how to convert propositions by learning the following operations: obversion, conversion, and contraposition.

You may be asking yourself why converting a proposition from one form to another is relevant and important to the study of deductive logic. There are two main reasons for learning to convert propositions. The first reason is because everyday language can be very unclear, convoluted, and difficult to present in logical form. Think about it: How often do you find arguments written in

IT'S MORE LIKELY THAT ARGUMENTS IN EVERYDAY ENGLISH WILL BE SIGNIFICANTLY MORE COMPLICATED THAN A SIMPLE *S IS P* PROPOSITION.

the form of *All S is P*? Very rarely. It's more likely that arguments in everyday English will be significantly more complicated than a simple *S is P* proposition. For example, what is logically being said in the following proposition?

> No pro-environmental activists are non-friends of humanity.

What about this?

> Some anti-smokers are not pro-prohibiting smokers in restaurants.

When we discuss things in everyday life, our language is frequently unpolished, convoluted, and filled with grammatical problems. As you explore the relationships of equivalence, you will study how to change propositions that may seem confusing into regular propositions. Doing so will allow you to clearly identify the matter at hand, which, as you'll recall, is essential to effective discussion.

The second reason learning to convert a proposition from one form to another is important is because the relationships of equivalence help us understand other propositions that are the equivalent to propositions that we might be considering. For illustration, consider the proposition "All good friends are good listeners." There are two other propositions that are equivalent to this proposition:

> No good friends are non-good listeners.

> All non-good listeners are non-good friends.

As you can see, equivalent propositions can sometimes be awkward. However, both the first and the second proposition are identical in meaning to the original proposition, and they are helpful because they allow you to examine the proposition from another point of view. As you may have noticed, the original proposition—"All good friends are good listeners"—examines the topic from a positive perspective. The equivalent propositions examine it from a negative perspective. You could say that both types of propositions—positive and negative—are different sides

of the same coin. Therefore, the relationships of equivalence help you gain a more complete view of your topic because they allow you to examine the topic from different angles.

In the next couple of chapters, as you examine three relationships of equivalence, remember their two purposes: 1) They can help you clarify more confusing propositions, and 2) they can help you to examine your proposition from different angles.

1. Explain how the relationships of equivalence differ from the relationships of opposition.

_____

_____

_____

_____

_____

_____

2. How can it be helpful to study relationships of equivalence?

_____

_____

_____

_____

_____

DEDUCTION IN ACTION

Logic and Math

As you study more about deductive logic, you may begin to notice some similarities between it and mathematics. This is because mathematics is logic. Remember that deductive logic operates by proceeding from *a priori* truths to new truths. This is exactly the way that mathematics works. Math works with numbers and mathematical laws that are certain. We construct formulas based upon these numbers and mathematical laws, and we arrive at new numbers, or new truths. For example, the entire study of geometry is based on axioms and postulates, which are mathematical laws about figures and shapes that we know are true. Mathematicians can figure out other properties about shapes and their relationship to other shapes based on these laws. As we proceed through the rest of this chapter, you will see several other connections between math and logic.

LESSON 6.3
The Obverse Relationship

POINTS TO REMEMBER

1. Every categorical proposition has an obverse relationship.
2. Obversion requires changing the quality of both the subject and predicate of the proposition. This is accomplished by:
    a. Changing the quality of the subject term from affirmative to negative or from negative to affirmative.
    b. Changing the quality of the predicate term to its **complement**.
3. If a term has two "nons" in it, the "nons" cancel each other out.
4. Use caution in using opposite terms as complements.

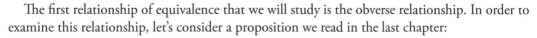

> ## FEAR NOT THOSE WHO ARGUE
> ## BUT THOSE WHO DODGE.
> ## —DALE CARNEGIE[1]

The first relationship of equivalence that we will study is the obverse relationship. In order to examine this relationship, let's consider a proposition we read in the last chapter:

No pro-environmental activists are non-friends of humanity.

As you can see, this proposition is a bit convoluted, and simplifying it would certainly be helpful. We can do this by using the relationship of obversion. The purpose of obversion is to change a proposition into an equivalent sentence. This can be very helpful because it can help you to simplify the proposition or to look at it from a different angle so that you can understand it better. That is, obversion will help you to discover simpler ideas that are equivalent to the confusing proposition. In addition, obversion, like all relationships of equivalence, can help you look at a subject from a different point of view.

Obversion can be used with all categorical propositions, which means that each categorical proposition has an obverse relationship. Before you learn how to simplify propositions using this relationship, let's take a minute to look at how the process of obversion works. It can be compared to the process of determining the answer to the following mathematical equation:

$x + 9 = 12$

What's the first step in solving this equation for the value of x? You must isolate x on one side of the equation, and then you need to isolate all of the constants on the other side of the equation. How is this accomplished? First, subtract 9 from the left side of the equation. If you remember your

pre-algebra, you know that what is done to one side of an equation must be done to the other side of the equation, which allows the equation to remain equivalent. So, if you subtract 9 from the left side of the equation, you must do the same to the right side as well. Here's what the equation looks like when these steps are taken:

$$x + 9 - 9 = 12 - 9$$

$$x = 12 - 9 \quad \text{(The 9s cancel each other out on the left side)}$$

$$x = 3 \quad \text{(12 minus 9 on the right side yields 3)}$$

That's a pretty easy equation to solve, isn't it? The process of finding x is similar to using the process of obversion on a proposition. Think of our proposition as a mathematical equation with two sides, just like the equation we just solved. Instead of an equal sign separating the two sides, we have a verb separating the subject from the predicate. In our example proposition, that means that the subject "No pro-environmental activists" is separated by the verb "are" from the predicate "non-friends of humanity."

Obversion requires changing the quality of both sides of the proposition, just like we had to subtract 9 from both sides of the mathematical equation to make it equivalent. So, how exactly do we accomplish obversion? We do it by following these two steps:

Step 1: Change the quality of the proposition. This means that affirmative (positive) propositions become negative ones and vice versa.

Step 2: Negate the predicate. That is, we change the quality of the predicate term. This operation is sometimes called **using the complement** and is always accomplished by adding the word "non" to the predicate.

The complement of a word is everything that is not represented by that word. We represent this by adding the word "non" before a word. For instance, the complement of the word "boy" would be "non-boy" because "non-boy" represents everything that is not represented by the term "boy." In the same way, if our word is "cat," its complement is "non-cat" because the term "non-cat" represents everything that is not represented by the word "cat." Therefore, to supply the complement of a word, you put the word "non" before it.

We will eventually look at how we can obvert our example proposition from the beginning of the lesson to make it less complicated and easier to understand, but first let's look at how obversion works with each of the different types of propositions (*A*, *E*, *I*, and *O*), starting with the *A* proposition. Note that obverting an *A* proposition involves changing "all" to "no" and adding "non" to the predicate. Symbolically, this means that the *A* proposition *All S is P* becomes *No S is non-P*. Let's look at this process using an actual *A* proposition. If we want to obvert the proposition "All boys are guitar players," we must do the following steps:

Step 1: "All" becomes "no."

Step 2: "Guitar players" becomes "non–guitar players."

Therefore, our new obverted proposition is "No boys are non-guitar players." (Of course, this proposition is not true, but remember that we're merely practicing the relationship of obversion. Don't worry about the truth-value of any of the propositions at this time.)

Now let's look at what we just did and relate it back to the math analogy we used earlier to explain conversion. First, we changed the term on the left side of the being verb "are." That is, we changed the term "all boys" to "no boys." This is like what we did in our original equation when we subtracted 9 from the left side of the equation. Now, because we changed "all boys" to "no boys," we need to do something with the term on the right side of the word "are," just as we had to subtract 9 from the right side of the math equation in order to keep the equation equivalent. In our proposition, we change the term "guitar players" to "non–guitar players."

If you think about it, we have now performed equivalent operations on the terms on both sides of the word "are." That is, we changed the quality of the term on the left side to its opposite quality. Then, we changed the term on the right side of the being verb to its complement, which represents everything that is not that term. For instance, "non–guitar players" represents everything that is not "guitar players." Therefore, both sides of the word "are" in our proposition have been equally changed, and the proposition "No boys are non–guitar players" is now truly equivalent to the original proposition "All boys are guitar players." This is just like what we did in the math equation when we subtracted 9 from both sides of the equal sign, making the new equation equivalent to the original equation.

THINK OF OUR PROPOSITION AS A MATHEMATICAL EQUATION WITH TWO SIDES.

Next, let's look at the *I* proposition. Note that obverting an *I* proposition involves changing the quality of the proposition by adding "not" to the "some are" phrase. Then we add "non" to the predicate to provide the complement. Therefore, the *I* proposition *Some S is P* becomes *Some S is not non-P*. Notice, once again, that in the process of obversion we equally change both sides of the proposition *Some S is P*, just as we did in our original mathematical formula. That is, we changed the quality of *S* to its opposite by adding the word "not," making the first part of the proposition *Some S is not*. Then we provided the complement of *P* by changing it to *non-P*, which includes everything that is not *P*. Because we changed both sides of the proposition, the new proposition is now equivalent to the old one.

Let's look at this process with a regular *I* proposition. Consider the proposition "Some caterpillars are future butterflies." Here are the steps for obverting this proposition:

Step 1: "Some caterpillars are" becomes "some caterpillars are not."

Step 2: "Future butterflies" becomes "non–future butterflies."

Our obverted proposition, therefore, becomes "Some caterpillars are not non–future butterflies."

Next, let's look at obversion with the *O* proposition. Even though this proposition is a negative proposition, we do the same thing we have done with the other propositions, changing both sides of the word "are" to produce a new equivalent proposition. Note that obverting an *O* proposition involves changing the quality of the proposition by removing the "not" from the "some are not" phrase. Then we add "non" to the predicate to negate the predicate, as we always do in the second step of obversion. Symbolically, this means that the proposition *Some S is not P* becomes *Some S is non-P*.

To practice this, look at the steps we would take to obvert the proposition "Some tennis players are not world champions."

Step 1: "Some tennis players are not" becomes "some tennis players are."

Step 2: "World champions" becomes "non–world champions."

Therefore, the new, equivalent proposition is "Some tennis players are non–world champions."

Lastly, let's consider the *E* proposition. Note that obverting an *E* proposition involves changing the quality of the proposition by changing "no" to "all." Then we add "non" to the predicate to negate the predicate. So, just as with all of the other obversions and our mathematical example, we are changing both sides of the word "are" to retain equality in the proposition. Symbolically, this means that *No S is P* becomes *All S is non-P*. Consider the process of obversion for the proposition "No sci-fi fanatics are dull":

Step 1: "No sci-fi fanatics" becomes "all sci-fi fanatics."

Step 2: "Dull" becomes "non-dull."

Therefore, our new proposition is "All sci-fi fanatics are non-dull."

Now that you have seen how obversion works, there are two interesting language issues related to it about which you need to know. The first occurs when we begin with a proposition that already has a "non" in it. For example, consider the following proposition:

No false rumors are non-important issues.

Notice what happens when we obvert this proposition:

All false rumors are non non-important issues.

If one of the main purposes of obverting a proposition is to simplify it, do you think we have accomplished that

here? Not really, right? People don't usually say things like "non non-important issues," do they? So, where does that leave us? Another math comparison may help you here. You might recall that in math, two negatives make a positive. Therefore, 2 − (-2) = 2 + 2. In other words, the negatives cancel each other out. It is the same with obversion. Therefore, the rather confusing proposition "All false rumors are non non-important issues" becomes more clear when we recognize that the two "nons" negate each other so that we end up with the following proposition: "All false rumors are important issues." This is still the obverse of the proposition "No false rumors are non-important issues." It's just a bit clearer. Keep in mind when using obversion that two negatives always cancel each other out. Therefore, two "nons" will cancel each other out. In addition, this is also true if you have a "not" and a "non" together. They also cancel each other out because they are both negative. For example, if you had the proposition "All mice are not non-cat-haters," by obversion this would become "All mice are cat-haters." If you keep in mind that two negative words cancel each other out, this will further help you in simplifying convoluted propositions.

Now we need to examine the second language issue related to obversion. Consider the following proposition:

All senators are wealthy people.

If we obvert this proposition, we get this new sentence: "No senators are non-wealthy people." This presents an interesting language/logic question: Could we replace the phrase "non-wealthy people" with "poor people"? It seems to make sense and to retain the same meaning, more or less, of the original proposition. The question, then, is this: Can the opposite of a term be used as its complement? The answer is a bit tricky. You have to be very careful when you use opposite terms. The reason for this is that the complement of a term should, technically, represent *everything* that falls outside of the class of that term. So, for instance, while "poor people" is the opposite of "wealthy people," it is not the true complement because the term "poor people" doesn't represent *everything* outside of the class of "wealthy people." For instance, it does not represent "middle-class people" who are neither poor nor wealthy. Therefore, the true complement to "wealthy people" is "non-wealthy people" because it contains everything that is not contained in the term "wealthy people."

Sometimes it may seem as though using the opposite term of another term is just as accurate as using the complement. After all, the phrase "No senators are poor people" certainly sounds close enough to the proposition "No senators are non-wealthy people." However, the concept "poor" is still quite a bit different from "non-wealthy" because it does not encompass everything that is not inside the class of "wealthy." Therefore, one proposition cannot replace the other. For example, a teacher or a pastor might say "I am non-wealthy." However, this certainly does not mean that they are poor. Therefore, it is clear that non-wealthy can mean other things besides poor, and this is why the word "poor" cannot work as a replacement for the phrase "non-wealthy."

In addition, using the opposite term in place of the complement of a term can often result in propositions that are patently misleading. Consider the following example, which is borrowed from David Kelley's book *The Art of Reasoning*: "No people in my family are thin." If we used the opposite term of "thin" in the obverse proposition, it would look like this: "All people in my family are fat."[2] As you can see, the meaning of this second proposition is quite different from the meaning of the original proposition. Just because people are not thin does not mean they are fat. This would be a misleading proposition. Therefore, we need to be very careful when we use opposing terms as complements. They can certainly help in clarifying a proposition and translating it into more ordinary English (after all, we do not ordinarily use terms like "non-wealthy" and "non-thin" in everyday conversation). However, if used carelessly, they may distort the meaning of the original proposition.

Now let's consider the proposition from the beginning of this lesson: "No pro-environmental activists are non-friends of humanity." Since this proposition is convoluted, we want to simplify it by using obversion. See if you can do it first on a piece of paper or in your head before you look at the following steps and the final answer.

Step 1: "No" becomes "all."

Step 2: "Non-friends of humanity" becomes "non non-friends of humanity."

Therefore, our new proposition is "All pro-environmental activists are non non-friends of humanity." We know that

we can simplify it further by allowing the two "nons" to cancel each other out. Therefore, our new proposition is "All pro-environmental activists are friends of humanity."

Let's consider one more example before we move on to the next lesson. Little Miss Cryptic is a very smart college student who loves debating with people in her ethics class. Furthermore, she loves to stump her opponents with convoluted, intellectual-sounding phrases. The other day, she and Nate were debating whether there should be a total free-market economy or whether the government should place significant regulations on corporations. At one point, Little Miss Cryptic said, "You know, Nate, no non-regulated economies are not acting in their own best interest." Nate, as you can imagine, was a bit mystified by that proposition. Can you help him out and use obversion to simplify Little Miss Cryptic's proposition? Do it first in your head or on a piece of paper. Then, check the following steps and final answer to see how you did.

Step 1: Change "no" to "all."

Step 2: Change "not acting in their own best interest" to "non not acting in their own best interest."

Your new proposition is this: "All non-regulated economies are non not acting in their own best interest." We know from previous examples that the two negatives—"non" and "not"—cancel each other out, so we end up with the following proposition: "All non-regulated economies are acting in their own best interest." As you can see, this is a much easier proposition for Nate to discuss.

Obversion is the first relationship of equivalence. Remember that the relationships of equivalence help you to determine other propositions that are equivalent to any particular proposition. This can be helpful when a proposition is very convoluted, as Little Miss Cryptic's was, or when you just want to look at a topic from a different point of view. The next relationship of equivalence we will examine is conversion.

REVIEW
DEFINE

1. Immediate Inference:

_____

_____

2. Obversion:

_____

_____

_____

EXPLAIN

Explain the two language issues of which you should be aware when using obversion.

_____

_____

_____

EXPLAIN (CONTINUED)

_____
_____
_____
_____
_____
_____
_____
_____
_____
_____
_____

PRACTICE

Explain the steps used to reach the obverse relationship for each of the following categorical propositions, and then write the obverse conversion for each.

1. *All S is P.*

_____
_____

Obverse Proposition: _____

2. *Some S is P.*

_____
_____

Obverse Proposition: _____

3. *Some S is not P.*

_____
_____

Obverse Proposition: _____

4. *No S is P.*

_____
_____

Obverse Proposition: _____

DETERMINE

Use obversion to determine equivalent propositions for each of the following propositions.

1. All watches are timekeepers. _____

2. Some baseball players are professional athletes. _____

3. No Italians are Romanians. _____

4. Some musicians are not studying at Juilliard. _____

5. No textbooks are non-interesting. _____

6. Everyone who studies is a non-failure. (Hint: To make this proposition easier to obvert, you may want to put it into categorical form first.) _____

   _____

7. A few pastors are not married. (Hint: Put this in categorical form before you obvert it.)

   _____

8. Some linguists are bilingual. _____

9. All Starbucks employees are non-volunteers. _____

10. No non-drivers are non-vehicle operators. (Two notes: 1. Determine if the statement needs to be changed into standard categorical form. 2. Don't allow yourself to get caught up in the truth-value of the statement as you work the problem. Remember, we are not trying to coerce the statement into becoming true if it is not. Allow the solution to reflect the original truth-value).

   _____

DEDUCTION IN ACTION
Little Miss Cryptic Strikes Again

Do you remember the discussion between Nate and Little Miss Cryptic from earlier in this lesson? Well, later on in the semester, they had another discussion. This time, it was over the issue of universalized healthcare in America. Little Miss Cryptic argued the following proposition in relation to universalized healthcare:

> All government handouts are not non-enabling people to be lazy.

Obvert this proposition and then write a paragraph in which you argue for or against the proposition. Use at least one syllogism in your argument. (Don't worry right now if it is structured correctly or not. Just use one that sounds logical to you).

LESSON 6.4
The Converse Relationship

POINTS TO REMEMBER

1. The converse relationship preserves equivalence for only *E* and *I* propositions.
2. Conversion is accomplished by switching the subject and predicate terms.
3. *A* and *O* propositions cannot use the converse relationship because switching their subject and predicate terms does not create a logically equivalent proposition.

> HE WHO ESTABLISHES HIS ARGUMENT
> BY NOISE AND COMMAND SHOWS THAT
> HIS REASON IS WEAK.
> —MICHEL EYQUEM DE MONTAIGNE[1]

The next relationship of equivalence we're going to study is the relationship of conversion. Unlike the obverse relationship, the converse relationship does not preserve equivalence for all categorical propositions. That is, it doesn't work on all of the propositions—it only preserves equivalence, or works, for *E* and *I* propositions. For an *A* or *O* proposition, you must use either obversion or contraposition (you'll learn about this in lesson 6.5) in order to maintain equivalence.

Conversion is the immediate inference that switches the subject and predicate terms of *E* and *I* propositions, allowing you to view the propositions from a different perspective while still maintaining the logical equivalence of the propositions. With conversion, the original proposition implies its converse. To help you understand what this means, consider the etymology of the word "imply." It comes from the Latin word *implicare*, which means "to involve."[2] An old-fashioned definition of imply is "to enfold, enwrap, or entangle."[3] In other words, when a second idea is implied by the first idea, it means that the second idea is involved, enfolded, and entangled with the first idea. This means that if a converse of a proposition is implied by the original proposition, it is involved, entangled, and wrapped up in the original proposition. You will start to see this more clearly with conversion as you begin to examine how it works.

If we look at conversion symbolically, this is how the propositions will appear:

E Propositions: *No S is P = No P is S.*

I Propositions: *Some S is P = Some P is S.*

Let's look at the conversion of some actual *E* and *I* propositions. If the original proposition is "No men are women," by conversion this proposition becomes "No women are men." That is, it is implied

that if no men are women, then no women could be men. Here's another example. If the original proposition is "Some ants are insects," its converse proposition is "Some insects are ants." It is implied that if some ants are insects, then some insects must be ants. As another example, consider the proposition "No planets are suns." By conversion, this proposition becomes "No suns are planets." It is implied that if no planets are suns, then there couldn't be any suns that are planets. As you can see, all of these propositions remain logically equivalent after swapping the subject and predicate terms.

Now let's examine why the converse relationship does not apply to *A* and *O* propositions. Switching the subject and the predicate of *A* and *O* propositions creates propositions that are not logically equivalent—the original proposition does not imply the converted proposition. For example, consider the *A* proposition "All pianists are musicians." By conversion, this proposition would become "All musicians are pianists." These propositions are not logically equivalent. Just because all pianists are musicians does not imply that all musicians are pianists. In fact, you can probably think of many musicians that are not pianists, such as violinists, harpists, drummers, and harmonica players.

Now let's look at the *O* proposition "Some berries are not blueberries." By conversion, this proposition would become "Some blueberries are not berries." In the same way that the *A* proposition we just looked at was no longer logically equivalent once we had converted it, this *O* proposition is not either. The fact that some berries are not blueberries does not imply that some blueberries are not berries.

There are some situations in which conversion can be very helpful. First, as we have mentioned before, the relationships of equivalence can help you examine ideas from different perspectives. For example, let's say that someone believes one of the following propositions: "No thoughtful people are Democrats" or "No thoughtful people are Republicans." If we convert these propositions, we have these new propositions: "No Democrats are thoughtful people" or "No Republicans are thoughtful people." Notice that when you switch the subject and the predicate, it forces you to think about your proposition from a different point of view. A person who makes such a proposition must consider whether or not he can truly say he has never met a thoughtful Republican or Democrat. You may notice that

the first wording of the proposition is a little more general (it's talking about people), but when the proposition is converted, it becomes more specific because it is talking about specific kinds of people (Democrats or Republicans).

You might remember that when we first introduced the relationships of equivalence, we said that these relationships can help you not only in simplifying convoluted propositions but also in looking at propositions from a different point of view. It is often helpful to look at a proposition from a different point of view because it can help you see how someone else might view what you are saying. So if you converted the proposition "No thoughtful people are Republicans" to "No Republicans are thoughtful people," it would make you think in a much more specific manner about individual Republicans. This specific view will challenge you to consider if you really mean what you originally stated. It's much easier to make strong negative generalizations about a group of people than to make a pointed negative comment about one person. Therefore, considering the converse of a proposition can force you to clarify your thinking.

Second, if you remember that conversion only works on *E* and *I* propositions, this may help you avoid an unwarranted inference. For instance, you are probably aware that many people have historically referred to God as "He" and have assigned Him male attributes. Some people have objected to this by claiming that "if God is male, then male is God." Think for a minute. What is the problem with this proposition? Well, you have probably figured out that the proposition "God is male" is an *A* proposition. Since conversion does not work on *A* propositions, the proposition "Male is God" is not equivalent to "God is male." The point here is not to argue about God's gender, but to note that if someone wanted to argue against the notion that God is male, it would not be logical to claim that "this means male is God" because the two propositions are not equivalent. Remembering the rules of conversion can help you avoid such mistakes.

Now that we have learned about obversion and conversion, we will be covering the last relationship of equivalence—contraposition—in the next lesson. You should find the relationship of contraposition fairly easy to understand because it combines obversion and conversion.

DEFINE

1. Obversion:

_____

_____

_____

2. Conversion:

_____

_____

_____

3. Immediate Inference:

_____

_____

_____

FIND

Find the immediate inferences for the following propositions using the named relationship.

1. **Obverse:** All creativity is genius.

_____

2. **Converse:** No terrorists are non-violent people.

_____

3. **Obverse:** No terrorists are non-violent people.

_____

4. **Converse:** Some vegetarians are egg-eaters.

_____

5. **Obverse:** Some vegetarians are egg-eaters.

_____

6. **Obverse:** All revolutionaries are freedom fighters.

_____

7. **Converse:** No Macintosh computers are inferior computers.

_____

8. **Obverse:** All Andorrans are Europeans.

_____

9. **Obverse:** Some otters are fish-eaters.

_____

10. **Converse:** Some otters are fish-eaters.

_____

129

PRACTICE
Part A: *Explain how to perform the obverse relationship and then write the obverse for each categorical proposition. (This is review, but you'll want to be proficient at obversion before we get to contraposition in the next lesson.)*

1. *All S is P.*

_____

_____

2. *Some S is P.*

_____

_____

3. *Some S is not P.*

_____

_____

4. *No S is P.*

_____

_____

Part B: *Explain why conversion only preserves equivalence for* E *and* I *propositions and not for* A *and* O *propositions.*

_____

_____

DEDUCTION IN ACTION
Logic and Math

Remember how we said that, since math is very logical, you are likely to see some similarities between math and logic? As you were reading about the relationship of equivalence, you might have been thinking about a mathematical law that is very similar to the law of conversion. Look up commutative, associative, distributive, and transitive laws at the following links:

<http://capress.link/dd0601>

<http://capress.link/dd0602>.

1. To which law is the relationship of conversion most similar? Why?

2. Will the mathematical law mentioned in the previous question work on all mathematical operations? How can you relate this to conversion? Explain your answer.

LESSON 6.5
The Relationship of Contraposition

POINTS TO REMEMBER

1. Contraposition applies only to *A* and *O* propositions.
2. Contraposition is achieved by performing a three-step process on standard categorical propositions:
   a. Obvert the original proposition.
   b. Convert the proposition.
   c. Obvert the proposition again.
3. *E* and *I* propositions cannot use contraposition because a logically equivalent proposition is not created.

> IT IS IMPOSSIBLE TO DEFEAT AN
> IGNORANT MAN IN ARGUMENT.
> —WILLIAM G. MCADOO[1]

Here's a question for you: If obversion works for all of the propositions, and if conversion works only for *E* and *I* propositions, for which propositions do you think contraposition will work? You guessed it! The final immediate inference we'll study—contraposition—preserves equivalence for only *A* and *O* propositions. Contraposition is actually a combination of the principles of obversion and conversion and requires three steps:

1. **Obvert the Proposition:** Change the quality of both the subject and the predicate. Remember, this means that you change the quantifiers "all" to "no" and "some" to "some . . . not." Next, you supply the complement of the predicate. Remember, the complement of a predicate is everything that is not in the class that the predicate represents. Therefore, we supply the complement of the predicate by adding a "non" to the predicate. For example, the complement of *P* is *non-P*.

2. **Convert the Proposition:** Switch the subject and the predicate terms. This means that *No S is P* becomes *No P is S*.

3. **Obvert the Proposition Once Again:** Change the quality of the subject and add the complement to the predicate by supplying the word "non."

Contraposition can be a bit tricky, so let's look first at how the process works with symbolic propositions. Let's first look at the process of contraposition with the *A* proposition in its symbolic form.

Original Proposition: *All S is P.*

Step 1 Obversion: *No S is non-P.*

Step 2 Conversion: *No non-P is S.*

Step 3 Obversion: *All non-P is non-S.*

Now let's look at contraposition symbolically with the *O* proposition.

Original Proposition: *Some S is not P.*

Step 1 Obversion: *Some S is non-P.*

Step 2 Conversion: *Some non-P is S.*

Step 3 Obversion: *Some non-P is not non-S.*

Now that you have seen how the process works with symbolic propositions, let's try a couple of propositions in regular, everyday language. We will start with the *A* proposition "All Andorrans are Europeans."

Step 1 Obversion: No Andorrans are non-Europeans.

Step 2 Conversion: No non-Europeans are Andorrans.

Step 3 Obversion: All non-Europeans are non-Andorrans.

Now let's step back for a minute and compare our end proposition to the original. Does it make sense? Our original proposition was "All Andorrans are Europeans." This is a true proposition, since Andorra is a country in Europe. Through contraposition, we inferred that people who are not Europeans are not Andorrans. Does the first proposition imply the last? Yes. Since Andorra is a European country, if someone isn't a European, he can't be an Andorran.

Now let's look at contraposition when we apply it to the *O* proposition "Some Buddhists are not Zen Buddhists."

Step 1 Obversion: Some Buddhists are non–Zen Buddhists.

Step 2 Conversion: Some non–Zen Buddhists are Buddhists.

Step 3 Obversion: Some non–Zen Buddhists are not non-Buddhists.

Once again, let's compare the last proposition to the original proposition. Does the first proposition imply its contraposition? Yes. Our original proposition was "Some Buddhists are not Zen Buddhists." This is a true

proposition, since Zen Buddhism is a school of Mahayana Buddhism. Our final proposition is "Some non–Zen Buddhists are not non-Buddhists." Since our original proposition implied that there are forms of Buddhism other than Zen Buddhism, it is implied that non–Zen Buddhists can be Buddhists (or "not non-Buddhists") as well.

You're right if you're thinking that contraposition can get very confusing. However, if you take each step one at a time and work through each proposition slowly and methodically, you will be able to figure it out. Don't rush! Once you reach the end of the process and have come up with a new proposition using contraposition, ask yourself if the new proposition is implied by the original proposition. If it is, then you'll know that you performed the process of contraposition correctly.

Let's try one more together. Our proposition is "All revolutionaries are freedom fighters." Remember, to perform contraposition, you need to obvert the proposition, then convert it, and then obvert it again. Why don't you do this on a separate piece of paper before you look at the final answer?

Step 1 Obversion: No revolutionaries are non–freedom fighters.

Step 2 Conversion: No non–freedom fighters are revolutionaries.

Step 3 Obversion: All non–freedom fighters are non-revolutionaries.

Did you get it? Does the first proposition imply the last? Think through it. If you claim that all revolutionaries fight for freedom, does that mean that if you're not fighting for freedom you're not a revolutionary? Yes, it does. You can't be a revolutionary without fighting for freedom.

Now that we have examined how contraposition works on *A* and *O* propositions, let's take a look at why it does not apply to *E* and *I* propositions. Let's try a couple and see if the original *E* or *I* proposition implies the contraposition proposition we create. First, let's look at the *E* proposition "No bicycles are four-wheeled vehicles." If we performed contraposition on this proposition, these are the steps we would follow:

Step 1 Obversion: All bicycles are non-four-wheeled vehicles.

Step 2 Conversion: All non-four-wheeled vehicles are bicycles.

Step 3 Obversion: No non-four-wheeled vehicles are non-bicycles.

Now let's compare our contraposed proposition to our first proposition. Our first proposition states "No bicycles are four-wheeled vehicles" (which we know to be true because by definition a bicycle is a two-wheeled vehicle). Our final proposition claims "No non-four-wheeled vehicles are non-bicycles." In other words, it is stating that there aren't any vehicles without four wheels. Not only is that proposition not true, but it's in no way implied in the original proposition. Once again, this is because contraposition does not work on *E* propositions. Now, let's look at why contraposition does not work on *I* propositions either. Consider the *I* proposition "Some coastal villagers are survivors of tsunamis." To make this easier to examine, let's restate this claim in standard categorical form: "Some villagers are tsunami survivors." Now let's look at what the proposition would look like if we performed contraposition on it:

Step 1 Obversion: Some villagers are not non–tsunami survivors.

Step 2 Conversion: Some non–tsunami survivors are not villagers.

Step 3 Obversion: Some non–tsunami survivors are non-villagers.

Let's compare the original proposition with the final one we came up with. Our original proposition was "Some villagers are tsunami survivors." This is a true proposition. Our contrapositive proposition is "Some non–tsunami survivors are non-villagers." This is also a true proposition. However, the first proposition only suggests what is true about villagers who are victims of a tsunami. It makes no implication about non-village survivors of other situations (non–tsunami survivors). Therefore, the contraposition

is not an immediate inference because it is not logically equivalent to the original proposition.

You might be thinking, "If we have obversion and conversion already, why do we need contraposition, especially since it is so complicated?" This is certainly a reasonable question. Think back to what we told you at the beginning of this chapter. The relationships of equivalence can help you to look at propositions in a different manner, and they also help you to simplify convoluted propositions. If this is the case, it can certainly help you to have several different ways of looking at a proposition, such as obversion, conversion, and contraposition. Furthermore, a proposition can sometimes be so convoluted that it needs two operations, rather than just one, to simplify it. This is why it is helpful for you to have several different operations of equivalence to use to examine a proposition, just as a carpenter or a doctor has several different tools or instruments to use in her work, depending on the job she is performing.

Before we conclude this chapter on contraposition, we need to make another important point about the word "non" that is specifically relevant to the relationship of contraposition. When you introduce the word "non" into a sentence as the complement of a word, it is important to notice that it is different from the word "not." The word "not" is part of the quality of a proposition, whereas the word "non" is actually a part of the predicate because it is denoting a class of things, such as *P* and *non-P*. Therefore, when you convert a proposition after you have obverted it, make sure the "non" moves with the whole predicate term.

Take, for example, the proposition "Some villagers are tsunami survivors." When we obvert this proposition, we introduce the term "non" into the predicate term, making it "non–tsunami survivors." It is important to note that the whole predicate is now "non–tsunami survivors." Therefore, when you convert the proposition again, the whole term is moved to where the subject "villagers" was. The converted proposition is "Some non–tsunami survivors are not

THE RELATIONSHIPS OF EQUIVALENCE CAN HELP YOU TO LOOK AT PROPOSITIONS IN A DIFFERENT MANNER, AND THEY ALSO HELP YOU TO SIMPLIFY CONVOLUTED PROPOSITIONS.

villagers." This important aspect of "non" is especially crucial to remember with the relationship of contraposition because when you perform the relationship of contraposition, you must both supply a complement when you obvert the proposition and also switch the subject and the predicate when you convert it. You aren't required to do both of these steps in either obversion or conversion. If you do not take the "non" with the rest of the predicate when you convert the proposition, it will mess up the meaning of your proposition. Therefore, remember that "non" becomes a part of the predicate term and travels anywhere that term travels.

Now that you understand how basic arguments are structured and how inference works with the square of opposition and the relationships of equivalence, it is time for us to return to syllogisms so that you can learn how to structure correct syllogisms and analyze them for validity. On to the next chapter!

REVIEW
DEFINE

1. Contraposition:

_____

2. Logically Equivalent:

_____

PRACTICE

Part A: *Explain how to perform contraposition, and then write the contraposition inference for each categorical proposition.*

1. *All S is P.*

_____

2. *Some S is not P.*

_____

Part B: *Explain why contraposition only preserves equivalence for* A *and* O *propositions and not for* E *and* I *propositions.*

_____

PRACTICE (CONTINUED)

Part C: Explain what you must remember about the word "non."

_____

_____

_____

Perform the immediate inference noted next to each categorical proposition. Be sure to translate each proposition into standard categorical form before attempting to create a logically equivalent proposition.

PERFORM

1. **Converse:** *No S is P.*

_____

2. **Contraposition:** *All S is P.*

_____

_____

3. **Obverse:** *Some S is P.*

_____

4. **Contraposition:** *Some S is not P.*

_____

_____

5. **Converse:** Some video games are graphically violent games.

_____

6. **Contraposition:** All yellow labs are hunting dogs.

_____

_____

7. **Obverse:** Some wristwatches are not radio-controlled watches.

_____

8. **Contraposition:** Some hiking trails are not blaze-marked trails.

_____

_____

9. **Converse:** No water-resistant boots are internally wet boots.

_____

10. **Obverse:** Some Presidential mountain peaks are lower than 6,000 feet.

_____

UNTANGLE

Little Miss Cryptic has, once again, been making convoluted declarations of her opinions. Read her propositions below. Then, use the relationship of equivalence indicated to untangle the boldfaced part of her tangled thoughts. Afterward, put the final proposition into your own words. If you are performing obversion or contraposition, make sure you show your work. That is, show the different steps of the operation. (Sounds like math again, huh?)

1. **Obversion:** Children shouldn't receive allowances. **After all, no non-allowance-receiving child is a deprived child.**

   _____

   _____

   _____

   _____

2. **Conversion: No non-private schools are not non-elite schools.** (Hint: Remember that "non" and "not" cancel each other out.)

   _____

   _____

   _____

   _____

3. **Contraposition:** All non-voters are non-patriotic citizens.

   _____

   _____

   _____

   _____

   _____

DEDUCTION IN ACTION
Forming an Argument

See if you can form a basic argument that offers support for the quote at the beginning of the lesson, or one that is for or against one of Little Miss Cryptic's propositions from the previous exercise. To do this, string together several propositions that people accept *a priori* and that lead to the conclusion. Remember, don't worry at this point if your argument is structured perfectly or if it sounds brilliant. This is just practice.

DIALOGUE 7.1
Introduction to Syllogisms and Validity

Nate catches up to Socrates as he is strolling around campus.

Nate: OK, Socrates, I think I'm finally ready.

Socrates: That's wonderful. For what are you ready, my friend?

Nate: Well, I think we've covered all of the basics of deductive logic. We've talked about mental apprehension, inference, and translating propositions into categorical form. We've also talked about the relationships of opposition and equivalence, which, by the way, have been very helpful with that girl in my ethics class. The last time she threw out one of her cryptic comments, I translated it into an equivalent proposition and then demonstrated the falsity of her proposition. I have to tell you, she was pretty shocked and has been a lot quieter lately.

Socrates: Exposing absurdity often has that effect on people.

Nate: It sure does. Well, now I am ready to learn about analyzing syllogisms. I want to know which syllogisms are valid and which ones are not.

Socrates: Very good. I love an eager student who knows what he does not know and desires to learn it. To get you started, let me ask you a few questions.

Nate: I would expect nothing less.

Socrates: Think back to our earlier discussions about deductive logic. If inductive logic is concerned with the *content* of an argument, what is the primary concern of deductive logic?

Nate: Well, I think deductive logic's primary concern must be its form, if I understand your question correctly.

Socrates: Very good. Let's consider what we mean when we say that we are examining the form of a syllogism. Let me go ahead and give you an example syllogism so that we can examine its form together. Let's see. . . . Oh, why not? Let's proclaim my mortality once again. Here is the syllogism:

> All men are mortal.
> Socrates is a man.
> Therefore, Socrates is mortal.

How many different terms do you see in this syllogism?

Nate: Well, I see three: "men," "mortal," and "Socrates."

Socrates: Excellent! In fact, all valid syllogisms contain three—and only three—terms. So, one characteristic of a syllogism's form is that it has three terms, correct?

Nate: It appears so.

Socrates: I want to see if you can figure out why this is so. Do you notice a term in the syllogism that is repeated twice in the premises but that is not in the conclusion?

Nate: Sure—the term "man."

Socrates: Very good. What seems to be the purpose of the term "man" in the premises? That is, what is it doing in the premises in relationship to the other terms, "Socrates" and "mortal"? It may help you to answer this if you think about why it is not in the conclusion.

Nate: Well, it seems as though in the premises, it is connecting the terms "Socrates" and "mortal," so it is not needed in the conclusion because it has already connected those terms. I guess its job is done.

Socrates: Very astute. It is almost as if you knew all of this information before and are merely recollecting it.

Nate: Well, I don't think I've learned it before. I think it's just your good questioning.

Socrates: As you say. Now, Nate, to help us in further discussions, it will be helpful for you to know the names of each of the terms in the syllogism. The term that is repeated twice in the premises but is not in the conclusion is called the **middle term**. The other terms are the **major term** and the **minor term**. The major term is the predicate of the conclusion, and the minor term is the subject of the conclusion.

Nate: Giving them names makes sense because that way it will be easier to keep track of which term is which.

Socrates: You're right, Nate, it does make it easier to keep track of the terms. So far, we have discussed two key aspects of the form of a syllogism. The first is that a syllogism has three terms: major, minor, and middle. The second is that the middle term connects the major and minor terms. Now, Nate, I want you to notice something else about the form of a syllogism. Do you see that in our Socrates syllogism, the middle term—"man"—is the subject of the first premise?

Nate: Sure, that's obvious. In the first premise, the term "man" is what the whole premise is about.

Socrates: What part of the premise is "man" in the second premise—subject or predicate?

Nate: Well, it's the predicate because it comes after the verb, and it describes the subject.

Socrates: Very good. Now, it's important for you to understand that the middle term could be arranged in a lot of different ways. For instance, the middle term could be the predicate of both premises or it could be the predicate of the first premise and the subject of the second. Can you see another possibility?

Nate: Sure, it could be the subject of both premises.

Socrates: Very good. We could say that another aspect of the form of a syllogism is the way that its middle term is arranged, correct?

Nate: That makes sense. After all, if the middle term of two different syllogisms is arranged in two different ways, the syllogisms are going to have different arrangements and appearances, even if they are alike in all other aspects. This means the form of the syllogisms would be different.

Socrates: Precisely. I also want you to notice something else about the propositions in the syllogism. Are the propositions all negative, all positive, or a combination of negative and positive?

Nate: They are all positive.

Socrates: Very good. What about the quantity of the propositions? Are they universal, particular, or a combination of the two?

Nate: They are all universal.

Socrates: Excellent. Now, Nate, let me ask you another question. Someone could, hypothetically, write a syllogism with all negative propositions, correct? For example, consider this syllogism:

> No men are mortal.
> Socrates is not a man.
> Therefore, Socrates is not mortal.

Someone could do this, correct?

Nate: Well, it sounds weird, but, yes, someone could do it.

Socrates: There are also other possible variations for syllogisms, too. For instance, a syllogism could have

a combination of positive and negative propositions, correct? Or a syllogism could have all universal or all negative propositions or a combination of them. Am I right so far?

Nate: Yes, hypothetically, a syllogism could have a combination of all of these different kinds of propositions.

Socrates: Very good. Wouldn't it be accurate to say, then, that the types of propositions a syllogism has—universal or particular, positive or negative—affects the form of a syllogism?

Nate: Sure. Once again, if you had two different syllogisms and they had identical terms, but their propositions were completely different in quality or quantity, then we would certainly say the forms of the syllogisms were different.

Socrates: Precisely. Let me ask you a final question. We know that when we analyze a syllogism for validity, we analyze it to make sure it is in the right form. We've been discussing many different aspects of a syllogism that affect the form of a syllogism. For instance, we discussed that the terms in a syllogism, the location of the middle term, and whether the propositions are universal or particular, or positive or negative, all affect the form of a syllogism. So, if I were to tell you that there were several basic rules that govern whether the form of a syllogism is valid, what would you expect those rules to be about?

Nate: Well, since the form of a syllogism is determined by its terms, the location of its middle term, and the types of propositions in it, it seems that the syllogism rules would have to be about the middle, major, and minor term, and the propositions.

Socrates: Excellent deduction, Nate!

Nate: So, what you are saying is that if I learn these different rules about the form of a syllogism, I will know which syllogisms are valid and which ones are not?

Socrates: Essentially, yes, although there are some other tools you can use to determine the validity of a syllogism as well.

Nate: This is great, Socrates! Thanks! I'm going to go study these rules. I feel like all of our discussions are really paying off!

Socrates: That's the beauty of the dialectic, my friend! Now, go and seek knowledge.

REVIEW
ANSWER

1. What types of things are we talking about when we discuss the form of a syllogism (list the three mentioned in this dialogue)?

a. _____

b. _____

c. _____

LESSON 7.2
Arranging the Syllogism

POINTS TO REMEMBER

1. An argument is a statement of rational reasons for or against an idea or action with the intent to persuade.
2. A syllogism is a formally arranged argument containing two premises (major and minor), a conclusion, and three—and only three—terms. Further, the syllogism is arranged in the following order: **major premise**, **minor premise**, conclusion.
3. A categorical syllogism is a syllogism in which the premises and the conclusions are written in standard categorical form, such as *S is P*.
4. A conclusion is the point of persuasion; it is that which the speaker is hoping his audience will be persuaded to do or believe; it is the last proposition in an argument.
5. A syllogism is limited to three terms identified by: 1) deciding on a simple subject and a simple predicate term for each sentence; and 2) using the same terms when possible throughout the syllogism.

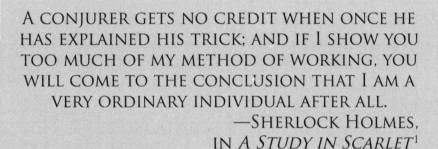

A CONJURER GETS NO CREDIT WHEN ONCE HE HAS EXPLAINED HIS TRICK; AND IF I SHOW YOU TOO MUCH OF MY METHOD OF WORKING, YOU WILL COME TO THE CONCLUSION THAT I AM A VERY ORDINARY INDIVIDUAL AFTER ALL.
—SHERLOCK HOLMES,
IN *A STUDY IN SCARLET*[1]

Now that we have examined the relationships of opposition and equivalence and we understand the process of inference, we can return to a discussion of more complex arguments. In chapter 3, we introduced the idea of an argument. An argument provides rational reasons for or against an idea or action with the intent to persuade. The way that an argument is constructed is the focus of this lesson. In previous lessons, we learned about organizing an argument's propositions into standard categorical form. In addition to being in standard categorical form, the propositions must also be placed in a particular order to form a **standard-form syllogism**. The next few lessons will show you how to discern the proper order for a standard-form syllogism.

Now, let's revisit a few of the terms and concepts we learned in chapter 3. We will also discover some new terms and concepts. As you will recall, a syllogism is a formally arranged argument

containing two premises (major and minor), a conclusion, and three—and only three—terms. The syllogism is arranged in the following order: major premise, minor premise, conclusion. The categorical syllogism is a syllogism in which the premises and the conclusions are written in standard categorical form, such as *S is P*. Since you are already familiar with translating ordinary-language sentences into standard categorical form, the next step is for you to learn how to place them into categorical syllogisms.

The following examples will show how an ordinary-language argument is arranged into a standard-form syllogism. (The lessons that follow will explain how to distinguish the major premise from the minor premise.) To get started, we will identify the conclusion, placing it last, and then translate each sentence from normal language into standard categorical form. Here's our first example:

> Most dangerous drivers speed down the road. Many highway motorists drive well over the speed limit. So, I think many highway motorists are dangerous drivers.

Remember, we must first break this argument into three separate sentences since our goal is to have a major premise, a minor premise, and a conclusion.

Sentence 1: Most dangerous drivers speed down the road.

Sentence 2: Many highway motorists drive well over the speed limit.

Sentence 3: So, I think many highway motorists are dangerous drivers.

Let's attempt to locate the conclusion and make sure that it is last in our lineup of propositions. Which one of the sentences do you think is the conclusion? Often, the concluding proposition will begin with a conclusion indicator such as "therefore," "so," or "thus." Do you see one of those words in our ordinary-language argument? That's right: the final sentence in the argument begins with the word "so," indicating that it is the argument's conclusion. Note that even if we didn't have a clue word (which in this case is "so"), we would still be able to locate the conclusion. A conclusion, by definition, is the point of persuasion—that which the speaker is hoping his audience will be persuaded

to do or believe. If an argument does not have an obvious conclusion indicator, you can determine the conclusion by asking yourself this question: What is it that the speaker is hoping you'll be persuaded to do or believe? In the case of our example argument, the speaker hopes to persuade his audience that many highway motorists are dangerous drivers. That means that the conclusion is "Many highway motorists are dangerous drivers."

Next, we need to write each of the three sentences in standard categorical form. Remember that a syllogism is limited to three terms, or nouns. We do this by: 1) deciding on a subject and a predicate term for each sentence; and 2) using the same terms consistently throughout the syllogism. As you are limiting the terms and using them consistently in the syllogism, you should also try to simplify your subject and predicate into as few words as possible, which helps to make constructing your syllogism much easier. The most common way to simplify subjects and predicates is to reword them and take out unnecessary words so that they are as short and clear as possible. Sometimes, you can shorten the subject and predicate to one word. Other times, you will need to keep an entire phrase in order to communicate the full idea of the subject or predicate. You'll see a few examples of this in the following paragraphs.

Consider the first sentence of our argument: "Most dangerous drivers speed down the road." "Dangerous drivers" is all we need for our subject. Therefore, we can simplify the subject by dropping "most" from the subject. Now, we need to separate the subject from the predicate with a being verb (remember, this is called the *copula*). The phrase "speed down the road" in our first sentence is not a noun phrase, but the idea here is that the dangerous drivers *are* speeders (there's our being verb). Therefore, we can simplify the predicate by substituting the noun "speeders" for the phrase "speed down the road." Finally, we need to determine the quantity of the proposition. Is the speaker stating that *all* dangerous drivers are speeders? No, the claim is "most," not "all." "Most" can be written as "some," so our first proposition can be written in this way: "Some dangerous drivers are speeders." There are two terms in this sentence—"dangerous drivers" (*D*) and "speeders" (*S*). Using those terms, we can translate our new proposition into symbolic form as *Some D is S*. We'll be looking for these terms in the other sentences of our argument as well.

Now, you might have noticed that although we have been using *S* and *P* to write propositions symbolically, in this sentence, we used the letters *D* and *S*. Can you guess why? You probably can. It's because our proposition is "Some dangerous drivers are speeders." Therefore, the *D* stands for the subject of the proposition—"dangerous drivers"—and the *S* stands for the predicate of the proposition—"speeders." While it is certainly fine to substitute *S* and *P* for every subject and predicate, it will probably help you remember the argument better if you use letters that represent the actual subject and predicate of the proposition. You will notice that we will do this often in the rest of the book.

Let's look at the next sentence in the argument: "Many highway motorists drive well over the speed limit." "Many" is a clue that the speaker isn't referring to *all* highway motorists, but to "some" again. "Some" will reflect the quantity of the proposition. "Highway motorists" will serve as our subject. "Drive well over the speed limit" is, again, a way of saying that they are speeders. Since the term "speeders" was used in the previous proposition, and there is the opportunity to use the same term here, we should do that. This simplifies our predicate and allows us to keep consistent terms throughout the syllogism. You must also include the *copula* to complete the categorical proposition. Our new proposition is "Some highway motorists are speeders." There are two terms in this sentence—"highway motorists" (*H*) and "speeders" (*S*). Using those terms, we can translate our new proposition into symbolic form as *Some H is S*.

Now let's look at our conclusion: "Many highway motorists are dangerous drivers." When we see that word "many," we know that we can indentify the quantity of our proposition as "some," since it indicates that only some, not all, highway motorists are dangerous drivers. The remainder of the sentence is already in the form of a categorical proposition. Note that the two terms in this proposition are "highway motorists" (*H*) and "dangerous drivers" (*D*), both of which are terms found in the other two propositions. Therefore, the subject and predicate of this proposition are already simplified. Our concluding proposition is "Some highway motorists are dangerous drivers," which we can translate into symbolic form as *Some H is D*. Note that there is a total of three terms in our argument: "dangerous drivers" (*D*), "speeders" (*S*), and "highway motorists" (*H*).

We can rewrite the argument as a syllogism as follows:

Some dangerous drivers are speeders.

Some highway motorists are speeders.

Some highway motorists are dangerous drivers.

Symbolically, this argument would look like this:

Some D is S.

Some H is S.

Some H is D.

Let's look at another example of this whole process. Let's say that someone makes this argument in everyday language:

CEOs of failing corporations should not get any bailout money through bonuses because people responsible for failing corporations should not be rewarded, and the CEOs are responsible for the failing corporations.

First of all, let's see if we can break up this syllogism into two premises and a conclusion. Can you find any premise or conclusion indicators? You might have noticed the word "because," which is a common premise indicator. The presence of that word lets us know that the sentence containing the word "because" is a premise. If you look at the sections of the sentence before and after the part starting with "because," it becomes clear that the section before is the conclusion, and the section after is another premise.

THE PRESENCE OF THE WORD "BECAUSE" LETS US KNOW THAT THE SENTENCE IS A PREMISE.

That is, this argument presents the conclusion first, and then it gives two premises to support the conclusion. Let's write the propositions in proper argument order:

> People responsible for failing corporations should not be rewarded.
>
> The CEOs are responsible for the failing corporations.
>
> CEOs of failing corporations should not get any bailout money through bonuses.

Now we need to translate these propositions into categorical from. The first proposition—"People responsible for failing corporations should not be rewarded"—is a little bit tricky. It looks like an *A* proposition because of the implication of the word "all," but it is really an *E* proposition because of the "[All] people . . . should not" phrase. The "all" lets us know the quantity is universal, and the "not" lets us know the quality is negative. When we insert the *copula*, the proposition can be worded like this: "No people responsible for failing corporations are people who should be rewarded."

The next proposition is a little tricky, too, since it says "the CEOs." It is unclear whether this is a universal or particular proposition until we realize that "the CEOs" refers to the CEOs of failing companies. When we realize this, the quality and quantity of the proposition becomes clearer, and we can state it this way: "All CEOs of failing corporations are people responsible for failing corporations."

The last sentence is tricky for several reasons, but it will be easier to figure out now that we have worked with the premises already. First, if we just supply a quantifier and a *copula*, we end up with this proposition: "All CEOs of failing corporations are people who should not get bailout money." However, we need to make the terms consistent with the terms in the original syllogism, and the original syllogism used the phrase "should not be rewarded" instead of "should not get any bailout money." Therefore, to make the syllogism consistent, we should reword the conclusion in this way: "All CEOs of failing corporations are people who should not be rewarded." In addition, we have the same problem with this conclusion as we did with the previous propositions. This proposition looks like an *A* proposition because of the word "all," but it is really an

E proposition because of the phrase "All . . . should not." So, now that we have figured that out, we can word it like this: "No CEOs of failing corporations are people who should be rewarded." Through making these changes, we make the terms of the syllogism consistent, and we put the propositions in categorical form.

Now we have our three propositions:

> No people responsible for failing corporations are people who should be rewarded.
>
> All CEOs of failing corporations are people responsible for failing corporations.
>
> No CEOs of failing corporations are people who should be rewarded.

You will notice that the subjects and predicates of each of these propositions were simplified enough that it was unnecessary to simplify them further. To change these propositions into symbolic form, we need to substitute the terms with symbols:

> CEOs of failing corporations = *C*
>
> People responsible for failing corporations = *P*
>
> People who should be rewarded = *R*

Therefore, our argument translated into symbolic form looks like this:

> *No P is R.*
>
> *All C is P.*
>
> *No C is R.*

Isolating the three premises and the three key terms of syllogisms is the most important step in both constructing and analyzing them. Before we look at the steps for analyzing the validity of a syllogism, we will examine major, minor, and middle terms in the next lesson.

DEFINE

1. Argument:

_____

_____

_____

2. Syllogism:

_____

_____

_____

3. Categorical Syllogism:

_____

_____

_____

4. Conclusion:

_____

_____

_____

CREATE

Create a syllogism for the following arguments by first separating each argument into two sentences and a conclusion. Then, translate each sentence into standard categorical form and place the conclusion last.

1. Most real Christmas trees are fire hazards. Placing electrical lights on dry trees is a fire hazard. Most real Christmas trees dry out in just a couple of weeks.

   Find the Conclusion: _____

   Sentence 1: _____

   Sentence 2: _____

   Translate to a Syllogism: *Be sure to determine the quantity of each proposition, limit yourself to three terms, and use a verb of being.*

   _____

   _____

   _____

CREATE (CONTINUED)

2. The best drinks on a cold day are warm ones. Hot cocoa is always piping hot. So, it's the best drink on a cold day.

   Find the Conclusion: _____

   Sentence 1: _____

   Sentence 2: _____

   Translate to a Syllogism: *Be sure to determine the quantity of each proposition, limit yourself to three terms, and use a verb of being.*

   _____

   _____

   _____

3. Some cell phone users are self-centered people. Some cell phone users talk on the phone during a movie. Only self-centered people would talk on their cell phones in the middle of a movie.

   Find the Conclusion: _____

   Sentence 1: _____

   Sentence 2: _____

   Translate to a Syllogism: *Be sure to determine the quantity of each proposition, limit yourself to three terms, and use a verb of being.*

   _____

   _____

   _____

ANSWER

1. Name the three types of propositions found in a syllogism. In what order should they be arranged?

_____
_____
_____

2. How many terms should a syllogism contain? How do you limit the number of terms?

_____
_____
_____
_____
_____

3. What are some clue, or indicator, words to look for when identifying the conclusion of an argument?

_____
_____
_____

FIGURE IT OUT

Did you know that logic even shows up in Garfield *comics every once in a while? Check out the* Garfield *comic at the following link and then answer the question that follows: <http://capress.link/dd0701>.*

Question: Jon, Garfield's owner, is actually using a syllogism in this comic strip, although one of the premises is implied rather than directly stated. See if you can figure out what the syllogism is and write it in the space provided below.

_____
_____
_____
_____
_____
_____
_____
_____

DEDUCTION IN ACTION

Socrates' Dialogue: The Crito

We have already read two Socratic dialogues: the *Apology* and *Euthyphro*. In this lesson, you are going to read the *Crito*. This dialogue takes place right before Socrates is about to die by swallowing poison (remember that he was condemned to death during the *Apology* for corrupting the youth of Athens). Crito is Socrates' friend who comes to Socrates' prison to talk with him before he dies. As you are reading, pay special attention to what Crito tries to persuade Socrates to do and how Socrates uses dialogue to demonstrate that Crito is incorrect and that his arguments are contradictory. Answer the questions that follow when you are done reading the dialogue. A copy of this dialogue can be found at the following link: <http://capress.link/dd0702>.

1. What does Crito try to persuade Socrates to do?

2. How does Crito use the allusion to the opinions of other people to try to convince Socrates to escape?

3. Explain the gymnast argument that Socrates uses to combat Crito's argument.

4. Socrates and Crito then explore whether or not it is right for Socrates to leave (and break Athenian law) because he has been given an unjust sentence. How does Socrates demonstrate that it is not right for him to do this?

LESSON 7.3
Categorical Syllogisms

POINTS TO REMEMBER

1. The major term is always found in the predicate of the conclusion. Because it's always the predicate term of the conclusion, the letter *P* is used to represent the major term of a syllogism.
2. The minor term is always found in the subject of the conclusion. Because it's always the subject term of the conclusion, the letter *S* is used to represent the minor term of a syllogism.
3. The middle is not found in the conclusion but is found in both premises. The letter *M* is used to represent the middle term of a syllogism.
4. The major premise, which contains the major term, should be the first premise listed.
5. The minor premise, which contains the minor term, should be the second premise listed.

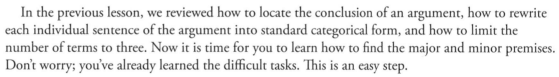

I AM NOBODY . . .
NOBODY IS PERFECT . . .
THEREFORE I AM PERFECT![1]

In the previous lesson, we reviewed how to locate the conclusion of an argument, how to rewrite each individual sentence of the argument into standard categorical form, and how to limit the number of terms to three. Now it is time for you to learn how to find the major and minor premises. Don't worry; you've already learned the difficult tasks. This is an easy step.

It is important that the premises of an argument are ordered in the standard fashion because it helps you to communicate about arguments more easily. Furthermore, having a syllogism properly outlined and ordered will be necessary for determining whether or not the syllogism is valid. (You'll be learning about validity in later chapters.)

With that in mind, let's revisit some of our examples from the review exercises in lesson 7.2.

The best drinks on a cold day are warm ones. Hot cocoa is always piping hot. So, it's the best drink on a cold day.

There are some words in these propositions that we can take out to simplify the subject and the predicate. First, let's pull out the conclusion: "(All) hot cocoa is the best drink on a cold day." So, now that we know the conclusion, we can construct the syllogism. It should look something like this:

All hot cocoa is a piping hot drink.

All piping hot drinks are the best drinks on a cold day.

(All) hot cocoa is the best drink on a cold day.

Determining the conclusion of an argument is central to the process of properly writing a syllogism. Failure to correctly determine the conclusion of an argument will lead to an incorrect rendering of the syllogism. In our example, the conclusion is "All hot cocoa is the best drink on a cold day." Now let's put that into symbolic form by determining the subject and predicate terms. In this proposition, "hot cocoa" is the subject term, so let's call it *S*. The predicate term is "the best drink on a cold day," and we'll call it *P*. It's important to identify the subject term and the predicate term of the conclusion because its predicate term is the major term and its subject term is the minor term. The major and minor terms are the key terms of a syllogism. They are the terms about which you are trying to make a point. The major term is contained in the major premise, and the minor term is contained in the minor premise. Therefore, identifying the major and minor terms of the conclusion helps us to identify the major and minor premises of the syllogism.

Once you have located the conclusion, your next step is to find the major and minor premises. When distinguishing the major premise from the minor premise, you will need to find in the remaining two propositions the major and minor terms. As we mentioned before, the major premise contains the major term, and the minor premise contains the minor term. Since the major premise comes first when ordering the syllogism, you need to look for the predicate of the conclusion in the two remaining propositions and locate the major term.

The predicate term of the conclusion of our example is "the best drinks on a cold day." Therefore, our major term is "the best drinks on a cold day." Now find the major premise by locating the major term in one of the two unidentified propositions in our example. Our major premise is "All piping hot drinks are the best drinks on a cold day." You will notice that the original syllogism places the major premise second, which means we'll need to rearrange the syllogism in order to put it in proper categorical form. This is an important note. Never assume that the major premise is stated first. Always identify the major premise by first determining the major term and working from there.

Next, let's find the minor term. We know that the minor term is the subject term of the conclusion, so if we look at our conclusion, then we can see that our minor term is "hot cocoa." Now locate the minor premise by finding the minor term. Our minor premise is "All hot cocoa is a piping hot drink."

We've found the major and minor terms and premises, but we're not quite done yet. Remember that a syllogism is an argument containing two premises, a conclusion, and three—and only three—terms. But so far we've only identified two terms: major and minor. What's the third term? The third term is known as the middle term. The middle term is the term that is found in both premises, but not in the conclusion. Do you see a term in our example that is used in both premises but not in the conclusion? That's right, the middle term in our example is "piping hot drink." When translating the middle term into symbolic form, we use the letter *M*. The middle term is important because it is the term that the major and minor premises have in common and, if the terms are correctly positioned, it is what ensures that the major and minor terms will be logically connected with one another in the conclusion.

Placing the premises and conclusion in the correct order yields the following:

Syllogism	Categorical Syllogism	Type of Categorical Proposition
All piping hot drinks are the best drinks on a cold day.	*All M is P.*	*A*
All hot cocoa is a piping hot drink.	*All S is M.*	*A*
All hot cocoa is the best drink on a cold day.	*All S is P.*	*A*

What has this exercise taught us? We know that, based on the conclusion, there is a relationship between the major term and the minor term. The validity of the relationship between the major and minor terms is determined by the relationship they each have with the middle term.

The terms of syllogisms are not always arranged in an order that yields a valid argument, but for now, let's not concern ourselves with validity. You'll learn in later lessons how to distinguish valid arrangements from invalid ones. Before we learn about validity, let's practice identifying all the pieces of the syllogism by taking a look at another example.

Since the philosopher Socrates was a man, and all men are mortal, Socrates is mortal.

Remember, your first job is to find your conclusion. In this example, the conclusion is "Socrates is mortal." Next, we want to identify the predicate term of the conclusion. In our example, it is "mortal." We know that the predicate term of the conclusion is called the major term. Now we want to find the subject term of the conclusion. It is "Socrates." The subject term of the conclusion is the minor term. Now that we have found these terms, we need to locate the major and minor premises. Remember, the major premise contains the major term, so our major premise is "All men are mortal." The minor premise contains the minor term, so our minor premise is "Socrates is a man." Now, we have just one more term to find. Do you remember what it is? That's right, it's the middle term, which is the term that our major and minor premises have in common with each other but not with the conclusion. Do you see that term? It is "man."

Now we want to write out our syllogism and then translate the sentences from normal English into standard categorical form. We will label each term accordingly: the major term as *P*, the minor term as *S*, and the middle term as *M*.

All men (*M*) are mortal (*P*)..............................*All M is P.*

Socrates (*S*) is a man (*M*)................................*All S is M.*

Therefore, Socrates (*S*) is mortal (*P*)................*All S is P.*

Once you get the hang of it, identifying the premises and conclusion, as well as the major, minor, and middle terms of a syllogism, isn't so tricky after all, is it? Now that you have these basics down pat, we're going to look at some tricky syllogisms that like to disguise themselves. One way they can disguise themselves is in the form of an **enthymeme**. We will look at enthymemes in the next lesson so that you can learn how to identify them properly.

REVIEW
DEFINE

1. Major Term:

_____

_____

2. Minor Term:

_____

_____

3. Middle Term:

_____

_____

4. Major Premise:

_____

_____

5. Minor Premise:

_____

_____

LABEL

First, identify each proposition as either an A, E, I, *or* O *proposition. Then, label the terms in each of the following syllogisms using the appropriate symbol (subject term =* S, *predicate term =* P, *middle term =* M*).*

1. *Some A is C.*   **Proposition Type:** _____
   Some B is A.   **Proposition Type:** _____
   Therefore, some B is C.   **Proposition Type:** _____
   Major Term (*P*): _____
   Minor Term (*S*): _____
   Middle Term (*M*): _____

2. *All boys are men.*   **Proposition Type:** _____
   All men are males.   **Proposition Type:** _____
   Therefore, all boys are males.   **Proposition Type:** _____
   Major Term (*P*): _____
   Minor Term (*S*): _____
   Middle Term (*M*): _____

3. *No women are kings.*   **Proposition Type:** _____
   Some men are kings.   **Proposition Type:** _____
   Therefore, some men are women.   **Proposition Type:** _____
   Major Term (*P*): _____
   Minor Term (*S*): _____
   Middle Term (*M*): _____

4. *All hurricanes are violent storms.*   **Proposition Type:** _____
   All tornadoes are violent storms.   **Proposition Type:** _____
   Therefore, all hurricanes are tornadoes.   **Proposition Type:** _____
   Major Term (*P*): _____
   Minor Term (*S*): _____
   Middle Term (*M*): _____

5. *Some pets are indoor pets.*   **Proposition Type:** _____
   Some dogs are pets.   **Proposition Type:** _____
   Therefore, some dogs are indoor pets.   **Proposition Type:** _____
   Major Term (*P*): _____
   Minor Term (*S*): _____
   Middle term (*M*): _____

151

PRACTICE *Translate the following arguments into syllogisms. Remember, to do this, you need to find the conclusion first and identify the major and minor terms. This will help you establish the major and minor premises. Once you have done this, translate the syllogisms into categorical syllogisms and label each line as an A, E, I, or O proposition.*

1. Sandra enjoys water-skiing. All water-skiers are good swimmers, so Sandra must be a good swimmer.

    a. **Original Proposition:** _____

      Categorical Proposition: _____

      Categorical Form: _____

      Proposition Type: _____

    b. **Original Proposition:** _____

      Categorical Proposition: _____

      Categorical Form: _____

      Proposition Type: _____

    c. **Original Proposition:** _____

      Categorical Proposition: _____

      Categorical Form: _____

      Proposition Type: _____

2. All eligible presidents of the United States must be at least thirty-five years old. Some US citizens are over thirty-five years old. Therefore some US citizens are eligible to be president of the United States.

    a. **Original Proposition:** _____

      Categorical Proposition: _____

      Categorical Form: _____

      Proposition Type: _____

    b. **Original Proposition:** _____

      Categorical Proposition: _____

      Categorical Form: _____

      Proposition Type: _____

    c. **Original Proposition:** _____

      Categorical Proposition: _____

      Categorical Form: _____

      Proposition Type: _____

Famous Syllogisms: *The following are arguments from famous past philosophers and theologians. See if you can detect the syllogism contained in each of these arguments. Write the arguments in standard syllogistic form.*

1. Augustine says, "To reach God with the mind is great happiness, to comprehend Him is impossible. Therefore happiness is without comprehension."[2]

_____

_____

_____

2. Thomas Aquinas, in his article "Whether one can be happy in this life" says, "For it is written: Blessed are the undefiled in the way, who walk in the law of the Lord. But this happens in this life. Therefore one can be happy in this life."[3]

_____

_____

_____

Logic and Fashion Wear: The logic quote about "nobody" at the beginning of the chapter is actually on a T-shirt that you can purchase. It is clever because it misuses a syllogism to make a startling and amusing point. Can you figure out how it cleverly manipulates the syllogism?

_____

_____

_____

_____

_____

This is the same problem with a syllogism we explored a couple of chapters back:

Time is money.
Money talks.
Therefore, time will tell.

As you can see here, the word "money" in the first premise is equivalent to the idea "the opportunity to earn income." In the second premise, the word "money" is equivalent to the idea of "the power of significant wealth." These two ideas are very different. Therefore, this syllogism actually has an extra term in addition to the middle, major, and minor terms. This disrupts the process of the syllogism. In a later chapter, you will discover that this is the **fallacy of four terms.**

DEDUCTION IN ACTION
Create Your Own Sherlock Holmes

As you have read Sherlock Holmes stories as part of the exercises in this book, you have probably noticed that Holmes uses a combination of deductive and inductive logic. Now it's your turn to create a fictional sleuth character and write a short mystery story. Your goal is to write a short story (about five pages or so) in which a mystery occurs and a person uses a combination of deduction and induction to solve the mystery. If you are having problems thinking about how to craft such a story, consider the ideas of possible sleuths and mystery ideas below. Choose one that appeals to you and just start writing. You may be surprised at how creative you are.

Possible Sleuths

1. A fifteen-year-old girl or boy in the tradition of Nancy Drew or the Hardy Boys

2. A cat or a dog (there are actually quite a few mystery books out today in which the sleuth is a cat)

3. A sweet, wise older lady or gallant, canny older gentleman in the tradition of Agatha Christie's Miss Marple or Hercule Poirot

4. A freelance detective in his or her twenties or thirties

5. A mom who solves problems in her neighborhood

6. A wise teacher who solves problems in her school

7. A policeman or policewoman

8. A male or female doctor

9. An average, ordinary person who just happens to be in the right place at the right time (or the wrong place at the wrong time, depending on how you look at it)

Possible Mysteries

1. A special school trophy goes missing.

2. A house is broken into and the only thing stolen is a book, which seems to be of no special significance.

3. A restaurant suffers a case of mass food poisoning, after which it becomes apparent that the food poisoning was specifically caused by someone for some unknown, evil purpose.

4. A family traveling on an Alaskan cruise finds a monkey wearing a ruby necklace in their room.

5. A school crossing guard is mysteriously run down by a car. Though she lives, suffering just a broken leg, she soon begins to receive threatening messages.

6. A friendly neighborhood cat investigates the death of several beloved neighborhood dogs.

7. A local sleuth figures out that a house in his or her neighborhood is actually the center of a local operation for shoplifting.

LESSON 7.4
Enthymemes

POINTS TO REMEMBER

1. Enthymemes are abbreviated forms of syllogisms.
2. Enthymemes either omit the conclusion of a syllogism or one of the premises.

> 'I STILL CAN'T BELIEVE YOU'RE GOING OUT ON A
>   BLIND DATE.'
> 'I'M NOT WORRIED. IT SOUNDS LIKE HE'S REALLY
>   GOOD LOOKING.'
> 'YOU'RE GOING BY SOUND? WHAT ARE WE, WHALES?'
>   —JERRY AND ELAINE,
>   IN "THE WINK," FROM *SEINFELD*[1]

We mentioned in the last chapter that syllogisms are sometimes in disguise. One common syllogism disguise is the enthymeme. In fact, you have probably already encountered enthymemes in everyday speech. Before we thoroughly explain this type of syllogism, consider this example:

I should study tonight because I want to get a good grade on my test.

Take a minute to think about the argument. What is it implying? That is, what is the person who is making the argument assuming about studying and getting a good grade on a test? This person is assuming that getting a good grade on a test is a result of studying. Now consider another question: How would you write this argument in syllogistic form? Remember, you need two premises and a conclusion. Here's one possible way you could write it:

All students who want to get good grades on their tests are students who should study.

I want to get a good grade on my test.

Therefore, I am a student who should study.

Now take a minute to compare the two versions of the argument. What differences do you notice between the two? You probably noticed that the syllogism written in syllogistic form includes one more proposition than is contained in the first version of the argument. That's because the proposition "All students who want to get good grades on their tests are students who should study" is implied in the first argument, but it is not explicitly stated. This argument is an enthymeme. In everyday life, you will run into enthymemes, which are a type of abbreviated argument. Enthymemes are basically syllogisms that have either an **implied premise** or an **implied conclusion**. Do you remember our discussion of the

ENTHYMEMES EITHER OMIT THE CONCLUSION OF A SYLLOGISM OR ONE OF THE PREMISES.

word "implied"? When a truth is implied by a proposition or argument, it means that it is contained in, or enfolded in, the proposition or argument. This means that enthymemes are arguments in which a hidden premise or conclusion is enfolded or contained. To help you better understand enthymemes, let's compare this argument in both forms: the full syllogism and the enthymeme. Here is the full syllogism:

> All students who want to get good grades on their tests are students who should study.
>
> I want to get a good grade on my test.
>
> Therefore, I am a student who should study.

Now look at the enthymeme form of this argument:

> I want to get a good grade on my test.
>
> I should study.

Notice that the enthymeme leaves out the entire first premise of the argument. Therefore, the enthymeme is an abbreviated form of a full syllogism.

Remember that with inductive logic, many arguments are based on generalizations. That is, we examine many different examples of a phenomenon and make a theory based on an observed pattern. In general, with inductive logic, the more examples a person includes, the stronger her conclusion is. However, there are times when a person doesn't necessarily have the time to go into an exhaustive list of examples, and, furthermore, it may not be necessary. Therefore, the arguer may just pick one excellent example to illustrate his point.

For example, if we are writing an essay about how caring for one's neighbor is a noble act, it is unnecessary for us to collect fifty or sixty examples to illustrate our point. Although that might be necessary for some arguments, one powerful illustration, such as the story of the good Samaritan, will suffice to illustrate our thesis in this

particular argument. In this case, our one example is a type of brief, but powerful, verbal shorthand that supports our argument. That one example is an abbreviated form of an argument from generalization or induction in the same way that an enthymeme is an abbreviated form of an argument from deduction.

When people are engaged in informal discussions or arguments, as many arguments are, they often use enthymemes rather than stating their point in a complete syllogism. For instance, if a person is arguing that it is necessary to repair broken windows in neighborhoods in order to prevent more vandalism, the person could argue this through a full syllogism such as this:

> All unrepaired acts of vandalism are things that can provoke more vandalism.
>
> This broken window is an act of unrepaired vandalism.
>
> Therefore, this broken window is a thing that could provoke more vandalism.

However, this syllogism would be a bit awkward to fit into an informal conversation. Therefore, it is likely that a person would abbreviate this argument and say it in a more informal manner, such as "We'd better fix this window or people will start breaking other windows." The same syllogism is implied, but the language is more informal.

Enthymemes function by the omission of either one of the premises or the conclusion of a syllogism. There are actually three types of enthymemes: **first-order enthymemes**, **second-order enthymemes**, and **third-order enthymemes**. A first-order enthymeme is a syllogism that omits the major premise. A second-order enthymeme is a syllogism that omits the minor premise. A third-order enthymeme omits the conclusion. Although it is not necessary in informal everyday language to know which type of enthymeme is being used in an argument,

sometimes it can be helpful for your own thinking and analysis to know what certain speech patterns are called.

You will remember that deductive arguments are rarely packaged in nice, neat syllogisms for you. This is because when we argue, we speak off the top of our heads and interject a lot of non-syllogistic descriptive phrases into our arguments. (We have examined some of the most common ways that we do this in past chapters.) We also tend to abbreviate our thoughts when we are speaking and/or arguing. The enthymeme is the most common way in which we do this. Recognizing enthymemes will help you spot deductive arguments more easily when they are disguised in the form of shorter propositions.

Now that you understand the basic format of a syllogism, even when it is disguised as an enthymeme, you need to learn some important terminology that will help you when you start to evaluate syllogisms for validity. These terms are **mood** and **figure**, and they will be the topic of our next lesson.

REVIEW
DEFINE

1. Enthymeme:

_____

_____

2. First-Order Enthymeme:

_____

3. Second-Order Enthymeme:

_____

4. Third-Order Enthymeme:

_____

5. Implied Premise:

_____

_____

6. Implied Conclusion:

_____

_____

TRANSLATE

Each of the following arguments is an enthymeme. Translate each into a syllogism by supplying the implied premise. In most cases, you will need to switch around the wording in order to put the argument into syllogistic form.

1. You shouldn't eat that. You will get sick.

_____

_____

_____

2. I want to be kind so that I will have lots of friends.

_____

_____

_____

3. We should care for our land, for our land is the source of our nourishment.

_____

_____

_____

4. You should stop being weird. You're scaring me.

_____

_____

_____

5. Human beings must be empowered to reach their full potential, for this allows them to contribute fully to society.

_____

_____

_____

TRICKY TRANSLATION

Each of the following arguments is an argument from a famous philosopher, politician, theologian, or cultural icon. Translate each into a syllogism by supplying the implied premise. In most cases, you will need to switch around the wording in order to put the argument into syllogistic form. A premise has been provided to get you started. See if you can complete the rest of the syllogism.

1. Augustine: "Now the end of life puts the longest life on a par with the shortest. For of two things which have alike ceased to be, the one is not better, the other worse."[2]
   Premise: Two things which both end are equal.

   _____

   _____

2. Augustine: "Concerning the love of praise, which, though it is a vice, is reckoned a virtue, because by it greater vice is restrained."[3]
   Premise: All things which prevent vice are virtues.

   _____

   _____

3. Sherlock Holmes: "About that chasm. I had no serious difficulty in getting out of it, for the very simple reason that I never was in it."[4]
   Premise: All chasms that I am out of are chasms easy to escape.

   _____

   _____

4. Homer Simpson: "English—who needs that? I'm never going to England!"[5]
   Premise: People who will go to England are people who need English.

   _____

   _____

DEDUCTION IN ACTION
Enthymemes and Julius Caesar

In a past lesson, we discussed that Shakespeare often used logic in his plays. You analyzed several passages in which he did this, often with humorous effect. It should come as no surprise to you that Shakespeare used enthymemes in his plays. One of the most famous enthymemes is from his play *Julius Caesar*, which describes the assassination of Julius Caesar and the events that ensued after the assassination. After Caesar was stabbed by senators (one of whom was his best friend, Brutus), Brutus gives a speech to the angry people of Rome in which he assures them that though Caesar was a great man and his personal friend, Caesar's assassination was necessary for the good of Rome. Brutus claims that Caesar had been too zealous for power.

To demonstrate good will, Brutus allows one of Caesar's other close friends, Mark Antony, to deliver Caesar's funeral oration. Mark Antony starts by praising the assassins as honorable men, which affirms that they must be correct in their assessment that Caesar was too zealous or ambitious for fame and glory. But then, as his speech goes on, he presents several examples that show the very opposite (that Caesar was not ambitious), one of which is the fact that Caesar refused to be crowned king of Rome. The following quote is a line from this speech. See if you can turn it into a full syllogism and then identify what kind of enthymeme it is (feel free to put it into more natural language when you turn it into a syllogism).

> "Mark'd ye his words? He would not take the crown. Therefore 'tis certain he was not ambitious."[6]

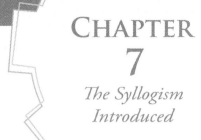

LESSON 7.5
Moods and Figures

POINTS TO REMEMBER

1. The **schema** of a syllogism is its pattern of organization identified by its mood and figure.
2. The mood of a syllogism refers to the combination and order of categorical propositions.
3. Figure is determined by the location of the middle term, designated *M* in the categorical syllogism. There are four possible combinations of middle term positions.

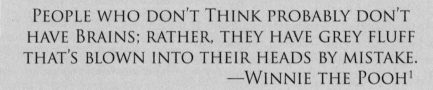

> PEOPLE WHO DON'T THINK PROBABLY DON'T
> HAVE BRAINS; RATHER, THEY HAVE GREY FLUFF
> THAT'S BLOWN INTO THEIR HEADS BY MISTAKE.
> —WINNIE THE POOH[1]

The following are the skills that you have learned so far in this unit:

1. Translate a sentence from normal English into standard categorical form.

2. Determine which proposition in an argument is the conclusion.

3. Identify the major and minor terms.

4. Identify the major and minor premises.

5. Identify the middle term.

6. Arrange the argument as a syllogism: major premise, minor premise, conclusion.

7. Translate the syllogism into a categorical syllogism of the form *S is P*.

8. Label each categorical proposition as an *A*, *E*, *I*, or *O* proposition.

As you start to write and examine more syllogisms, one of the things you will notice is that they often follow familiar patterns. For instance, can you note any similarities between the following two syllogisms?

Syllogism	Categorical Syllogism	Type of Categorical Proposition	Syllogism	Categorical Syllogism	Type of Categorical Proposition
All men are males.	*All M is P.*	*A*	All rectangles are four-sided figures.	*All M is P.*	*A*
All boys are men.	*All S is M.*	*A*	All squares are rectangles.	*All S is M.*	*A*
Therefore, all boys are males.	*All S is P.*	*A*	Therefore, all squares are four-sided figures.	*All S is P.*	*A*

At first glance, these syllogisms look very different from each other. However, if you look at the second two columns of the tables, you will detect some similarities. For instance, notice that both of the syllogisms have three *A* propositions in them. Furthermore, note that the *M*s, *P*s, and *S*s are each in the same places in both syllogisms. In fact, you will notice that, structurally, these two syllogisms are exactly alike. The major terms occur in the same places, as do the minor terms and middle terms. Both syllogisms contain three universal affirmative propositions. These two syllogisms have the same schema. In other words, these two syllogisms are organized in exactly the same way.

When we want to determine the schema of a syllogism, there are two components that must be examined. These components are mood and figure, and once an argument has been converted into a categorical syllogism, one can find these two components. The mood of a syllogism refers to the combination and order of categorical propositions. The two aforementioned syllogisms have the same mood—*AAA*—denoting that all three of their premises are *A* propositions. Can you determine the mood of the following syllogisms?

> No people under the age of thirty-five can be president. Some voters are thirty-five years old. Therefore, some voters can be president.

Syllogism 1	Categorical Syllogism	Type of Categorical Proposition
No under-thirty-five-year-olds can be president.	*No M is P.*	E
Some voters are under-thirty-five-year-olds.	*Some S is M.*	I
Some voters can be president.	*Some S is P.*	I

The mood of this syllogism is *EII*. Let's look at another example:

> Some phones are portable phones. No rotary phones are portable phones. Therefore, some phones are not rotary phones.

Syllogism 2	Categorical Syllogism	Type of Categorical Proposition
No rotary phones are portable phones.	*No P is M.*	E
Some phones are portable phones.	*Some S is M.*	I
Some phones are not rotary phones.	*Some S is not P.*	O

The mood of this syllogism is *EIO*.

Note that it is not necessary for you to translate a syllogism into symbolic form in order to determine its mood. That is, you can find it just by examining the original premises to determine what kind of propositions they are. However, translating a syllogism into symbolic form can make it easier for you to determine mood, especially when you are just learning about mood. Let's look at an example of a syllogism in everyday language and then determine its mood. Consider the following syllogism:

> Everyone should grow a backyard garden because anything that can cut costs in hard economic times is something people should do, and growing a garden in your backyard certainly does this.

Let's find the conclusion first. If you look at the first proposition, you will notice that it makes a claim: "Everyone should grow a backyard garden." After this first proposition, you have the word "because," which is a premise indicator that signals that the next two propositions will support the first proposition. Therefore, let's write out the basic propositions in syllogistic form, making the first proposition the conclusion.

> Anything that can cut costs in hard economic times is something people should do.
>
> Growing a garden in your backyard certainly does this.
>
> Everyone should grow a backyard garden.

If we simplify the terms, make them consistent, and supply the correct quantifiers, we would have a syllogism like this:

> All cost-cutting practices are practices all people should adopt.

Growing backyard gardens is a cost-cutting practice.

Growing a backyard garden is a practice all people should adopt.

We can simplify this symbolically if we substitute the following letters for each of the terms: *C* = "cost-cutting practices," *P* = "practices all people should adopt," and *G* = "growing a backyard garden." Here is the symbolic form of this syllogism:

All C is P.

All G is C.

All G is P.

Once we have translated this everyday argument into categorical form and then symbolic form, it is easy to see its mood: It is an *AAA* syllogism. You will notice that the process for determining the mood of an everyday argument is the same for determining the mood of an argument written in categorical form. Now that we have examined mood, let's examine figure.

The second indicator used to determine the schema of a syllogism is its figure. Figure is determined by the location of the middle term, which, as you know, is designated *M* in the categorical syllogism. Look at the two previous examples. Notice that not only do they have different moods, but the position of their middle term is also different.

There are four possible middle term positions:

	Figure 1		Figure 2		Figure 3		Figure 4	
Major Premise	*M*	*P*	*P*	*M*	*M*	*P*	*P*	*M*
Minor Premise	*S*	*M*	*S*	*M*	*M*	*S*	*M*	*S*

This table may seem a bit confusing at first, so to help you understand it better, let's take a look at what's in it. Each figure has two rows that represent the two premises in a syllogism. The top row of the table, which represents a premise, contains the letters *S*, *P*, or *M* in some order. The bottom row, which also represents a premise, contains those same letters in some order. As you have already learned, the *M* stands for the middle term of a syllogism, the *P* stands for the predicate of a proposition, and

the *S* stands for the subject of a proposition. Once you understand this, you can begin to understand what each figure in the chart represents.

In the first figure, the middle term is the subject of the first premise and the predicate of the second premise. This is why the *M* is first in the proposition in the first column and second in the proposition in the second column. (Remember, in a proposition, the subject is always first in a proposition, and the predicate is always second.) In the second figure, the middle term is the predicate of both the first and second premises. In the third premise, the middle term is the subject of both the propositions. In the fourth figure, the middle term is the predicate of the first premise and the subject of the second premise. You can see that the middle term switches place in each of the figures so that each of the figures has a different pattern that distinguishes it from another.

Now that we have examined figure and understand how the four figures work, let's look back at our syllogisms about presidents and phones. What is the figure of the first syllogism about presidents? In the major premise, the middle term is the subject term. In the minor premise, the middle term is the predicate term. Therefore, the first syllogism is figure 1. The schema of the first syllogism is a combination of its mood and its figure, and it is written this way: *EII-1*. The schema will always be written as the three letters of the syllogism's mood followed by the number representing its figure.

What is the figure of the second syllogism about phones? In this case, the middle term is the predicate term in both the major and minor premises. Therefore, the second syllogism is figure 2. The schema of the second syllogism is *EIO-2*.

And what about our syllogism about backyard gardens? If you look at it again, you will notice that the middle term—"cost-cutting practices"—is the subject of the first premise and the predicate of the second premise. Therefore, this syllogism is figure 1.

Being able to detect the mood and figure of a syllogism can be extremely helpful for several reasons. One reason is that it is good to be able to assign a name to different types of syllogisms. Another reason mood and figure can be helpful is because they can help you to figure out whether

or not a syllogism is structured correctly. To illustrate this better, we want to introduce you to a clever memory device that people in the Middle Ages devised to use mood and figure in order to identify correctly structured syllogisms. Before we introduce this device, we want to introduce two terms that we will discuss more thoroughly in the next chapter: valid and invalid. We use the term "valid" to describe a syllogism that is structured correctly. That is, a valid syllogism is one that is logical, or one that works. On the other hand, an invalid syllogism is a syllogism that is not structured correctly. That is, it is illogical, and it does not work properly.

Logicians in the Middle Ages wanted a way to remember all of the valid combinations of mood and figure, so they developed a memory device (a **mnemonic**) to help them do this. It looks really alien and incomprehensible at first, but soon you will understand how it works. Here it is:

Barbara, Celarent, Darii, Ferio *que prioris*

Bramantip, Camenes, Dimaris, Fesapo, Fresison[2]

Now, don't be scared. It's not as mysterious as it seems. This is how it works:

The first line of the memory device represents the first figure. Remember, that is the figure in which the middle term is the subject of the first premise and the predicate of the second. In fact, each of the different lines in the memory device represents a different figure (the first line is the first figure, the second line is the second figure, etc.). We have figure, but what about mood? After all, with syllogisms, figure is only one half of the equation. Here's where those medieval logicians got really clever. All of the vowels of the names in the first line are the moods valid in the first figure. That is, the three *A*'s in "Barbara" stand for the mood *AAA*. The *EAE* in "Celarent" stand for the mood *EAE*. The *AII* in "Darii" stand for the mood *AII,* and so on. The words *que* and *prioris* are Latin for "and" and "first," as in "first figure." Therefore, here are all the valid moods in first figure: *AAA, EAE, AII, EIO.* You will note that these vowels match exactly the vowels in the names in the first line.

The valid moods in the second figure are represented by the second line of the mnemonic. The word *secundae* at the end of the second line is Latin for "second," as in "second figure." Remember that the second figure is the figure in which the middle term is the predicate of both the first and second premises. Now let's look at mood. The vowels in "Cesare" stand for the mood *EAE*. The vowels in "Camestres" stand for the mood *AEE*. The vowels in "Festino" stand for the mood *EIO*. You get the idea. Here are all of the valid moods in second figure: *EAE, AEE, EIO, AOO.* You will note that these vowels match exactly the vowels in the names in the second line.

By now, you are probably getting the hang of this, so it is not going to surprise you when we tell you that the valid moods in the third figure are represented by the third line and a little into the fourth line of the mnemonic, up to the word *habet*. By the way, the word *tertia* at the beginning of the third line means "third" in Latin, as in "third figure." Don't confuse it with a name. The third line starts with the name "Darapti." Here are the valid moods in the third figure: *AAI, IAI, AII, EAO, OAO, EIO.*

The valid moods in the fourth figure are found in the last line of the mnemonic. The phrase *Quarta in super addit* means "the fourth," as in "fourth figure," "in addition adds." These are the valid moods in the fourth figure: *AAI, AEE, IAI, EAO, EIO.*

You have to admit that it's ingenious, if not also a bit crazy. Now, to be honest, very few logic students memorize this entire mnemonic device today. However, it may be helpful to some of you. Its usefulness lies in the fact that once you have it memorized, you can immediately spot an invalid syllogism because you can compare its mood and figure to the list of valid moods and figures you have memorized. Furthermore, if you want to write a syllogism, you can immediately choose from the available syllogism schemas listed in the device, and you will always know when you have chosen a valid syllogism.

However, some people find this memory device extremely difficult to memorize, so let us clue you in on something that may make it more reasonable for you. The first line of the memory device contains some of the most common syllogisms you will encounter, especially the first two schemas—*AAA* and *EAE*. For instance, you might

have recognized that the first mood and figure—*AAA-1*—is the mood and figure for the famous "Socrates is mortal" syllogism. The point is that if you memorize just this first line, you will know the mood and figure for the syllogisms you will encounter most frequently. Therefore, if you are analyzing a syllogism that has one of these schemas, which is likely, you will automatically know that it is valid. Furthermore, if you are making an argument and want to construct a valid syllogism, you will automatically have five valid schemas from which to choose. What if even memorizing the first line is difficult because the names are so odd? Even memorizing the first two syllogism schemas—Barbara and Celarent—can be of great help. In fact, medieval logicians developed a way to use the relationships of equivalence to convert any syllogism to these first two syllogisms. We won't include that process here, but it does demonstrate how helpful it is to know those first two schemas.

Some people find that, while memorizing this entire device can be daunting, memorizing part of it is helpful, especially for constructing syllogisms. To be honest, there are much easier ways to analyze a syllogism's validity, and you will be introduced to these in the next few lessons. After you have learned all of these techniques, you will notice that some help you construct syllogisms easily, while others help you analyze syllogisms easily. Keeping several techniques in mind will make the world of syllogisms easier and more accessible for you.

REVIEW
DEFINE

1. Mood:

_____

_____

_____

2. Figure:

_____

_____

_____

_____

_____

3. Schema:

_____

_____

_____

DEFINE (CONTINUED)

4. Major Term:

_____

_____

_____

5. Minor Term:

_____

_____

_____

6. Middle Term:

_____

_____

_____

7. Major Premise:

_____

_____

_____

8. Minor Premise:

_____

_____

_____

9. Valid:

_____

_____

_____

10. Invalid:

_____

_____

_____

COMPLETE

Complete the figure table.

	Figure 1		Figure 2		Figure 3		Figure 4	
Major Premise	*M*	_____	*P*	_____	*M*	_____	_____	*M*
Minor Premise	_____	*M*	*S*	_____	_____	*S*	_____	*S*

Create four schemas with the same mood but that have four different figures. Then, create four schemas with the same figure but different moods. Translate all eight syllogisms into categorical syllogisms.

PRACTICE

1. **Same Mood, Different Figures:**

a. _____

_____

_____

_____

b. _____

_____

_____

_____

c. _____

_____

_____

_____

d. _____

_____

_____

_____

PRACTICE (CONTINUED)

2. **Same Figure, Different Moods:**

a. _____

_____

_____

_____

b. _____

_____

_____

_____

c. _____

_____

_____

_____

d. _____

_____

_____

_____

DEDUCTION IN ACTION
Logic and Medieval Memory Devices

One of the best ways for you to get comfortable with syllogisms is to practice writing a lot of them—both valid and invalid. As you do this, you will start to develop an intuitive feeling for whether a syllogism is structured correctly or incorrectly. Pick four of the syllogisms from the medieval mnemonic you learned about earlier in this lesson—the ones in the first line of the mnemonic will work well—and write these syllogisms on a separate piece of paper. Then, come up with four syllogisms that aren't valid and write these on the same piece of paper. You will see that it is easy to determine invalid syllogisms from the memory device. All you have to do is choose a mood that is not a valid mood in a figure. For example, the valid moods in figure 1 are *AAA*, *EAE*, *AII*, and *EIO*. You could write all of your valid syllogisms based on these first-figure moods. To write invalid syllogisms, you could pick any four moods in first figure that are not *AAA*, *EAE*, *AII*, or *EIO*. For example, here are four moods in first figure that would be invalid: *EEA*, *AEE*, *III*, and *OIO*.

LESSON 8.1
Validity and the Counterexample Method

POINTS TO REMEMBER

1. **Valid syllogisms** are syllogisms that are structured properly.
2. **True syllogisms** are syllogisms that are factually accurate and correct.
3. **Sound syllogisms** are syllogisms that are both true and valid.
4. It is possible to have a syllogism that is valid but not true.
5. It is possible to have a syllogism that is true but not valid.
6. To construct a sound syllogism, make sure that your premises are true and that the syllogism is structured validly.
7. The **counterexample method** is one method used to examine the validity of a syllogism.

> 'WHO WAS BARBARA?' ASKED HARRIET QUICKLY.
>
> 'OH, A GIRL. I OWE HER QUITE A LOT, REALLY,' REPLIED WINSEY, MUSINGLY. 'WHEN SHE MARRIED THE OTHER FELLOW, I TOOK UP SLEUTHING AS A CURE FOR WOUNDED FEELINGS, AND IT'S REALLY BEEN GREAT FUN, TAKE IT ALL IN ALL. DEAR ME, YES—I WAS VERY MUCH BOWLED OVER THAT TIME. I EVEN TOOK A SPECIAL COURSE IN LOGIC FOR HER SAKE.'
>
> 'GOOD GRACIOUS!'
>
> 'FOR THE PLEASURE OF REPEATING "BARBARA CELARENT DARII FERIO . . ." THERE WAS A KIND OF MYSTERIOUS ROMANTIC LILT ABOUT THE THING WHICH WAS SOMEHOW EXPRESSIVE OF PASSION. MANY A MOONLIGHT HAVE I MURMURED IT TO THE NIGHTINGALES WHICH HAUNT THE GARDENS OF ST. JOHN'S . . .'
>
> —FROM *STRONG POISON*,
> BY DOROTHY L. SAYERS[1]

Now that you understand how to structure a syllogism and determine its mood and figure, it's time to learn how to determine whether or not an argument is valid. As we mentioned in the Deduction in Action section in the last lesson, you can use mood and figure to determine the validity of a syllogism. As we also mentioned, in the past, many people memorized the "Barbara, Celarent . . ." mnemonic

device in order to help them determine validity for syllogisms. This is certainly one way of doing it, but it's probably not the easiest way for most people. Therefore, we want to teach you several other ways in which you can determine the validity of syllogisms, so that you will have a variety of tools at your disposal. In this lesson, we want to introduce you to the counterexample method.

Before we introduce this method to you, we need to explore the terms "valid" and "invalid," along with a few other related terms, a little more thoroughly than we did in the previous chapter. First, it is important for you to know that validity and truth are not the same thing. That is, you can actually have an argument that is valid logically but not true. You can also have an argument that's true but not valid. It's important to understand this because people often casually misuse the term "valid" in everyday conversation. For example, you've probably heard someone say, "You make a valid point," or "That's a valid argument." When people use the term "valid" in this manner, they are misusing the term to mean "worthwhile" or "good." While that may be fine in everyday conversation, it can be confusing in your study of logic if you do not gain a clear understanding of the word "valid." Therefore, let's take a minute to look at the word "valid," as it is used in logic, along with several other common terms.

First of all, let's make sure that we have a clear understanding of what the word "valid" means logically, rather than what it means in everyday conversation. In logical terms, a valid argument is one in which the conclusion follows logically from the premises. Just in case you have forgotten, remember that "premises" are the first two propositions of a syllogism, which form the basis of the conclusion. When propositions are by themselves, such as, for example, when we are stating the proposition that is the main idea of an argument, they are often referred to simply as propositions. However, when we are speaking about propositions that are the basis of an argument, rather than just single claims, we call them "premises." So, when we say that a valid argument is one in which the conclusion follows logically from the premises, we mean that a valid argument is structured in such a way that if the premises are true, the conclusion will also be true. For example, consider the Socrates argument with which you are familiar:

All men are mortal.

Socrates is a man.

Therefore, Socrates is mortal.

This is a valid argument because the conclusion follows logically from the premises. Note that the premises are true, and so the conclusion should be true, too—which it is. Another way of describing a valid argument is to say that the argument is structured correctly. However, remember that the validity of a deductive argument has more to do with the arrangement and construction of the various pieces of the syllogism than with the content of that argument. This is why, as we said earlier, you can have a valid argument that isn't true. For example, consider the following argument:

All men are elephants.

Santa Claus is a man.

Therefore, Santa Claus is an elephant.

This syllogism is obviously false. We know men are not elephants, and we all know that the fictional character Santa Claus is not an elephant. However, although this syllogism is false, it is valid. If you think back to our definition of the word "valid," you will see why. That is, consider that if, hypothetically, the premises of this syllogism *were* true, the conclusion would have to be true as well because the conclusion follows logically from the premises. In other words, if it is true that all men are elephants, and if it is true that Santa Claus is a man, then it must be true that Santa Claus is an elephant. In fact, you may have figured it out already, but this syllogism is structured just like the syllogism about Socrates. That is, both of them have an *AAA* mood, and both of them are first-figure syllogisms. (You may also recall from the mnemonic device that this is a "Barbara" syllogism, which is one of the valid syllogisms in the first figure.)

The term "valid" is one important term to consider when analyzing syllogisms. Two other important terms are "true" and "sound." The term "true" means just what you probably think it means. Premises or syllogisms that are true are factually accurate, correct, or right. They are not false statements. Our first syllogism about Socrates was true because it was factually accurate, correct, and right. The

syllogism about elephants was false because we obviously know that men are not elephants. The term "sound" is one with which you are probably not as familiar. When we say that an argument is sound, we simply mean that it is both true and valid. Therefore, the argument about Socrates is sound because it is true and valid. The argument about elephants and Santa Claus is valid but not sound.

You may be asking yourself, "Well, what good is deductive logic if you can have a deductively valid syllogism that is completely unsound?" To understand the answer to that, consider that throughout this book, we have stated that deductive arguments begin with *a priori* assumptions about which everyone generally agrees. Now that you understand the terms "valid," "true," and "sound," you can better understand why it is important to start with *a priori* assumptions or truths when you are arguing deductively. If you start with falsehood or nonsense, you will end with falsehood and nonsense even if your argument is perfectly valid. Therefore, from now on, when you make deductive arguments, you need to make sure of two things: First, that your premises are true, and second, that you are structuring your syllogisms in a correct or valid manner. In addition, when you critique someone else's deductive arguments, you should critique them in the same manner. That is, you should ask yourself if the premises are true, and you should also ask yourself if the syllogism is structured validly. Later, in chapter 9, we will show you how you can go about critiquing the truth of deductive premises.

You should also remember that when people argue, they often use a combination of inductive and deductive logic. Therefore, it is highly recommended that, if you have not done so already, you study inductive arguments and inductive fallacies, which are invalid inductive arguments.[2] This chapter describes how to test deductive arguments for validity, as well as some common invalid forms. You will also be learning about what are referred to as **formal** (and entirely deductive) **fallacies**, which are the key ways in which the structure of a deductive argument can go wrong.

For the rest of this book, you will be learning how to critique arguments for validity, as well as truth. These skills, along with the skills you have learned in the chapters on inference, will help you to interact with your own thinking, as well as the thinking of others, in a powerful and effective

manner. In this lesson, you will learn the first technique you can use to critique syllogisms. Have you heard of the phrase "There are many different ways to skin a cat"? Well, similarly, there are many different ways to analyze syllogisms for validity. You have already learned one: analyzing a syllogism's mood and figure for validity. The next method you will learn is called the counterexample method. When you use the counterexample method to determine if a syllogism is valid, you construct another syllogism with the same exact schema as the syllogism that you are examining. However, when you construct the counterexample that is in the same schema as the first syllogism, you must construct a syllogism that has true premises that lead to a false conclusion.

To understand this method and why you would want to construct a counterexample syllogism that has true premises that lead to a false conclusion, consider something you learned in the last chapter: A syllogism with true premises must have a true conclusion. That is, if a syllogism has true premises and a false conclusion, it is an indication that the syllogism is invalid. To use this method, you find terms that make both of the premises true. If the conclusion that follows happens to be false when those terms are inserted into it, then the argument is invalid. You know this because of the definition of validity. Recall that for all valid arguments, if the premises are true, then the conclusion will be true by necessity. If the premises are true, but the conclusion is false, then you can be sure that your argument is invalid.

Let's look at an example to understand the counterexample method more clearly. Consider the following syllogism:

E: No postmen are bus drivers.

E: No blind people are postmen.

E: Therefore, no blind people are bus drivers.

Now, on the surface, this syllogism seems to make sense. That is, the first two premises are true, the conclusion is true, and the conclusion seems to follow the premises. But, if you are like a lot of people who are new to deductive logic, you probably feel a lot less confident about this syllogism than you did about the "All men are mortal" syllogism. The validity of that one seems obvious, but with this syllogism, it is not as obvious. To test the validity of this syllogism, we can use the counterexample method. To

 YOU SHOULD NEVER STOP AT JUST ONE ATTEMPT AT A COUNTEREXAMPLE IF YOUR FIRST ATTEMPT SEEMS TO INDICATE THAT IT IS A VALID SYLLOGISM.

do this, notice that this syllogism is an *EEE-1* syllogism, meaning that its mood is *EEE* and it is a first-figure syllogism. To use the counterexample method to determine the validity of this argument, we want to see if we can make another syllogism with true premises, in the same mood and figure, which has a false conclusion. Let's see if we can do it:

No cats are dogs.

No golden retrievers are cats.

Therefore, no golden retrievers are dogs.

Aha! This new syllogism shows that our previous syllogism is invalid. Because we were able to construct an identical syllogism, with the same mood and figure, with an obviously untrue conclusion, we know that our original syllogism is invalid. Our cat and dog syllogism is an *EEE-1* syllogism, which is identical in schema to the bus driver and postman syllogism. Also notice that the premises for our cat and dog syllogism are undeniable *a priori* premises. No one would disagree with them. However, the conclusion is definitely false. Therefore, this kind of syllogism—an *EEE-1* syllogism—must be invalid because the premises were true, but the conclusion was false. In fact, if you look back at the mnemonic device, you will, indeed, find that *EEE* is not a valid mood in the first figure. Remember that for a syllogism to be valid, the conclusion must be true if the premises are true. That is obviously not the case in our cat and dog syllogism.

Let's try another one. Look at the following syllogism:

Some bankers are corrupt.

Some bankers are athletes.

Therefore, some athletes are corrupt.

Once again, on the surface of it, this syllogism seems fine. After all, the premises are certainly true, and the conclusion is true. But something just doesn't seem right about this syllogism. So, let's apply the counterexample method and see if we can discover whether it is valid or not.

First of all, notice that this syllogism is an *III-3* syllogism. So, in order to use the counterexample method to disprove its validity, we need to write a syllogism with true premises in an identical mood and figure that has a false conclusion. Can we do it? Here's our counterexample:

Some French citizens are chefs.

Some French citizens are babies.

Therefore, some babies are chefs.

This type of syllogism—*III-3*—must be invalid because the premises are indisputably true, but the conclusion is false. If you look back at the mnemonic device, you will find that, indeed, *III* is not a valid mood in the third figure.

Now, we have to admit, we make this counterexample method look pretty easy, but that's just because you didn't see how long it took us to come up with a true counterexample. Be assured, it took us a couple of tries before we came up with a counterexample that had true premises and a false conclusion. You should know that you have to be careful with the counterexample method because sometimes when you are trying to come up with a counterexample to a syllogism, you first come up with several more syllogisms that have true premises and conclusions before you find one that has true premises and a false conclusion. If you stop early in the process, you might convince yourself that a syllogism is valid when it's really not.

For example, consider the second example with which we tried the counterexample—the *III-3* one. When we first tried to come up with a counterexample, this is what we came up with:

Some bankers are corrupt.

Some men are corrupt.

Therefore, some men are bankers.

Notice, that this supposed counterexample is not a counterexample at all. It's just another example of the same

syllogism schema, which also has true premises and a true conclusion. Furthermore, even though the *III-3* syllogism is an invalid mood and figure, this supposed counterexample seems to indicate that it actually is a valid mood and figure. Therefore, if you use the counterexample method to disprove the validity of a certain mood and figure, make sure that you try it a couple of times if your first couple of counterexamples seem to indicate the syllogism schema is valid. Otherwise, you might actually deceive yourself with the counterexample method. At this point, you might be thinking to yourself, "This whole counterexample method seems really frustrating and time-consuming!" This can definitely be true—it can be very time-consuming to come up with a counterexample. In fact, the best time to use the counterexample method is when you can automatically, or very quickly, think of a counterexample that disproves the validity of a syllogism. We will discuss why this is so a little bit later in this lesson.

Consider one more example. Let's say you have an *AAA-2* syllogism like this:

All feathered creatures are birds.

All ravens are birds.

Therefore, all ravens are feathered creatures.

This is another example of a syllogism that seems valid. If we use the counterexample method, we could even find another *AAA-2* syllogism that seems valid because it has true premises and a true conclusion. Here's an example:

All criminals are lawbreakers.

All thieves are lawbreakers.

Therefore, all thieves are criminals.

This syllogism seems to show us that the *AAA-2* syllogism is legitimate after all. But be careful. You should never stop at just one attempt at a counterexample if your first attempt seems to indicate that it is a valid syllogism.

For example, try writing another syllogism in this mood and figure. This time, use the term "pigs" for the minor term, "cows" for the major term, and "livestock" for the middle term.

All cows are livestock.

All pigs are livestock.

Therefore, all pigs are cows.

This second attempt at a counterexample demonstrates that the *AAA-2* syllogism is, indeed, invalid. Therefore, keep in mind that if at first you try a counterexample and come up with another premise with true premises and a true conclusion, try, try again. Just because the first counterexample attempt seems to confirm the validity of a syllogism does not mean the syllogism is actually valid.

To be perfectly honest, creating counterexamples can be a time-consuming process, as we mentioned before. In addition, while you can use this method to determine the invalidity of a syllogism, it is impossible to absolutely guarantee the validity of a particular mood and figure using the counterexample method. Why is this? Well, think about it. Remember that it is possible for you to come up with quite a few examples of an invalid syllogism schema that actually appear to be valid, that is, a syllogism that has true premises and a true conclusion. Technically, if you are using the counterexample method alone, you would have to try all of the possible syllogisms in the world to know with 100 percent certainty that a mood and figure was valid.

Now, of course, if you try fifteen or ten or even five different syllogisms with different moods and figures and you always have true premises leading to true conclusions, then it is certainly likely that the mood and figure is valid. However, you can't be 100 percent certain using the counterexample method alone. For this reason, the best time to use the counterexample method is when you are wondering if a syllogism schema is valid and you can automatically, or very quickly, think of a counterexample syllogism in the same schema that has true premises leading to a false conclusion. If you can think of a counterexample quickly, you will know automatically that the syllogism schema is invalid. If not, you really don't want to spend a lot of time going through a bunch of different syllogisms to see if you can find a true counterexample. In this case, there are other methods that are much quicker for determining validity. Another, simpler, way to determine validity is to use the seven rules of validity, to which you will be introduced in the next couple of lessons.

DEFINE

Provide a proper definition for each of the following terms as they apply to syllogisms.

1. Valid:

_____

_____

2. True:

_____

_____

3. Sound:

_____

_____

4. Counterexample:

_____

_____

_____

EXPLAIN

1. In the space provided, explain how someone can structure a valid deductive argument that is false or nonsensical. Illustrate this by writing a nonsensical valid syllogism to illustrate your point. (Hint: Write a nonsensical *AAA-1* syllogism like the one in this lesson.)

_____

_____

_____

_____

_____

_____

2. In the space provided, explain why it is important to start a deductive argument using *a priori* premises.

_____

_____

_____

_____

3. Explain what a counterexample is and how it works.

_____

_____

_____

_____

EXPLAIN (CONTINUED)

4. Explain why counterexamples alone can never demonstrate, with 100 percent certainty, the validity of a certain kind of syllogism schema.

_____

_____

_____

_____

_____

PRACTICE

The following syllogisms are invalid, but their premises and conclusions are true. Identify the mood and figure of each syllogism. Then, construct a counterexample that has true premises and a false conclusion. Remember, you may have to try several times to find an actual counterexample.

1. Some artists are moody.
   Some actors are moody.
   Some actors are artists.

   Mood: _____ **Figure:** _____

   Possible Counterexample:

   _____

   _____

   _____

2. No professional singers are people with severely damaged larynxes.
   No presidents are people with severely damaged larynxes.
   No presidents are professional singers.

   Mood: _____ **Figure:** _____

   Possible Counterexample:

   _____

   _____

   _____

3. Some conspiracies are things broadcasted over the television.
   Some bank robberies are things broadcasted over the television.
   All bank robberies are conspiracies.

   Mood: _____ **Figure:** _____

   Possible Counterexample:

   _____

   _____

175

DEDUCTION IN ACTION
Exploring a Topic Deductively, Part 1

Throughout the Deduction in Action sections in this book, you have explored many different angles of deductive logic. Now it is time for us to start pulling together all of the different skills you have learned. The last couple of chapters in this book will focus on constructing and critiquing your own sound arguments, as well as critiquing other people's deductive arguments for soundness. Therefore, as you learn these skills, these Deduction in Action sections will help you apply the skills to an actual argument. Consider the following argument proposition:

> The most important goal of education should be to train students to be effective, powerful thinkers.

This thesis statement reflects a continual debate in educational circles. What *is* the most important purpose of education? Some people argue that the highest goal of education is teaching people how to think well, while other people believe that the key purpose of education is to help people to get a good job. Other people believe the main priority of education is something different, such as helping students to discover themselves, to participate in American democracy, or to comprehend and embrace the riches of Western and American cultural heritage.

People who believe these purposes have strong reasons for believing them, and we will look at some of those reasons later. Right now, we want you to explore what *you* think about education. Now, you may believe that the statement above about education and thinking is true, or you may believe that it is false. We don't expect you to know what you believe with certainty right now. In addition, if you do think you know what you believe, you may not know why you believe it. That's OK. We're at the exploration stage right now, which means that we want you to take some time to think about what you believe about this statement and why you believe it. Don't worry about making a brilliant argument for your case at this moment. That will come later. Right now, take some time to jot down a few thoughts on a separate piece of paper in response to the following questions:

1. Do you agree with the proposition? If so, make sure you actually do agree. That is, do you really think that training students to be effective, powerful thinkers is a higher goal than helping them to get a job? Is there any other goal that is more important than training students to be effective, powerful thinkers? If so, what is it? If there is no higher goal, why is effective, powerful thinking of such supreme importance?

2. If you disagree with the proposition, why do you disagree with it? In other words, why shouldn't effective, powerful thinking be the supreme goal of education? What should be the supreme goal?

3. Now that you have a better idea of what you think about the proposition, why do you think that people who believe differently from you believe as they do? In other words, if you agree with this proposition, why do you think people might disagree with it? If you disagree with it, why do you think people might agree with it?

LESSON 8.2

Evaluating Validity:
Terminological Rules 1 and 2

POINTS TO REMEMBER

1. There are seven rules for determining the validity of a syllogism.
2. The first four rules are terminological rules.
3. The last three rules are qualitative rules.
4. The first rule of validity is: There are only three terms in a syllogism.
5. The second rule of validity is: The middle term cannot be in the conclusion.

> 'BRILLIANT,' SAID HERMIONE. 'THIS ISN'T MAGIC—
> IT'S LOGIC—A PUZZLE. A LOT OF THE GREATEST
> WIZARDS HAVEN'T GOT AN OUNCE OF LOGIC,
> THEY'D BE STUCK HERE FOREVER. . . .'
> —HERMIONE GRANGER, IN *HARRY POTTER
> AND THE SORCERER'S STONE*[1]

Thus far, you have learned how to analyze a syllogism using mood and figure and the counterexample method. In this chapter, you will be introduced to the seven rules of validity. Once you learn these rules, you can analyze any syllogism using them, and you will know, with absolute certainty, whether, that syllogism is valid or not.

Let's look at the seven rules:

Rule 1: There are only three terms in a syllogism.

Rule 2: The middle term cannot be in the conclusion.

Rule 3: The middle term must be distributed at least once.

Rule 4: If a term is distributed in the conclusion, it must be distributed in the premises as well.

Rule 5: No conclusion can follow two negative premises.

Rule 6: If the premises are positive, the conclusion must be positive.

Rule 7: If either premise is negative, the conclusion must be negative.

You may not have realized it when you read through the rules, but the first four rules apply to the terms in a syllogism. The last three rules apply to the quality of the premises in a syllogism. Therefore, we will refer to the first four rules as the **terminological rules** and the last three rules as the **qualitative**

rules. When you first look at the rules, it may not seem obvious why a syllogism must follow them in order to be valid. However, as you study the rules in light of how a syllogism is structured, it will become a matter of common sense to you. Understanding each of the rules will help you memorize them more easily. In this lesson, we will look at the first two terminological rules.

Rule 1: There are only three terms in a syllogism.

In order to understand this rule, let's compare deductive logic to math again. We did this in the chapter on relationships of equivalence, and it will be helpful here as well. You may be familiar with the transitive law of mathematics, which looks like this:

If A = B, and B = C, then A = C.

If you notice, this is very similar to the way in which a syllogism works. You have two terms—major and minor—that are related to a third term—middle term—in some way. Because the major and minor terms are related to the middle term, they are also related to each other in some way. If you keep this idea of how a syllogism works in mind, it becomes clear why a syllogism can only have three terms. In fact, let's take our old Socrates syllogism, which we're all so fond of by now, and insert a fourth term into it to see what happens. Here it is:

All men are mortal.

Socrates is a philosopher.

Therefore all philosophers are men.

As you can see, this syllogism just doesn't work. In no way is it implied that philosophers are men just because Socrates is a philosopher and all men are mortal.

As another example, consider this syllogism, which also violates the first rule of validity because it has four terms:

All dogs are canines.

All golden retrievers are good pets.

Therefore, all good pets are canines.

As you can see, when you insert a fourth term into a syllogism, it totally disrupts the process of deductive inference because the process naturally works by relating two terms to one another through a third term. When you interject a fourth term, it disrupts the relationship of the two terms through this third term.

Think of it this way: The entire purpose of the middle term is to act like a link directly between the major and the minor terms. So, in a way, the middle term acts like a conductor. For example, in order to cook food effectively, you need to have a source of heat, food, and some sort of metal pan that can conduct the heat to the food in order to cook it. We could say that the pan connects the heat to the food, just as the middle term connects the major and minor terms. Now, imagine if you introduced a fourth element. For instance, let's say that instead of putting the food directly in the pan, you put a piece of wood in the pan and put the food on top of it. It would disrupt the pan's ability to transfer heat to the food, wouldn't it? In the same way, although we would not say that a middle term conducts heat in a syllogism, it does connect the major and minor terms in the same way that the pan connects the food with the heat. If you stick another term in the syllogism, it disrupts this connection, just like sticking a block of wood in the pan disrupts the connection between the heat and the food. That is, when you interject a fourth term into a syllogism, the middle term can't do its job of connecting the major and minor terms. In fact, there is no middle relating term anymore. You just have a major term in a premise with another term and the minor term in a premise with another term, and they can't relate to each other at all.

When a syllogism has four terms, it is invalid. This is called the fallacy of four terms. The fallacy of four terms is one of the most common validity rules that is violated when an invalid syllogism is constructed. However, it is important to note that people often commit the fallacy of four terms without knowing it, or they commit it in a way that is not immediately detectable to other people. One common way people do this is to use one term in two different ways. When they do this, they commit a fallacy called **equivocation**, which is a way of committing the fallacy of four terms. To understand this fallacy better, consider the following argument that some people might make in support of legalizing the drug marijuana, a debate that has been going on for some time in various states.

Our Declaration of Independence states that life, liberty, and the pursuit of happiness are natural rights of men. If smoking marijuana makes people happy, then it is our patriotic duty to let them pursue this method of happiness. Therefore, marijuana should be legalized.

If we were to write out this argument in syllogistic form, it might look something like this:

All pursuits of happiness are pursuits that are natural rights of men.

Smoking marijuana is a pursuit of happiness.

Therefore, smoking marijuana is a natural right of men.

If you analyze this syllogism, you will realize that this is an *AAA-1* syllogism, which means it has a valid mood and figure. Furthermore, the premises are true. Our Declaration of Independence does state that the rights of men are "life, liberty, and the pursuit of happiness."[2] It is also true that, at least temporarily, smoking marijuana does make some people happy. Therefore, on the face of it, this syllogism seems to be sound, meaning it seems to be both valid and true. However, there is a problem with it. It actually commits the fallacy of four terms.

It certainly doesn't seem like it when you first look at the syllogism. After all, it seems to have very clear middle, major, and minor terms: "pursuit of happiness," "natural rights of men," and "smoking marijuana." But look at the term "pursuit(s) of happiness." This phrase is actually being used in more than one way. Consider this: It is very likely that murdering, stealing, and lynching people makes some people happy. Unfortunately, we see evidence of this in the news on a regular basis. Is it likely that the authors of the Declaration intended to condone such pursuits? Hardly. When our founding fathers used the phrase "pursuit of happiness," they were not referring to any fancy that might strike someone no matter how illegal or socially undesirable it may be. A better interpretation of this phrase in our Declaration would be "any pursuit that is lawful." We can be assured that when our founding fathers penned the Declaration as war with England ensued, they were not planning to fight England for the right of any willy-nilly pursuit of happiness, such as consuming harmful drugs or

murdering people. Therefore, while this syllogism seems to contain only three terms, it actually contains four because the middle term is used in two different ways. To refer back to the term "equivocation," which was mentioned a few paragraphs previously, this syllogism equivocates, or uses in two different ways, the phrase "pursuit of happiness." In the first premise, it refers to "the pursuit of happiness through lawful, socially constructive means," while in the second premise, the pursuit of happiness seems to refer to "whatever floats my boat no matter if it is illegal or socially undesirable."

As mentioned earlier, when someone uses two different terms in a way that makes it seem as though they are the same term, they are committing a fallacy called equivocation. The word "equivocation" comes from the Latin words *aequus*, which means "equal," and *vocare*, which means "to call." When you equivocate, you call two different things equal or the same thing. In other words, when you equivocate, you are using one term for two different meanings. In the previous syllogism, the arguer used the same term—"pursuit of happiness"—in two very different senses, discussing two different concepts. The fallacy of equivocation is another way a person can commit the fallacy of four terms. Sometimes people blatantly commit the fallacy of four terms by using four distinctly different terms in a syllogism; however, more commonly, a person commits this fallacy subtly by using one term in two slightly different manners. The fallacy of equivocation demonstrates why it can be difficult to catch the fallacy of four terms, even though it seems like an easy fallacy to spot. In chapter 9, we will teach you about the art of definition, which can help you not only to spot this fallacy more clearly in your own reasoning, but also to recognize it in the reasoning of others. As a second example, consider a student who makes this argument to his teacher:

Allan: Mrs. Jefferson, you believe that killing is ethically wrong, right?

Mrs. Jefferson: Of course, Allan.

Allan: Well, Mrs. Jefferson, this writing assignment is killing me! Therefore, this writing assignment is ethically wrong, and you should cancel it!

Mrs. Jefferson: Nice try, Allan.

179

If we wrote out Allan's argument as a syllogism, it would look like this:

All killing is morally wrong.

This assignment is killing me.

Therefore, this assignment is morally wrong.

See if you can spot the term with which Allan is equivocating. It's "killing," of course. In the first premise, Allan is using this word to refer to the actual act of taking someone's life. In the second premise, he is using the word colloquially, or as a slang expression. When we say, colloquially, that something is killing us, we mean that it's really annoying or painful. For instance, someone might say, "My back is *killing me*!" or "We have got to paint this kitchen! This shade of green is *killing me*!" When someone uses the phrase "killing me" as a slang expression, no one really believes the person is in danger of losing his life. It's merely an expression of annoyance. Therefore, in Allan's argument, he speaks as though he is talking about one thing—the act of taking a life—when he is actually speaking about two things—the act of taking a life and the feeling of being annoyed.

In a syllogism, we know that it is important to have only three terms: middle, major, and minor. Not only is it important to have the right number of terms, but it is also important to put them in the right places. The second terminological rule addresses this issue.

Rule 2: The middle term cannot be in the conclusion.

Remembering how a syllogism is structured will help you understand this rule. A syllogism works by relating two terms—major and minor—through a third term, the middle term. The job of the middle term is to relate the major and minor terms in the premises so that these terms can be connected in the conclusion. Once the middle term has done this, its job is finished, and it drops out of the conclusion. For instance, in our Socrates syllogism, the job of the middle term "man" is to connect "Socrates" and "mortal" so that they can relate in the conclusion. So, once it has done that, the middle term "man" drops out of the conclusion.

All *men* are mortal.

Socrates is a *man*.

Therefore, Socrates is mortal.

Notice that the term "man," which appears in both premises, is not in the conclusion. Now imagine what would happen if, instead of dropping out, the middle term "man" showed up in the conclusion again. It would look something like this:

All *men* are mortal.

Socrates is a *man*.

Therefore, some *men* are not Socrates.

Or it might look like this:

All *men* are mortal.

Socrates is a *man*.

Therefore, some mortal things are *men*.

As you can see, when someone makes the mistake of putting the middle term in the conclusion, he misses the whole point of the syllogism. That is, he tries to make a statement about the middle term in the conclusion, when, in actuality, the syllogism is about the major and minor terms, not the middle term. Let's relate this back to our analogy of the heat, the food, and the pan. Once the food is cooked, we don't need the pan anymore, right? We don't have to try to eat the pan along with the food in order to keep it warm, do we? Of course we don't. The pan has done its job in connecting heat with the food, and now that it has performed that function, we don't need it anymore. In the same way, once the middle term has done its job in the premises, we don't need it in the conclusion.

It probably seems obvious that the middle term does not belong in the conclusion. In fact, it may seem like such an obvious concept that no one would make this mistake in real life. However, consider that sometimes when we are making a deductive argument on the spot, we can get sidetracked from our original argument and may introduce irrelevant items or attempt to make connections between terms that are not really connected or between which we have not actually established a clear connection. Furthermore, when we really want to prove a point, we are more apt to make inferential leaps between points that really cannot be justified.

To understand how this can happen, imagine a little old lady, Mrs. Ellen Chester, who lives by herself and spends her day watching the comings and goings of her neighbors. Mrs. Chester has an active imagination (she aspires to be a mystery novelist), and she has become especially curious about a certain neighbor of hers, Mr. Lambert, who comes and goes at all hours of the night. (Mrs. Chester doesn't sleep very well, so she's often up at odd hours.) Furthermore, she notices that Mr. Lambert often comes home in disguise. Once he came home wearing a dark fedora (hat) and sunglasses; another time, he arrived home wearing a sultan's turban and robe; and one other time, he entered his house wearing a chef's outfit. One day, Mrs. Chester had this conversation with her daughter, Ellie, about Mr. Lambert.

Ellie: How have your neighbors been, Mother? That Mr. Lambert seems really nice. He keeps his lawn very well manicured.

Mrs. Chester: *(with excitement)* Yes, he is very nice, but, my dear, I think my neighbor Mr. Lambert must be a government agent.

Ellie: Oh, Mother, surely not! You must be imagining things.

Mrs. Chester: I thought so, too, at first, but as I have observed him over these past few weeks, I have become increasingly convinced.

Ellie: But, Mother, why do you think Mr. Lambert is a government agent?

Mrs. Chester: Well, first there is the fact that he is extremely secretive. He comes and goes at all hours of the night and keeps his curtains drawn day and night. Then there is the fact that he comes home in all sorts of disguises. Now, of course, not all secretive people are government agents, but obviously, some secretive people are, because . . . well, government agents, if nothing else, are secretive. Through studying Mr. Lambert, I have come to the conclusion that Mr. Lambert is one of those secretive people who is a government agent.

Mrs. Chester, bless her heart, has made a common mistake that we all make from time to time. She has gotten caught up in an exciting idea and, in her excitement to express her reasoning, has gotten sidetracked and has made unwarranted inferential leaps. Mrs. Chester seems to have several flaws in her reasoning, but one of those flaws is that she is basing her conclusion on a syllogism that violates the second rule of validity. This is what her argument looks like as a syllogism:

My neighbor is a secretive person.

Some secretive people are not government agents.

Therefore, some secretive people are government agents.

From this, she concludes that Mr. Lambert is one of the secretive people who is a government agent. As you will notice, Mrs. Chester starts her reasoning process by noticing that her neighbor is secretive and that it is true, she admits, that not all secretive people are government agents. But then she concludes that some secretive people *are* government agents and that this proves her point that Mr. Lambert is a government agent. If you notice, her middle term was "secretive people," but instead of this term acting as a type of connecting term between the major and minor terms, it ends up in her conclusion again.

Here's another example of how someone might accidentally end up putting the middle term in the conclusion. Imagine that someone makes the following argument:

All heroic people are *brave people*.

No *brave people* are dishonorable.

Therefore, all *brave people* are honorable.

This conclusion seems true, but it doesn't follow from the premises, and the person has gotten sidetracked in the process of the argument—she lost track of the ideas she was trying to connect. The argument should have looked something like this:

All heroic people are *brave people*.

No *brave people* are dishonorable.

Therefore, no heroic people are dishonorable.

To help you remember these syllogism rules, keep the role of the middle term clear in your mind. The only job of the middle term is to connect the minor and major terms. Furthermore, the only way that a syllogism can work is by connecting two terms through a third term. If you introduce a fourth term or put the middle term in the conclusion, the syllogism falls apart. If you keep these two ideas in mind, you won't have any problems with violating these two rules in your own syllogisms, and it will help you to spot these errors in other people's syllogisms. These two rules are both terminological rules. We have two other terminological rules to cover in the following lesson.

REVIEW
FILL IN THE BLANK

Fill in the blanks below to complete the two rules of validity you have learned thus far.

1. There are only _____ terms in a syllogism.

2. The _____ cannot be in the conclusion.

DEFINE

1. Fallacy of Four Terms:

_____

_____

_____

2. Equivocation:

_____

_____

_____

EXPLAIN

1. Explain why the inferential process of a syllogism is disrupted when there are four terms. (Hint: You may want to use the analogy of conduction to help you clarify your answer.)

_____

_____

_____

_____

_____

_____

_____

EXPLAIN (CONTINUED)

2. Explain why the inferential process is disrupted in a syllogism when the middle term appears in the conclusion. (Hint: You may want to make use of the conduction example again.)

_____

_____

_____

_____

_____

_____

_____

EVALUATE

All of the following fallacies are invalid because they break either the first or second rule of validity. Examine each of the following syllogisms and then circle either rule 1 or rule 2 to indicate which rule the syllogism breaks. In the space provided, supply a brief explanation of how the syllogism breaks that rule. Circle "fallacy of four terms" if a syllogism commits just the regular fallacy of four terms. Circle "equivocation" if a syllogism commits the fallacy of equivocation. If a syllogism commits equivocation, identify the equivocated word and its two different meanings in the space provided.

1. All cows are mammals.
   All mammals are warm-blooded.
   Therefore, cows are mammals.

   Rule 1: There are only three terms in a syllogism.

   • Fallacy of Four Terms

   • Equivocation _____

   _____

   Explanation: _____

   _____

   Rule 2: The middle term cannot be in the conclusion.

   Explanation: _____

   _____

   _____

EVALUATE (CONTINUED)

2. Some people are villains.
   Some heroes are unknown.
   Therefore, some people are unknown villains.

Rule 1: There are only three terms in a syllogism.

   • Fallacy of Four Terms

   • Equivocation _____

   _____

Explanation: _____

   _____

Rule 2: The middle term cannot be in the conclusion.

Explanation: _____

   _____

   _____

3. All wounds are potentially disease causing.
   Your words cause wounds.
   Therefore, your words are potentially disease causing.

Rule 1: There are only three terms in a syllogism.

   • Fallacy of Four Terms

   • Equivocation _____

   _____

   _____

   _____

Explanation: _____

   _____

Rule 2: The middle term cannot be in the conclusion.

Explanation: _____

   _____

   _____

EVALUATE (CONTINUED)

4. No heroes are villains.
   Some villains are jugglers.
   Therefore, all villains are jugglers.

Rule 1: There are only three terms in a syllogism.

- Fallacy of Four Terms

- Equivocation _____

_____

Explanation: _____

_____

Rule 2: The middle term cannot be in the conclusion.

Explanation: _____

_____

_____

5. All lost people should stay right where they are.
   I am lost in my classes.
   Therefore, I should stay right where I am.

Rule 1: There are only three terms in a syllogism.

- Fallacy of Four Terms

- Equivocation _____

_____

_____

_____

Explanation: _____

_____

Rule 2: The middle term cannot be in the conclusion.

Explanation: _____

_____

_____

EVALUATE (CONTINUED)

6. Some U.S. citizens are postmen.
   Some homicidal maniacs are not U.S. citizens.
   Therefore, some U.S. citizens are homicidal maniacs.

Rule 1: There are only three terms in a syllogism.

   • Fallacy of Four Terms

   • Equivocation _____

   _____

Explanation: _____

   _____

Rule 2: The middle term cannot be in the conclusion.

Explanation: _____

   _____

   _____

7. No treasure chests are worthless.
   Some pirates are treasure hunters.
   Therefore, no pirates are worthless.

Rule 1: There are only three terms in a syllogism.

   • Fallacy of Four Terms

   • Equivocation _____

   _____

Explanation: _____

   _____

Rule 2: The middle term cannot be in the conclusion.

Explanation: _____

   _____

   _____

186

Writing Syllogisms: *One of the best ways to get into the habit of spotting valid and invalid syllogisms is to practice writing them a lot. Therefore, use the form provided to help you write two valid syllogisms. Remember that you need to have two premises, a conclusion, and three—and only three—terms. (Note: If it works best for your syllogism to change the tense of the verbs, feel free to do so.)*

1. All _____ are _____.
   _____ is a _____.
   Therefore, _____ is _____.

2. No _____ is _____.
   All _____ are _____.
   Therefore, no _____ are _____.

DEDUCTION IN ACTION

Exploring a Topic Deductively, Part 2

In the last lesson, you explored different purposes for education, and you thought about which purpose of education you believed was the most important. In this lesson, you will decide for certain which purpose of education you want to argue for as the primary purpose of education. Furthermore, you will choose another purpose of education against which you want to argue. That is, you will choose at least one other purpose of education that you think is the least important. To help you in this process, the following are brief explanations of some of the key purposes of education that people have advocated over the years.

1. **The most important goal of education should be to train students to be effective, powerful thinkers:** Some people have argued that training students how to think well is the most important goal of education. They stress this because students who know how to think well can learn and understand any subject well, and they can easily adapt to new situations that require new learning skills and conceptual acquisition. Therefore, these people argue, training students how to think well is the best education for life because it prepares them to be lifelong learners, a skill that is necessary for survival and fulfillment in the world.

2. **Education as economic preparation:** Some people have argued that the most important purpose of education is to prepare students to enter the workforce and make money. People who advocate economic preparedness as the key purpose of education would emphasize the three Rs (reading, 'riting, and 'rithematic) and would often advocate vocational programs in schools that train students in specific job skills.

3. **Education as a cultivation of humanity:** Some people have argued that the most important purpose of education is to help students become better, whole human beings. People who advocate this type of education often promote a liberal arts curriculum in which students study all of the subjects of mankind: science, literature, art, math, physical education, history, languages, etc. Students in this type of environment often study the great philosophic questions of humanity and discuss what it means to be fully human and to be an excellent human.

DEDUCTION IN ACTION (CONTINUED)

4. **Education as the nurturing of democratic values:** Some people believe the most important job of education is preparing students to participate in democracy. People who advocate democratic training as the key purpose of education would certainly want students to have all the basic skills, but they would also train students thoroughly in American civics and government and would emphasize other skills pertaining to functioning well in a democracy, such as cooperating in a group and making decisions for the betterment of the community.

5. **Education as the transmission of cultural heritage:** Some people advocate that the key purpose of education should be to transmit the heritage of culture. (In our case, we would study Western culture.) Students at schools that have this goal spend a lot of time reading and learning about the great ideas of their culture. They read a lot of classic literature, listen to classical music, view classical art, and learn the key mathematical and scientific ideas that have shaped their culture. The goal in these schools is for students to understand, appreciate, and even critique the influences and ideas that have made their culture what it is.

6. **Education as an exploration of self-identity:** People who advocate the development of a student's identity and uniqueness as the main goal of education often make education very personal and unique. If you have heard of Montessori schools, you may be aware that they take this type of approach. Students in this type of school spend a lot of time exploring and discovering their personal interests and talents, often at their own pace. Exploration, discovery, and personal growth are the key emphases of this type of education.

These explanations are certainly simplified (and they are not an exhaustive list of educational purposes), but they do indicate some of the most commonly stated purposes of education for which people argue. In addition, it is important to note that many schools embrace a combination of these purposes as their educational values. Now it's time for you to think through these. In order to help you do this, consider the following questions.

1. If, in the previous lesson, you determined that you believe that teaching students how to think is the most important goal of education, do you still believe that after reading through the provided list of key purposes? If so, list two or three reasons why you believe this. In addition, which of the goals of education provided in this exercise do you disagree with most? This doesn't mean that you think it is necessarily a bad goal, it just means that you think it is the least important goal for education. Why do you think this? List three reasons. (Note to student: You may believe that the most important goal of education is something different from what is provided in the list. If so, feel free to argue for what you believe, even if it is not represented in the list.)

2. If, in the previous lesson, you determined that you do not believe that teaching students how to think is the most important goal of education, what *do* you think is the most important goal? List two or three reasons for why you think this. Why do you think that teaching students how to think is not the primary purpose of education? (Note to student: You may believe that the most important goal of education is something different from what is provided in the list. If so, feel free to argue for what you believe, even if it is not represented in the list.)

3. At this point, you now know what you think is the most important goal of education, and you also know why you don't think at least one of the other goals of education is the most important goal. Now that you know these things, construct a syllogism that argues for the purpose that you advocate as the most important purpose of education.

LESSON 8.3

Evaluating Validity:
Terminological Rules 3 and 4

POINTS TO REMEMBER

1. The terminological rules pertain to the number and distribution of terms in a syllogism.
2. In universal affirmative *A* statements, the subject term is **distributed**, but the predicate term is **undistributed**.
3. In universal negative *E* statements, both the subject and predicate terms are distributed.
4. In particular affirmative *I* statements, the subject and the predicate terms are undistributed.
5. In particular negative *O* statements, the subject term is undistributed, but the predicate term is distributed.

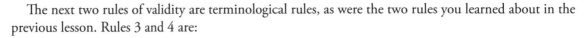

> THE WISE SPEAK ONLY OF WHAT THEY KNOW.
> —J.R.R. TOLKIEN[1]

The next two rules of validity are terminological rules, as were the two rules you learned about in the previous lesson. Rules 3 and 4 are:

Rule 3: The middle term must be distributed at least once.

Rule 4: If a term is distributed in the conclusion, it must be distributed in the premises as well.

As you may notice, both of these rules contain the word "distributed" and are concerned with the proper distribution of terms. Therefore, before you can grasp these rules, it is important that you understand what the word "distributed" means. A term in a syllogism is considered distributed if it refers to all the members of its class. For instance, if a proposition contains the subject "all men," then that subject is distributed because it is talking about *all* men. If a proposition is talking about "No men," then that term is also distributed because it is still talking about *all* men—we are denying something about all of them.

On the other hand, a term is considered to be undistributed when we are only talking about *some* of the class. For instance, if a proposition contained the subject "some men," then that subject is undistributed because it is only talking about *some* of the members in a class. Now let's look at the four propositions symbolically to see if we can start to understand distribution:

All S is P.
Some S is P.
No S is P.
Some S is not P.

If you notice, it is easy to determine the distribution of the subject term in all of the propositions because of the quantifiers "all," "some," "no," and "some . . . not." For example, the quantifiers "all" and "no" let us know that the subject term for the *A* and the *E* statements is distributed because we are

saying something about every single item in a class. In the *A* statement, we are confirming something about every single item in the class: *All S*. In the *E* statement, we are denying something about every single item in the class: *No S*. But whether we are confirming or denying, we are certainly talking about all the members of a class; therefore, the subject of *A* and *E* statements is distributed.

Next, consider *I* and *O* statements. The quantifier "some" lets us know that the subject term of *I* and *O* statements is undistributed because we are only talking about some of the members of the class. In *I* statements, we are confirming something about some of the members of the class: *Some S*. In *O* statements, we are denying something about some of the members of the class: *Some S is not*. In both the *I* and *O* classes, we are only talking about some; therefore, the subject term of *I* and *O* statements is undistributed.

We can see how quantifiers make it easy to determine the distribution of the subject term in the four statements, but what about the predicate term? Since the quantifier only applies to the subject, it will not help us in determining the distribution of the predicate term, and, to be honest, it can be a bit difficult to figure out the distribution of the predicate term just by looking at it. In fact, the best way to understand the distribution of the predicate term is to use a special type of diagram called a **Venn diagram** to help you do it. John Venn, an English mathematician and logician, invented the concept of the diagrams to represent the way in which sets of items are related to each other.[2] Venn diagrams use circles that represent an entire class of items to demonstrate how terms relate to each other in propositions and, as we will learn in an upcoming lesson, in syllogisms.

For instance, if we are diagramming a proposition with the terms *S* and *P* in the proposition, we place two interlocking circles, one that illustrates all of the class of *S* and one that illustrates all of the class of *P*. We make them interlocking because the terms are interrelated through their connection in the proposition. Here's what this looks like:

Figure 1

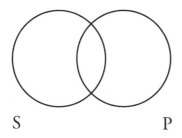

Notice that once we have done this, we have created three important areas: the area on the left, which is *All S and no P*; the area in the middle which is *S and P*; and the area on the right which is *All P and no S*. It is important to remember that a Venn diagram of two interlocking circles has these three areas. When you are using Venn diagrams to illustrate propositions, it is important that the circles always overlap in this manner because we will use these three areas to illustrate the relationship between the terms in a proposition.

We also need a way to distinguish whether there are items in a class or not. Therefore, when we want to indicate that there are no items in a class, we shade the circle. For instance, if we wanted to say that there are no items in class *S*, we would shade it like this:

Figure 2

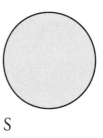

On the other hand, when we want to illustrate that there are some items in a class, we put an *X* in it. For instance, if we were to say that there were some items in class *P*, we would illustrate it like this:

Figure 3

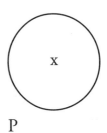

Now that we have looked at what different shading patterns in single circles mean, let's look at the two common shading patterns in overlapping circles. For instance, consider the diagram below:

Figure 4

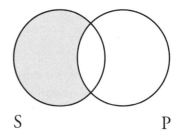

You will notice that all of *S* is shaded out except for the part that is overlapping with P. This can be a little confusing because, since most of the diagram is shaded out, it can seem like this diagram is saying that there are no *S*s, or that there are only a few *S*s. However, what this diagram is actually showing is that there are no *S*s that are not also *P*s. This makes sense if you think about it because not all of the *S* circle is shaded out—only the part of *S* that does not intersect with *P*. So, it is showing that there are, indeed, *S*s, it's just that all of the *S*s are *P*s. In other words, what this diagram is showing is that all *S is P*.

Now let's look at the second common shading pattern with the interlocking circles of a Venn diagram.

Figure 5

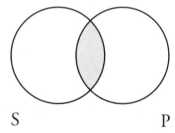

You will notice that in this diagram, the only part that is shaded out is the area in which *S* and *P* overlap. The rest of *S* and *P* is not shaded out. This means that there aren't any *S*s that are *P*s or, for that matter, any *P*s that are *S*s. What this is demonstrating is that *No S is P*. If you understand the four circle types we have just examined (the two single circle types and the two interlocking circle types), you will be able to understand how Venn diagrams work to illustrate a proposition.

Now that you have a basic understanding of how Venn diagrams work, let's look at them to examine distribution in each of the propositions. Let's begin with the *A* statement. Consider the familiar proposition "All men are mortal." This is how this proposition would look using two interlocking circles:

Figure 6

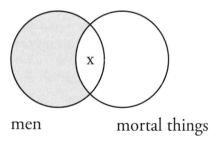

You will probably notice right away that this statement is similar to the first overlapping Venn diagram that illustrated the proposition *All S is P*. Remember from that discussion that when we say *All S is P*, this means that there are no *S*s that are not also *P*s. Therefore, we shaded out all of the area of *S* that did not overlap with *P*. In the same way, when we say "All men are mortal," we are saying that there are no men that are not also mortals. Therefore, we shade out the area of "men" that is not mortal. Remember from our discussion of distribution that the subject in *A* propositions is distributed because of the quantifier "all." What our diagram shows is that all men, or every single man, are mortal because the only section of "men" not shaded out is the one that intersects with the "mortal" circle. In addition, we learned in our study of the square of opposition that the particular is implied by the universal, so we must also place an *X* in the part of the diagram where "men" and "mortal" overlap. We want to do this so that we diagram any proposition that another proposition implies.

Now let's look at what the Venn diagram shows us about the predicate term. As you will notice from the figure 6 diagram, every member of "men" is accounted for. We see that all men are mortal things because we have shaded out any part of men that does not cross over with mortal things. Therefore, we know something about all men: that they are mortal. But does this mean that we know something about all mortal things? No, it does not mean that. Notice that while some of the circle of mortal things is taken up by men—the part that interlocks with the "men" circle—there are other mortal things that are not men. If you look at the diagram, you will notice that there's a lot of space in the mortal things circle that we don't know about. That is, we don't know what that space represents. On the other hand, we have shaded out the entire "men" circle because we know something about every single man—that they are mortal. Therefore, the predicate term of the *A* statement is not distributed because we are only talking about some of the mortal things—the some that are men

Now let's examine the *E* statement form of our familiar proposition: "No men are mortal." Of course, you will notice that this proposition is false. For the sake of learning how Venn diagrams work, we are going to ignore, for the time being, the truth-value of the proposition. We are merely using this proposition in order to understand how

we construct Venn diagrams for all of the propositions. In order to diagram this proposition, we need to shade out the area on the diagram in which the circle of men and the circle of mortal things intersect. Why? We do this because the diagram tells us that no men are in the mortal things category. This intersecting region represents the area of men that are mortal things. Since our proposition is telling us that there are no men that are mortal things, we shade this section out. In addition, because the particular statement— "Some men are not mortal"—is implied in the universal statement, we need to place an *X* somewhere clearly in the "men" circle. Remember, we want to make sure that we fully illustrate all that a proposition implies. Our Venn diagram of this *E* statement looks like this:

Figure 7

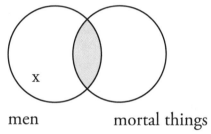

men   mortal things

You will remember from our discussion about quantifiers and distribution that the quantifier "no" in the *E* statement tells us that the subject is distributed. Venn diagrams demonstrate that this is so because the diagram for "No men are mortal" shows us that every single man is not in the category of mortal things. Therefore, we can see that the subject is distributed because we are talking about every single man. What does the diagram show us about the predicate? If you notice, the diagram also shows us something else about every single man: that they are not mortal. We know this because all of the area in which mortal things meets men has been shaded out. Therefore, the predicate term of the *E* proposition is also distributed because we are talking about all mortal things: that they are not men.

If you think back to the relationships of equivalence, it may help you understand this even better. Remember that the *E* proposition is one of the only two propositions on which we can perform conversion; that is, we can switch the subject and the predicate terms of *E* propositions. For example, the statement "No men are mortal creatures" is equivalent to the statement "No mortal creatures are

men." The reason that we can perform conversion on the *E* statement is because both of the terms in the statement have the same distribution—we are talking about "all" with both terms. Therefore, since we are denying something exclusively about both of the classes, we can legitimately perform conversion on them.

So far, we have examined the universal statements. Now let's look at the particular statements. You will notice that it is easier to understand the particular statements now that we have examined the universal statements. First, we will examine the *I* statement "Some men are mortal things." Notice how we diagram this statement:

Figure 8

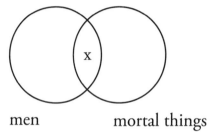

men   mortal things

This diagram shows that both the subject and the predicate terms are undistributed. Why is this? Well, the *X* in the center of the diagram shows that we are only talking about *some* men and *some* mortal things because, while the interlocking area represents both men and mortal things, it only represents some of men and some of mortal things. That is, we have done nothing with the rest of the men circle and the rest of the mortal things circle. If we were talking about all of men or all mortal things, we would have shaded out one or both of the rest of these circles. But, as it is, we only know something about some of both of these classes of things: that some men are mortal and that some mortal things are men. Therefore, both the subject and the predicate of the *I* statement are undistributed.

By the way, you will remember that the *I* statement is the only other proposition, along with the *E*, that can be converted. The reason the *I* statement can also be converted is because both of the terms in the *I* proposition are undistributed. Therefore, since we are only talking about some of both classes, the terms can be converted. This means that the statement "Some men are mortal things" can be converted to "Some mortal things are men," and that the two statements are equivalent.

Let's look at our final proposition: the *O* proposition. The *O* proposition is "Some men are not mortal." Let's look at the Venn diagram for this statement:

Figure 9

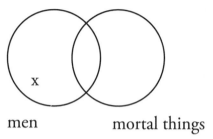

men   mortal things

Notice that we must put an *X* in the men circle because all we know is that some—the *X* represents some—men are not mortal. This *X* doesn't tell us about any of the other "men." The *X* only represents *some* men, and when we remember the quantifier "some," we realize that the subject term is undistributed. What about the predicate? This one is a little tricky, so make sure you pay attention. Notice that we have done absolutely nothing with the mortal things circle. We haven't shaded any of it, we haven't put an *X* in it—nothing. Does this mean we know nothing about the mortal things circle? It may seem like it, but think about this question: Considering where the *X* is, what do we know that all of the mortal things circle is not? Did you get it? Here's what we know: We know that none of the mortal things circle is the *X*, which is in the men circle.

Another example may help to clarify this. Let's give the *X* a name. We'll call it "Superman." What does this mean? Well, it means that our statement "Some men are not mortal" really means that "Some men, namely Superman, are not mortal." Now that we have given a name to our "some men," we can say that we know one thing about all of the mortal things: They are not Superman. Therefore, though it may not seem like it at first, the predicate term in the *O* statement is distributed because we are saying something about all of the predicate term: that it is not the *Some S*.

Let's review, in table form, what we have learned about all of the propositions and the distribution of their subject and predicate terms:

Now that you understand distribution, the next two terminological rules of validity should make better sense. Here are the rules again:

Rule 3: The middle term must be distributed at least once.

Rule 4: If a term is distributed in the conclusion, it must be distributed in the premises as well.

Let's look at rule 3: The middle term must be distributed at least once. Remember that we have talked about the fact that the middle term acts as a connecting term between the major and minor terms. In valid syllogisms, there is not only a relationship between the major term and the minor term in the conclusion, but the middle term also acts as the link that connects these two terms in the major and minor premises. Because the middle term is acting as a connecting term, it must refer to all of its class at least one time. Think of it this way: Imagine that we make the claim "All girls in the world have brown hair." Now, imagine that we have a group of some girls. What do you know about these girls? That's right. You know that these girls have brown hair because we already told you that *all* girls have brown hair. A syllogism based on this scenario would look like this:

All girls are people with brown hair.

These people are girls.

Therefore, these people are people with brown hair.

Notice that because we stated a quality about every single girl in the first premise, we automatically knew something about the group of girls in the second premise. That is, we knew something about them because they belonged to a group about which we knew something regarding every member. In this syllogism, the term "girls" is the middle term that connects the term "people"—the minor term—with the term "people with brown hair"—the major term. Because we know something about all of this middle term at least once, it is distributed at least once. In other words, it can properly connect the minor and major terms. How do you know that "girl" is distributed at least once? Well, take a look at the distribution table we just provided. "Girl" is the subject of the first premise, which is an *A* proposition, and we know from the table that the subjects of *A* propositions are always distributed. In the second premise, "girls" is the predicate of the proposition,

	Universal Affirmative *A*	Universal Negative *E*	Particular Affirmative *I*	Particular Negative *O*
Subject Term	**Distributed**	**Distributed**	**Undistributed**	**Undistributed**
Predicate Term	**Undistributed**	**Distributed**	**Undistributed**	**Distributed**

which is an *I* proposition. We know from our table that the predicates of *I* propositions are always undistributed. But it is OK that "girls" is undistributed in the second premise because it is distributed in the first premise, and rule 3 says that a middle term must be distributed at least *once*. Our syllogism meets that criterion, so it is a valid syllogism.

Now imagine if we changed the syllogism to look like this:

Some girls are people with brown hair.

These people are girls.

Therefore, these people are people with brown hair.

Now we have a problem. Can you see it? Our problem is that we only know that *some* of the girls in the world are people with brown hair. We don't know about the other girls. They may have blond hair, black hair, red hair, or no hair. We don't know. In the second premise, we have a group of some girls—"these people." Can we be certain that they have brown hair? No, we can't. They may be in the group of "some girls" that have brown hair, or they may be in the other group of girls that have hair of a different color or no hair at all. Because we don't know something about all of the middle term "girls," it cannot act as a proper connecting term between the major and minor terms. In other words, because the middle term "girls" is not distributed at least once in this syllogism, it cannot act as a proper middle connecting term.

It is important to determine the distribution of the middle term because when a syllogism fails to distribute its middle term at least one time, the syllogism commits the **fallacy of the undistributed middle**. As another example of validity rule 3 and its corresponding fallacy, consider this proposition: "All U.S. presidents are at least thirty-five years old." Now, consider the next proposition: "Barack Obama is a U.S. president." Notice that in the first premise, the term "U.S. president" is distributed—it is talking about all U.S. presidents. Now, because it is talking about all U.S. presidents when it says that they are thirty-five years old, we can automatically infer that Barack Obama is at least thirty-five years old, once the fact that he is a U.S. president is established. What if we changed the first proposition to an *I* proposition: "Some U.S. presidents are at least thirty-five years old"? Notice that in this statement, the term "U.S. presidents" is undistributed. Now, consider

the next proposition in relation to our new proposition: "Barack Obama is a U.S. president." Notice that in this proposition, the term "U.S. president" is undistributed as well. Therefore, we cannot infer from these premises that Barack Obama is at least thirty-five years old because neither premise is talking about *all* U.S. presidents at least one time.

Let's look at a syllogism that commits this fallacy. Its schema is *AIA-4*:

All flowers are plants.

Some plants are hydrangeas.

Therefore, all hydrangeas are flowers.

Notice that although the premises and conclusion are true, the argument is invalid because the conclusion doesn't logically follow from the premises. The middle term—"plants"—is not distributed in either premise. We know this because the predicates of *A* propositions and the subjects of *I* propositions are always undistributed. Because, in our syllogism, we don't know something about *all* plants but rather only something about *some* plants, we can't, therefore, infer from the premises that all or even some hydrangeas are flowers because we only know things about *some* plants. Don't let the truth of a syllogism fool you into thinking it is valid. As we noted with an example in the lesson on counterexamples, sometimes invalid syllogisms have true premises and conclusions. However, remember that what we are most concerned about in a syllogism is not the truth of the premises and conclusion but whether or not the conclusion can be inferred from the premises.

Here is another example of a syllogism that commits the fallacy of the undistributed middle.

All college professors are educated people.

All well-read people are educated people.

Therefore, all well-read people are college professors.

Notice that the middle term—"educated people"—is undistributed in both of the premises. Because of this, the middle term cannot link the minor and major terms, and the conclusion cannot be inferred from the premises. This syllogism illustrates one of the most common ways in which

people commit the fallacy of the undistributed middle. If you notice, the reasoning of this syllogism is basically that because two kinds of people—college professors and well-read people—belong to the same group of people—educated people—they are equivalent to each other. Someone would be reasoning this same way if he reasoned like this:

> All right-wing militia members are politically conservative.
>
> All Republicans are politically conservative.
>
> Therefore, some Republicans are right-wing militia members.

If you notice, the conclusion cannot be inferred from the premises because the middle term—"politically conservative"—is undistributed in both premises. The fallacy of the undistributed middle reminds us that just because two terms may have something in common does not mean they are equivalent or connected to each other. For example, just because right-wing militia groups and Republicans are both politically conservative does not mean they are connected to each other in any way.

Now that we have covered validity rule 3 and its related fallacy, let's consider validity rule 4, the other terminological rule that deals with distribution: If a term is distributed in the conclusion, it must be distributed in the premises as well. Take, for example, the following syllogism:

> Some bank robberies are violent events.
>
> No picnics are bank robberies.
>
> No picnics are violent events.

This example breaks rule 4. What term in the conclusion is distributed? First, notice that the conclusion is an *E* proposition. You will remember that both the subject term and the predicate term of *E* propositions are distributed. Notice that our minor premise is also an *E* proposition, which means that both "picnics" and "bank robberies" are distributed. However, if you check the major premise, you'll notice that the term "violent events" is not distributed in this premise. This is because the major premise is an *I* statement, and the predicate term is undistributed in *I* statements. If you will think about what we discussed with rule 3, you will see why this is a

problem. You cannot infer that an individual member of a group has a certain quality if you only know that *some* of the group as a whole have this quality.

For instance, in our previous syllogism, we are talking about *all* violent events in the conclusion (the predicate of *E* statements is always distributed), but in the premises we have only been discussing *some* violent events (the predicate of *I* statements is always undistributed). In other words, in the conclusion, the major term is distributed, but in the major premise, this term is undistributed. This syllogism is guilty of **illicit major**, which means the major term is distributed in the conclusion but not in the major premise. The word "illicit" means "wrong, illegal, or improper." Therefore, when we make an improper inference from the major premise to the major term in the syllogism, we call it an illicit major because we are making a wrong or improper inference with the major term.

If illicit major occurs when we make an improper inference with the major term, can you guess what an **illicit minor** is? That's right, an illicit minor occurs when we make an inappropriate inference with the minor term. Let's look at a syllogism that commits illicit minor:

> All triathletes are cross-trainers.
>
> Some marathon runners are cross-trainers.
>
> Therefore, all marathon runners are triathletes.

Notice that the conclusion of this syllogism is an *A* proposition, which means that the subject term is distributed and the predicate is undistributed. However, you will notice that the minor term—"marathon runners"—is distributed in the conclusion, but it is undistributed in the minor premise. The minor term is the subject of an *I* proposition, and we know that the subjects of *I* propositions are always undistributed. This syllogism demonstrates the same problem we discussed with the last syllogism. That is, we are making an inference about *all* marathon runners when we have only discussed *some* marathon runners in the premise. Since it is the minor term that is making this improper inference, we call it an illicit minor.

So far, we have discussed four terminological rules:

Rule 1: There are only three terms in a syllogism.

Rule 2: The middle term cannot be in the conclusion.

Rule 3: The middle term must be distributed at least once.

Rule 4: If a term is distributed in the conclusion, it must be distributed in the premises as well.

In addition to the four terminological rules of validity, there are also three qualitative rules. The next lesson will deal with these last three rules.

DEFINE

1. Validity:

_____

_____

2. Distributed Terms:

_____

_____

3. Undistributed Terms:

_____

_____

4. Venn Diagrams:

_____

_____

_____

PRACTICE

Part 1: Distribution Table

Fill in the blanks to complete the distribution table.

	Universal Affirmative *A*	Universal Negative *E*	Particular Affirmative *I*	Particular Negative *O*
Subject Term				
Predicate Term				

Part 2: Middle Term Figure Table

Fill in the blanks to complete the middle term figure table. (Hint: You learned this table in lesson 7.5.)

	Figure 1		Figure 2		Figure 3		Figure 4	
Major Premise								
Minor Premise								

Analyzing Syllogisms for Validity: First, determine the schema of each syllogism. Next, identify and circle the validity rules that are broken in each of the following syllogisms. Please note there may be more than one rule broken in each syllogism and you should identify all the ways the syllogism is invalid. If the syllogism breaks rule 4, circle either illicit minor *or* illicit major *to indicate the problematic term. In this exercise, if a syllogism does not break any of the four rules of validity, it is valid and you should circle the word "valid."*

ANALYZE

1. All indoor games are boring games.
   Some video games are indoor games.
   Therefore, all video games are boring games.

Schema: _____

Rule 1: Fallacy of Four Terms Equivocation	**Rule 2:** Middle Term in Conclusion	**Rule 3:** Undistributed Middle	**Rule 4:** Illicit Minor Illicit Major	**Valid**

2. Some lilies are flowers.
   Some lilies are pinkish things.
   Therefore, some pinkish things are flowers.

Schema: _____

Rule 1: Fallacy of Four Terms Equivocation	**Rule 2:** Middle Term in Conclusion	**Rule 3:** Undistributed Middle	**Rule 4:** Illicit Minor Illicit Major	**Valid**

3. All rainy days are happy days.
   This day is a rainy day.
   Therefore, rainy days are not sad days.

Schema: _____

Rule 1: Fallacy of Four Terms Equivocation	**Rule 2:** Middle Term in Conclusion	**Rule 3:** Undistributed Middle	**Rule 4:** Illicit Minor Illicit Major	**Valid**

4. No wild parties are good environments for contemplation.
   All drunken revels are wild parties.
   Therefore, no drunken revel is a good environment for contemplation.

Schema: _____

Rule 1: Fallacy of Four Terms Equivocation	**Rule 2:** Middle Term in Conclusion	**Rule 3:** Undistributed Middle	**Rule 4:** Illicit Minor Illicit Major	**Valid**

5. Some gray squirrels are not park dwellers.
   Some park dwellers are not rodents.
   Therefore, some rodents are not gray squirrels.

Schema: _____

Rule 1: Fallacy of Four Terms Equivocation	**Rule 2:** Middle Term in Conclusion	**Rule 3:** Undistributed Middle	**Rule 4:** Illicit Minor Illicit Major	**Valid**

197

ANALYZE (CONTINUED)

6. It's dangerous to go near a tornado.
   My room looks like it was hit with a tornado.
   Therefore, it looks like it's dangerous to go near my room.

Schema: _____

Rule 1: Fallacy of Four Terms Equivocation	Rule 2: Middle Term in Conclusion	Rule 3: Undistributed Middle	Rule 4: Illicit Minor Illicit Major	Valid

7. No edible things are toxic things.
   All candles are toxic things.
   Therefore, no candles are edible things.

Schema: _____

Rule 1: Fallacy of Four Terms Equivocation	Rule 2: Middle Term in Conclusion	Rule 3: Undistributed Middle	Rule 4: Illicit Minor Illicit Major	Valid

8. All chocolate brownies are tempting desserts.
   All ice cream is a delicious treat.
   Therefore, all delicious treats are tempting desserts.

Schema: _____

Rule 1: Fallacy of Four Terms Equivocation	Rule 2: Middle Term in Conclusion	Rule 3: Undistributed Middle	Rule 4: Illicit Minor Illicit Major	Valid

9. All bestsellers are moneymaking books.
   All bestsellers are highly publicized books.
   Therefore, some highly publicized books are moneymaking books.

Schema: _____

Rule 1: Fallacy of Four Terms Equivocation	Rule 2: Middle Term in Conclusion	Rule 3: Undistributed Middle	Rule 4: Illicit Minor Illicit Major	Valid

10. All bank robbers are audacious characters.
    Some professional bikers are audacious characters.
    Therefore, all professional bikers are bank robbers.

Schema: _____

Rule 1: Fallacy of Four Terms Equivocation	Rule 2: Middle Term in Conclusion	Rule 3: Undistributed Middle	Rule 4: Illicit Minor Illicit Major	Valid

Writing Syllogisms: For each of the following schemas below, write a syllogism that illustrates the schema, and then write which syllogism rule is being broken in the space provided. All of the following schemas will break one of the validity rules.

WRITE

1. *IEO-1*

   a. **Example Syllogism:**

   _____

   _____

   _____

   b. **Rule Broken/Fallacy:**

   _____

   _____

   _____

2. *AII-2*

   a. **Example Syllogism:**

   _____

   _____

   _____

   b. **Rule Broken/Fallacy:**

   _____

   _____

   _____

3. *IAA-3*

   a. **Example Syllogism:**

   _____

   _____

   _____

   b. **Rule Broken/Fallacy:**

   _____

   _____

WRITE (CONTINUED)

4. *OIO-3*

a. **Example Syllogism:**

_____

_____

_____

b. **Rule Broken/Fallacy:**

_____

5. *IEO-2*

a. **Example Syllogism:**

_____

_____

_____

b. **Rule Broken/Fallacy:**

_____

6. *AII-4*

a. **Example Syllogism:**

_____

_____

_____

b. **Rule Broken/Fallacy:**

_____

CREATE

Create a Venn diagram for each of the following statements. Then identify which terms are distributed and which terms are undistributed.

1. All women are shoppers.

Women = _____

Shoppers = _____

CREATE (CONTINUED)

2. Some summer days are hot days.

Summer days = _____

Hot days = _____

3. Some mathematicians are not math teachers.

Mathematicians = _____

Math teachers = _____

4. No military officers are civilians.

Military officers = _____

Civilians = _____

5. All moons are satellites.

Moons = _____

Satellites = _____

6. Some moons are satellites.

Moons = _____

Satellites = _____

7. Some rooms do not have windows.

Rooms = _____

Windows = _____

CREATE (CONTINUED)

8. No rooms have windows.

Rooms = _____

Windows = _____

DEDUCTION IN ACTION
Exploring Your Ideas Through Socratic Dialogue

We're going to continue our exploration of the proposition about education that we have been discussing for the last several lessons. Do you remember what it is? It is "The most important goal of education should be to train students to be effective, powerful thinkers."

In lesson 8.1, you decided whether or not you agreed with this proposition. In lesson 8.2, you were given some additional information about this and other propositions regarding education, and you decided which proposition was the one with which you agree. You also chose one other purpose of education with which you disagree.

In this lesson, you will practice writing a Socratic dialogue about your perspective. In the last lesson, you wrote a valid syllogism with true premises supporting your point. This will become the basis of your dialogue. For this assignment, structure a dialogue between two people. One person will agree with your viewpoint; the other person will agree with another viewpoint (i.e., they will believe that the purpose of education is different from what you believe it is). Use the ideas expressed in your syllogism and the other reasons you listed in support of your thesis to shape the structure of your dialogue. Remember the following points for your dialogue:

- Jump right into your dialogue. To do this, have the person who supports a different purpose of education than the one you have chosen to support state that he heard you talking about your views on the purpose of education the other day, and, since he believes the purpose of education to be different than your view, he was wondering if you would explain yours.

- Remember to ask questions, rather than arguing your point.

- Use the inchworm approach. That is, start with a point about which both of you can obviously agree. Then move on to the next point about which you obviously agree and so on. If you ask a question to which the answer is not necessarily obvious, then it means you need to back up and find intermediary points about which both of you can agree.

- Cover only one or two small points, rather than large points, in your dialogue. The more points you want to cover, the longer the dialogue you need to write.

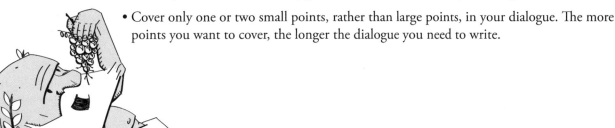

202

LESSON 8.4
Evaluating Validity:
Qualitative Rules

POINTS TO REMEMBER

1. No conclusion can follow two negative premises.
2. There must always be one affirmative premise in a syllogism.
3. If the premises are positive, the conclusion must be positive.
4. If either premise is negative, the conclusion must be negative.

> IRON SHARPENS IRON,
> SO ONE MAN SHARPENS ANOTHER.
> —PROVERBS 27:17, NASB

So far, we have covered the four terminological rules of validity. Now we need to explore the last three rules of validity, which are the qualitative rules. They are:

Rule 5: No conclusion can follow two negative premises.
Rule 6: If the premises are positive, the conclusion must be positive.
Rule 7: If either premise is negative, the conclusion must be negative.

In order to better understand rule 5, imagine that a guy says this to a girl: "You know, they say that no guys who use cheesy pickup lines on girls are classy. Well, I don't use cheesy pickup lines." This guy seems to be hoping that the girl will assume that he is classy, but can she infer that conclusion from the premises? If you read his statement again, you will notice that this guy hasn't affirmed anything in the premises from which the girl can then draw an inference. He has denied that guys using cheesy pickup lines are classy, and he has denied that he uses cheesy pickup lines. But he has affirmed nothing about himself. Furthermore, just because no guys who use cheesy pickup lines are classy and just because he doesn't use cheesy pickup lines, it does not follow that he is classy.

For example, he could refrain from using cheesy pickup lines but still not be classy because he's cruelly sarcastic, he interrupts people when they are speaking, or he rambles on about paranoid conspiracy theories. Here's the point: You can't infer a further truth from two denials. It would have been different if he had said, "All guys who avoid cheesy pickup lines are classy. I avoid cheesy pickup lines." Then, the girl could have rightly inferred that he was classy (although she might have quibbled with the truth of his premises). Or, consider if she was with a friend, and that friend said, "No guys who use cheesy pickup lines are classy. That guy over there uses cheesy pickup lines." She could have inferred something from her friend's statements: namely, that the guy to whom her friend referred was not classy. It's important to note that in a syllogism, you must affirm something at least one time, or you have no basis from which to draw a conclusion, and you commit the **fallacy of two negative premises**.

Consider another example. Let's say that you meet someone for the first time, and you say, "Tell me something about yourself." The person responds, saying, "Well, I don't have brown hair. I didn't grow up in North Dakota, and let's see . . . oh, yes, I have never met the president of the United States." Could you infer anything else about that person than what has already been stated? You certainly cannot, because we infer truths from connecting previous *a priori* truths to new ideas. Therefore, if all we have are denials of something, then we cannot infer anything new. Keeping this truth in mind will help you to understand our next syllogism.

As a reminder of how the inference process occurs, consider this syllogism:

> All weather alerts should be heeded.
>
> This alarm is a weather alert.
>
> This alarm should be heeded.

Notice that this syllogism affirms something about an entire class of things: weather alerts. Then, it affirms that this alarm is a weather alert. Through these two affirmative premises, we can infer the conclusion, which is also affirmative. Now consider another syllogism:

> No Platonist despises beauty.
>
> I am a Platonist.
>
> Therefore, I do not despise beauty.

You will notice that this syllogism is different because it denies something about a whole category—Platonists—first, and then it affirms "I am a Platonist." Therefore, through the denial of one truth and the affirmation of a second, we can infer the conclusion. It is still a valid syllogism. You will notice that both of our example syllogisms function by first affirming or denying something about an entire category of items and then, second, by placing something else in that category. Keeping that in mind, take a look at this syllogism:

> No icemakers are quiet appliances.
>
> This is not an icemaker.
>
> Therefore . . .

Notice that we deny a truth in the first premise, and then we deny another truth in the second premise. This leads us nowhere. That is, we have denied something about a category of things, but then instead of placing an item in that category to make an inference, we have just denied

something about another category of things. In essence, we have destroyed the connection created by the middle term, which in this syllogism is "ice maker." Therefore, no inference can be made. Consider another syllogism that also commits the fallacy of two negative premises:

> No women are librarians.
>
> No librarians are loud people.
>
> Therefore . . .

Notice that once again, we have denied something about an entire category of things—"women." We have denied that they are librarians. Now, if we affirmed that something was in the category of women, we could make an inference. For instance, if we said, "No women are librarians, and Angela is a woman," we could then make the inference that Angela is not a librarian. But we have not placed anything in the category of "women" to enable us to make an inference. Instead, we have merely denied something about another category of items—"librarians." Therefore, we have destroyed the connecting power of the middle term.

Another way of looking at this is to say that it is never reasonable to infer what something is by only stating what it is not. If your friend were to tell you that he didn't like pizza or hamburgers, what conclusion could you draw besides what has already been stated? Could you infer that he *did* like any other specific food, such as broccoli or ice cream? No. You can't even infer that he doesn't like cheese or meat (some of the ingredients of pizza and hamburgers) because he may actually like these food items when he eats them by themselves and just not when they are in the form of pizza or hamburgers. This shows how important it is to note that a valid argument will always include at least one affirmative statement.

Let's examine the next qualitative rule: If the premises are positive, the conclusion must be positive. This rule should make more sense now that we have discussed rule 5. Remember that one way that syllogisms work is by affirming something about that category and then placing something in that category. Consider one of the examples we used for our previous rule:

> All weather alerts should be heeded.
>
> This alarm is a weather alert.
>
> This alarm should be heeded.

Notice that since the syllogism affirms something about weather alerts—that they should be heeded—and we have affirmed that this alarm is a weather alert, it only makes sense to then make an affirmative inference for the conclusion. When premises are affirmative, which means they only *confirm* truths about categories of things, it only makes sense that the conclusion is also a positive inference. For instance, it certainly wouldn't make sense for us to infer from the premises of the example syllogism that "This alarm should not be heeded," would it? As another example of this rule, consider this syllogism:

All philosophy PhD candidates are people who read a lot.

Andrew is a philosophy PhD candidate.

Therefore, Andrew reads a lot.

Notice that the first two premises affirm something about two categories of things—that philosophy PhD candidates read a lot and that Andrew is a philosophy PhD candidate. It would be ridiculous, then, to infer that Andrew does not read a lot. Two positive premises always lead to a positive inference in the conclusion.

Now let's consider the final qualitative rule, which expresses the opposite idea: If either premise is negative, the conclusion must be negative. Now that you understand rules 5 and 6, you can probably see why this is so. Consider one of our previous example syllogisms:

No Platonist despises beauty.

I am a Platonist.

Therefore, I do not despise beauty.

Notice that this syllogism works by denying something about an entire category of things and then placing something in that category. The only thing that makes sense is for the conclusion, the final inference, to be negative as well. For instance, it would not make sense for us to conclude from the premises that "I do despise beauty." Consider another syllogism that follows this pattern:

No fireman avoids fires.

Jared is a fireman.

Therefore, Jared does not avoid fires.

In this syllogism, we have denied that any fireman avoids fires, and we have affirmed that Jared is a fireman. The obvious conclusion is that Jared does not avoid fires. In a valid syllogism, if one of the premises denies something (is negative), then your conclusion will always be negative.

As you have probably noticed, the qualitative rules of validity all tend to revolve around similar concepts, and by understanding one, it is much easier to understand the other two. Thus far, you have learned three different ways of testing syllogisms for validity: the mood and figure mnemonic device, counterexamples, and the seven validity rules. In appendix C, you will find a syllogism evaluation form that will help you to evaluate syllogisms according to mood and figure and the seven rules of validity. Using a methodical check sheet or process such as the counterexample method, the mnemonic device, or the validity rules can be very helpful when analyzing syllogisms. Once you get the hang of evaluating them, you will likely find that you can do this process in your head.

In the next lesson, you will explore how you can use Venn diagrams, which you have already learned about a little bit, as the final test of the validity of a syllogism.

FILL IN THE BLANK

Fill in the blanks for each of the syllogism rules you have learned thus far:

1. There are only _____ terms in a syllogism.

2. The _____ cannot be in the conclusion.

3. The middle term must be _____ at least once.

4. If a term is distributed in the _____, it must be distributed in the _____.

5. No conclusion can follow two negative _____.

6. If the premises are positive, the conclusion must be _____.

7. If either premise is negative, the conclusion must be _____.

EXPLAIN

1. Explain why no conclusion can follow two negative premises in a syllogism.

_____

_____

_____

_____

2. Explain why the conclusion of a syllogism must be positive if the premises are positive.

_____

_____

_____

_____

EXPLAIN (CONTINUED)

3. Explain why the conclusion of a syllogism must be negative if either premise is negative.

_____

_____

_____

_____

_____

_____

_____

_____

_____

_____

_____

_____

_____

_____

_____

_____

REVIEW   *Determine the schema of each of the following syllogisms, and then analyze each for validity. If the syllogism is invalid, circle the rule it breaks or the fallacy it commits. If the syllogism is valid, circle the word "valid." Some syllogisms may break more than one rule. If that is the case, you only need to circle one rule that it breaks.*

   1. No wooden objects are glass objects.
      Some glass objects are not tables.
      Therefore, some tables are wooden objects.

   Schema: _____

   Rule 1: Fallacy of Four Terms

   Rule 3: Undistributed Middle

   Rule 5: Conclusion from Negative Premises

   Rule 7: Positive Conclusion After a Negative Premise

   Valid

   Rule 2: Middle Term in Conclusion

   Rule 4: Illicit Minor or Illicit Major

   Rule 6: Negative Conclusion from Positive Premises

   2. All indoor games are boring games.
      Some video games are indoor games.
      Therefore, all video games are boring games.

   Schema: _____

   Rule 1: Fallacy of Four Terms

   Rule 3: Undistributed Middle

   Rule 5: Conclusion from Negative Premises

   Rule 7: Positive Conclusion After a Negative Premise

   Valid

   Rule 2: Middle Term in Conclusion

   Rule 4: Illicit Minor or Illicit Major

   Rule 6: Negative Conclusion from Positive Premises

   3. Some lilies are flowers.
      Some lilies are pinkish things.
      Therefore, some pinkish things are flowers.

   Schema: _____

   Rule 1: Fallacy of Four Terms

   Rule 3: Undistributed Middle

   Rule 5: Conclusion from Negative Premises

   Rule 7: Positive Conclusion After a Negative Premise

   Valid

   Rule 2: Middle Term in Conclusion

   Rule 4: Illicit Minor or Illicit Major

   Rule 6: Negative Conclusion from Positive Premises

REVIEW (CONTINUED)

4. Some gray squirrels are not park dwellers.
   Some park dwellers are not rodents.
   Therefore, some rodents are not gray squirrels.

Schema: _____

Rule 1: Fallacy of Four Terms

Rule 2: Middle Term in Conclusion

Rule 3: Undistributed Middle

Rule 4: Illicit Minor or Illicit Major

Rule 5: Conclusion from Negative Premises

Rule 6: Negative Conclusion from Positive Premises

Rule 7: Positive Conclusion After a Negative Premise

Valid

5. No edible things are toxic things.
   All candles are toxic things.
   Therefore, no candles are edible things.

Schema: _____

Rule 1: Fallacy of Four Terms

Rule 2: Middle Term in Conclusion

Rule 3: Undistributed Middle

Rule 4: Illicit Minor or Illicit Major

Rule 5: Conclusion from Negative Premises

Rule 6: Negative Conclusion from Positive Premises

Rule 7: Positive Conclusion After a Negative Premise

Valid

6. All birds are feathered creatures.
   Some feathered creatures are not flying creatures.
   All flying creatures are birds.

Schema: _____

Rule 1: Fallacy of Four Terms

Rule 2: Middle Term in Conclusion

Rule 3: Undistributed Middle

Rule 4: Illicit Minor or Illicit Major

Rule 5: Conclusion from Negative Premises

Rule 6: Negative Conclusion from Positive Premises

Rule 7: Positive Conclusion After a Negative Premise

Valid

REVIEW (CONTINUED)

7. No cowboys are animal haters.
   Some cowboys are not vegetarians.
   Therefore, some cowboys are vegetarians.

Schema: _____

Rule 1: Fallacy of Four Terms

Rule 3: Undistributed Middle

Rule 5: Conclusion from Negative Premises

Rule 7: Positive Conclusion After a Negative Premise

Valid

Rule 2: Middle Term in Conclusion

Rule 4: Illicit Minor or Illicit Major

Rule 6: Negative Conclusion from Positive Premises

8. Some flag burners are violent protestors.
   No extreme patriots are flag burners.
   Some extreme patriots are not violent protestors.

Schema: _____

Rule 1: Fallacy of Four Terms

Rule 3: Undistributed Middle

Rule 5: Conclusion from Negative Premises

Rule 7: Positive Conclusion After a Negative Premise

Valid

Rule 2: Middle Term in Conclusion

Rule 4: Illicit Minor or Illicit Major

Rule 6: Negative Conclusion from Positive Premises

9. All happy feelings are mental states.
   All sad feelings are mental states.
   All sad feelings are happy feelings.

Schema: _____

Rule 1: Fallacy of Four Terms

Rule 3: Undistributed Middle

Rule 5: Conclusion from Negative Premises

Rule 7: Positive Conclusion After a Negative Premise

Valid

Rule 2: Middle Term in Conclusion

Rule 4: Illicit Minor or Illicit Major

Rule 6: Negative Conclusion from Positive Premises

REVIEW (CONTINUED)

10. Some religions are violent.
    All religions are belief-based systems.
    All belief-based systems are violent.

Schema: _____

Rule 1: Fallacy of Four Terms   **Rule 2:** Middle Term in Conclusion

Rule 3: Undistributed Middle   **Rule 4:** Illicit Minor or Illicit Major

Rule 5: Conclusion from Negative Premises   **Rule 6:** Negative Conclusion from
                                                              Positive Premises
Rule 7: Positive Conclusion After a Negative Premise

Valid

11. Some shy people are librarians.
    All introverts are shy people.
    All introverts are librarians.

Schema: _____

Rule 1: Fallacy of Four Terms   **Rule 2:** Middle Term in Conclusion

Rule 3: Undistributed Middle   **Rule 4:** Illicit Minor or Illicit Major

Rule 5: Conclusion from Negative Premises   **Rule 6:** Negative Conclusion from
                                                              Positive Premises
Rule 7: Positive Conclusion After a Negative Premise

Valid

12. Some superstitious people are people who have seen ghosts.
    All people who have seen ghosts are unusual people.
    No unusual people are superstitious people.

Schema: _____

Rule 1: Fallacy of Four Terms   **Rule 2:** Middle Term in Conclusion

Rule 3: Undistributed Middle   **Rule 4:** Illicit Minor or Illicit Major

Rule 5: Conclusion from Negative Premises   **Rule 6:** Negative Conclusion from
                                                              Positive Premises
Rule 7: Positive Conclusion After a Negative Premise

Valid

REVIEW (CONTINUED)

13. Some pro-war people are not naturally aggressive people.
    Some pro-war people are military people.
    Some military people are not naturally aggressive people.

Schema: _____

Rule 1: Fallacy of Four Terms

Rule 3: Undistributed Middle

Rule 5: Conclusion from Negative Premises

Rule 7: Positive Conclusion After a Negative Premise

Valid

Rule 2: Middle Term in Conclusion

Rule 4: Illicit Minor or Illicit Major

Rule 6: Negative Conclusion from Positive Premises

14. No myths are stories totally devoid of reality.
    Some myths are not true.
    Therefore, some myths are reality.

Schema: _____

Rule 1: Fallacy of Four Terms

Rule 3: Undistributed Middle

Rule 5: Conclusion from Negative Premises

Rule 7: Positive Conclusion After a Negative Premise

Valid

Rule 2: Middle Term in Conclusion

Rule 4: Illicit Minor or Illicit Major

Rule 6: Negative Conclusion from Positive Premises

15. Some insensitive people are malicious people.
    No philanthropists are malicious people.
    Some philanthropists are not insensitive people.

Schema: _____

Rule 1: Fallacy of Four Terms

Rule 3: Undistributed Middle

Rule 5: Conclusion from Negative Premises

Rule 7: Positive Conclusion After a Negative Premise

Valid

Rule 2: Middle Term in Conclusion

Rule 4: Illicit Minor or Illicit Major

Rule 6: Negative Conclusion from Positive Premises

REVIEW (CONTINUED)

16. All thoughts are subjective experiences.
    Some subjective experiences are false perceptions.
    Some false perceptions are thoughts.

Schema: _____

Rule 1: Fallacy of Four Terms   **Rule 2:** Middle Term in Conclusion

Rule 3: Undistributed Middle   **Rule 4:** Illicit Minor or Illicit Major

Rule 5: Conclusion from Negative Premises   **Rule 6:** Negative Conclusion from
                                           Positive Premises

Rule 7: Positive Conclusion After a Negative Premise

Valid

17. All segregation is evil.
    You are segregating your things from my things.
    Therefore, you are evil!

Schema: _____

Rule 1: Fallacy of Four Terms   **Rule 2:** Middle Term in Conclusion

Rule 3: Undistributed Middle   **Rule 4:** Illicit Minor or Illicit Major

Rule 5: Conclusion from Negative Premises   **Rule 6:** Negative Conclusion from
                                           Positive Premises

Rule 7: Positive Conclusion After a Negative Premise

Valid

18. All ethical obligations are serious matters.
    No serious matter is an avoidable responsibility.
    All avoidable responsibilities are ethical obligations.

Schema: _____

Rule 1: Fallacy of Four Terms   **Rule 2:** Middle Term in Conclusion

Rule 3: Undistributed Middle   **Rule 4:** Illicit Minor or Illicit Major

Rule 5: Conclusion from Negative Premises   **Rule 6:** Negative Conclusion from
                                           Positive Premises

Rule 7: Positive Conclusion After a Negative Premise

Valid

REVIEW (CONTINUED)

19. All hockey players are skilled ice-skaters.
    Bob is a hockey player.
    Therefore, Bob is a skilled ice-skater.

Schema: _____

Rule 1: Fallacy of Four Terms   **Rule 2:** Middle Term in Conclusion

Rule 3: Undistributed Middle   **Rule 4:** Illicit Minor or Illicit Major

Rule 5: Conclusion from Negative Premises   **Rule 6:** Negative Conclusion from Positive Premises

Rule 7: Positive Conclusion After a Negative Premise

Valid

20. Some birthday parties are traumatic events.
    Some birthday parties are surprise events.
    Therefore, some surprise events are not traumatic events.

Schema: _____

Rule 1: Fallacy of Four Terms   **Rule 2:** Middle Term in Conclusion

Rule 3: Undistributed Middle   **Rule 4:** Illicit Minor or Illicit Major

Rule 5: Conclusion from Negative Premises   **Rule 6:** Negative Conclusion from Positive Premises

Rule 7: Positive Conclusion After a Negative Premise

Valid

DEDUCTION IN ACTION
Arguing the Opposite Side

Aristotle once said, "The mark of an educated man is that he can entertain an idea without accepting it." The reason that this ability is the mark of educated people is because it allows them to be able to examine ideas from all sides. The more angles from which you can explore an idea, the better you understand it, and the more thorough is your reasoning concerning that idea. Therefore, in this exercise, you are going to do just that: entertain an idea without accepting it. That is, you are going to examine the other side of the argument about the purpose of education you made in the previous lesson. You wrote a Socratic dialogue in which one character argued for your thesis statement about education, and the other character disagreed with your thesis. In this lesson, you will write another Socratic dialogue, but this time you will write it from the point of view of the person in the previous lesson's dialogue who did not agree with your thesis about education.

When you do this, it may be tempting to make your opponent's viewpoints very weak. After all, you don't agree with his side, so it will be natural for you to make his arguments less than convincing. However, if you do this, you are not really acting the part of an educated person. That is, you are not really entertaining an idea without accepting it. You should approach this task by imagining that you actually believe what this person is saying and then constructing the best, most convincing, most logical arguments for his side. This will be tricky, but you may even find that you are really provoking yourself to think deeply about this topic, which is certainly one of the goals of this exercise.

214

LESSON 8.5

An Introduction to the Venn Diagramming Method of Establishing Validity

POINTS TO REMEMBER

1. Venn diagrams are another method for testing the validity of a syllogism.
2. When you use Venn diagrams to test the validity of a syllogism, you use three interlocking circles that help you to examine the relationship between terms in the premises and conclusion of a syllogism.

> AN IDEA, LIKE A GHOST, MUST BE SPOKEN TO
> A LITTLE BEFORE IT WILL EXPLAIN ITSELF.
> —CHARLES DICKENS[1]

You now know three ways to test the validity of a syllogism: mood and figure, counterexamples, and the seven rules of validity. Next, you are going to learn the fourth and final way to test the validity of a syllogism: Venn diagrams. You were briefly introduced to Venn diagrams in lesson 8.3, in which distribution was discussed. In that lesson, we used Venn diagrams to examine propositions, but in this lesson, we will use a more complex version of Venn diagrams to examine syllogisms. A Venn diagram is a great pictorial representation of a syllogism and can establish the validity or invalidity of a syllogism with **certainty**. At first, it may seem to take more effort to use the diagrams to determine validity than it does to use the rules method, but using Venn diagrams can yield a better understanding of the relationship between the two premises of the syllogism. In addition, some people find that having a pictorial diagram of an argument helps them grasp validity or invalidity more effectively.

Venn diagrams are based on the essential idea of a syllogism, which we have discussed several times already. Remember that when you construct a syllogism, you draw a conclusion from the available premises. In a valid syllogism, the conclusion does not go any further than the premises. In other words, the conclusion is contained in, or implied by, the premises. This concept is reflected when you use a Venn diagram to examine a syllogism. When you use a Venn diagram in this way, you implement three interlocking circles, each of which represents a class of items, or a term. Then, you diagram the two premises on the Venn diagram in the way that we diagrammed propositions in the lesson on distribution.

After you have diagrammed the premises, you inspect the Venn diagram to determine if the conclusion has also been diagrammed. If your syllogism is valid, you will have already diagrammed your conclusion by diagramming the premises because, as we noted previously, in a valid syllogism, the conclusion is implied by, or contained in, the premises. If you find that your conclusion has not been diagrammed in the process of diagramming the premises on the Venn diagram, then you know the syllogism is invalid.

Before we look at how this process works with a syllogism, let's review how each of the propositions looks when diagrammed with two interlocking Venn circles. This is important because when we diagram a syllogism, we will basically be diagramming three separate propositions on the same diagram and then examining the diagram to see how the propositions relate to each other.

Here's an example of the *I* proposition *Some S is P*.

Figure 1

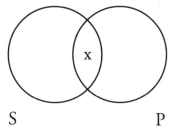

You will notice that we have placed an *X* in the overlapping space of *S* and *P*. This *X* represents the some *S*. Notice that we don't know anything else about *S* or *P*, so we have left the rest of these circles alone.

Here is an example of the *O* proposition *Some S is not P*.

Figure 2

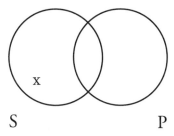

You will notice that we have placed one *X* in *S*. This *X* represents the some *S* that is not *P*. You will notice that we don't know about any of the other *S*s and *P*s, so we have left the rest of these circles alone.

Here is an example of the *A* proposition *All S is P*.

Figure 3

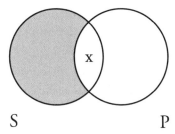

You will notice that we have shaded out every part of *S* that is also not *P*. We have done this because our proposition says that all of *S* is *P*; therefore, there is no *S* that is not *P*. In addition, because the particular proposition (e.g., *Some S is P*) is always implied in the universal proposition (e.g., *All S is P*), we have placed an *X* in the overlapping region to illustrate that implication. We want to make sure our diagram reflects no more and no less than what our proposition implies.

Here is an example of the *E* proposition *No S is P*.

Figure 4

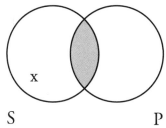

You will notice that in this diagram, we have shaded out the part where *S* and *P* overlap. This area represents the *S*s that are *P*s (and, if you remember how conversion works, it also represents the *P*s that are *S*s). We have shaded out this area because there are no *S*s that are *P*s, and there are no *P*s that are *S*s. In addition, because the particular proposition *Some S is not P* is implied in the universal proposition *No S is P*, we have put an *X* in the *S* circle to represent the some *S* that is not *P* implied in the universal proposition *No S is P*.

Now that you have reviewed how to diagram each of the propositions using Venn diagrams, let's examine how to diagram syllogisms. We will first examine valid syllogisms, and then we will examine invalid syllogisms. In addition, we will start with syllogisms that contain all universal premises rather than a mixture of particular and universal premises. That is because syllogisms containing all universal premises are a little easier to diagram. Let's begin with a syllogism that we already know to be valid: the *AAA-1* syllogism. This is what it looks like in symbolic form:

> *All S is P.*
>
> *All Q is S.*
>
> *Therefore, all Q is P.*

The first thing that you need to do is create three interlocking circles that are each labeled with one of

the terms—*S*, *P*, or *Q*—in the syllogism. This is what it looks like:

Figure 5a

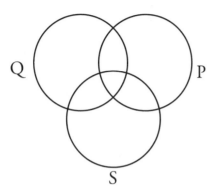

For Venn diagrams, the top left circle should represent the minor term, the top right should represent the major term, and the bottom circle should represent the middle term. Now, don't be confused because a third circle has been added. As you create the diagram, you will be concentrating on the two terms of one proposition at a time, so it isn't as confusing as it looks. That is, just diagram one proposition at a time. You have already done this with each of the propositions in the lesson on distribution, so you are doing what you already know how to do—you are just doing it twice with two different propositions.

Let's look at the first premise: *All S is P*. You will notice that the two circles on the bottom and top right represent this proposition. You will also notice that this is an *A* proposition. Therefore, we want to diagram it just like we diagramed the *A* proposition in figure 3 at the beginning of this lesson. Remember, this means that you must shade out all of the area of *S* that does not intersect with *P* because there are no *S*s that are not *P*s. Look at how we do this in the diagram below:

Figure 5b

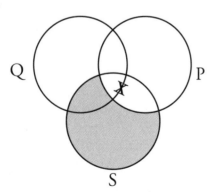

Notice that in shading out the area of *S* that does not overlap with *P*, we have already shaded some of the area overlapping with *Q*. It's OK—this is how a syllogism works. Remember, in diagramming our premises, we will also diagram our conclusion. We are starting to do that already. In addition, note that we have put an *X* in the overlap of *S* and *P*. Remember, we do this because the particular proposition *Some S is P* is implied in the universal proposition *All S is P*, and we want to diagram no more and no less than what a proposition implies. Notice that we have placed the *X* on the line where *Q* intersects the overlap of *S* and *P* and, essentially, divides the overlap of *S* and *P* in half. We must put the *X* on the line because we don't know exactly where this *X* goes right now. That is, we might find out in the second premise that one of these halves is shaded out and that the *X* can't be in that half. So, for right now, we will put it on the line.

Now, let's look at our next premise: *All Q is S*. Notice that this is an *A* proposition as well. To diagram this, we want to focus on the circles representing *Q* and *S*. We want to shade out everything in the *Q* circle that does not overlap with *S*, and we want to place an *X* in the overlap between *Q* and *S* because the particular proposition *Some Q is S* is implied in the universal proposition *All Q is S*. It looks like this:

Figure 5c

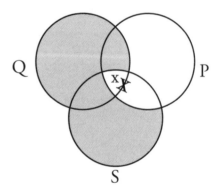

Now that we have diagrammed our premises, let's look at our conclusion: *Therefore, all Q is P*. You will notice that this is another *A* proposition. If our syllogism is valid, the area of *Q* that is not *P* should all be shaded out, and there should be an *X* in the overlap section between *Q* and *P*. This conclusion was diagrammed on the Venn diagram when we diagrammed the premises. Because of this, we know that this syllogism is valid.

You may note that some of the overlap section between *Q* and *P* has been shaded out as well. The premises of a syllogism may or may not imply more than what the conclusion implies, which is fine. A syllogism can still be valid even if the premises imply more than the conclusion implies. For instance, consider the syllogism "All men are mortal. Socrates is a man. Therefore, Socrates is mortal." This syllogism also implies that "no men are non-mortal" by conversion of the first premise. This is not stated in the conclusion, but it is certainly implied by the premises. Therefore, the premises of a valid syllogism will often imply more than the conclusion. However, they must *at least* imply the conclusion. That is, a syllogism is invalid if the premises imply less than what the conclusion implies or, in other words, if its conclusion is not already implied in the premises.

Let's try diagramming another syllogism. Since our last syllogism had all positive premises, this time we will diagram a syllogism with a negative premise so that you can see the difference. This syllogism has the schema *EAE-2*. Here is the syllogism in symbolic form:

No P is Q.

All R is Q.

Therefore, no R is P.

This is how our Venn diagram will look before we diagram the premises:

Figure 6a

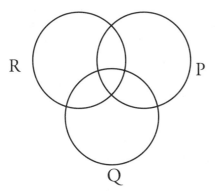

Since you are still figuring out how Venn diagrams work, let's take this syllogism one premise at a time. Our first premise is an *E* proposition: *No P is Q.* Remember that when you are diagramming a syllogism, you look at one premise at a time, which means that you examine the relationship between two circles (e.g., *P* and *Q*) at a time. Then, you examine the relationship between one of those circles and another circle (e.g., *R* and *Q*). Remember that when we have an *E* proposition, we are saying that the two terms in the proposition do not overlap or intersect at all. Therefore, for our proposition, we want to shade out any part of *P* that overlaps with *Q* and we also want to put an *X* in the *P* circle because the particular proposition *Some P is not Q* is implied by the universal proposition *No P is Q.* The question is: Where in the *P* circle should the *X* go? After all, the part of the *P* circle that has not been shaded out is intersected by the *R* circle into two parts. Since the proposition does not tell us that we need to put the *X* in one part or another, we should put it on the line where circle *R* intersects circle *P.* It looks like this:

Figure 6b

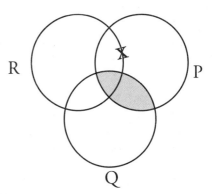

You will notice, once again, that in diagramming the relationship between *P* and *Q*, we have also shaded in some areas of the circle representing *R*. Remember that it is normal to affect the third circle as you are diagramming the relationship between two of the other circles in a Venn diagram. This is because all of the terms are working together in a syllogism. They are all connected, so it is natural that what affects one or two of them is going to affect another. In other words, when you are diagramming something about two of the terms in a syllogism, you are going to be implying things about a third term, so it is natural that this will show up in your diagram.

Also, remember that when we mark an *X* in circle *P*, we need to put it on the line of circle *R* where it intersects *P.* We must do this because we may find out in our second premise that one of the regions created by the intersection of *P* by circle *R* is shaded out and, therefore, the *X* cannot be in that region. If we put it on the line, we will avoid this problem.

Now let's look at our second premise: *All R is Q.* Because this is an *A* proposition, we know that all of *R* that is not *Q*

needs to be shaded out. In addition, the shading of *R* tells us that the *X* in the *P* circle cannot be in that part of *P* that overlaps with *R*. So we should put the *X* back in the *P* circle that is still unshaded. This is how it looks:

Figure 6c

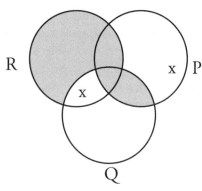

If you look at our conclusion, *No R is P*, we can conclude that this syllogism is also valid because we have already diagrammed the area *No R is P* through our diagramming of the premises. This means that our premises implied our conclusion, thus making the syllogism valid. This syllogism illustrates something about the *X*s you may want to keep in mind. Because it can be difficult to know in which part of the diagram to place *X*s, one way to handle this is to do any shading for both premises of a syllogism before you place any *X*s. This is because if you are wondering in which of two parts of an overlap section or a circle you should put the *X*, diagramming the shaded part of both of the premises may help you better determine where the *X* goes. However, another method of handling it—the method we used in the last syllogism—is to place an *X* on a dividing line if you are not sure where it goes and then move it once an area is shaded. Either method for figuring out where to place the *X*s is acceptable.

Now that we have practiced diagramming syllogisms with all universal propositions, let's practice some syllogisms that contain both universal and particular propositions. These can be a little bit trickier. When you are only considering one particular proposition and, therefore, two interlocking circles, it's pretty obvious where to put that *X*—you just stick it in the middle of the overlap section between the two circles. On the other hand, when you are using *X*s with three interlocking circles, sometimes it can be a little confusing where to place the *X*. We alluded to this idea when we diagrammed universal propositions

that imply particular propositions, but we will examine the concept more fully now. For example, let's consider an *AII-1* syllogism. Here it is in symbolic form:

> *All P is Q.*
>
> *Some R is P.*
>
> *Therefore, some R is Q.*

Since we have already done two Venn diagrams from start to finish, we will speed up the process a little bit. So, here is the Venn diagram of our syllogism with the first premise—*All P is Q*—diagrammed.

Figure 7a

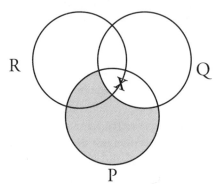

Next, let's look at the proposition *Some R is P*. You already know that when you diagram an *I* proposition, you put the *X* in the overlapping area between the two circles, and you also know you have to be careful where in the overlap you put the *X*. But if you look at this diagram, you will see that one of the halves of the overlap between *R* and *P* is already shaded out because of the universal premise *All P is Q*. Therefore, you must put the *X* in the other half. This is how our diagram should look at this point:

Figure 7b

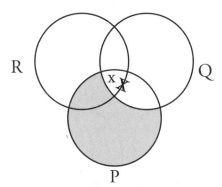

Now that we have diagrammed the premises, we must see if the conclusion *Some R is Q* has been diagrammed as

well. Has it? Yes, because in diagramming the premises, we have also placed an *X* in the overlap between *R* and *Q*, which designates the existence of some *R* that is *Q*. This syllogism is valid.

This syllogism illustrates another important point to remember when diagramming syllogisms. If you have a syllogism with both a particular and a universal premise, always diagram the universal premise first, even if it is not the first premise or the major premise. The reason it is wise to diagram the universal premise first is because it implies more than the particular premise, and so it affects more space on the Venn diagram than the particular premise. This is significant because sometimes, when you diagram a universal premise, it will shade out sections of the diagram that then help you know how to diagram the second premise properly. For example, in our previous syllogism, we knew where to put the *X* in the overlap of *R* and *P* for the second premise because we had already shaded out part of the overlap when we diagrammed our first premise, which was universal. If we had not diagrammed the universal premise first, we would not have known where to put our *X*. Therefore, in a syllogism with a universal and a particular premise, always diagram the universal premise first, whether it is the first or second premise.

Before we look at some invalid syllogisms, let's examine the Venn diagram of one more valid syllogism with a mixture of universal and particular propositions. Consider an *EIO-1* syllogism:

> *No P is Q.*
>
> *Some R is P.*
>
> *Therefore, some R is not Q.*

We know that we need to diagram the universal proposition first for this syllogism, so here is a Venn diagram with the first proposition, the universal proposition *No P is Q*, diagrammed:

Figure 8a

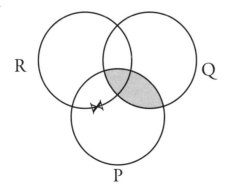

As with the other *E* propositions we have diagrammed, notice that we shaded the area in which *P* and *Q* overlap because this indicates that the *P* and *Q* categories do not intersect at all. We have also placed an *X* in the *P* circle because the particular proposition *Some R is P* is implied in the universal proposition. We also put this *X* on the circle where *R* intersects *P* because we want to make sure we don't put it in a region that will be shaded out by a later premise. Putting it on the line solves this problem. Now that we have diagrammed the universal proposition, placing the *X* for the particular proposition will be easier. We want to diagram the proposition *Some R is P*. Here is what this proposition looks like diagrammed with the first proposition:

Figure 8b

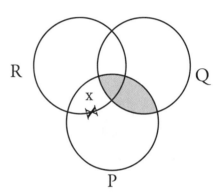

Notice that because we diagrammed the universal premise first, we now know where the *X* for *Some R is P* goes because one half of the overlap has already been shaded out. Therefore, we knew to put the *X* in the part that was not shaded out. Also, notice that by diagramming the premises, we already diagrammed our conclusion *Some R is not Q*, thus indicating that this is a valid syllogism.

Now that we have examined several Venn diagrams of valid syllogisms, let's evaluate some Venn diagrams of invalid syllogisms. First, we will look at a syllogism with the schema *AAA-2*. If you were to write a syllogism with this schema and analyze it according to the validity rules, you would realize that it is an invalid schema because it has an undistributed middle term. Let's assign this schema symbolic terms:

> *All P are Q.*
>
> *All R is Q.*
>
> *Therefore, all R is P.*

Let's look at what it looks like as a Venn diagram. Because we have already explained how the Venn diagram process works with the previous four syllogisms, we will simply analyze the full diagram (the end product) of the *AAA-2* syllogism:

Figure 9

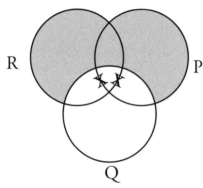

Inspecting the diagram above should make it obvious that this argument is invalid. If this one were valid, what should the diagram look like? You will notice that since the conclusion is *All R is P*, all of the *R* section that is not *P* should be shaded out. However, if you look at the Venn diagram above, you will notice that a large bottom section of *R* is not shaded out. This is because the conclusion is not implied by the premises, and, as such, this syllogism is invalid. On our Venn diagram, this means that we did not diagram our conclusion when we diagrammed our premises, which indicates that it is an invalid syllogism.

Let's examine one last example of an invalid syllogism. Consider an *IEO-4* syllogism with these terms:

> *Some P is Q.*
>
> *No Q is R.*
>
> *Therefore, some R is not P.*

Now let's look at what a Venn diagram of this syllogism would look like:

Figure 10

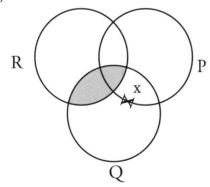

Is the conclusion of this syllogism implied in the premises? No, it is not. The conclusion is *Some R is not P*. Therefore, there should be an *X* in circle *R* demonstrating the some *R* that is not *P*. Notice that we did not diagram this *X* as we were diagramming the premises. Therefore, this syllogism is invalid because the conclusion was not implied by, or contained in, the premises.

We want to do one last thing before we have you practice Venn diagrams on your own in the review exercises. So far, we have only diagrammed syllogisms in symbolic form. Now we want to practice diagramming a syllogism that actually contains terms. Therefore, we will close the lesson with two of these. Of course, we can't leave our friend Socrates out, so we will first diagram our model syllogism: "All men are mortal. Socrates is a man. Therefore, Socrates is mortal." By now, you know that this is an *AAA-1*, Barbara syllogism that is valid. Here is what the Venn diagram looks like for this syllogism:

Figure 11

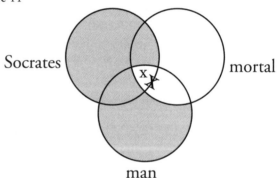

You will notice that this Venn diagram shows that the Socrates syllogism is, indeed, valid. Our conclusion is "Socrates is mortal," so in diagramming the premises, we should have shaded out all of the area of the circle "Socrates" that does not intersect with the circle "mortal", and there should be an *X* in the overlap between Socrates and mortal. We did, indeed, diagram this when diagramming the premises. Therefore, the syllogism is valid. (Note: You will also notice that in diagramming the premises, we also shaded part of the overlap between "Socrates" and "mortal." Remember that not only will the conclusion be implied in the premises of a valid syllogism, sometimes more than the premises will be implied, which is fine. This is what this syllogism shows. The premises imply the conclusion and a little more as well.)

We diagrammed a valid syllogism with terms, so let's diagram an invalid syllogism with terms as well. We will diagram one of the invalid syllogisms you saw in an earlier lesson: "No guys who use cheesy pickup lines are classy guys. I am not a guy who uses cheesy pickup lines. Therefore, I am a classy guy." This is an *EEA-1* syllogism, which is invalid because it draws a conclusion from two negative premises. Examine the Venn diagram of this syllogism below:

Figure 12

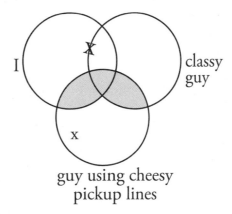

Our conclusion is "I am a classy guy," so if this were a valid syllogism, in diagramming the premises, we would have shaded out all of the circle of "I" that does not overlap with the "classy guy" circle, and there would be an *X* in the overlap between "I" and "classy guy." Notice that when we diagrammed the premises, we did neither of these things. Therefore, as we already knew, this syllogism is invalid.

You now know four different ways in which you can analyze the validity of a syllogism: the counterexample method, the mnemonic device (mood and figure) method, the seven rules of validity method, and the Venn diagram method. With these four different methods, you will be able to find what works well for you when you assess a particular syllogism. You have made a great deal of progress in learning the art and science of deductive logic. In the next lesson, you will review all of the skills you have learned thus far, and then, in the last chapter, we want to examine some final tricky situations in which you might find yourself as you make your way in the world of deduction.

REVIEW
PRACTICE

For the following five exercises, write a standard-form syllogism using the terms S, P, *and* M, *and then determine whether or not each is valid or invalid using the Venn diagram method.*

1. *EAE-3*
   Proposition 1: _____
   Proposition 2: _____
   Conclusion: _____
   Valid or Invalid: _____

PRACTICE (CONTINUED)

2. *EIO-2*

Proposition 1: _____
Proposition 2: _____
Conclusion: _____
Valid or Invalid: _____

3. *AOO-3*

Proposition 1: _____
Proposition 2: _____
Conclusion: _____
Valid or Invalid: _____

4. *OIO-2*

Proposition 1: _____
Proposition 2: _____
Conclusion: _____
Valid or Invalid: _____

5. *AEE-3*

Proposition 1: _____
Proposition 2: _____
Conclusion: _____
Valid or Invalid: _____

DEDUCTION IN ACTION
Summarizing Your Final Argument

Throughout chapter 8, you have used deduction and Socratic dialogue to explore the purpose of education from several angles. Hopefully, as you challenged yourself through Socratic dialogue, you gained a deeper understanding of this topic. To summarize your findings, write an essay that argues for what you believe is the most important purpose of education. In addition, you should argue against another purpose of education and demonstrate why it is not the most important purpose. Your essay should contain the following items:

• A clear thesis statement (this is a proposition)

• A valid syllogism that supports your thesis statement

• A brief demonstration that your premises are true

• An explanation of another purpose that some people claim as the most important purpose of education. (this should be stated in the form of a proposition)

• A discussion of some of the strengths of this proposition that supports the other purpose of education. (remember, you should be able to do this since you have entertained this idea in a Socratic dialogue already)

• A brief explanation of why, ultimately, this proposition that supports the other purpose of education you are discussing is false

• A conclusion proposition (this should be the same as your original proposition)

LESSON 8.6
Combining the Skills

POINTS TO REMEMBER

1. In analyzing a proposition or argument, you must often use multiple logic procedures to determine the meaning of the proposition or argument.
2. When analyzing a complex argument, determine first what logic procedures need to be used, and then perform them one at a time.

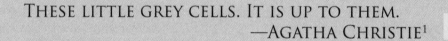

THESE LITTLE GREY CELLS. IT IS UP TO THEM.
—AGATHA CHRISTIE[1]

If you look back at what you have learned so far in this book, you will realize that you have accomplished quite a bit. So far, you have learned about four kinds of propositions, and you have learned how rules of inference are guided by relationships of opposition and equivalence. In addition, you know what a syllogism is, and you know four different ways in which you can test the validity of a syllogism. You also know how to construct a valid syllogism. Furthermore, you certainly know how to analyze syllogisms when they are in symbolic form, but you also know how to analyze them when they are in everyday language.

Now that we have explored these basic skills of categorical logic, it is time to combine them into a useful set of methods for analyzing propositions and arguments. To do this, we are going to look at arguments that require multiple operations in order to make sense of them or to examine them for validity. For instance, we may have syllogisms that require you to use the laws of equivalence in order to translate them into arguments that can be analyzed. In many ways, what we will be doing is similar to solving a math problem that requires several different operations to figure out the answer (yes, math again!). Remember that when you encounter a math problem like this, which requires many different steps to figure out the answer, you must stop, analyze it, and take it one mathematical operation at a time. You will do this same thing with a complex argument: stop, take time to analyze it, isolate the different operations required to solve it, and then perform them one at a time.

Consider someone who makes the following statement: "Only those students who achieved higher than a 3.5 GPA in their high school programs were admitted to Wallace University." Consider what this sentence means, and try to translate it into standard form. It has the same meaning as "Every person admitted to Wallace University earned a GPA of 3.5 or better." This can be simplified and put into this logical form: *All W is P*, with *W* meaning "those admitted to Wallace University" and *P* meaning "earned a GPA of 3.5 or better."

Now consider a different but related claim: "Some people who were not admitted to Wallace University had GPAs of 3.8 or better." In attempting to maintain consistent terms, this one would translate into symbolic form as *Some non-W is E,* with *W* meaning "those not admitted to Wallace University" and *E* meaning "performers of 3.8 or better." Notice that this proposition is not quite in standard logical form. To put it in standard form, we must change the *non-W* to *W* somehow in order to maintain consistency among the terms. What method should we use to do so? What kind of operation can we perform on an *I* proposition to change it into a different but equivalent proposition? Conversion is one option, because we know we can use conversion on *I* propositions, so let's see what we get when we convert the proposition.

Original Proposition: *Some non-W is E.*

Converted Proposition: *Some E is non-W.*

As you can see, the process is not complete because we still have that *non-W* in there. The other operation we should use here is obversion because it works on all of the propositions. Furthermore, we know that if we obvert the proposition, we will change the quality of the subject and negate the predicate *non-W,* and doing so will cancel out the "nons," thus simplifying the proposition. So let's go ahead and obvert the proposition, replacing the negation of *W—non-W—*with its complement, *W.*

Converted Proposition: *Some E are non-W.*

Obverted Proposition: *Some E are not non-non-W.*

If we simplify this further, we now have this statement: *Some E are not W.* As you can see, this sentence is much easier to understand than the original sentence was.

Let's practice on another proposition related to this argument. Consider the proposition "Having rich relatives who made large endowments to Wallace University didn't count toward favored admission." This seems to imply that Wallace University did not give preferential treatment to anyone who had relatives who gave big donations to the college. We could word this proposition this way: "No people whose relatives gave big cash endowments are people given preferential status." This can then be translated into

the symbolic proposition *No B is P,* with *B* meaning "people whose relatives gave big cash endowments" and *P* meaning "given preferential status."

But let's say that someone argues that because no people whose relatives gave big cash endowments are people given preferential status, this means that everyone given preferential status at Wallace University is not a person whose relatives gave large cash endowments. Can this be inferred from the previous proposition? How can you determine this? If you guessed that we should use a relationship of equivalence to see if this new statement can be inferred, you are correct. To determine if the statement is equivalent, first determine what the new proposition—"Everyone given preferential status at Wallace University is not a person whose relatives gave large cash endowments"—looks like when arranged categorically. The best arrangement is *All P is non-B.* Next, using equivalence operations, you can infer this:

Original Proposition: *All P is non-B.*

Obverted Proposition: *No P is B.*

It's been a while since you did the operation of obversion, so let's review it. Remember, when you obvert a proposition, you change the quality of the subject and negate the predicate. Therefore, the proposition *All P is non-B* would become *No P is non non-B.* The two "nons" cancel each other out, so the final proposition is *No P is B.* Then, when we convert the proposition, we switch the subject and the predicate.

Converted Proposition: *No B is P.*

As you can see from the converted proposition, you *can* infer this conclusion from the proposition, which tells us that these propositions are logically equivalent. If you had only inspected the ordinary-language propositions, you may not have been able to discern that the conclusion could be inferred, but by using these methods, you can easily draw this conclusion. As you can see, applying the methods you have learned can be handy in making ordinary-language propositions easier to understand so that you can examine them for inference, either as single propositions or as the premises of an argument, which we will look at next.

To continue the honing of your skills, let's take these methods one final step further and analyze an argument that might appear in ordinary language. Consider the following:

> If cruelty to animals is taking place, then those concerned about animal welfare will want to stop it. Many corporate farms force animals into confined quarters where they endure harsh conditions. Consequently, those who are concerned for animal welfare should also take a stand against many corporate farms.

This argument should not be too difficult to translate and evaluate for validity. There are two premises and a conclusion. The conclusion is indicated by the word "consequently." The other two propositions are the premises. The first premise can be interpreted to mean "All times when animal cruelty is taking place are times that those concerned about animal welfare oppose it." In standard form, it can be stated this way: *All C is W*, with *C* referring to "animal cruelty taking place" and *W* to "animal welfare advocates who oppose it."

The second premise's translation is determined by how one interprets the word "many." Do you think "many" means "all" or "some"? That's right, "many" means "some." Therefore, we would translate that premise so that it looks like this: "Some corporate farms are farms that use confined quarters and harsh conditions." However, note that the person making this argument seems to imply that the "confined quarters and harsh conditions" are cruel treatment. So, in standard form, this premise will read: *Some F is C*, with *F* standing for "corporate farms" and *C* for "animal cruelty taking place," as it did when we translated the first premise.

Finally, let's consider the conclusion. The manner in which this proposition is phrased may be confusing. Should it be translated as an *A* proposition or as an *I* proposition? Admittedly, there are no easy rules that you can follow to figure out which way a proposition like this should be translated. It's really just a matter of becoming a careful reader and interpreter. Let's look at this proposition more closely. Because it addresses *some* corporate farming operations, we know that it is either an *I* or an *O* proposition. Which do you think it is? That's right, it's the

particular affirmative *I* statement. The best interpretation of this proposition is probably "Some corporate farms are those that animal welfare advocates should oppose." In standard form it is *Some F is W*, with *F* meaning "corporate farms," as in the previous proposition, and *W* meaning "animal welfare advocates who oppose it," as in the first proposition.

Now that we have translated all of the propositions in this syllogism, we can proceed to making an evaluation. Let's begin by writing the entire syllogism in standard form:

> *All C is W.*
>
> *Some F is C.*
>
> *Some F is W.*

If you analyze this syllogism for mood and figure and validity, you will see that it is an *AII-1* syllogism (Darii) that follows all of the rules for validity. The subject of the major premise is a distributed middle term, and there are no distributed terms in the conclusion with which you should be concerned. Now let's test the validity with the Venn diagram method:

Figure 1

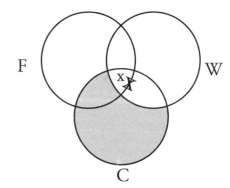

As you can see, the diagram affirms that this syllogism is valid.

One thing that you must note is that not all arguments in ordinary language will be as easy to write in standard form as this one was. What's more, you will come across some arguments that you will not be able to translate into standard syllogistic form. Because the more rigid format of categorical logic limits what arguments you can translate into standard syllogistic form, logicians have developed propositional logic, which is designed to be able to translate a wider variety of everyday arguments into logical format.

At this point, you should feel very proud of your ability to analyze propositions and arguments according to the rules of inference and validity. In the final chapter of this book, you will learn how you can critique an argument that is valid but unsound. Once you tackle this chapter, you will have a firm foundation in handling many of the deductive arguments that come your way.

REVIEW
CUMULATIVE REVIEW

Read the directions for each of the following exercises and complete the activities called for in each one.

1. Consider the following argument: "There aren't any poverty-stricken congressmen because every congressman is wealthy, and no wealthy people are poverty-stricken." Place this argument into standard categorical form, state its mood and figure, and evaluate it for validity using at least one of the four evaluation methods.

   Standard Categorical Form:

   _____

   _____

   _____

   Mood and Figure:

   _____

   _____

   Evaluate for Validity:

   _____

   _____

   _____

CUMULATIVE REVIEW (CONTINUED)

2. Is the proposition *All P is Q* logically equivalent to the proposition *All Q is P*? Use any of the methods you have learned in this book to answer. Be sure to provide a clear explanation of your answer.

3. What are the four kinds of propositions in categorical logic? Name the ones that distribute the predicate term.

4a. Translate the meaning of the following into standard form: "Few college graduates are illiterate people."

4b. Because the *I* proposition implied in the above question is true, what can be concluded about the truth-value of the proposition "No illiterate people are college graduates"? (Hint: Use the square of opposition.)

CUMULATIVE REVIEW (CONTINUED)

5. The proposition "No professional landscapers are people who always work inside" is obviously a true *E* statement. Please state its corresponding categorical propositions and their truth-values. (Hint: Think *A*, *E*, *I*, and *O* propositions.)

   A Proposition:

   _____

   _____

   Truth-Value: _____

   I Proposition:

   _____

   _____

   Truth-Value: _____

   O Proposition:

   _____

   _____

   Truth-Value: _____

6. What is the best way to translate "To err is human" into standard form? Explain your answer.

   Translation: _____

   Explanation:

   _____

   _____

   _____

   _____

   _____

7. Translate the following into standard form: "For truly moral people, violence can only be used as a last resort in the advancement of good."

   _____

   _____

CUMULATIVE REVIEW (CONTINUED)

8. Explain the meaning of the term "validity." Please also show one circumstance in which a valid argument can lead to a false conclusion.

_____

_____

_____

_____

_____

_____

_____

_____

_____

_____

9. Explain the concept of soundness, being sure to explain its relationship to validity.

_____

_____

_____

_____

_____

_____

_____

_____

_____

_____

_____

CUMULATIVE REVIEW (CONTINUED)

10. How does formal logic differ from informal logic? What is at least one advantage of learning about formal logic?

11. Show that the *AAA-3* syllogism is invalid using the counterexample method and the Venn diagramming method. To do this, use the following *AAA-3* syllogism:

    All pianos are percussive instruments.
    All pianos are large instruments.
    All large instruments are percussive instruments.

CUMULATIVE REVIEW (CONTINUED)

12. Explain, using diagrams if necessary, why the converse relationship preserves validity for *E* propositions but not *A* propositions.

_____

_____

_____

_____

_____

_____

_____

_____

CUMULATIVE REVIEW (CONTINUED)

13. Is the proposition *Some non-H is C* logically equivalent to the proposition *Some C is H*? Show your work.

_____

_____

_____

_____

_____

_____

_____

14. Translate the following proposition into standard categorical form: "Those who are wealthy are successful."

Standard-Form Proposition:

_____

15. **Part 1:** Write the following in standard form and determine its contrapositive: "Some people who don't eat meat are people who are activists for animal rights."

Standard Form:

_____

_____

Contrapositive Proposition:

_____

_____

_____

_____

Part 2: Does the contrapositive of our proposition preserve equivalence?

_____

_____

CUMULATIVE REVIEW (CONTINUED)

16. If given the proposition "All who are human are those who make mistakes," experience tells us that its truth-value is _____. This being the case, "Some humans are not those who make mistakes" has a _____ truth-value. We can certainly know this through experience, but we can also determine its truth-value through _____ from the square of opposition.

17. According to the square of opposition, if the statement "All heroes are immortal" is false, then what can be concluded about its corresponding *E* proposition, "No heroes are immortals"?

_____

_____

_____

18. Use any of the methods to determine the validity of the following:

    Some P is not Q.
    All R is Q.
    Some R is not P.

_____

_____

_____

_____

_____

_____

_____

_____

CUMULATIVE REVIEW (CONTINUED)

19. Using both a Venn diagram and the rules for determining validity, discuss the following syllogism:

    All P is Q.
    Some R is not Q.
    Some R is not P.

_____

_____

_____

CUMULATIVE REVIEW (CONTINUED)

20. Using all of the methods necessary, determine the validity of the following syllogism:

    Since no non-citizens are voters and no citizens are non-residents, one concludes that all voters must be residents.

DEDUCTION IN ACTION
Self-Love and Propositional Analysis

In the previous lesson, you thoroughly explored the concept of education and developed an argument in which you defended a proposition about the purpose of education. Through this process, you not only defended your idea, but you also entertained opposing ideas. In other words, you acted as an educated person by entertaining an idea without accepting it (unless, of course, you eventually change your mind). As you can imagine, cultivating this habit takes practice. Therefore, we want you to walk through this process a second time.

In chapter 9, you will be exploring the following proposition: "To be a good friend, a person must love himself or herself the most." Now, if you are like many people, you probably experienced a mixed reaction to this statement. For instance, you might have thought something like, "I don't want to be friends with someone who is in love with herself. She would be really stuck up and arrogant—especially if she loves herself best of all." On the other hand, you might have thought, "That makes sense. After all, it's a drag to hang around someone who hates himself and is self-loathing all the time. If someone hates himself, how good a friend can he really be to someone else?"

As you can see, although this may seem like a simple proposition, it becomes more complicated once you examine it from several different angles. In the next few lessons, you will try to do just that: look at the matter from several different angles. Right now, consider this proposition much as you did when you first explored your beliefs about the purpose of education. To do this, consider the following questions and jot down in response:

1. Do you think that a person must love himself in order to be a good friend? Why or why not?

2. In what ways, if any, can a person love herself that will make her a good friend? In what ways, if any, can a person love herself that will make her a bad friend?

3. Is there any way in which a person could love himself best of all and be a good friend?

DIALOGUE 9.1
Introduction to Definitions and Disagreements

Nate and Socrates are sitting under a tree in the campus commons.

Nate: Socrates, I can't believe how much our discussions about deductive logic have helped me over the past couple of months. I can really tell a difference in my thinking and speech, as well as in the way in which I listen to and comprehend other people's arguments.

Socrates: I'm so glad to hear it, Nate! It's always a pleasure to examine life and search for truth, especially with one so eager to find it.

Nate: I have just one final question about deductive logic. I think I already know the answer to it, but I wanted to double-check with you to make sure I'm correct.

Socrates: Wonderful! Proceed. I'm eager to hear what you have to say.

Nate: OK, well it actually has to do with a conversation Tiffany and I had the other day.

Socrates: Tiffany—delightful girl!

Nate: Yes, well, you would be proud of her. That girl knows her deductive logic, and she's getting better at arguing all the time. I need all of these private logic lessons with you just so I can keep up with her. Anyhow, the other day, we were discussing universalized healthcare. You've probably heard that this is a big topic in the United States right now. Some people say that the government should provide healthcare for all people, while others say that people should have to purchase healthcare on their own or receive it from their employers.

Socrates: Yes, I do believe I've heard something to this effect. Very strange system you have nowadays.

Nate: Yes, well, Tiffany made the following argument:

All basic living necessities are necessities to which people are entitled.
Healthcare is a basic living necessity.
Therefore, healthcare is a necessity to which people are entitled.

Socrates: Very good. As you can see, this syllogism is structured like the syllogism about my mortality, which we examined in our last dialogue.

Nate: Yes, it is. It's what is called, I believe, an *AAA-1* syllogism.

Socrates: Ah, yes. I've read about this way of classifying syllogisms. Very clever. Wish I had thought of it myself.

Nate: Yes, well, as you know, this is a valid syllogism.

Socrates: Of course.

Nate: So I cannot critique its validity.

Socrates: That is correct. There is no fault in its form or structure. It is a valid argument.

Nate: Right. So let's say I still disagree with it. I could critique its content, right? For instance, I could show that even if it is valid, one of the premises is wrong or something else about the content of the argument is off, right?

Socrates: You are correct, Nate. That's an excellent observation. Of course, true deductive logic proceeds by moving from *a priori* truth to *a priori* truth. In that case, you need never question the content of the argument because the truth of the premises is, ideally, already established. However, there are certainly times when someone constructs an argument upon premises that he believes are *a priori* truths, but they actually are not *a priori* truths. In such a case, you must critique the truth-value of the proposition to demonstrate that the proposition is false or that it is not an *a priori* truth.

Nate: Right. So, for instance, with Tiffany's syllogism, I could either show that it is false that basic living necessities are necessities to which all people are entitled, or I could show that it is false that healthcare is a basic living necessity.

Socrates: That is correct. That is one way you could critique it. Very good. Another common way to critique a syllogism is to demonstrate that a word is being used improperly. That is, you can demonstrate that the way a person is defining a word is incorrect. In addition, sometimes a premise makes an assumption about the world that is not correct. I believe these assumptions are sometimes referred to as "presuppositions." You can also demonstrate that the presupposition behind a proposition is incorrect.

Nate: That makes sense. I think I finally understand how all the parts of deductive logic fit together.

Socrates: I must admit, I am a little sad that our deductive logic sessions are coming to a close. So, now, let on old philosopher offer a parting wish for you: May you be beautiful inside. May your external possessions be in harmony with your soul. May you consider wisdom riches.

Nate: I think that's about the best wish I have ever heard. Thank you, Socrates.

REVIEW
ANSWER

1. If a syllogism is valid but you still disagree with it, what is one way in which you can disprove or critique it?

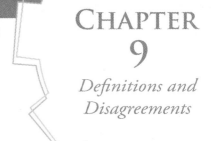

LESSON 9.2
Types of Disagreements

POINTS TO REMEMBER

1. There are several steps for critiquing an argument:
   a. Identify the deductive argument and analyze it for validity.
   b. If the syllogism is invalid, demonstrate this in a method that your opponent can understand.
   c. If the syllogism is valid but you still believe the conclusion is false, you need to determine if it is an **empirical**, **definitional**, or **presuppositional dispute** and critique it accordingly.
2. An empirical dispute is a dispute over facts.
3. A simple empirical dispute can be easily resolved by checking the facts.
4. A **complex empirical dispute** is a factual dispute that can be difficult to resolve because it involves many complex variables that make its truth difficult to determine.
5. A person may need to use inductive logic to examine the evidence supporting a complex empirical dispute.

> IN A FALSE QUARREL THERE IS NO TRUE VALOR.
> —WILLIAM SHAKESPEARE[1]

Throughout this book, you have learned how to analyze arguments for validity. This is an important skill for using logic in everyday life because it helps you to construct your own arguments and to critique other people's arguments. However, analyzing an argument for validity is only one part of the process of logic. As you know, a deductive argument can be valid but not sound. That is, someone can have a perfectly well-structured, valid argument, but because he starts from false or incorrect premises, the conclusion is false. Therefore, not only is it important for you to be able to demonstrate whether an argument is valid or not, it is also important for you to be able to identify whether an argument is sound or not. Remember, if an argument is sound, this means it is both true and valid. It is important for you to be able to critique an argument for truth as well as validity.

Furthermore, if you critique an argument and decide that the premises are false, then you need to be able to identify why this is so, since there are several different ways in which premises can be false. It is also important for you to offer sound premises or syllogisms as an alternative to the unsound ones. After all, if your only logic skill is pointing out the flaws and fallacies of another person's argument, your opponents will likely find you more cynical than thoughtful.

In these final lessons, you will learn some tips for understanding the types of disagreements and argument pitfalls you might encounter and how you can respond in each of these situations. There are several basic steps for grappling with a deductive argument—several of which you know and several of which you don't. They are:

1. Identify the deductive argument and analyze it for validity.

2. If the syllogism is invalid, demonstrate this in a method that your opponent can understand. Venn diagrams and counterexamples are often useful for this step. (You can probably imagine that springing the Barbara mnemonic device on the average, unsuspecting person may not be helpful in resolving an argument.)

3. If the syllogism is valid, but you still believe the conclusion is false, you need to show how the syllogism is unsound or how the premises are wrong. In order to do this, you must determine what type of dispute you have with one of the premises and proceed accordingly:

   a. It may be an empirical dispute in which case you need to verify the facts of one or both of the premises.

   b. It may be a definitional dispute, in which case you need to clarify the key term or terms of the premises and select the most accurate description for the terms under discussion.

   c. It may be a presuppositional dispute—an argument about the basic assumptions or beliefs contained in one of the premises. In this case, you need to use Socratic dialogue to help your opponent realize the error, contradiction, or weakness of his presupposition.

   d. It may be a combination of any of these types of disputes, in which case you need time, patience, and a proper application of these basic steps.

If you have no actual opponent, such as in a debate, discussion, or you are merely writing about a topic and exploring it from all sides, you can still critique arguments using these basic steps.

Before we discuss these different types of disputes, however, you should become familiar with the phrase "Pyrrhic victory." A Pyrrhic victory is one in which the winner of a battle incurs such heavy losses during battle that the victory nearly ruins him. This phrase is an allusion to King Pyrrhus, a Greek ruler whose armies, though they won a battle against Rome, suffered such heavy losses that Pyrrhus said about the battle, "Another such victory over the Romans and we are undone."[2] If you are wondering how Greeks, Romans, and ruinous battles apply to deductive logic, consider this: If you approach arguments and disagreements with the sole desire of proving your opponent wrong, no matter what the cost, your discussion with the other person could be so devastating to your relationship that your win becomes a Pyrrhic victory.

For example, if you and your friend who disagree about politics are debating about the next presidential candidate, you could do some serious damage to your relationship if your single goal in the conversation was to show your friend the ridiculousness of his political views. If that were your goal, you would likely come across as obstinate, arrogant, and as someone who insults, misunderstands, and alienates anyone else who dares to disagree with you. "But wait," you may be thinking, "Isn't learning logic supposed to help me win arguments?" Actually, the ultimate goal of learning logic is to help you discover truth. Think back to Socrates. In the dialogues you have read as you have progressed through this book, you learned that while he certainly demonstrated to people the error of their thinking, much to their chagrin, his one true goal was to discover the truth. His dialogues are a model of people seeking truth together.

This was the goal of early philosophers and logicians who attempted to organize logic into a clear system that could be taught. There may be times in your discussions that you, indeed, are right and the other person is wrong, and you may be able to use logic to show that person, gently, the error in her thinking. However, it is always wise to do this with humility and civility because it is likely that just as often, your friends will need to show you the error of *your* thinking. Therefore, if you approach arguments with the desire to seek truth rather than to win at all costs, you will likely find truth and avoid Pyrrhic victories in which you win arguments but alienate everyone around you.

In addition, consider that it is not only wise for you to approach arguments with humility and civility, but it is also wise for you to determine whether or not the person with whom you are arguing has these goals as well. For example, let's say that you have decided to place the search for truth as the ultimate goal of your discussions but your opponent approaches the argument with the sole purpose of winning. You can imagine that this may hinder the effectiveness of the discussion. Only when two people are willing to analyze their own arguments and admit possible weaknesses, as well as critique the other person's argument, can a true discussion take place. If you know your opponent only desires to win rather than to seek the truth, you may still decide to have the discussion. However, you may find yourself playing much the same role that Socrates did with Euthyphro, and even if you show the person the contradiction in his thinking, he may not admit it. Some people really enjoy dialogue similar to that between Socrates and Euthyphro, but other people do not enjoy this type of dialogue. Therefore, it is wise to discern, if you are able, the goal of the person with whom you are arguing. In this way, you can determine whether or not you really want to argue with that person.

As we have mentioned, if you know that a syllogism is valid but you still disagree with its conclusion, it means that you believe that the syllogism is unsound. There are several ways in which you can still dispute the premises and, ultimately, the argument. There are three main types of disputes: empirical, definitional, and presuppositional. We will focus on empirical disputes in this lesson and definitional disputes in a few of the lessons after that. Lastly, we will examine presuppositional disputes.

Let's examine empirical disputes. An empirical dispute is a disagreement about the facts of the argument. If both parties involved in an argument maintain level heads, these types of disputes should be fairly easy to settle by one or both parties looking up the disputed fact in a book or some other source. This is the best way to handle an empirical dispute, since few things could be more ridiculous than arguing vehemently about the facts when consulting a reference book or an authority can settle the matter. Consider this argument:

Matthew: I think the government is covering up some secret about who really shot John F. Kennedy. Did you know that the government won't release any documents pertaining to JFK's assassination?

Nate: Actually, that's not true. In 2004, the National Archives released a bunch of never-before-released information pertaining to his death.

Matthew: I don't believe it. There's no way the government released any information about the assassination. They have too much to cover up.

Nate: I'm serious. I don't know what all of the information was, but I know they did release it. It made national news.

Matthew: I seriously doubt it.

As you can see from this argument, there is a clear, factual dispute present: whether or not the National Archives released documents in 2004 about JFK's assassination. Furthermore, consider that Matthew and Nate can easily resolve this dispute by looking up this information on the Internet or in a database at a library. Therefore, because Matthew and Nate can look up this information and discover which statement is accurate, it is silly for them to waste time debating this issue.

As another example, if you were to disagree with someone about how many World Series the Yankees had won, this would be a factual dispute, and it would be needless to spend too much time discussing this issue because you could easily find the answer in the library or on the Internet. The point is, if you are arguing with an opponent over factual information, and you can find this information in a book or on the Internet, you are engaging in needless and unproductive debate. Therefore, if you are debating with someone and you determine that you are having an empirical dispute, you should stop the discussion and look up the facts in question in order to resolve the dispute.

It is important to note that while some disputes are, indeed, factual, they may not be as easy to resolve as the disputes about the JFK files and the number of championships the Yankees won. For example, consider the following conversation:

Matthew: I am really concerned about the general income level in the United States. Although it certainly looks as though our incomes have risen

over the last thirty years, when you look
at the increase in the cost of living, this actually
is not the case.

Nate: That doesn't seem right. We have an
unprecedented level of wealth in the United States.
Surely we must be better off now than we were
several decades ago.

Whether or not Americans have generally higher
incomes today than they did thirty years ago is a factual
dispute. However, it may be difficult to discover the facts,
even in a trustworthy source, because it is difficult for the
average individual to gain a clear picture of this matter.
It involves complex issues, such as inflation, as well as
other issues, such as taxes, food, housing, and gas prices,
which all affect the standard of living. As another example
of a tricky factual dispute that cannot be resolved easily,
consider another argument between Matthew and Nate:

Nate: I read recently that groups who are predominantly
vegetarian, such as the Seventh-Day Adventists, are
generally healthier than the rest of the population.
I think vegetarianism must be the ideal diet for
human beings.

Matthew: I don't think so. After all, the people with
the longest life spans are from the island of
Japan and the Mediterranean, and those people
eat meat, or at least fish and some poultry. So,
I don't think that vegetarianism is necessarily
the healthiest diet for humanity.

This argument does contain a factual dispute: whether or
not vegetarianism is the best diet for humanity. However,
it is impossible to resolve this dispute by just looking for
the answer in a book or on the Internet because, as you
probably know from hearing about or reading reports on
diets and eating habits, for every book you find promoting
one type of diet or eating plan, you will find as many books
promoting some other type of dietary plan. This argument,
although it is factual in nature, has been difficult for even
highly trained physicians to resolve because there are many
variable issues involved in this debate, such as the genetic
dispositions of people, their environmental conditions, and
psychological and emotional conditions as well.

As you have probably been able to determine from these
examples, when a factual dispute involves a single issue or
fact, such as the examples about government files being
released or about the number of times the Yankees have
won the World Series, it can be easily clarified through
consulting reference materials. However, when the factual
dispute involves multiple issues or variables, such as the
issue of the best diet, it can be extremely difficult to solve.
So how should you handle an argument that involves
complex facts that are under debate and cannot be easily
solved by consulting reference material? It's important to
note that for some arguments, you may not be able to settle
the matter entirely. That is, you may not be able to figure
out the complete truth or answer about an issue.

However, just because you cannot figure out the entire
answer doesn't mean you shouldn't use logic to figure out
what you *can* discover. For example, though doctors and
nutritionists have been unable to definitively establish the
ideal diet for everyone, there are some facts upon which
all doctors and nutritionist agree, such as the fact that it is
good for everyone to eat lots of vegetables, that drinking
lots of soda pop is bad for everyone, and a diet based on an
abundance of fast food is going to be nutritionally deficient
for all people. The point is that if you have an argument
based on a complex factual debate, you can often figure out
some, or even most, of the answers, even if you can't figure
out all of the answers. Therefore, look up what you can, use
logic to figure out what you can, and accept that you may
not be able to find the definitive answer.

In addition, when you are considering a premise that is
a part of a syllogism based on a complex, or tricky, factual
dispute such as we have been discussing, you may not
be able to determine whether the premise is 100 percent
accurate or not, but it is certainly possible to examine
whether or not the evidence supporting the premises is
strong or weak. For example, consider this argument, which
relates to the argument about vegetarianism:

A diet that encourages the greatest health is the
optimal diet for humans.

A vegetarian diet encourages the greatest health.

Therefore, a vegetarian diet is the optimal diet
for humans.

Notice that few people, if any, would dispute the first premise. In fact, it is a clear *a priori* proposition. Of course the diet that encourages the greatest health is the optimal diet for humans. After all, who would argue that a diet that encourages bad or mediocre health in humans is the optimal diet? No one would argue that way. However, the second premise—"A vegetarian diet encourages the greatest health"—is certainly open to dispute. This premise is not an *a priori* truth. Therefore, if you disagree with this premise, how do you go about disputing it? Note that this is a complex empirical dispute. You are not going to be able to look this up in a medical book and find whether or not this premise is true or false. Even if you find a doctor who claims this statement is true, you will find another doctor who claims it is false. Therefore, you cannot verify the truth-value of this premise with 100 percent certainty. However, you can do research to determine if the evidence to back this premise is strong or weak.

When you read the phrase "strong or weak" in the last sentence, did it ring a bell? You may recall from the beginning of this book that deductive arguments are either valid or invalid, whereas inductive arguments are strong or weak. Therefore, in order to dispute this premise, you would need to use inductive logic (see appendix D for more information on how to use inductive logic to dispute an argument). It is important to note that if you use inductive logic to dispute a premise, you cannot demonstrate with 100 percent certainty that the premise is wrong and that the whole syllogism is, therefore, unsound. However, you can certainly undermine the credibility of the premise and demonstrate that the soundness of the syllogism is questionable.

Empirical disputes are often the source of disagreements in everyday life. Many empirical disputes, especially those revolving around a simple factual claim, can be resolved through consulting reference material. Some empirical disputes, however, deal with complex issues involving multiple variables and intertwining issues. It may be impossible to resolve these types of disputes completely. However, it is possible to evaluate the relative strength or weakness of a claim and to determine some facts and truths, even if you can't figure out all of them. If you can demonstrate that the evidence supporting a particular premise is weak, you can claim that the syllogism is unsound.

Now that we have examined how to handle an empirical dispute, we need to look at the next type of dispute: a definitional dispute. This type of dispute is a little trickier to handle. We will examine this type of dispute in the next couple of lessons.

REVIEW
EXPLAIN

1. If you disagree with the conclusion of a syllogism, but you know that the syllogism is valid, what is your other option for showing the unsoundness of the argument?

LIST

1. List the three types of disputes people can have:

   a. _____

   b. _____

   c. _____

DEFINE

1. Empirical Dispute:

_____

_____

_____

_____

_____

_____

_____

2. Complex Empirical Dispute:

_____

_____

_____

_____

_____

_____

_____

_____

DETERMINE

Simple or Complex Empirical Disputes: *For each of the following disputes, determine if it is a simple empirical dispute that can be resolved by consulting a book (or the Internet or some other resource) or a complex empirical dispute, which will be harder to resolve. Circle which type of dispute it is.*

1. **Nate:** Our movie starts at 7:00, so we'd better get going so we can get good seats.
   Tiffany: It's at 7:30, not at 7:00.
   Nate: I'm sure it's at 7:00.

         Simple Empirical Dispute   Complex Empirical Dispute

2. **Matthew:** I wonder how our forty-second president will fare?
   Nate: Do you mean President Obama?
   Matthew: Yeah.
   Nate: Well, he's our forty-fourth president.
   Matthew: No way. We're only on president number forty-two. I memorized a list of the presidents in eighth grade; I'm sure it's forty-two.
   Nate: Sorry, dude. It's forty-four. Better go work on memorizing the list again.

         Simple Empirical Dispute   Complex Empirical Dispute

3. **Julie:** The Iraq War is just like the Vietnam War all over again.
   Tiffany: Hmm. I don't really think they're alike at all.
   Julie: I do. Same reasoning, same problems. They're so similar, it's scary.
   Tiffany: I'm pretty sure there are some significant dissimilarities.

         Simple Empirical Dispute   Complex Empirical Dispute

DETERMINE (CONTINUED)

4. **Tiffany:** I've decided to give up all coffee for my New Year's resolution. I've heard that it can raise cholesterol and can be bad for your health in other ways, too.

   Nate: Wow. That's interesting. I was just listening to a radio show the other day, and the radio host said that caffeine can make you smarter and help your health.

   Tiffany: I doubt it. I'm certain it's bad for you.

   Nate: I'm not convinced. Healthy people in many countries drink coffee as a regular part of their diets and actually seem to benefit from it.

   Tiffany: I'm skeptical.

   Simple Empirical Dispute   Complex Empirical Dispute

5. **Matthew:** Hey, Nate, did you finish your application to the University of Kentucky graduate program yet?

   Nate: No, I have plenty of time. The deadline isn't until January 10.

   Matthew: That's not right. It's December 10.

   Simple Empirical Dispute   Complex Empirical Dispute

DEDUCTION IN ACTION
Determining the Basis of a Dispute

In lesson 8.6, this proposition was introduced: "To be a good friend, a person must love himself or herself the most." If one person believed that this proposition was true but another believed it was false, which type of dispute do you think that they might be having: empirical, presuppositional, or definitional? Now we know that so far we have only discussed empirical disputes in detail, so to help you think through this issue better, answer the following questions:

1. Is there some kind of fact in this proposition that can be disputed? That is, could someone go find the exact answer to this question in a book? Could someone do research to demonstrate that the evidence behind this statement is strong or weak? If not, why not?

2. Is there a vague or ambiguous word in this premise that is the cause of the dispute? That is, is there a word that people could define in more than one way and could therefore cause differing interpretations of the proposition?

3. Is there some kind of basic presupposition (personal belief) about the world, humans, and the way things work that is at the heart of this question? That is, is this presupposition based on a basic belief about the world?

4. Is this dispute a combination of disputes? If so, which ones?

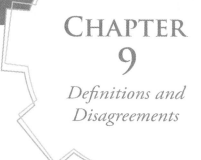

LESSON 9.3
Rules for Defining Words

POINTS TO REMEMBER

1. Definitional disputes are disputes that arise over the meaning of words.
2. There are seven rules for defining words:
   a. The key content rules are:
      Rule 1: As much as possible, the definition should contain the essential primary characteristics, not the secondary accidental characteristics, of the term.
      Rule 2: The definition should not be circular.
      Rule 3: The definition should not be too broad or too narrow.
      Rule 4: The definition should prefer positive comparisons to negative ones.
   b. The key language rules are:
      Rule 5: The definition should be clear.
      Rule 6: The definition should avoid unnecessarily emotive language.
      Rule 7: The definition should define the term as the correct part of speech.
3. Equivocation occurs when a person uses a word in two different ways in an argument but argues as though he is only using one meaning for the word.

> WHAT DO YOU MEAN ['GOOD MORNING']? DO YOU WISH ME A GOOD MORNING, OR MEAN THAT IT IS A GOOD MORNING WHETHER I WANT IT OR NOT; OR THAT YOU FEEL GOOD ON THIS MORNING; OR THAT IT IS A MORNING TO BE GOOD ON?
> —J.R.R. TOLKIEN[1]

> THOSE WHO PREFER THEIR ENGLISH SLOPPY HAVE ONLY THEMSELVES TO THANK IF THE ADVERTISEMENT WRITER USES HIS MASTERY OF THE VOCABULARY AND SYNTAX TO MISLEAD THEIR WEAK MINDS.
> —DOROTHY L. SAYERS[2]

We know that arguments can be based on empirical disagreements, and sometimes these empirical disputes can be simple, as in the case of how many World Series the Yankees have won, or complex, as in the best kind of diet for all human beings. Another type of dispute that can be both simple and complex is a definitional dispute. It may seem like definitional disagreements would always be easy to solve. After all, can't we just look up the proper definition in the dictionary? This is not always the easy answer it may seem. One reason that definitions can be so tricky is that many debates revolve around different *interpretations* of words. For instance, consider the following argument Nate and Tiffany had the other day when they met at a local coffee shop to study:

Nate: *(frustrated)* Tiffany, I told you to get here early. We have a lot of studying to do for our philosophy class tomorrow, and I have to go to swim practice soon.

Tiffany: Nate, what are you talking about? I *am* early. You said we should meet at 4:30, and it's 4:23. That's early.

Nate: That's not early! That's just getting here a few minutes before we planned to meet. When I say early, I mean "early early," like 4:00 or 4:10. I've been waiting for you for over fifteen minutes.

Tiffany: Well, sorry I can't read your mind, Nate. I didn't know that you meant "early early" when you said "early." I guess I was just thinking "early."

As you can see, this argument revolves around different interpretations of the word "early." This is a common definitional problem that people encounter in debates. They use words that have somewhat vague or abstract meanings but they argue using a very specific definition of the word that the other person involved in the argument may or may not know.

Vague and abstract words are not the only definitional problems that occur in debates. Consider this argument that Nate had with his friend, Matthew, before the philosophy test the next day:

Nate: Hey, Matt, do you think you are ready for the philosophy test?

Matt: Well, I guess it doesn't matter, does it? I mean, it is what it is.

Nate: Wait, what does that mean?

Matt: It just means that I'm going to get what I'm going to get, so it doesn't really matter.

Nate: Do you mean you don't think you really have any control over what you're going to get?

Matt: *(thinks for a moment before answering)* Yeah, I guess I do mean that. I have a certain intelligence level that I really can't control, and I have circumstances in my life that I can't control that determine how much I can study. So, it is what it is.

Nate: Whoa, dude, why such a bleak outlook all of a sudden? When you say you can't control the circumstances, do you mean that you can't change them if you want to?

Matt: Well, I could change them if I wanted to, but other factors control what I want. For instance, I could have not played five hours of video games last night and studied if I had wanted to, but other factors in my life have determined that I wanted to play video games for five hours instead of studying, so I really didn't have control over that.

Nate: I see. The picture is becoming a little clearer now. If someone had put a gun to your head and told you to study instead of playing video games, would you have suddenly wanted to study?

Matt: Well, sure.

Nate: If someone had offered you $1,000 to study instead of playing video games, would you have studied then?

Matt: Can you make it $2,000?

Nate: Very funny. So, when you say you can't control the fact that you wanted to play video games for five hours instead of studying, what you are really saying is that you didn't have sufficient motivation to study, right?

Matt: Well, yeah, but I couldn't really control whether or not I had sufficient motivation to study. Other factors in life determined my motivation level.

Nate: Oh, good grief.

This is a somewhat lighthearted example of how we often quibble over words and their meanings, but it illustrates an important point about words and definitions. As you can see from this argument, the argument between Nate and Matt stems from their interpretation of words such as "control" and "motivation." It is in arguments such as these that definitions become really tricky. For instance, consider the word "control" in the previous argument. You can see that Nate and Matt seem to be defining this word in two different, but legitimate, ways. Nate believes a person has control when he can act differently if he chooses to do so, while Matt seems to define control as wanting to do what he should do when he should do it. That is, Nate believes Matt has control over whether or not he plays video games for five hours because he could have stopped playing if he chose to do so. Matt, on the other hand, believes that he did not have control because he wanted to play video games more than he wanted to study. Therefore, although Matt and Nate's different definitions of control are legitimate, their legitimacy actually complicates, rather than settles, the argument.

As a final example of a verbal dispute, consider the following scenario. Imagine that two people—James and Emma—have been dating during their senior year of high school, but they plan to go to different colleges after they graduate. James really cares about Emma, but he is a chivalrous guy. He wants Emma to be able to fully experience college and not worry about taking the time to see him on the weekends. Furthermore, he knows Emma is very smart and can go far in college, and he doesn't want the emotional complications of their relationship to get in the way of her excelling in college. Therefore, James convinces himself that it will benefit Emma if he breaks up with her, at least for their time at college. As you can imagine, if Emma really cares about James, she is not likely to see this break in their relationship as a benefit. And, in fact, if James and Emma were to have an argument over whether or not breaking up before college is a benefit to Emma, they are likely to run into several difficulties because the word "benefit" has so many different meanings in our language. For instance, look at just a few of the most common uses of the word "benefit":

- Her parents' love of books was a great *benefit* to her as she was growing up.

- He *benefited* by cheating on his income taxes.

- The chemotherapy, though it made her horribly sick, *benefited* her.

Although we can see how the word "benefit" certainly implies some kind of advantage in each of these sentences, it is also clear that it can be used in many different, even opposing, contexts. After all, in the first sentence, the word "benefit" is obviously coupled with something, such as a love of books, that would unanimously be considered a good thing in our culture. Then in the next sentence, we have the word "benefit" coupled with an action that is unanimously considered wrong—cheating on income taxes. In the final sentence, the word "benefit" is linked with horrible sickness as a result of a treatment, which is bad, but that bad thing is actually something that leads to some type of good. As you can see, the word "benefit" is not as straightforward as it may first appear. Because it can be used in so many different types of contexts, it can cause problems in arguments, although it is a perfectly legitimate word to use.

These examples demonstrate that it is highly important to define your words well because even simple words can carry a lot of different meanings and can add layers of complexity and potential misunderstanding to even simple debates. Because of this, in the next few lessons, you are going to learn the most common and useful definition devices that can be used in clarifying your own main terms, as well as in understanding other people's terms. Before we begin exploring those devices, let's take a look at a list of guidelines for constructing effective word definitions. These rules can be divided into two categories: four rules about the *content* of the definition and three rules about the *language* used to create the definition.

The key content rules for definitions are as follows:

Rule 1: As much as possible, the definition should contain the essential primary characteristics, not the secondary accidental characteristics, of the term. This rule can actually be a difficult one to follow completely, because the question of what those essential characteristics are can be a difficult one. However, there are certainly some primary characteristics that people can generally agree upon. For example, if we were to define a "house," we would say that its primary characteristics are that it is a building with

four walls and a roof in which human beings dwell. The fact that some houses are small, some are large, some are brick, some are wood, some are white, some are brown, some are expensive, and some are cheap are all secondary accidental characteristics, so we would not include those characteristics in the definition of "house."

Rule 2: The definition should not be circular. One of the most common ways in which a definition can be circular is if it contains the word being defined in the definition. Thus, if we were to define the verb "hasten" as "to act with haste," it would be unlikely that others would find our definition very helpful. Therefore, one of the best ways to follow this rule is to avoid defining a word with that word itself. Always use other examples and synonyms to define the word. For example, consider the word "cheater." If we defined the word "cheater" as "someone who cheats on a test," this would be a circular definition because the word "cheat" is a form of "cheater," and so our definition doesn't really clarify the word. Instead, a better definition for the word "cheater" would be something like this: "Someone who deceives by trickery or swindle."[3] This is a much better definition because it shows what a cheater does without using the word "cheat" in the definition itself. It is important to note that many times dictionary definitions use circular definitions along with various other definitions. This is because one thing that dictionary definitions do is show different forms of words. Therefore, a dictionary might define a cheater as "one who cheats" because it is showing that both "cheater" and "cheat" are forms of the same word. Therefore, while it is often good to start with a dictionary to help you define a word, you may have to consult other sources eventually to construct a proper definition. (We will discuss these other sources later.)

Rule 3: The definition should not be too broad or too narrow. For example, it would be inappropriate to define "woman" as "a human being with long hair," because not all women have long hair, and, therefore, this definition is too narrow. (Note: This definition also breaks rule 1.) However, if you defined "woman" as "a female," this would be too broad, because there are female dogs, peacocks, and frogs, and these are certainly not women. Instead, a proper definition for the word "woman" should be broad enough to include all possible kinds of female humans; however, it should be narrow enough that it excludes non-human

females. One of the definitions for "woman" in Merriam-Webster Online Dictionary is "an adult female person," a definition that satisfies both of these requirements.[4]

Rule 4: The definition should prefer positive comparisons to negative ones. Most of the time, it's hard to get much use from a definition that only tells you what something is not. Thus, a definition of "table" as "a piece of furniture that isn't a chair" would be distinctly unhelpful. (Remember from our discussion about syllogisms that you can't figure out what something is from just knowing what it isn't.) After all, there are many pieces of furniture that are not tables but are also not chairs. For instance, a couch is neither a table nor a chair. A refrigerator is neither a table nor a chair. A much better definition for a table would be: "A piece of furniture consisting of a smooth, flat slab fixed on legs."[5] Notice that this definition is positive, rather than negative. It tells what a table is, rather than what a table is not. However, there are some exceptions to this rule. For example, a definition of "fallacy" as "an argument that does not follow the rules of sound reasoning" would be fairly acceptable, even though it is a negative definition. As another example, consider this definition of "pacifist:" "Someone who does not fight in wars because of personal beliefs." Even though this is not a complete definition for pacifist, it is fairly accurate. The point is that there are some things or people whose essence is, actually, what they are not or what they do not do, such as a fallacy and a pacifist. In these cases, using a negative definition may be an acceptable definition technique.

The previous four rules pertain to content. The following are the key language rules:

Rule 5: The definition should be clear. This rule should be fairly self-explanatory: A definition should differentiate what is being defined from other things and should also avoid ambiguity. For instance, remember that Nate and Tiffany had an argument over the meaning of the word "early." Since words like "early" can have a wide range of meanings to different people, it is wise to avoid them when you are formulating your arguments. Other ambiguous words similar to "early" are "good," "bad," "nice," and "beneficial."

Rule 6: The definition should avoid unnecessarily emotive language. A definition that is emotive is called a **persuasive definition** and is actually a rhetorical, or speech,

device that can slant an argument, usually in an unfair manner. A good arguer should try to avoid such slanting tactics whenever possible. For example, consider someone who is arguing that school destroys students' individuality. Imagine if the person offered the following definition of school: "School is a controlling and repressive institution that manufactures cookie-cutter robots by forcing students to conform to culturally accepted standards." As you can see, a definition like this is blatantly emotive and biased. Furthermore, it pretty much guarantees that there is no possibility of reasonable discussion. No matter how strongly you feel in favor of or against an idea you are debating, it is wise to establish a neutral, objective definition from which you can make further points. Therefore, avoid emotive language as much as possible when creating your definitions.

Rule 7: The definition should define the term as the correct part of speech. This is a common mistake that many young logic students make. For example, students who have this problem with definitions might define the fallacy of illicit major this way: "Talking about all of a term in the predicate of the conclusion when you have only talked about some of the term in the premise." You will notice that this student has actually taken something that is a noun and defined it as if it were a verb. A better definition of this fallacy would be: "A fallacy that occurs when the predicate term of a conclusion in a syllogism is distributed, although that same term is undistributed in the premises." Another example of this problem would be if someone defined the verb "scold" as this: "A lecture intended to improve someone's behavior." As you can see, this definition is a definition for a noun. In fact, this would be the proper definition of the noun form of the word "scold," which is "scolding." However, since "scold" is the verb form, the definition should also be in the verb form, like this: "To lecture with the intent to improve someone's behavior." One way you can avoid breaking this rule is to avoid using the word "when" in your definition. For instance, imagine if someone defined a "table" as: "When you have a flat slab on top of four legs." As you can see, a table is not "when" anything. It is a thing—a noun. Although using "when" in a definition may be appropriate for some words (adverbs, for instance), often when students use it, they are defining a word as the wrong part of speech.

Therefore, it is better to avoid using "when" in definitions if at all possible.

Learning to use proper definition techniques will certainly head off a lot of unnecessary disputes, but it is also important for avoiding and detecting a more subtle source of many definitional disputes: equivocation. The first syllogism rule you learned is that there are three—and only three—terms in a syllogism. However, as we discussed previously in this book, sometimes it can seem as though a syllogism has only three terms in it, but it actually has four terms because one of the terms is used in two different ways. When a syllogism has a term like this, we say that the syllogism *equivocates* with the term. Remember that the word "equivocate" comes from two Latin words meaning "to call equally." Therefore, an **equivocating term** is one term used to refer to two different ideas. (While equivocation is actually a validity problem, it also pertains to definitions, so we will discuss it in this chapter as we are dealing with the soundness of arguments.)

It may seem as though it would be very difficult to commit this formal fallacy and get away with it. After all, no one is going to call both a cat and a dog a cat, for example. These are two obviously different animals. However, if you think about the illustrations that we used at the beginning of this lesson, you will recall that sometimes we use terms, such as "benefit," in very different ways in everyday conversation. If we are not careful with these fine shades of meaning, it can be easy to equivocate. For instance, consider the following syllogism, which equivocates with the word "benefit":

No benefits are destructive activities.

Chemotherapy is beneficial.

Therefore, no chemotherapy is destructive.

Most people would probably agree with the premises of this syllogism, but most people would disagree with the conclusion. This is a valid, *EAE-1* syllogism, and the premises are factually correct. So if the premises are correct, and it is a valid syllogism, where is the problem? If you analyze the syllogism carefully, you will soon discover that it equivocates with the word "benefit." In the first premise, the word "benefit" is used to refer to things that bring us happiness or blessing. In the second premise, it is used to

mean something that helps in the long run (even if it is painful, and even destructive, in the short run). Therefore, this is actually an invalid syllogism because it commits the fallacy of four terms, which in this case is equivocation. It is important to keep an eye out for equivocation whenever you are arguing deductively. Sometimes, the different definitions of words are so subtle that people can commit the fallacy of equivocation without intending to, and, in fact, this can cause valid and seemingly sound syllogisms to imply problematic conclusions.

Though it may seem as though defining words properly is a very easy task, it can be tricky because words take on a lot of different nuances as they are used in everyday conversation. Learning how to define words properly, as well as how to detect the definitions behind your opponent's key terms, will help you to handle these disputes. Now that you have examined some general rules that can guide you in constructing definitions, in the next lesson, you will look at a few types of common definitions.

REVIEW
DEFINE

1. Definitional Dispute:

_____

_____

_____

2. Equivocation:

_____

_____

_____

FILL IN THE BLANK

Reviewing the Seven Definition Rules: Each of the following sentences represents one of the seven definition rules. Fill in the blanks with the appropriate word or words to complete the sentence.

1. The key content rules for definitions are:

    Rule 1: As much as possible, the definition should contain the _____ _____ characteristics, not the _____ _____ characteristics, of the term.

    Rule 2: The definition should not be _____.

    Rule 3: The definition should not be too _____ or too _____.

    Rule 4: The definition should prefer _____ comparisons to _____ ones.

2. The key language rules for definitions are:

    Rule 5: The definition should be _____.

    Rule 6: The definition should avoid unnecessarily _____ _____.

    Rule 7: The definition should define the term as the correct part of _____.

See if you can identify which of the seven rules each of these definitions breaks. Be sure to explain how the definition breaks the rule(s). (Note: A definition could break more than one rule.)

IDENTIFY

1. Rotation: The action of rotating.

Rule(s) Broken: _____

Explanation:

_____

_____

_____

2. Dog: A floppy-eared, carnivorous animal.

Rule(s) Broken: _____

Explanation:

_____

_____

_____

3. Foot: A unit of measurement that isn't as big as a yard.

Rule(s) Broken: _____

Explanation:

_____

_____

_____

4. Starvation: Not being fed enough.

Rule(s) Broken: _____

Explanation:

_____

_____

_____

IDENTIFY (CONTINUED)

5. Democratic Party: The brave party of the working poor.

Rule(s) Broken: _____

Explanation:

_____

_____

_____

6. Republican Party: The political party of liberty, justice, and the American way.

Rule(s) Broken: _____

Explanation:

_____

_____

_____

7. Catapult: A military machine.

Rule(s) Broken: _____

Explanation:

_____

_____

_____

CREATE

Using Definition Techniques: *For each of the following words, create a definition that adheres to the seven definition rules. Write your definition first. Then, look up the word in the dictionary and write the dictionary definition down to see how your definition compares.*

1. School:

Your Definition:

_____

_____

_____

Dictionary Definition:

_____

_____

CREATE (CONTINUED)

2. Neighbor:

Your Definition:

_____

_____

_____

Dictionary Definition:

_____

_____

_____

3. Holiday:

Your Definition:

_____

_____

_____

Dictionary Definition:

_____

_____

_____

4. Book:

Your Definition:

_____

_____

_____

Dictionary Definition:

_____

_____

_____

CREATE (CONTINUED)

5. Lock:

Your Definition:

_____

_____

_____

Dictionary Definition:

_____

_____

_____

_____

ANSWER

Argument Analysis: *Hopefully by now you are beginning to understand how important it is to properly define key words in arguments and debates. The following exercise will help you continue to explore this concept. First, answer the question at the beginning of this dialogue. Then, read the dialogue and answer the questions at the end.*

1. How would you define the word "friend"?

_____

_____

Friends, Puppies, and Bank Robberies

Julie: I've decided that the man I marry has to be my best friend. He needs to support me in all my decisions and always take my side when I have arguments with other people. He also needs to encourage me to do whatever makes me happy.

Tiffany: Wait, that doesn't sound like a friend. That sounds like a pet. I think you mean that you want a husband who is like a puppy that will follow you around and be at your beck and call.

Julie: That's harsh. What's wrong with wanting a best friend who supports you in everything you do?

Tiffany: Well, I don't think a best friend should support you in *everything* you do. I mean, what if you decided to rob a bank? Shouldn't a true friend tell you that you are out of your mind and about to ruin your life?

Julie: Oh, come on, Tiffany. That's an absurd example. I'm never going to rob a bank.

Tiffany: Probably not, but don't you think it's possible that you'll do something wrong someday?

Julie: Well, of course. Everyone does.

ANSWER (CONTINUED)

Tiffany: Well, then, don't you think a best friend should call you on it? If a friend is really a friend, he should tell you when you are being an idiot, shouldn't he?

Julie: No, I don't see it that way. I think a friend should always love and support you.

Tiffany: Boy, I think you and I have really different ideas of the words "friend" and "love."

1. How do Julie and Tiffany define the word "friend" differently?

_____

_____

_____

_____

_____

2. Look up the word "friend" in the dictionary, and in the space provided below, write at least three of the definitions you find. Which definition, Julie's or Tiffany's, seems to best fit the dictionary definition of friend? Do they both match definitions from the dictionary?

_____

_____

_____

_____

_____

_____

_____

_____

_____

ANSWER (CONTINUED)

3. Which definition of "friend," Julie's or Tiffany's, do you believe is the more accurate definition? Why?

_____

_____

_____

_____

_____

_____

_____

_____

_____

_____

DEDUCTION IN ACTION
Defining Love

In this chapter, we are exploring the proposition "To be a good friend, a person must love himself or herself the most." Eventually, you will craft a deductive argument that argues for or against this premise. Answer the following questions as a way of further exploring your thoughts on this proposition.

1. How do you define the verb form of "love"?

2. List two common definitions of the noun form of the word "love."

LESSON 9.4
Types of Definitions

POINTS TO REMEMBER

1. A **lexical definition** is a definition from the dictionary.
2. A **theoretical definition** is a definition proposed by a certain school of thought.
3. A **précising definition** reduces ambiguity and shows how a word is used in the world.
4. A **stipulative definition** is a definition that is created on the spot in order to add more clarity.

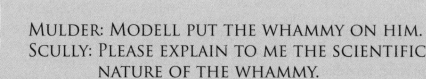

> MULDER: MODELL PUT THE WHAMMY ON HIM.
> SCULLY: PLEASE EXPLAIN TO ME THE SCIENTIFIC
> NATURE OF THE WHAMMY.
> —FROM *THE X FILES*[1]

"Look it up in the dictionary." How many of us have inquired after the meaning of a word, only to have a teacher or parent tell us this very thing? The dictionary is, indeed, a great place to start as you are trying to determine the definition of a term. After all, people who write dictionaries have spent a great deal of time studying the usage of words in everyday conversations, as well as the etymological origins and historical backgrounds of words. The dictionary definition of a word is called its lexical definition (another name for "dictionary" is "lexicon"). Since everyday word usage changes and has a good deal of flexibility, most dictionaries have more than one definition for each word. In fact, many words have, in common usage, more than one completely, at least seemingly, unrelated definition. Ascertaining a term's intended meaning is often an important endeavor. After all, a lexical definition reflects how the word is used in everyday life.

It is important to note, however, that the dictionary is just one place people look to understand how to define a word in a debate. To be honest, because the space in the dictionary is limited, lexical definitions often have to be very limited and do not always represent the full meanings of words as they are used in all possible contexts. Therefore, it is important to understand several other types of definitions and where they can be found.

One of the most common definitions is a theoretical definition. A theoretical definition tries to characterize something's fundamental nature. It naturally assumes a certain philosophical view of that word. It is not likely that you, as a student, will construct theoretical definitions because you are not necessarily familiar with different philosophical schools of thinking on certain subjects. However, it is good to know that this type of definition exists so that if you disagree with a person's definition, you will know that you may be quibbling with his or her theoretical use of the word. Theoretical definitions can be extremely complex. In fact, philosophers, scientists, theologians, and people in other fields of study can write entire essays, dissertations, and books surrounding the theoretical definition of a word.

To help you understand theoretical definitions better, consider a modern philosophic debate: Can computers think? To answer this question, people have to define the word "think." Before you read any further, stop and consider how *you* would define the word "think." Some philosophers have defined the essence of thought as being able to convince other human beings that thinking is occurring. Based on this definition, they argue that computers can think because it is possible to program a computer with such complexity that if someone is talking with a computer in another room and doesn't know it is a computer, that person could think that he was talking to a human being. As you can imagine, you are certainly not going to find this theoretical definition of "think" in the dictionary. Nevertheless, if you were arguing with someone about whether or not computers can think, and she defined "thought" with this particular definition, it would be necessary for you to know this definition in order to have any kind of discussion.

You have actually already been exposed to theoretical definitions in your reading of Plato's dialogue *Euthyphro*. Do you remember for what word Socrates was seeking a definition in this dialogue? It was the word "piety." You might recall that Euthyphro offered several theoretical definitions for the word "piety." The first definition Euthyphro offered for the word "piety" was what he was doing—prosecuting his father for murder. However, Socrates quickly demonstrated that this definition was an inadequate theoretical definition. Another definition he offered for piety was that piety is what the gods love, but Socrates disproved this. You may recall that Socrates and Euthyphro never actually settled on a theoretical definition of piety in this dialogue. However, this definition is what they were searching for because they were attempting to find a definition that would capture the essence of piety.

Consider one final example. In the book *The Myth of Religious Neutrality*, philosopher Roy Clouser defines "religion" as "an understanding of the Divine and of man's relationship to it."[2] It is interesting that Clouser's theoretical definition of the word "religion" is worded in such a way that it could include an atheistic idea of the cosmos because although they do not believe that God exists, atheists certainly have an understanding of the divine and of man's relationship to it. This is a novel definition for the word "religion," since most people use this word to refer to a system of beliefs in God, gods, or some kind of spiritual reality governed by an absolute entity. Therefore, you can see that if someone wanted to dispute the key ideas or claims in Clouser's book, he would certainly want to understand Clouser's theoretical definition of the word "religion" because any conclusion Clouser makes about religion will be significantly affected by this definition.

You can probably see that the theoretical definitions used in logic often intersect with other fields of study, such as science, philosophy (particularly the branch of philosophy called metaphysics), and politics. Obviously, you cannot be aware of every possible theoretical definition someone may bring into an argument. However, it is important to note that people often use theoretical definitions that differ widely. If you sense during an argument that someone is using a term in a manner very different from common usage, it is likely he is using a theoretical definition, and you simply need to ask him to explain how he is defining the word. Furthermore, if you ever build an argument on a theoretical definition with which the common person is unfamiliar, be sure to explain the definition you are using.

Another kind of common definition is the précising (prey-SEE-ing) definition. A précising definition is one that is designed to reduce vagueness. A term is vague if it is unclear to which examples and/or situations it applies. When it is unclear to which cases a certain term applies, those cases are known as **borderline cases**. Précising definitions can clear up such cases. Definitions that reduce the vagueness of a term and demonstrate to which examples or situation a term applies are called précising definitions because they define clearly and exactly what that term means and in which situations it should be used. For example, we know that in the area of politics, different political parties often discuss issues pertaining to the rich and the poor. When, for instance, the Democrats refer to a Republican desire to have tax cuts for the rich, the Republicans are likely to respond that their proposed tax cuts are even more beneficial for the middle class or even the working poor. It can get very confusing if the two parties make the claim that their policies, which are very different, both help the middle class or the poor working class. As you can see, terms like "rich" and "poor" are often used in a vague manner, and one person's idea of who is

poor or rich may be completely different from another person's idea of who is poor or rich.

In cases like this, it would be helpful for these groups to use précising definitions to clarify what they mean by "middle class" and "poor." As you can imagine, the dictionary is not going to be helpful in this type of situation because it will offer a general definition for these two words, whereas this type of debate calls for extremely precise and specific definitions of these two words based on a specific dollar figure. For instance, some social agencies have been able to determine the minimum income a person in the United States must have in order for their basic survival needs—food, clothing, and shelter—to be met. These social agencies give the précising definition to the word "poor" as anyone who falls below this specific income level.

Précising definitions are very common and useful in the area of law. To ensure how the courts will interpret laws, key terms are often carefully defined within statutes. For example, in the U.S. criminal code, two different forms of theft from a bank are carefully distinguished and defined. "Bank robbery" involves theft through "force or coercion," whereas "bank larceny" involves theft without the use of force or coercion.[3] Since the two offenses have different penalties (violent crimes are generally punished more harshly), this is a very important distinction for judges and lawyers to understand.

A good précising definition succeeds in its goal of increasing clarity and/or aiding in interpretation. Once again, it is not necessary for you to know every possible précising definition for a certain debate. It is only necessary for you to understand that a person may be basing an argument on a précising definition or you yourself may need to use a précising definition for a term in your own argument.

The last type of general definition technique we want to cover is a stipulative definition, which is a definition arbitrarily suggested for a particular word. This definition of stipulative definitions can be a little confusing, so we want to be precise about what we mean when we say that stipulative definitions arbitrarily assign a definition to a word. After all, this sounds like a shady thing to do in an argument. For example, let's say that someone wanted to argue that cats are incredibly loud, noisy animals and then

assigns a stipulative definition to cats as creatures that bark and growl. This seems to match the idea of a stipulative definition—a meaning being arbitrarily assigned to a word. However, everyone will realize that this is a ridiculous and dishonest thing to do in an argument. This is not what we mean by the term "stipulative definition."

To help you better understand what a stipulative definition is, it may be helpful for you to understand two reasons for using these types of definitions. The first reason to use a stipulative definition is to define a new word. For instance, we often need new words to name newly discovered objects, new inventions, or to name a concept that is either new or that could be referred to more efficiently if a new name were selected for it. For example, in the past, the word "typewriter" was created as the new name for an invention that allowed someone to write mechanically in type. Lately, the term "worldview" has become common to describe someone's general philosophy of life. You can certainly see how the term "worldview" is much easier to use in a conversation than "general philosophy of life."

A humorous example of a stipulative definition comes from an episode of the show *Gilmore Girls*, which originally aired on the WB network. One of the main characters of this show, Lorelai Gilmore, loves takeout food and is especially good at finding excellent takeout joints. The first night she takes her daughter, Rory, to college, she invites a bunch of Rory's floormates over to sample takeout food from all over the city so that they can determine which of the takeout restaurants are the best. The next morning, Rory's floormates bring her coffee and tell her that they "Lorelaied" the best coffee place on campus.[4] As you can see, these girls created a new word: the verb "Lorelai." Then they provided a stipulative definition for their verb: "to scope out and find the best takeout joints." Although this is a humorous example of the creation of a new word and a definition to go along with it, this is, essentially, how the process works in real life when people create new words and stipulative definitions to go along with them.

Sometimes in a debate, you are discussing a concept for which no word exists or that has a definition with which you are unfamiliar. In such a case, you may have to create an appropriate term and assign a stipulative definition to

it. A stipulative definition of this type is not in itself either right or wrong; it should be treated as a suggestion for assigning meaning to a word. Sometimes you have to do this to clarify a term so that both people involved in the argument can proceed in a more informed manner. For example, consider a later discussion that Julie and Tiffany had about love and husbands:

Julie: Hey, Tiffany, I was thinking about our conversation about love and friendship and husbands that we had the other day, and I think I thought of a way to express my thoughts better.

Tiffany: Cool. I'm interested in hearing your ideas.

Julie: Well, I learned this word in English class the other day: "ameliorate." It means "to make better."

Tiffany: OK, I'm with you so far.

Julie: Well, I've created a new word phrase to help define the type of love about which I have been talking. The kind of love that I want my husband to have is "ameliorative love." What I mean by "ameliorative love" is the kind of love that will make me a better person.

Tiffany: Well, that makes sense so far, but if your husband had "ameliorative love" for you, wouldn't he tell you if you were doing something wrong, rather than taking your side?

Julie: Well, I don't see it that way. In my past experience, just lecturing someone about what she is doing wrong doesn't make her a better person. In fact, it often just makes her more stubborn and stuck in her ways. But if my husband had ameliorative love for me, he would make me a better person by talking with me, supporting and being patient with me, and helping me see the error of my ways by sticking with me as I learned from my mistakes. This is the kind of love that makes a person better, rather than making her stubborn.

Tiffany: Well, I guess if you define "ameliorative love" in that manner, your argument makes sense. I still don't know if I totally agree with it, but it definitely makes more sense.

As you can see, when Julie created a new term— "ameliorative love"—and provided a definition for it—"love that makes a person better"—it helped her to communicate better with Tiffany. This is often the case with stipulative definitions.

Another reason for using a stipulative definition would be to stipulate a specific definition, meaning that you would employ a stipulative definition in the case of a word that has more than one definition. In this case, the definition is being used to reduce ambiguity. Problems sometimes occur when people use terms in their arguments that are ambiguous, or which have more than one possible correct meaning. Clarifying ambiguity always clarifies discussions. Sometimes, the way you do this is to explain what you mean by an ambiguous term. When you do this, you are assigning a stipulative definition to a term to reduce ambiguity. For instance, think back to the argument Nate and Tiffany had about the word "early." If Nate had clearly stipulated what he meant by the word "early," the disagreement would not have occurred. Stipulative definitions can help to simplify an argument.

As you can imagine, the type of general definition technique you use depends on the topic under discussion. If you are arguing about a generally well-established, simple topic, you will likely use a lexical definition. If you are arguing about a more abstract topic, the key words of which appear in many different contexts, you may need to use a précising or theoretical definition. If you are arguing about a topic that has many different interpretations, you may need to use a stipulative definition in order to establish the particular interpretation from which you are arguing. It is equally important to be aware of the type of definitions your opponent is using in any given argument. Because you may need to create terms and assign stipulative definitions in a debate, or analyze someone else's stipulative definitions, in the next lesson you will learn how to create definitions that are clear, precise, and thorough.

DEFINE

1. Lexical Definition:

_____

_____

_____

2. Theoretical Definition:

_____

_____

_____

_____

3. Précising Definition:

_____

_____

_____

_____

4. Stipulative Definition:

_____

_____

_____

_____

EXAMINE

Examining Theoretical Definitions: *When people create theoretical definitions, they propose definitions that capture the essence of a word or a concept. As you can imagine, sometimes this is very tricky to do and can lead to a lot of controversy, especially when people propose several different theoretical definitions for the same word. In the following exercises, you will see several words for which people have proposed various theoretical definitions over the years. For this exercise, pretend you are a philosopher or specialist who is attempting to create a theoretical definition that captures the essence of the word. In the space provided, write at least two different definitions for the word that demonstrate two different theoretical perspectives.*

1. Educated Person:

_____

_____

_____

_____

_____

EXAMINE (CONTINUED)

2. Obscenity:

_____

_____

_____

_____

_____

3. Green (as it applies to products considered environmentally sound):

_____

_____

_____

_____

_____

4. Justice:

_____

_____

_____

_____

_____

EXPLORE

Exploring Précising Definitions of Crime: *Throughout history, societies have attempted to provide précising definitions for the word "crime" so that they can be just and fair in meting out punishment to criminals. For example, for many years in England, courts sentenced people to death for all sorts of crimes from petty theft to heinous murder. Eventually, many people started to believe that death was too harsh a penalty for some crimes, and so they began to create different classifications of crimes so that the punishment would fit the crime, so to speak. The American justice system is highly influenced by the British legal system. Check the links below and read about the précising definitions courts, judges, and lawyers have created in order to apply justice more appropriately. After you read this information, write a précising definition for the words "misdemeanor" and "felony." In your definitions, you should define each word precisely so that it is clear how they are different from each other.*

<http://capress.link/dd0901>

<http://capress.link/dd0902>.

EXPLORE (CONTINUED)

1. Misdemeanor:

_____

_____

_____

2. Felony:

_____

_____

_____

CREATE

1. What if you were debating whether or not a healthy diet is important for every teenager? Create a stipulative definition for "a healthy diet."

_____

_____

_____

_____

2. Imagine you are debating this proposition: Lying is never right. Create a stipulative definition for "lying."

_____

_____

_____

3. Consider if you wanted to make an argument based on the following proposition: Arrogance is always a bad quality in a person. Provide a stipulative definition for "arrogance."

_____

_____

_____

DEDUCTION IN ACTION
Love, Friendship, and Aristotle

Believe it or not, Aristotle himself pondered the very proposition we are considering in this chapter. In the excerpt below, read Aristotle's summary of the two views of the matter and then answer the questions that follow.

> The question is also debated, whether a man should love himself most, or someone else. People criticize those who love themselves most and call them self-lovers, using this as an epithet* of disgrace, and a bad man seems to do everything for his own sake, and the more so the more wicked he is—and so men reproach him, for instance, with doing nothing of his own accord—while the good man acts for honor's sake, and the more so the better he is, and acts for his friend's sake and sacrifices his own interest.
>
> But the facts clash with these arguments, and this is not surprising. For men say that one ought to love best one's best friend, and a man's best friend is one who wishes well to the object of his wish for his sake, even if no one is to know of it; and these attributes are found most of all in a man's attitude toward himself, and so are all the other attributes by which a friend is defined. . . . All the proverbs, too, agree with this, e.g. "a single soul," and "what friends have is common property," and "friendship is equality," and "charity begins at home"; for all these marks will be found most in a man's relation to himself; he is his own best friend and therefore ought to love himself best. It is therefore a reasonable question, which of the two views we should follow, for both are plausible?[5]

*Epithet: A name associated with a person; a curse.

1. In the first paragraph, Aristotle says that people who love themselves most are criticized by others. What reason does Aristotle give for people criticizing people who love themselves most?

2. In the second paragraph, Aristotle critiques the idea that self-lovers are wicked people and, instead, says that there is evidence that good people love themselves best and that this is right to do. What explanation does he give for this view?

3. In the space provided below, write a summarizing syllogism for both of the two views presented here by Aristotle.

4. Now that you have examined two different ways of looking at this issue, courtesy of Aristotle, take a minute to think about which viewpoint you favor more. That is, do you think it's right or wrong for a person to love himself or herself best? Explain your answer. Make sure you have a specific reason or example to back up your answer.

LESSON 9.5
Extension vs. Intention

POINTS TO REMEMBER

1. There are both extensive and intensive definitional techniques.
2. The extension of a term is the sum total of all of the members of that class.
3. The intension of a term is the sum total of qualities that identify which entities are members of that class.

> SPOCK: FASCINATING IS A WORD I USE FOR THE UNEXPECTED. IN THIS CASE, I SHOULD THINK 'INTERESTING' WOULD SUFFICE.
> —"THE SQUIRE OF GOTHOS"[1]

In the last lesson, we discussed several broad categories of definitions: lexical, theoretic, précising, and stipulative. We also mentioned that often when you are in a debate, you must create stipulative definitions, either because you need to create a new term to clarify a concept in the debate or because you must clarify an ambiguous term already present in the debate. In order to help you understand how such an instance would unfold, let's look at a dialogue Matt and Nate had one afternoon about a certain aspect of the environmental movement.

Matt: I have to say, Nate, this whole environmental movement is really getting on my nerves. It's a total fad and people are just joining it to be cool. We should all just ignore the environmental people; maybe they'll go away.

Nate: Could you clarify what you mean by the term "environmental movement," or could you clarify exactly what part of it annoys you? After all, it's a pretty big movement, and sometimes people who are involved with one part of it, such as protecting endangered species, aren't necessarily involved in another part of it, such as advocating for sustainable agricultural practices.

Matt: Yeah, you're right. I should be clearer. By "environmental movement," I mean the "save the earth people."

Nate: Again, you are going to have to be a little clearer. That phrase is still really broad.

Matt: OK, when I say "save the earth people," I mean the people who tell us we have to stop driving cars and eating so much beef because both cars and cows put out dangerous gases into the air. I guess I'm talking about the people who believe that a crisis is imminent because of global warming, and so we all have to radically change our lives or we'll all die.

Nate: So, right now, you are criticizing people who want to make possibly drastic changes in our lives, such as driving less, inventing more fuel-efficient cars, regulating industrial pollution, and changing other things that contribute to global warming, right?

Matt: Yes, those are all good examples.

Nate: And you say that these "save the earth people" are getting on your nerves right now because they do what they do because it's a fad. That is, it's currently popular to want to save the earth, and, therefore, they are saving the earth to be popular, correct?

Matt: Well, not all of them, but most of them. Yes, that's what I mean.

Nate: Does this mean that you think we shouldn't do things if they are popular? For instance, if voting in a presidential election becomes popular, we shouldn't do it, or if helping little old ladies across the street is popular, we shouldn't do it because it is popular?

Matt: Well, no. I guess I think people are fighting global warming because it's popular, not because it's been proven that it is really happening. I don't think we should make such big lifestyle changes that could drastically affect us, and even cost us lots of money, if there's no proof the thing is happening.

Nate: What do you mean by the word "proven"? For instance, someone can say, "I can *prove* I have a worse scar than you," and then show you his leg. Or someone can say, "I can *prove* that Frankfort is the capital of Kentucky," and then point out this fact in a book. Or someone could say, "I can *prove* I can juggle," and then do it. Do you mean "prove" in the sense of showing it, such as with the examples of juggling or looking a fact up in a book, or do you mean something else by the word "prove"?

Matt: Well, I mean that scientists haven't been able to demonstrate conclusively that global warming is happening and that it is happening because of the fumes and gases humans are putting into the air.

Nate: When you say scientists haven't demonstrated conclusively that global warming is happening and

that human beings are doing it, I am wondering what you mean by the word "conclusive."

Matt: By "conclusive," I mean evidence that is scientifically tested and proven to be 100 percent certain—like gravity.

Nate: I see. So what you are saying is that you get annoyed by people who join a movement and try to influence other people in a certain way because the movement is popular, rather than because its beliefs have been proven 100 percent certain, as gravity has been proven.

Matt: I guess that's what I mean.

This discussion is a good example of a discussion two people might have in everyday life. You will notice that even though Matt was using fairly common words, such as "environmental movement," "prove," and "conclusive," it was crucial for his discussion with Nate that he *stipulated* his meaning for those terms. If he hadn't done this, it would have been impossible for him to discuss these issues with Nate. After all, as Nate mentioned, the environmental movement has many different facets, and if Nate thought Matt was discussing one aspect of the movement, but Matt was actually discussing another aspect of the movement, this wouldn't have been helpful for either of them in pursuing the truth.

When two people are discussing a matter, it is common and important for them to stipulate definitions for different terms in the discussion. Because this is the case, the question becomes, "How do you create a definition that is accurate and relevant to the discussion at hand?" As you will remember, in categorical logic, we are focusing our efforts at definition on words (or terms) that represent categories of things. When examining the meaning of these terms or trying to construct an appropriate definition, logicians often distinguish between two different types of meaning: **extension** (also called **denotation**) and **intension** (also called **connotation**). Both of these types of meaning are very important to understand when defining words properly, as well as when you are trying to understand other people's definitions. Therefore, before we look at the specific definition techniques you can use, it is important for you to understand the difference between extension and intension.

"Extension" (or denotation) is the first term we will examine. The extension of a term is the sum total of all of the members of that class. In a sense, the extension of a term is the *breadth* of that term. A term can be said to have great extension if the class that it represents has a great many members. Thus, the class "human" has a greater extension than the class "Pennsylvanian" because there are far fewer items in the class "Pennsylvanian" than there are in the class "human." In much the same way, the class "animal" has a greater extension than the class "Siberian tiger." In fact, if we were to go through the various members of this class in between these two classes in order of increasing extension, it could look something like this: Siberian tiger, tiger, great cat, feline, carnivore, mammal, animal.

As another example, consider the term "environmental movement," a term Matt used in the dialogue at the beginning of the lesson. This has much less extension than the general term "social movement" because there are all kinds of social movements: prohibition, abolition, feminism, civil rights, etc. In contrast, the environmental movement, though it may have different facets and sub-movements within it, is just one movement, meaning that it has much less extension than the term "social movement" does. Let's consider the word "friend," which we defined in a previous lesson, as another example. The word "friend" has a smaller extension than, for example, the word "acquaintance." The class "acquaintance" can contain enemies, mortal enemies, friends, associates, neighbors, third cousins, and so on. On the other hand, the class "friend" cannot contain enemies and some of the other terms in the class "acquaintance," such as third cousins and associates, unless you have a pleasant, familiar, and productive relationship with these people.

When you are attempting to determine the extension of a word, you may be able to figure it out on your own. For instance, if you were trying to determine the extension of the word "vehicle," you could probably think up all, or most, of the different types of vehicles. On the other hand, if you were trying to think of the extension for a word such as "vertebrate," you might not be able to recall many of the items that make up the extension of this word. Therefore, you might need to consult a source, such as a dictionary or encyclopedia. It's important to realize that when you are providing an extensive definition for a word,

it is not necessary to list every single example that makes up the extension of that word. Instead, providing three to five examples is often sufficient. Listing a few examples is satisfactory because the purpose of an extensive definition is to provide some examples that clarify what kind of thing you are talking about, rather than constructing a comprehensive list of all possible examples of that term. Therefore, when you construct an extensive definition of a term, it is perfectly fine to think of them yourself or to consult a dictionary or encyclopedia to find several good examples.

If the extension of a term is the sum total of all of the members of a class, the intension[2] (or connotation[3]) of a word is the sum total of qualities that identify which entities are members of that class. A term can be said to have great intension if that list of qualities is very specific. Note that *the greater the intension of a term, the less its extension and vice versa.* This makes sense, because the more specific you are about what qualities define a class, the smaller that class will be. Thus, if we were to take one of the examples we used to explain extension and listed its classes in order of increasing *intention*, it would simply be reversed like this: animal, mammal, carnivore, feline, great cat, tiger, Siberian tiger.

In a sense, the intension of a term is the *depth* of it. As an example, consider the intension of the term "environmental movement." Characteristics of the environmental movement are that it is a social movement, it is focused on preserving and purifying the resources and habitats of the earth, and it promotes societal and individual changes that benefit the earth, such as recycling, reusing materials, and reducing consumption. It also has several different facets, such as reversing global warming, protecting endangered species, creating sustainable living communities, and promoting sustainable agricultural practices. If you notice, all of these words and phrases are describing what the environmental movement is. Rather than listing different parts or sub-movements in the environmental movement as an extensive definition would do, the intension of the phrase "environmental movement" attempts to broaden our view of what the environmental movement is by providing descriptive phrases and synonyms that illustrate it. This is the purpose of intensive definitions.

As another example, consider the word "friend." Its intension includes these items: a being (for both people and animals can be friends), acquaintance, kind feelings

and behavior, and interaction. In order for someone or something to be a friend, it must have all of these characteristics. You will notice that, once again, instead of listing types of friends, as an extensive definition would do, these intensive terms describe and illustrate the term more deeply so that we can gain a full picture of what it is, rather than what kinds of things or people fall under that term.

When you are creating new definitions, it's important to realize that because definitions have both extension and intension, there are different definition techniques that correspond to these two different modes of definition. That is, there are both **extensive definitions** and **intensive definitions**.

Extensive definitions list or point out examples of the term and, thus, give it a certain degree of concreteness. There are several different types of extensive definitions. One kind of extensive definition is the **ostensive** or **demonstrative definition** (from the Latin words *ostens*, meaning "display," and *demonstro*, meaning "I point out"). An ostensive definition is essentially what people do when they are teaching a new (or first) language: They point to something and give the word for it. Whenever people use ostensive definitions, they point to, or in some other way indicate, an example of a word. For example, if Matt and Nate had been watching a movie about global warming and then Matt stated that he was annoyed by the "save the earth people," he could have pointed to someone in the movie as an example of this type of person. As you can imagine, using ostensive definitions may not be an adequate definition technique because the object at which we point to serve as an example of a term may not fully represent that term. Therefore, it is usually wise to use ostensive definitions with other definitional techniques.

Another type of extensive definition is the **enumerative definition**, which is a listing of examples that illustrate the word you are trying to describe. For example, if Matt wanted to better explain what he meant by "save the earth people," he could have pointed out several prominent people who represent this type of person, such as former vice president Al Gore, writer Wendell Berry, and various high-profile movie stars, such as Leonardo DiCaprio, who support the environmental movement. This definition still would not have been fully adequate, but it would have painted a clearer picture for Nate.

The last type of extensive definition, **definition by subclass**, is a listing of various subclasses that fit into that class. This is a very helpful type of extensive definition to use for terms that have many different components or facets. For instance, you will remember that Nate asked Matt to use this technique to define what he meant by the term "environmental movement," because there are a lot of subclasses within this term. Matt, indeed, did this when he stipulated the anti–global warming movement as the subclass of the environmental movement to which he was referring. As a simpler example, consider that a definition by subclass of the term "vehicle" could include these terms: car, bus, train, boat, airplane, etc. As mentioned earlier when you were first introduced to extension, it is not necessary to list all possible subclasses of a term. Instead, it is adequate to use your life experience, a dictionary, an encyclopedia, or another reliable source to help you find several subclasses that illustrate a term.

As mentioned before, just as there are extensive definitions for a term, there are also intensive definitions. It is usually wise to use a combination of both of these types of definition techniques when you are defining a term. This is because using both extensive and intensive definitions together will give you a deeper, fuller understanding of the word. Intensive definitions will help you understand what a word is by providing description and explanation, while extensive definitions will give you examples of the word by listing specific instances of this word or pointing out items that fit into the category described by the word. Intensive definitions indicate what qualities should be assigned to a term.

One technique that can be used to create intensive definitions is **definition by synonym**, which supplies words that are the same as, or similar in meaning to, the original word you are trying to define. This is basically the approach taken by a thesaurus. For example, some synonyms for the term "environmental movement" are "green movement" and "sustainable movement." Matt could have used these synonyms to clarify his terminology, although he also would have needed to use other extensive and intensive definition techniques. If we wanted to think of synonyms for the word "friend," some good ones would be "pal," "comrade," "buddy," and "kindred spirit." For some words, you may already know several synonyms that you can use to create an intensive definition. However, if you do not already know

synonyms for a word, you can use a thesaurus to find them. Once again, it is not necessary to create an exhaustive list of synonyms—two or three will suffice.

Another type of intensive definition technique is the **operative definition**, which gives a set of procedures (or "operations") that can affirm if a term has the necessary qualities to fit into a given class. For instance, if Matt wanted to use a non-emotional operative definition to define the environmental movement, he might have said something like this: "The environmental movement is a social and cultural movement in which people advocate for behavioral changes in society and the individual that will protect and conserve the earth's resources, such as food, water, animals, and land." As you can see, this gives a procedure or a way in which people in the environmental movement operate to help us identify this movement more accurately. You can often develop an operational definition from your general knowledge of a term. However, if you do not know enough about a term to create an operational definition, you can consult a dictionary or encyclopedia to help you gather information that will help you construct this type of definition.

Sometimes, when you have a complex term, simply defining it with a synonym or with an operational definition is inadequate. In such an instance, another helpful definitional technique of intension would be **genus and difference**, a definitional technique that is often used by philosophers to create theoretical definitions. When we attempt to construct a definition from genus and difference, we start by saying what type of thing it is that we are describing or into what larger class it fits. Then, we name a feature that sets it apart from other things within that category. For example, the genus, or the larger group, of the environmental movement is "social movement." The feature that sets the environmental movement apart from other social movements is that it is focused on the preservation of the earth and its resources. This is its difference. The difference of a term is the distinguishing characteristics that set it apart from other terms in a genus.

Determining genus and difference is often a matter of common sense. That is, you can often figure out genus and difference just by thinking about the matter and determining to what larger category something belongs.

For example, if you are trying to figure out the genus of "car," it is a matter of common sense that a car is a type of vehicle. That is, the genus of "vehicle" is the genus to which the word "car" belongs. In addition, if you have the term "woman," it is a matter of common sense that the genus to which "woman" belongs is "human being." For words like this, it is pretty simple to determine the genus. However, consider the term "snail." Do you know to what genus a snail belongs? If you're like most people, you aren't totally sure. In this case, you could just do research on the Internet, in an encyclopedia, or in a dictionary to determine that snails are a part of the genus of "mollusk."

In the same way, determining difference is often a matter of common sense. For example, let's say you were trying to determine the difference of the term "woman" and you asked yourself, "What is it that sets women apart from other human beings?" You would probably be able to list several characteristics, such as that women are female and they are adults. You could probably also easily determine the difference of cars from other vehicles. For instance, you would probably be able to say that cars are different from other vehicles because they are smaller, four-wheeled vehicles that can drive on a highway and hold multiple passengers. You can easily think up characteristics like this without any research.

However, if you tried to figure out the difference for the term "snail," you would, once again, probably have to do some research to figure out that snails are different from other mollusks like octopi because they have a shell, and they emit slime, which helps them crawl. Therefore, if you cannot think of the genus and difference of a term on your own, it is perfectly legitimate to consult an outside source, such as the Internet, a dictionary, or an encyclopedia. As another example of genus and difference, consider the word "friend." The genus of the word "friend" is "associate" or "acquaintance." The features, or difference, that set a friend apart from other associates or acquaintances is that a friend is an acquaintance with whom you share a pleasant rapport, common interests, and a certain level of intimacy. As a final example, consider the word "bicycle." The genus of "bicycle" is "vehicle." The distinguishing features—difference—that set a bicycle apart from other vehicles, such as motorcycles or cars, is that a bicycle has two wheels, and it is propelled by human energy, rather than by electrical

SOMETIMES, WHEN YOU HAVE A COMPLEX TERM, SIMPLY DEFINING IT WITH A SYNONYM OR WITH AN OPERATIONAL DEFINITION IS INADEQUATE.

energy. Using a genus and difference definition can help you paint a clearer picture of what kind of thing something is, as well as what sets it apart from other things like it.

Now that you have explored several different types of extensive and intensive definitions, let's consider how you might use these different definitional techniques together. Let's consider the word "love." To get a better understanding of what the word "love" is, we might first consider what genus love fits under. In considering common sense and our experience, we can easily determine that love fits into the genus of "emotions," which also includes hate, joy, sadness, fear, and hope. However, the difference of love is that it is an emotion of affection, kindness, and even passion toward another person. Indeed, synonyms for love are "affection," "passion," "solicitude," and "tenderness."[4]

In addition, it may be helpful to list some different kinds of love. People often refer to the three types of love represented by the Greek words *philos*, *eros*, and *agape*. *Philos* represents brotherly love. *Eros* represents passionate or romantic love. *Agape* represents sacrificial, unconditional love. Listing these different types of love would be an example of an enumerative definition. Furthermore, we could also use an operational definition for love that would go something like this: "When someone loves another person, he regards that person with affection, tenderness, and even passion. He focuses on the other person's needs and interests and unselfishly puts that person's needs and interests above his own." If we put all of these definitional techniques together, our definition of love might look something like this:

> Love is an emotion, such as joy, hope, sadness, or hate. It is differentiated from other emotions by feelings of tenderness, affection, and even passion toward another person. There are three common different types of love, often represented by the three Greek words *philos*, *eros*, and *agape*. *Philos* is brotherly love such as what siblings or friends might have for one another. *Eros* is passionate

or romantic love such as what lovers or spouses might have for one another. *Agape* is sacrificial, unconditional love such as what a parent might have for a child. When someone loves someone else, he focuses on the other person's needs and interests and unselfishly puts that person's needs and interests above his own.

As you can see from this brief definitional paragraph, using a variety of extensional and intensional definition techniques in conjunction with each other can be a very effective way of clearly illustrating the meaning of a word. When defining a word, it is not necessary to use every single possible definitional device. Instead, you should just choose several that seem to work best in illustrating the word you wish to define.

Now that you have examined the different types of definitional techniques, it is important for you to learn how to critique someone's argument if it is a definitional dispute. There are several different reasons you might critique an opponent's definitions. First, you might believe that he is equivocating with a word in an argument. If so, you need to point out the two different definitions being used. Second, you might believe that the definition is just plain inaccurate. In such a case, you need to show the person why her definition is inaccurate by showing examples of the word that do not fit the definition. Third, you might believe that a person's definition is incomplete and that it fails to represent a word or concept fully. In such a case, you would suggest a broader, more inclusive definition.

In previous lessons, you have spent a lot of time learning about the characteristics of a good definition and appropriate definitional techniques. This is important because definitional disputes are some of the most common disputes people have. Furthermore, they can often be frustrating unless people pay close attention to words and understand how they are being used in an argument. In the next lesson, we will examine the last type of dispute: a presuppositional dispute.

DEFINE

1. Intention:

_____

_____

2. Extension:

_____

_____

3. Extensive Definition:

_____

_____

4. Ostensive Definition:

_____

_____

5. Enumerative Definition:

_____

_____

6. Definition by Subclass:

_____

_____

7. Intensive Definition:

_____

_____

8. Definition by Synonym:

_____

_____

9. Genus and Difference:

_____

_____

ANSWER

1. Give several of the subclasses between "white pine" and "plant" in order of increasing *intention*.

_____

_____

2. Give several of the subclasses between "white pine" and "plant" in order of increasing *extension*.

_____

_____

PRACTICE

Practicing Definition Techniques: *For each of the following words, provide the type of definition listed in parentheses.*

1. Television Shows (Enumerative):

_____

_____

2. Enemy (Synonym):

_____

_____

3. Planet (Enumerative):

_____

_____

4. Courage (Lexical):

_____

_____

5. Student (Operative):

_____

_____

Define the following items using the technique of defining by genus and difference.

APPLY

1. Cherry Pie:

_____

_____

2. Sports Car:

_____

_____

3. Sport-Utility Vehicle (SUV):

_____

_____

4. Sewing Machine:

_____

_____

5. Laser Printer:

_____

_____

_____

6. Now choose a term of your own and define it using the technique of genus and difference.

_____

_____

_____

WRITE

Writing Definition Paragraphs: In order to better understand a word, it is often wise to look at it from several angles. One way you can do this is to write a paragraph in which you use several definition techniques to define the word. In the space below, an example has been provided for you of a definition paragraph that explores the word "integrity." Read this example paragraph and then, on a separate piece of paper, write a similar paragraph on the word "love." This paragraph should contain an introduction, a conclusion, and at least five definition techniques. You may use any of the definition techniques you have learned about thus far in the book. It will help if you brainstorm your ideas first by jotting them down without worrying about how they sound (you can do this in words or phrases). Then, once you know what you are going to say, go ahead and write the paragraph.

Integrity is a very important characteristic to have. Integrity can be defined as soundness, incorruptibility, and firm adherence to a code, especially of artistic or moral values; completeness; it is the quality or state of being complete or undivided.[7] To have integrity, people must know in which principles they believe, and they must adhere to those principles at all times, whether someone is watching or not. Some common synonyms for integrity are honesty, sincerity, and honorableness.[8] Integrity is a virtue, like faithfulness, kindness, and peacefulness. However, it differs from these other virtues because, rather than characterizing how a person acts toward other people, integrity pertains to an overarching belief system and how a person adheres to that belief system. Some people throughout history who have been characterized as having integrity are George Washington, Abe Lincoln, Mother Theresa, and Gandhi. Integrity is an excellent quality that all people should develop, which will help them in all areas of their lives.

DEDUCTION IN ACTION
Writing an Argument to Support Your View

So far, you have looked at the proposition "To be a good friend, a person must love himself or herself the most" from several different angles. You have examined definitions of "love" and "friendship." You have looked at reasons to agree with this proposition and reasons to disagree with it. You have read and summarized some arguments by Aristotle, supporting both sides of the issue as he presented it. Lastly, you have constructed syllogisms that support both sides of the proposition.

Now that you have accomplished all of this, it is time for you to write a paragraph in which you state whether or not you agree with the proposition and then present a syllogism and evidence to support your belief.

On a separate piece of paper, please follow these steps, which will help you accomplish this task:

1. Make a brief outline for your paragraph. This outline can have Roman numerals and letters, bullet points, or check marks. The format of the outline is not as important as is the process of getting your thoughts down on paper.

2. In your outline, state whether or not you agree with the proposition "To be a good friend, a person must love himself or herself the most." You can do this by stating, "It is true that to be a good friend, a person must love himself or herself the most," or, "It is false that to be a good friend, a person must love himself or herself the most." Then, write the syllogism that supports your viewpoint. Next, write at least three facts or examples or a combination of the two to support your syllogism. The purpose of these three facts and/or examples is to support and illustrate your premises fully. (You may use one of the syllogisms that you constructed in the last lesson, or you may create another syllogism that supports your reasoning.)

3. Write a paragraph that has a topic sentence, your syllogism, your three supporting facts and/ or examples, and a conclusion.

LESSON 9.6
Presuppositional Disputes

POINTS TO REMEMBER

1. Presuppositional disputes center around people's opinions or views of the world.
2. Socratic dialogue is an effective method for showing contradiction in ideas.
3. Sometimes disputes contain a combination of all three types of disputes.

> LOVE IS COMPOSED OF A SINGLE SOUL
> INHABITING TWO BODIES.
> —ARISTOTLE[1]

Empirical disputes arise from a disagreement of fact. Definitional disputes arise from disagreements over definition. Our third type of disagreement, as we mentioned in the first lesson in chapter 9, is the presuppositional dispute. These disputes arise because of a disagreement regarding a belief or value. For example, consider the following argument between Julie and Tiffany about the political stances regarding the distribution of wealth held by Senator Jacobson and Senator Abernathy:

Julie: I am all for Senator Jacobson's plan to redistribute wealth in the United States. After all, we do have a widening gap between the rich and the poor in this country. I've been reading this book that argues that the gap between the wealthy and poor is destructive to democracy because it concentrates power in the hands of the very wealthy. It is our government's duty to do all that it can to promote democracy. Therefore, spreading wealth throughout the United States promotes democracy because it decreases the gap of inequality and, therefore, decreases the concentration of power in the hands of a few.

Tiffany: I completely disagree with you. The idea of distributing wealth is destructive to a true democracy, as Senator Abernathy has repeatedly argued. Besides, if people work hard, they can pull themselves up by their bootstraps, and they can become self-sufficient and independent. A self-sufficient and independent population is the heart of a democratic nation. If the government offers handouts to everyone, people won't be self-sufficient. It will make them dependent on the government, which will give the government too much power.

Notice that the disagreement between Julie and Tiffany is not an empirical dispute, because there is nowhere Julie and Tiffany can look to find out, once and for all, if the government should spread the wealth, if the poor can pull themselves up by their bootstraps, or if a gap between the rich and the poor is destructive to democracy. This is not a complex empirical dispute either, because, for instance, you can't really research to discover whether or not there is strong or weak evidence to support the notion that government should equally distribute wealth. Furthermore, Julie and Tiffany are not having a definitional dispute, because, for instance, they are both defining the word "democracy" as a government that is ruled

279

by the people, and providing more specific definitions is not going to clear up their dispute.

Julie and Tiffany are disagreeing because they have significantly different views or attitudes about the role of the government in the nation, as well as the cause of poverty. In other words, this is a presuppositional argument that stems from Julie and Tiffany's different beliefs regarding certain components of the world, namely, government, poverty, and wealth. A **presupposition** is a belief that someone already holds and subsequently brings into an argument. As you can imagine, these types of disagreements can be much harder to resolve than empirical or definitional disputes.

Not only that, but people don't always recognize the presuppositions that they bring into a situation, which can often cause problems. For instance, consider two people named Sarah and Christopher who get married. Imagine that Sarah believes that all dishes should be done every night before she and Christopher go to bed. Christopher, on the other hand, strongly believes it's OK to leave the dishes unwashed overnight, especially if people have had a really stressful day. You can imagine that these different presuppositions could cause Sarah and Christopher to disagree. The disagreements could become especially significant if Sarah and Christopher fail to realize that these are beliefs they have, which may or may not be right, and instead view them as ironclad rules or principles that govern reality (i.e., Sarah believes the universe will implode if dirty dishes remain in the sink overnight; Christopher believes washing dishes after a difficult day will provoke respiratory arrest or mental insanity).

In some ways, presuppositions are like preferences, but they are much stronger than preferences. For example, people prefer certain colors. If Sarah prefers the color green, she may desire to make this the general color scheme of her house; however, she will likely be willing to compromise with Christopher if he really dislikes the color green. This is because she does not likely view the issue of color as a moral issue (e.g., green is right, but blue is wrong). On the other hand, if she feels very strongly that all of the dishes should be washed before she and Christopher go to bed at night, it is likely that she views this as a moral issue.

How can washing the dishes at night be a moral issue? Well, it is likely that Sarah believes that keeping a clean house is morally excellent and that letting dishes go unwashed overnight is an act of laziness or irresponsibility, which is morally reprehensible to her. On the other hand, Christopher may believe that it is really important and even morally necessary to relax, be peaceful, and take care of himself. He may believe that it is wrong to "sweat the small stuff" and that maintaining peace of mind is the most important thing in life. In this case, as you can see, Sarah and Christopher's fundamental beliefs about the nature of the world and reality will cause them conflict because their ideas conflict.

It is important to note that presuppositions can be especially tricky in the areas of religion, morality, and ethics. This is because people's religious beliefs often flow from their belief in whether or not there is a God, and if there is, what kind of God He is. However, it is impossible to prove scientifically or philosophically, once and for all, whether there is a God or not. Therefore, this can complicate discussions about morality, ethics, and religion. (For further discussion on how to solve these dilemmas, see appendix E.)

Furthermore, people's presuppositions often flow from their religious beliefs and are highly influenced by religious systems and documents. For instance, because of a Hindu's religious system and the texts he holds as sacred, he will likely have many different presuppositions than, for example, an atheist or a Christian, who have completely different religious systems and texts that they hold sacred. In the same way, someone who is a devout Wiccan will hold many different presuppositions than a Hassidic Jew or a Shiite Muslim. When people hold significantly different presuppositions, it can lead to significant disagreements, because they believe very different things about the nature of reality and morality. It is interesting to note that many political disagreements arise from presuppositional disputes, because traditional conservatives and liberals often view life in very different manners. Presuppositional beliefs are often tied to our own religious, ethical, or moral code and the attitude we developed about the world as we were growing up.

Let's consider Julie and Tiffany's argument about wealth, poverty, and democracy. Many people in the United States have presuppositions similar to those of both Julie and Tiffany. Some people believe that the role of government is to stay out of people's lives as much as possible, while others believe that the role of government is to help people as much as possible. Furthermore, some people believe that

the main cause of poverty is a character flaw in individuals, such as laziness or poor money management, while others believe that the main cause of poverty is governmental and societal injustice, such as prejudice, greed, and corporate corruption. As you can imagine, presuppositional disagreements such as these can make it difficult for people to debate, because these presuppositions significantly affect the way in which people view the world and can cause them to talk past one another. In other words, because they come at a subject from completely different viewpoints, they often cannot even grasp the arguments or logic of their opponent.

So how should you handle presuppositional or attitudinal disputes? The good news for you is that deductive logic is one of the most useful tools for working through presuppositional disputes, because presuppositions are propositions that are held *a priori*. Remember, this means that people accept these presuppositions as true already. Therefore, if two people agree to search for truth and carefully and honestly examine their propositions together, it is possible to determine if a proposition leads to contradiction or absurdity. This is where your exposure to Socratic dialogue and discussion will come in handy. Throughout this book, you have read several Socratic dialogues recorded by Plato. You have also read several dialogues set in modern times that dealt with modern issues. You have also had the opportunity to write several dialogues yourself. Through this reading and writing of dialogues, you have already gained a strong sense of ways in which you can approach presuppositional disputes.

To explore this more, consider the Socratic dialogue *Euthyphro*, which you read at the beginning of this book. (If you have not read it, you might consider reading it now; however, the following discussion will still be helpful to you, even if you have not read it.) Remember that in *Euthyphro*, Euthyphro is a young priest who is prosecuting his father for murder. (Note: Euthyphro's father had a slave who slit another slave's throat. Euthyphro's father bound the murdering slave and threw him in the ditch, leaving him there until he could consult a priest or a magistrate about what should be done with the murderer. In the meantime, the slave died from exposure.) Euthyphro believes he is being pious through his actions. This leads Socrates to question him about what piety truly is.

Now, here is where we relate this back to presuppositional arguments. Euthyphro first tells Socrates that piety is what is loved by the gods. This is a presupposition that Euthyphro holds. However, in questioning him, Socrates also discovers that Euthyphro holds another presupposition: that the gods are often at war with each other and that they quarrel about the things that they love and hate. Can you remember (or figure out) what comes next? Socrates points out to Euthyphro that the pious cannot be what the gods love because the gods war and fight about what they love and hate. Notice that what Socrates did here was examine the implications of two presuppositions that Euthyphro held and show that the two presuppositions were incompatible. (If you remember from your lessons on the square of opposition, they defied the law of contrary statements.)

As another example, consider another way in which Socrates refuted Euthyphro's claim that what is loved by gods is piety. For the sake of argument, Socrates says, in essence, to Euthyphro, "OK, Euthyphro, let's pretend that the gods do all love at least some things and that these things that they all love are pious." Euthyphro affirms that this, indeed, is what he believes. Then, through a series of questions, Socrates discovers that Euthyphro believes that what is loved by the gods is loved because the gods love it. However, Euthyphro also believes that what is pious is loved by the gods because it is pious. What this means is that what is god-loved and what is pious are not the same thing. In essence, the first (what is god-loved) is made lovable by the gods loving it but the second (what is pious) is loved because it is lovable (good). What is happening here is that Socrates is showing Euthyphro that the two things Euthyphro believes are equivalent (the god-loved and the pious) are not equivalent at all, because Euthyphro himself has given them two different definitions.

How do these examples help us? Consider Socrates' statement at the end of *Euthyphro*:

Socrates: And are you not saying that what is loved of the gods is holy; and is not this the same as what is dear to them—do you see?

Euthyphro: True.

Socrates: Then either we were wrong in former assertion; or, if we were right then, we are wrong now.[2]

Socrates' last statement gives us insight into how we can handle presuppositional disputes. When people discuss their presuppositions and are using logic properly, the discussion will show them that their presuppositions are either contradictory or consistent. If the discussion demonstrates a contradiction between presuppositions, this means that either the two parties made some logical error during the argument or that the conclusion is somehow wrong. Let's look at a later discussion Julie and Tiffany had about poverty to see how an argument might work in this manner.

Julie: Tiffany, I have been thinking about the debate we had earlier about the government redistributing wealth in America. You said that the poor need to pull themselves up by their bootstraps and that giving them money is harmful. Am I remembering this correctly?

Tiffany: I think that's a good summary of my views, yes.

Julie: Well, I have a scenario to pose to you.

Tiffany: Go for it.

Julie: Imagine that a child is born to impoverished parents who had dropped out of high school. Would you agree with me that this child is probably not going to be interacted with and shaped in the same way as that of a child who is born to highly educated, wealthy parents?

Tiffany: Sure. That seems pretty obvious.

Julie: Let's say that the impoverished parents take drugs to escape the unpleasantness of their poverty. Let's also say that because of their lack of education and their drug addiction, they create an extremely erratic home life for their child. They don't have regular mealtimes, and, in fact, there are times when they don't have meals at all. In addition, they are out during all hours of the night, and the child does not have regular sleeping patterns. Would you say that these patterns would likely have a negative affect on the child's ability to concentrate and perform in school?

Tiffany: I don't see how it could be otherwise.

Julie: Would you agree with me, Tiffany, that the child cannot help these factors in his life? That is, do you agree that he cannot help that his parents are poorly educated, impoverished, have a drug problem, and keep wildly erratic meal and sleeping schedules?

Tiffany: Certainly not when he is younger. Younger children are, for better or worse, at the mercy of their parents in these matters.

Julie: Would you agree with me that a child's habits and modes of acting are strongly shaped during the first years of his life? That is, if a child has been read to, spoken to, and nurtured from an early age, do you agree that this is going to form extremely different habits than those in the child who has been neglected and deprived of proper nutrition, sleep, and nurturing?

Tiffany: I think that's accurate.

Julie: Would you also agree that the child who has been nurtured and educated from birth would find excelling at school much easier than the child who has been neglected educationally and deprived of proper nutrients?

Tiffany: Well, you couldn't say that is the case all the time. There are exceptions, but I think that it would be safe to say that's true.

Julie: Would you say that in many cases, when a child has been neglected from childhood by impoverished parents, that this child may find himself so far behind where he should be that the frustration is overwhelming?

Tiffany: That's certainly possible.

Julie: Would it be possible that this child could find school so bewildering and overwhelming that he might eventually drop out?

Tiffany: Once again, that is certainly possible.

Julie: Would you agree that someone who drops out of high school is often going to find it hard to get a job and be financially successful?

Tiffany: Certainly.

Julie: Would it be right to say that our hypothetical person became poor due, in large part, to his dropping out of school?

Tiffany: Yes.

Julie: Would it also be safe to say that while dropping out of school was his choice, this decision was strongly influenced by the home environment his parents had created for him?

Tiffany: I think we could say that.

Julie: Could we say, then, that his poverty, later in life, was largely due to the home environment his parents created for him when he was a child?

Tiffany: It's not totally due to that, but it is largely influenced by that.

Julie: Would you agree that, although not impossible, it would be hard for him to overcome this influence and pull himself up by his bootstraps?

Tiffany: It's not impossible, but it would certainly be harder.

Julie: Would it be right, also, to say that the person who was nurtured from an early age has an advantage over the person who grew up with an erratic and impoverished home life?

Tiffany: I think so.

Julie: Is not advantage a type of strength? That is, someone who has great advantage will be stronger, and someone who has great disadvantage will be weaker?

Tiffany: That's generally the case.

Julie: Is it not noble and right for the stronger to help the weaker? For instance, say someone is lost. Shouldn't those who know the way help him find his way? Or, for instance, isn't it right and good for an older adult to help and care for a young child in trouble?

Tiffany: Certainly.

Julie: Then isn't it just for those who have been able to gain much wealth, largely because of the influence of a good upbringing, to monetarily help those who have been deprived of wealth, largely due to the influence of an impoverished upbringing?

Tiffany: Hmmm. Those are some interesting points, Julie. I certainly agree with much of what you are saying, but some of it doesn't seem right. Mind if I think about it more and get back to you?

Julie: Sure. Thanks for the discussion.

Notice that in this dialogue, Julie challenges Tiffany's presupposition that the poor should pull themselves up by their bootstraps and that it is wrong to give them money. Julie does this by demonstrating that this belief, ultimately, seems to conflict with another belief upon which she and

Tiffany agree: that it is extremely difficult for many people to overcome their impoverished upbringing, and it is right for the stronger to help the weaker. Because Tiffany agreed with each of Julie's points along the way, Tiffany now has two options: She can either amend or relinquish her earlier presuppositions about the poor, or she can go back through the chain of reasoning and find weaknesses in it (possibly empirical or definitional problems). If she amends her former belief, she will have changed a presupposition and now she will view the world in a different manner.

It is important to note that people *can* change their presuppositions. However, they usually only do it when they realize for themselves that their beliefs are contradictory, rather than when people simply tell them they are wrong. Therefore, Socratic dialogue is one of the best tools for dealing with presuppositional disputes because it allows people to realize for themselves when their presuppositions are contradictory. Unfortunately, people with presuppositional disputes often engage in shouting matches or name-calling, rather than reasonable dialogue. Just look at a televised political debate, and you'll see that this is true. Too often political candidates spend their time making accusations and hurling insults at one another, rather than pursuing truth. When you engage in dialogue with a person, and you treat her with dignity, it is ultimately a more effective tool for reaching common ground. It is important to note that there may be times when you must critique the presuppositions of an argument but you cannot use Socratic dialogue to do so. For instance, if you are writing a critique of an argument, it will likely be impractical (and unnecessary) for you to formulate your critique in terms of a Socratic dialogue. Instead, you can reach the same end by presenting your critique in a written essay format.

For instance, if Julie was writing her critique of Tiffany's argument, rather than dialoguing directly with Tiffany, Julie would include the chain of reasoning that she used in the dialogue, but she would not include Tiffany's comments. That is, she would start with point A, her first point, with which even most of her opponents would agree: that children raised in an educationally impoverished home will find school more difficult. Then, she would move to point B, which would be closely related to or implied by point A. This would lead to a point C, D, and E (or however many points she needs), which would all be closely related to or implied by previous points. Finally, this moving from point-to-point would eventually lead to her conclusion, which would be a critique of the opposing viewpoint. In this way, someone could critique a presupposition in writing, rather than in Socratic dialogue.

Before you finish this lesson, let's explore one other type of dispute. In this chapter, we have examined empirical, definitional, and presuppositional disputes. It is important to note that sometimes a dispute is a combination of all three of these disputes. As you can imagine, this kind of dispute can be like a piece of yarn that has become all knotted and tangled. It takes a lot of time to unravel it and to get it into some kind of sensible shape. When you run into these kinds of arguments, verify your facts, ask your opponent to clarify what he means by his terms, and be patient with dialogue as you work through each step of the dispute. The fact that you realize there are different types of disputes will be extremely helpful to you in this process.

To sum this lesson up, it is good to remember that many disputes are presuppositional in nature. That is, they deal with disagreements proceeding from different values or beliefs. Socratic discussion, in which two people examine the natural conclusion of their beliefs or propositions, is one of the most useful tools for resolving presuppositional disputes. Socratic dialogue is also extremely helpful when you get involved in a disagreement that features all three kinds of disputes.

REVIEW
EXPLAIN

1. Explain what a presuppositional or attitudinal dispute is.

_____

_____

_____

_____

2. Explain why presuppositional disputes can be so hard to resolve.

_____

_____

_____

_____

EXPLAIN (CONTINUED)

3. Explain how people should handle an argument that is a combination of all three types of arguments—empirical, definitional, and presuppositional.

_____

_____

_____

_____

_____

_____

_____

DETERMINE

What Kind of Dispute Is It? *Read each of the following arguments and determine whether the dispute is definitional, empirical, or presuppositional, and explain why you answered the way you did. That is, if you said it was a definitional dispute, be able to identify the word that is at the center of the dispute. If you identified it as a presuppositional dispute, be able to explain the presupposition that is at the center of the dispute. If you identified it as an empirical dispute, identify the fact that is at the center of the dispute*

1. **Argument 1:**

Person 1: Religion will soon become a thing of the past. We are living in a scientific and technological age in which science will be able to provide us with the answers to all of the mysteries of the universe.

Person 2: I think that idea attributes far too much credit to science. Science will never be able to answer some mysteries of the universe, although it certainly provides us with a lot of important knowledge.

Person 1: That's nonsense. Science's horizons are expanding every minute, and they will soon encompass everything.

Type of Dispute:

_____

_____

_____

_____

DETERMINE (CONTINUED)

2. **Argument 2:**

Person 1: My son's art book is obscene! It has a picture of some statue called *David* in it. That statue is completely naked! I can't believe the school would approve of such obscenity.

Person 2: That statue is not obscene. It's a famous Renaissance sculpture by Michelangelo and is a humanistic interpretation of the glory of man.

Person 1: I don't care who sculpted it! It's obscene!

Type of Dispute:

_____

_____

_____

_____

_____

_____

3. **Argument 3:**

Person 1: George Washington was such a great leader! After all, even when he was a little boy, he demonstrated great integrity and told his father he chopped down a cherry tree, even though he knew he would get in trouble for it.

Person 2: Wait . . . George Washington didn't chop down the cherry tree. It was Abraham Lincoln.

Person 1: No, I'm pretty sure it was George Washington.

Type of Dispute:

_____

_____

4. **Argument 4:**

Person 1: I just listened to Bob Dylan's new CD. It's great!

Person 2: Dude, Bob Dylan is dead.

Person 1: I'm pretty sure he's not.

Type of Dispute:

_____

_____

DETERMINE (CONTINUED)

5. **Argument 5:**

Emily: That's no fair! You'll let Sara go see the new James Bond movie, but you won't let me go.

Mom: Emily, it's completely fair. Sara is eight years older than you are, and she is old enough to see some movies that aren't appropriate for an eight-year-old girl like you to see. When you are Sara's age, you will be able to see more movies, too.

Emily: I still don't think it's fair.

Type of Dispute:

_____

_____

WRITE

Socratic Dialogue and Presuppositional Disputes: Earlier in this lesson, you read Julie and Tiffany's Socratic dialogue about their presuppositions about the government's responsibility to the poor. As you may recall, through her dialogue, Julie attempted to demonstrate to Tiffany that some poor people are in weakened financial positions largely because of factors outside of their control. Furthermore, she argued that it was noble for the strong to help the weak.

While there are many good points in this case, it is also wise to examine the opposite side, as well, to form an educated opinion. Now that you have gained practice in writing Socratic dialogue, see if you can write, on a separate piece of paper, a dialogue from Tiffany's point of view, supporting her presupposition that it is wrong for the government to give handouts to the poor.

DEDUCTION IN ACTION

Explore and Critique the Other Viewpoint

In the previous lesson, you wrote your opinion about the proposition "To be a good friend, a person must love himself or herself the most." At this point, you probably know that it is not enough to merely explore your own opinion about the matter—you must also entertain the opposing idea and consider it fairly. As you do this, be fair to the opposing viewpoint. It's easy, when you are examining a viewpoint with which you disagree, to make a silly caricature of the view. In other words, you might summarize the opposing viewpoint in a way that is so silly that it is patently false.

This is actually a logical fallacy called a **straw man fallacy**. The name "straw man" presents a great image to help you remember what this fallacy is. Consider this: If you were going to fight with another person, who would be easier to fight—a real person or a scarecrow? Of course, the scarecrow would be easier because scarecrows aren't real people; therefore, they are easy to knock down. In the same way, when someone commits the straw man fallacy, he turns the opposition's argument into a silly argument that is a pretend argument, lacking any real substance, just like the scarecrow is a pretend man, lacking any real substance. The argument is much easier to defeat this way.

DEDUCTION IN ACTION (CONTINUED)

For instance, if someone wanted to make a straw man out of the opposition's viewpoint in our argument, he might write something like this: "Oh, yeah, people who love themselves are *excellent* friends! After all, who doesn't love someone who talks about himself all the time, brags about his accomplishments, and spends all day looking at himself in the mirror?" Now, of course, this is ridiculous. Who would want to hang around someone like this? No one would. So, this argument is easily defeated, right? On the contrary, the opponent's argument has not been defeated because this is not a true argument. No one would make such an argument.

The point is, when you are entertaining the opposing viewpoint in an argument, you need to be fair and treat your opposition with respect. Make sure that when you critique the opposition's argument, you are actually critiquing a fair representation of the argument or an argument that an intelligent person from the opposition might make. If you craft the opposition's viewpoint as though he were a five-year-old, this is not a true discussion.

In order to write a fair critique of the opposing viewpoint, use the following steps to help you outline the argument:

1. Use one of the arguments Aristotle summarized as your argument to critique (obviously, you want to choose the one that represents the viewpoint that opposes your own), or make up another opposing argument that an intelligent, logical person might make.

2. Write this argument in the form of a syllogism (of course, if you use Aristotle's argument, this was already done in a previous lesson, and you can use that syllogism).

3. Almost all arguments have at least something good about them. Find one good thing about this argument or one element of truth it contains. State at least one strength of this argument in a complete sentence.

4. Now figure out why you disagree with this argument. Is it an empirical dispute? Is it a definitional dispute? Is it a presuppositional dispute? Is it a combination of these types of disputes? In your outline, write what kind of dispute you have with this argument and identify the specific areas around which the dispute revolves. For instance, you would write down the specific fact, word, or presupposition with which you disagree.

5. Now, in a couple of sentences, write a critique of the argument by focusing on the point about which you disagree. For instance, if a factual dispute is involved, explain what fact is incorrect and provide the correct factual information. If you are disputing a definition, identify the term and write the correct (or better) definition and explain why it is better or more correct. If it is a presuppositional dispute, identify which presupposition you believe is incorrect and write an explanation that shows why this presupposition is contradictory. (Hint: Remember that this debate likely revolves around definitional and presuppositional disputes, with definitional disputes being the major issues. Keep this in mind as you do this part.)

6. After you have constructed your outline, write a paragraph that contains all of these items and is neatly tied together with an introduction and a conclusion. The following are the items you should have in your paragraph:

   • An introductory sentence

   • The opposing view stated in a syllogism

   • An explanation of one strength of this viewpoint

   • An identification of the problem in this argument

   • A better view of this problem area

LESSON 9.7
Pursuing Truth

> "YOU CAN ONLY FIND TRUTH WITH LOGIC IF YOU
> HAVE ALREADY FOUND TRUTH WITHOUT IT.
> —G.K. CHESTERTON[1]

It's time to celebrate. You have reached the end of *The Discovery of Deduction* and have accomplished quite a bit:

- You know the difference between induction and deduction.

- You know how to identify single propositions and make inferences using the square of opposition and the relationships of equivalence.

- You know how to identify deductive categorical arguments and analyze them for validity using the Barbara mnemonic device, counterexamples, the seven validity rules, and Venn diagrams.

- You know how to critique an argument when it is valid but you believe it is unsound.

- You know how to construct valid deductive arguments.

- You know how to use Socratic dialogue to discuss a deductive argument.

These skills that you have learned will help you in any walk of life in which you find yourself, whether you are discussing ideas with a friend, writing a paper for a class, watching ads on television, or thinking about your goals in life. The skills you have learned in this book will give you a leg up in almost any profession you choose to pursue, especially those involving law, philosophy, and mathematics. Special emphasis is given to logic in these fields, but you will have an advantage in any profession by understanding and applying logic.

Because the study of logic is so integral and important to everyday life, we highly encourage you to pursue your logic studies by taking logic classes, participating in debate and mock trial clubs, and discussing and debating all the time with your friends. Practice makes perfect.

As this book comes to a conclusion, we would like to leave you with a parting story from our friend Socrates, as recorded by Plato. It is often referred to as the "Allegory of the Cave." This story is not only a captivating myth, but it also carries important implications concerning the things you have been learning in this book. The following is a retelling of Socrates' work. You can find the original in book 7 of Plato's book *The Republic*. Read the myth and then answer the questions that follow. Once you have answered the questions, read the discussion of the story at the end of the lesson.

The Allegory of the Cave

Once upon a time, there was a cave, and in this cave, there were a group of people who were captives. They had been there since birth and knew no other life. Indeed, they did not even know they were captives. These captives were chained in such a way that they were always looking at the wall directly in front of them. They could neither look to the right nor to the left. Behind and back a ways from these captives, there was a great bonfire that burned continually and cast shadows upon the wall at which the captives continually looked.

The captors of these people in the cave were strange people and took to educating the captives in a strange way. Daily, they paraded items behind the captives but in front of the bonfire so that the items cast shadows upon the wall. For instance, they paraded a large cutout of a horse in front of the bonfire, and it cast the shadow of a horse onto the wall. The captors said to their prisoners, "This is a horse." Next, they paraded the cutout of a tree in front of the bonfire so that it cast the shadow of a tree upon the wall. The captors said to the captives, "This is a tree." The captors did this every day with many different objects, and the captives, in this way, gained an understanding of the world. But it was a shadowy, flat, deceptive view of the world and all that was in it. This was the world that the captives knew: a world of shadows.

One day, one of the captives escaped from the cave and climbed out into the world. As he encountered the real world, he felt nothing but terror and anguish at first. The blazing sunlight pierced his eyes, and he was as a blind man. The rushing sounds of life assaulted his ears until he thought he would go insane. Then, as his eyes grew accustomed to the light of the sun, and he began to see, new terrors (or were they wonders?) barraged his mind. His brain couldn't process what was happening to him. All around him, he saw colors and shapes, depth and breadth, and he was amazed (when he was no longer terrified) at the richness and fullness of life. He remembered the world of shadows in which he had lived so long and wept for the years he had lost.

Once the man had adjusted to the real world and could begin to grasp the truth of reality, he realized that he had to go back and tell his fellow captives and friends about what he had seen. He could not leave them to reside in the land of shadows, cut off from the color, mystery, and beautiful agony of real life. Rallying his strength, he found the entrance of the cave and crept back down into it, proceeding with fear and trembling lest he should be caught and imprisoned once again. When he reached the captives, he hid himself and bided his time until the captors were away and he could speak to the prisoners alone.

He crept up to the nearest captive, and said, "Friend, you must let me free you, and you must come with me. I have escaped into the world above, and it is so beautiful that words cannot express it! There are colors, shapes, and sounds you could never imagine. The trees are not flat and black: They are majestic, full, and living! And the sea! You can't imagine!"

And on and on he went until he realized his friend was gazing at him with confusion and pity. The friend said, "You certainly have gone mad. There is no world above. You have been chasing fantasies. Come back and be with us where you belong."

The captive who had escaped was crestfallen. Why could he not explain things right? Why wouldn't his friend believe? He spoke to several of the other captives, telling them the same story but trying to explain better, to be more specific, so that they would understand and leave with him. He even tried to loosen the manacles that bound them so that they were always facing the wall. He thought if he did this, they would begin to taste freedom and want more. But the other captives only laughed at him and told him he was crazy, just as the first had done.

Finally, fearing that he might be discovered by the guards and imprisoned once again, he crept away in the darkness and found the passage leading up to the world above. He scaled the passage with sadness for his friends, but with gladness that he was leaving the kingdom of shadows and would enter the realm of beauty and light again. He determined he would do all he could to go back one day and lead his friends away from the shadows and into the land of light.[2]

Before you read the conclusion of this lesson, take a few minutes to stop and reflect on this story and its connection to what you have learned in logic. Use the following questions to help you in this reflection.

1. This story is an allegory, which means that the different elements of the story are symbolic of different things in life. What are some different things that this story could correspond to in real life?

_____

_____

_____

_____

_____

_____

_____

2. How could the story symbolize the process of learning and correctly applying logic?

_____

_____

_____

_____

_____

_____

_____

Now that you have considered these questions on your own, we would like to offer these concluding thoughts to you about your journey into the realm of thinking and truth. As you mature and learn more about the world, you will find that there are many people and things in the world that desire to give you false messages. False friends will try to manipulate you for their selfish ends. Greedy advertisers will attempt to feed you lies and fuzzy thinking to persuade you to buy their products. Well-meaning people tell you wrong or illogical things sometimes, just because they are human.

One way that you can interpret the cave in this story is that it is the realm of bad logic, distortion, lies, and falsehood. When you escape from the cave into the light, you are escaping the realm of false thinking and bad logic and entering the realm of truth, logic, and, hopefully, happiness. After all, all humans desire happiness, and finding truth is one of the greatest parts of finding that happiness. Therefore, we encourage you to use the knowledge of logic you have gained in this book (and any past books) to escape the cave of false thinking, distortion, and bad logic and to journey into the world of right thinking.

This process is not always easy. Sometimes, we grow very attached to our illogical and contradictory views of life, and seeing the real world in all of its complexity can be painful. Furthermore, sometimes when we try to share what we have learned with our friends, they laugh at us in disbelief, or worse, tell us we are crazy. Always remember that deductive logic will only get you truth if you start with truth. If you start with false premises, you will end up with false conclusions. Therefore, always be open to reconsidering the truth of your premises when they lead you in ways that seem wrong or harmful.

As G.K. Chesterton said, "You can only find truth with logic if you have already found truth without it." The journey toward logic and truth is certainly not easy, but it is worth it. We hope that you will continue on your journey of logic, and we wish you well on your way!

Looking to the Future

The authors hope that your discovery of deduction was enjoyable as well as informative. Learning how to think well can be both useful and enjoyable, assisting us in becoming rational, thoughtful, and, hopefully, happy people. This foray into logic is just one installment in Classical Academic Press's logic series (see also *The Art of Argument* and *The Argument Builder*, which deal with inductive logic). The next step in deductive logic is the study of propositional logic. For a taste of propositional logic, consider the following argument from the famous children's book *Alice's Adventures in Wonderland*:

> A pigeon says to Alice: "You're a serpent; and there's no use denying it. I suppose you'll be telling me next that you never tasted an egg!"

> "I have tasted eggs, certainly . . . but little girls eat eggs quite as much as serpents do, you know."

> At this, the pigeon exclaims: ". . . If they do, why then they're a kind of serpent, that's all I can say."[3]

This is a common type of propositional argument called a hypothetical syllogism. Here is a common, valid symbolic form of a hypothetical argument:

> If A, then B.
> A.
> Therefore, B.

Notice that this was the form of the pigeon's argument to Alice:

> If you eat eggs, you're a serpent. (If A, then B.)
> Alice eats eggs. (A is true.)
> Therefore, Alice is a serpent. (Therefore, B is true.)

From your studies in this book, you can probably figure out that the problem with this hypothetical syllogism is that the first premise—"If you eat eggs, you're a serpent"—is not true. You will learn about hypothetical syllogisms and other propositional arguments as you continue to progress in your logic studies.

DEDUCTION IN ACTION

What Aristotle Has to Say

Now that we have examined both sides of the argument about our proposition "To be a good friend, a person must love himself or herself the most," let's look at what Aristotle has to say about the matter. Read the following argument carefully, out loud if necessary, and then answer the questions at the end.

> Perhaps we ought to mark off such arguments from each other and determine how far and in what respects each view is right. Now if we grasp the sense in which each school uses the phrase "lover of self," the truth may become evident. Those who use the term as one of reproach ascribe self-love to people who assign to themselves the greater share of wealth, honours, and bodily pleasures; for these are what most people desire, and busy themselves about as though they were the best of all things, which is the reason, too, why they become objects of competition. So those who are grasping with regard to these things gratify their appetites and in general their feelings and the irrational element of the soul; and most men are of this nature (which is the reason why the epithet has come to be used as it is—it takes its meaning from the prevailing type of self-love, which is a bad one); it is just, therefore, that men who are lovers of self in this way are reproached for being so. That it is those who give themselves the preference in regard to objects of this sort that most people usually call lovers of self is plain; for if a man were always anxious that he himself, above all things, should act justly, temperately, or in accordance with any other of the virtues, and in general were always to try to secure for himself the honourable course, no one will call such a man a lover of self or blame him.

> But such a man would seem more than the other a lover of self; at all events he assigns to himself the things that are noblest and best, and gratifies the most authoritative element in and in all things obeys this; and just as a city or any other systematic whole is most properly identified with the most authoritative element in it, so is a man; and therefore the man who loves this and gratifies it is most of all a lover of self. Besides, a man is said to have or not to have self-control according as his reason has or has not the control, on the assumption that this is the man himself; and the things men have done on a rational principle are thought most properly their own acts and voluntary acts. That this is the man himself, then, or is so more than anything else, is plain, and also that the good man loves most this part of him. Whence it follows that he is most truly a lover of self, of another type than that which is a matter of reproach, and as different from that as living according to a rational principle is from living as passion dictates, and desiring what is noble from desiring what seems advantageous. Those, then, who busy themselves in an exceptional degree with noble actions all men approve and praise; and if all were to strive towards what is noble and strain every nerve to do the noblest deeds, everything would be as it should be for the common weal, and every one would secure for himself the goods that are greatest, since virtue is the greatest of goods.

> Therefore the good man should be a lover of self (for he will both himself profit by doing noble acts, and will benefit his fellows), but the wicked man should not; for he will hurt both himself and his neighbours, following as he does evil passions. For the wicked man, what he does clashes with what he ought to do, but what the good man ought to do he does; for

DEDUCTION IN ACTION (CONTINUED)

reason in each of its possessors chooses what is best for itself, and the good man obeys his reason. It is true of the good man too that he does many acts for the sake of his friends and his country, and if necessary dies for them; for he will throw away both wealth and honours and in general the goods that are objects of competition, gaining for himself nobility; since he would prefer a short period of intense pleasure to a long one of mild enjoyment, a twelvemonth of noble life to many years of humdrum existence, and one great and noble action to many trivial ones. Now those who die for others doubtless attain this result; it is therefore a great prize that they choose for themselves. They will throw away wealth too on condition that their friends will gain more; for while a man's friend gains wealth he himself achieves nobility; he is therefore assigning the greater good to himself. The same too is true of honour and office; all these things he will sacrifice to his friend; for this is noble and laudable for himself. Rightly then is he thought to be good, since he chooses nobility before all else. But he may even give up actions to his friend; it may be nobler to become the cause of his friend's acting than to act himself. In all the actions, therefore, that men are praised for, the good man is seen to assign to himself the greater share in what is noble. In this sense, then, as has been said, a man should be a lover of self; but in the sense in which most men are so, he ought not.[4]

1. In the first paragraph, what kind of lover of self does Aristotle agree is bad?

2. In the second paragraph, there is another lover of self that Aristotle believes is the true lover of self. What is that person like?

3. Why is the good man a true lover of self?

4. Why shouldn't the evil man love himself?

5. How is the good man different from the evil man, besides the fact that one is good and the other bad? How does this support Aristotle's original idea that good men should love themselves?

6. Do you agree with Aristotle's assessment? If so, what do you think are the greatest strengths of his argument, and why do you think that? If not, what type of dispute do you have with Aristotle: empirical, definitional, or presuppositional? Propose an alternate fact, definition, or presupposition that you think clarifies the matter.

APPENDIX A
Figure and Mood

FIGURE

	Figure 1		Figure 2		Figure 3		Figure 4	
Major Premise	M	P	P	M	M	P	P	M
Minor Premise	S	M	S	M	M	S	M	S

MNEMONIC

Barbara, Celarent, Darii, Ferio *que prioris*; Cesare, Camestres, Festino, Baroco *secundae*; *Tertia*, Darapti, Disamis, Datisi, Felapton, Bocardo, Ferison, *habet*; *Quarta in super addit* Bramantip, Camenes, Dimaris, Fesapo, Fresison

MOOD

Figure 1	AAA	EAE	AII	EIO		
Figure 2	EAE	AEE	EIO	AOO		
Figure 3	AAI	IAI	AII	EAO	OAO	EIO
Figure 4	AAI	AEE	IAI	EAO	EIO	

APPENDIX B
Venn Diagrams of Valid Syllogisms Based on Mnemonic

FIRST-FIGURE SYLLOGISMS

Barbara

All M is P.
All S is M.
All S is P.

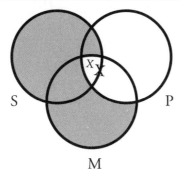

Celarent

No M is P.
All S is M.
No S is P.

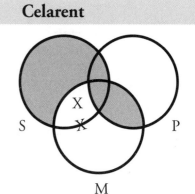

Darii

All M is P.
Some S is M.
Some S is P.

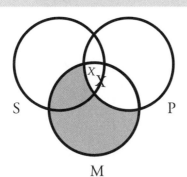

Ferio

No M is P.
Some S is M.
Some S is not P.

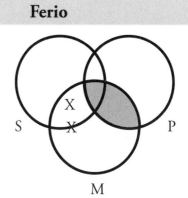

SECOND-FIGURE SYLLOGISMS

Cesare

No P is M.
All S is M.
No S is P.

Camestres

All P is M.
No S is M.
No S is P.

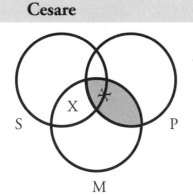

SECOND-FIGURE SYLLOGISMS (CONTINUED)

Festino	Baroco

No P is M.
Some S is M.
Some S is not P.

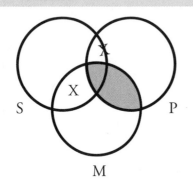

All P is M.
Some S is not M.
Some S is not P.

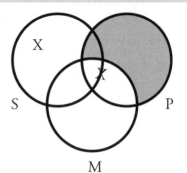

THIRD-FIGURE SYLLOGISMS

Darapti	Disamis

All M is P.
All M is S.
Some S is P.

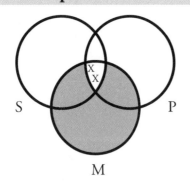

Some M is P.
All M is S.
Some S is P.

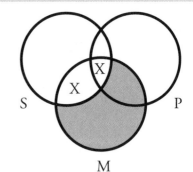

Datisi	Felapton

All M is P.
Some M is S.
Some S is P.

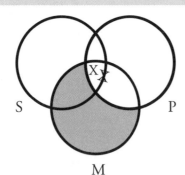

No M is P.
All M is S.
Some S is not P.

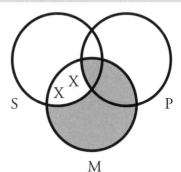

THIRD-FIGURE SYLLOGISMS (CONTINUED)

Bocardo

Some M is not P.

All M is S.

Some S is not P.

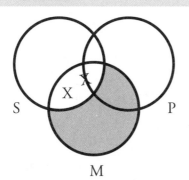

Ferison

No M is P.

Some M is S.

Some S is not P.

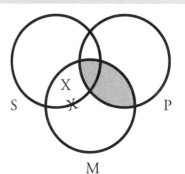

FOURTH-FIGURE SYLLOGISMS

Bramantip

All P is M.

All M is S.

Some S is P.

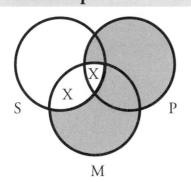

Camenes

All P is M.

No M is S.

No S is P.

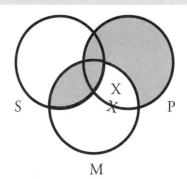

Dimaris

Some P is M.

All M is S.

Some S is P.

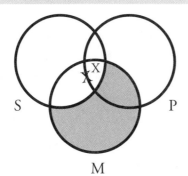

Fesapo

No P is M.

All M is S.

Some S is not P.

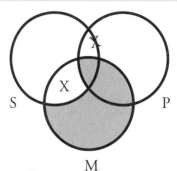

Fresison

No P is M.

Some M is S.

Some S is not P.

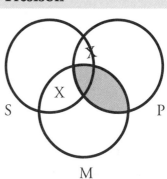

Name: _____ Date: _____

APPENDIX C
Syllogism Evaluation Form

Part A: Write Out the Syllogism

_____

_____

_____

_____

Part B: Convert to Categorical Form
Hint: Fill in the conclusion line first and work up.

_____ is _____.

_____ is _____.

Therefore, _____ is _____.

Part C: Schema
Reminder: Simply rewrite the syllogism, but substitute **S**, **M**, *and* **P** *for the terms.*

_____ is _____.

_____ is _____.

Therefore, _____ is _____.

Part D: Mood and Figure

_____ _____ _____ – _____

Part F: Circle the Fallacies, If Any:

Rule 1: _____

• Fallacy of Four Terms   • Equivocation

Rule 2: _____

Rule 3: _____

Rule 4: _____

Major? _____   Minor? _____

Rule 5: _____

Rule 6: _____

Rule 7: _____

299

APPENDIX D
Analyzing Arguments Inductively

Sometimes it can be very difficult to determine whether or not a fact is 100 percent true or 100 percent false. For instance, consider the following statements: Meat is never an optimal food for humans; meat is an optimal food for humans. Eating any fast food is horrible for your health; fast food can be part of a healthy diet. God exists; God doesn't exist. All people have guardian angels; guardian angels are fictitious, imaginary creatures. There is intelligent life on other planets; there is no intelligent life on other planets.

All of these statements are factual statements. They are propositions. Therefore, they are either true or false. However, as you can imagine, it is very difficult to prove the truth or falsity of these propositions with 100 percent accuracy. This is because some of these propositions, like the first couple about the effects of eating meat or fast food, contain so many variables that it is extremely difficult to determine their truth-value with 100 percent certainty.

The truth-value of statements like the last two about God and extraterrestrial life is difficult to prove because of several different reasons. We don't have tests or technology at this time that can measure these types of things. Furthermore, many people would argue that science doesn't have the capability, and never will, to measure spiritual or religious matters, such as whether God exists or not. What, then, do we do in situations in which we cannot determine the truth-value of a proposition with 100 percent certainty? We use inductive logic to examine whether the evidence supporting a proposition or argument is strong or weak.

You probably already know how to use inductive logic to some degree because you use it in your everyday life. For example, you may recall that inductive logic is based on generalization. That is, people make observations in everyday life, notice a pattern, and then make an inductive generalization based on the pattern they note. What kind of observations do people make? They might make an observation of cause-and-effect relationships. For example, a person might notice that when people study, they tend to get good grades, or when they smoke, they tend to get more diseases, such as lung cancer. That is, the person notices that one factor causes the other factor.

People might also generalize from examples or illustrations. For instance, someone might notice examples of absolute monarchs in history who are tyrannical, and she might generalize that absolute monarchs abuse power. She has generalized this from the historical examples she has examined. Another type of generalization someone might make is from expert opinion. For example, if a person is curious about the cause of poverty, he might read a lot of books on this subject. In his reading, he might notice that almost all experts agree that a lack of education is a common cause of poverty. Therefore, he might generalize that failure to graduate from high school is a common cause of poverty. These types of arguments—cause and effect, examples, and expert opinion—are just three types of generalizations people make. (If you are interested in learning other generalization techniques, you can study them in *The Argument Builder*, published by Classical Academic Press.)

In reading these examples of different types of generalizations, you probably realized that you do this quite a bit in your thinking and discussion already. In fact, almost everybody reasons this way.

That is, people naturally reason by making generalizations based on daily observations. However, although generalization is a common and helpful reasoning tool, it is possible to make faulty or illogical generalizations. For example, one common inductive fallacy is **illegitimate appeal to authority**. This occurs when someone makes a generalization from authorities that are not authorities in the area about which they are speaking. For instance, let us say that Dr. Phillips, who has a doctorate in physics, mentions offhandedly in his physics class that one of the main causes of poverty is a very poor education. If a student in Dr. Phillips's class later cited Dr. Phillips's statement in a paper on the causes of poverty and relied on Dr. Phillips's expertise to prove this statement, she would be committing the fallacy of an illegitimate appeal to authority because Dr. Phillips, while certainly an expert of some kind, is not an expert on the causes of poverty. He is only an expert in physics. There are many types of common inductive fallacies, and learning them can be a great aid in helping you to think more clearly. (If you would like to learn more about the inductive fallacies, you should consult *The Art of Argument* or *The Argument Builder*.)

Now that you have a basic idea of what generalization is and what a logical fallacy is, you can better understand how you might use inductive logic to dispute the soundness of a premise in a syllogism when it involves a complex empirical dispute. You would examine the evidence behind the premise to see if the inductive evidence supporting it is strong or weak. There are several different ways you can do this. You can demonstrate that the evidence supporting a premise is weak because the examples used to support the generalization are inadequate, misunderstood, or misrepresented. You can demonstrate that the evidence supporting the premise is factually incorrect. You can also demonstrate that the evidence supporting the premise commits a logical fallacy. Critiquing the evidence behind a premise inductively can be a very effective method for disputing arguments.

Through *The Discovery of Deduction*, you have learned that deductive logic works though inference from *a priori* propositions. However, you have also learned that sometimes people believe that the propositions in their arguments are *a priori* propositions when they actually are not. One way that you can critique an argument

that has questionable *a priori* propositions as premises is to use inductive logic to demonstrate that the evidence supporting the proposition is weak. In this way, you effectively use a combination of induction and deduction to critique the argument.

APPENDIX E
Handling Religious, Moral, and Ethical Disputes

One of the most difficult kinds of disputes to handle is a religious dispute or a dispute over the morals and ethics that flow out of religious beliefs. Many people feel that we shouldn't even argue about religious beliefs. After all, some people will ask, aren't all religions equally true?

As we have mentioned in this book, deduction works from inference from *a priori* premises. However, as we mentioned in the appendix on induction (appendix D), sometimes people believe the propositions in their arguments are *a priori* propositions when they really are not. One way you can critique an argument such as this is to use inductive logic to demonstrate that the evidence supporting a proposition is weak (see appendix D for an explanation of this process).

This is fairly easy to do when propositions pertain to matters such as eating habits, physical health, and causes of poverty, but what about propositions pertaining to religious issues, such as whether or not God exists, whether lying is wrong or not, or whether or not angels exist? After all, aren't all religious beliefs equal? Can we really critique the truth-value of propositions that pertain to people's religious beliefs? Furthermore, if we do attempt to critique the truth-value of a religious belief, aren't we being intolerant?

The truth is that we can and even *should* critique religious beliefs, but civility and wisdom should certainly accompany any discussion of this kind. However, while tolerance, or civility, is important, it is not necessary to accept all religious beliefs as equally valid in order to be tolerant. In fact, declaring all religious beliefs as equally true can lead to contradiction and illogic, which are never helpful in the search for truth.

First of all, before we discuss religious beliefs and how and why we should critique them, it is important to clarify the difference between beliefs that are preferences and beliefs that are based on propositions that have a truth-value. For example, let's say that a guy named Drew says, "I believe that green is the best color in the world," but his friend, Jennifer, contradicts him, saying, "Blue is the best color in the world." Would we be justified in saying, in this scenario, that both of them are right because Drew has his own favorite color, and Jennifer has her own favorite color? It seems like the answer should be "yes," but in this scenario, it is actually misleading to use the word "right" to describe Drew and Jennifer's declarations.

You might remember that in our discussion of propositions earlier in this book, we discussed that only propositions can have truth-values and that propositions are statements that can be proven true or false. Whether or not a color is the best color in the world cannot be proven true or false because there is no such thing as a "best color," unless you are using the phrase "best color" in the context of which color best compliments another color. But that is not the context in which Drew and Jennifer are using the phrase "best color" in the illustration above.

In essence, both Drew and Jennifer are stating their color *preference*. That is, they are *self-reporting* on their favorite color. Self-reports are not debatable because we generally assume someone's self-report is true. In other words, they believe what they say they believe. Therefore, although it would

be incorrect to say that both Drew and Jennifer's beliefs are "right," we could say, "Drew and Jennifer, you are both allowed to have your own favorite color, and it is silly to fight over this issue because favorite colors are preferences, not scientific facts. So, be kind to each other, and enjoy your own favorite color."

The point of this illustration is to demonstrate that people are entitled to their own preferences, and they should be respectful of other people's preferences. However, preferences are self-reports and do not contain truth-values and, therefore, it is incorrect to say that both people's preferences are "right," or true.

It is important to realize that while some religious beliefs may be preferences, many religious beliefs are based on propositions with truth-values. For example, let's consider the statement "God exists." Let us say that you have two people: one who believes that God does exist and one who believes that God does not exist. As we know from the square of opposition, it is impossible for both of these beliefs to be true at the same time because it is impossible for something to exist and not exist at the same time. Therefore, if one person believes that God does exist, and one person believes that God does not exist, one of them is right and one of them is wrong. However, it is likely impossible to prove which one is which with 100 percent accuracy, given our current scientific and logical tools. Even philosophers and scientists generally agree that it is impossible to design a scientific experiment or develop a philosophical argument that irrefutably proves or disproves the existence of God. Therefore, while the proposition "God exists" certainly has a truth-value, it is impossible to determine this truth-value beyond a shadow of a doubt with any current scientific or logical tools.

People often have very strong opinions about the truth-value of the proposition "God exists." Religious beliefs usually proceed from either a belief in God's existence and how we believe He has told us how to act or from a disbelief in God's existence. To illustrate the difficulty of analyzing religious beliefs, consider the act of lying. Someone might say, "Lying is always wrong," and another person might say, "Sometimes lying is not wrong." These statements are contradictory, meaning that if one is true, then the other is false. We cannot do a scientific test

to prove any truth about lying, but these statements do contain truth-values—they are not merely preferences or self-reports.

Let us say, for example, that God does exist, and that He is, indeed, all-knowing and perfectly good. If this is so, then God is the ultimate source of moral standards because He always knows what is right in all situations. Therefore, people would look to God's wisdom or commands in order to determine the truth-value of the propositions about lying. On the other hand, let us say that God does not exist and that there is no ultimately wise, ultimately perfect being who knows the ultimate good. Then, people would have to set forth another standard that would guide their decisions about lying. For instance, they might say that whether or not lying is good or bad always depends on the culture and what is best in that culture. Or they might argue that for all cultures, lying is generally bad for the community, but there are a few exceptions. This does not exhaust all the possible beliefs about God and lying, but it does illustrate some possible positions people might hold.

It is important to realize that although we cannot prove whether or not God exists with 100 percent accuracy, we can use logic to determine whether or not it is likely that God exists. If we can use logic to determine the likelihood of God's existence, we can also use logic to determine the likelihood that beliefs that flow from a belief or disbelief in God are true or false.

Although we can use logic to do these things, you may be wondering if it is really worthwhile to do so. After all, why not just "live and let live," as the saying goes? It is important to realize that if some religious beliefs are based on propositions with truth-values, then those beliefs are our guide about what is right, true, good, and beautiful. Whether or not we do what is right, good, or true certainly affects our lives, our families, our neighborhoods, and our societies, which is why it is good and even necessary to discuss and debate these ideas.

The point is that there is a right and a wrong answer about many religious issues, as well as the morals and ethics that flow from them. However, we cannot design a test or check a fact in a book to prove irrefutably the truth-value of such issues. Therefore, we must decide what we believe to be true, using logic as well as advice from our parents and

mentors, and we must treat each other with kindness and civility when we disagree.

The United States has had a long tradition of religious freedom, which is a good thing because, frankly, you can't force someone to believe what he doesn't believe. We may hope to convince people that our belief is correct or, just as importantly, we may desire to recognize the flaws in our own belief system. The only way we can do this is to have productive, thorough, and clear discussions that help us search for the truth. Civility and kindness promote this type of discussion, whereas rudeness and hate disrupt it.

Interestingly, treating propositions that have truth-values as though they were only self-reports or preferences (i.e., claiming that everyone's belief is equally right) can also disrupt this type of discussion because it leads to contradiction and logical absurdities. Furthermore, it reduces all moral and religious beliefs to mere preferences, and it is silly, in most cases, to argue about preferences. After all, if, for example, all political beliefs have equal truth-values and are just preferences, we wouldn't need to waste time watching presidential debates and discussing political platforms with our friends and family.

However, we recognize, inherently, that this is not how it is. We do believe that our beliefs, and the actions that flow from our beliefs, do make a difference in the world around us. They contain truth-value. Therefore, the best type of tolerance is the kind that recognizes that all *people* are equally valuable, but not all *beliefs* are true. We should engage in actions that promote reasonable, civil, and thorough discourse, because this is what helps us to discover truth. (For more information on engaging in productive debate and discussion, see Classical Academic Press's text *Everyday Debate & Discussion: A Guide to Socratic Conversation, Informal Discussion, and Formal Debate*.)

ENDNOTES

Note: Some of the endnote numbers will appear to skip. This is because the missing numbers apply solely to the teacher's edition.

Lesson 1.1: Formal vs. Informal Logic

1. Louis P. Pojman, *Classics of Philosophy*, vol. I, *Ancient and Medieval*, Plato, the *Apology* (New York: Oxford University Press,1998), n.p.

2. C.L. Hamblin, *Fallacies* (London: Methuen, 1970), n.p.

3. Bryan Magee, *The Story of Philosophy* (New York: Dorling Kinserly, 2001), 86.

4. Joel Feinberg and Russ Shafer-Landau, *Reason and Responsibility: Readings in Some Basic Problems of Philosophy* (Belmont, CA: Thompson Wadsworth, 2008), 130-131.

5. Descartes actually considered his famous statement "I think; therefore I am" as a matter of intuition, rather than deductive inference. In other words, he believed that we all have an intuition—a clear, distinct and undeniable conception of our existence. For Descartes, this conception was innate, or inside all of us as an undeniable reality that leaves no room for doubt. Even to say, "I doubt that I exist" shows that someone (the "I" in the statement) is doing the doubting and that the doubter must therefore exist! As shown in the syllogism, it is also possible to turn Decartes' statement into an example of a deductive syllogism by adding the first premise "All beings that think are (exist)."

Lesson 1.2: Deductive vs. Inductive Reasoning

1. John Locke, "Quotes from John Locke," *ThinkExist.com*, <http://thinkexist.com/quotation/logic_is_the_anatomy_of/170278.html>.

2. A good example of this would be an in-depth study of scientific reasoning using John Stuart Mill's Canons fof Induction, as is done in Copi's logic curriculum *An Introduction to Logic*.

3. Peter Kreeft, *Socratic Logic: A Logic Text Using Socratic Method, Platonic Question, and Aristotelian Principles*, 3rd ed. (Sound Bend, IN: St. Augustine's Press, 2008), 358.

4. Pojman, 11.

Lesson 1.3: Categorical vs. Propositional Logic

1. The "being" verbs are: am, is, are, was, were, be, being, been.

2. Andrew Carnegie, "Famous Andrew Carnegie Quotes," <http://www.quotes.net/quote/3069>.

3. One recent (and excellent) text written by Paul Herrick for college-level students, entitled *The Many Worlds of Logic*, uses a very similar analogy by comparing the different types of logic to different worlds. It is very good for exploring many different types of logic that we don't have time for in this curriculum.

4. The previously mentioned text, Herrick's *The Many Worlds of Logic*, in fact, is an example of a textbook that takes this approach.

5. "She's a Witch," *Monty Python and the Holy Grail*, transcript, from <http://www.youtube.com/watch?v=zrzMhU_4m-g>.

Lesson 2.1: Part I: Artistotle Gets the Ball Rolling

1. Michael Moncur, "Michael Moncur's (Cynical) Quotes," Quotation #1152, Aristotle, <http://www.quotationspage.com/quote/1152.html>.

2. When seventeenth-century English scholar Francis Bacon wrote about the need to put more emphasis on inductive logic (and experimental science) and less emphasis on deductive logic, he entitled his work *Novum Organum*, or "new instrument," to indicate his belief that a new tool was needed to push forward the frontiers of human knowledge.

3. Morton L. Schagrin, "Logic," in *World Book Encyclopedia* (New York: Scott Fetzer Company, 1992), 429.

4. Magee, 32-35.

5. *Stanford Encyclopedia of Philosophy*, s.v. "Ancient Logic," <http://plato.stanford.edu/entries/logic-ancient/> (accessed July 27, 2009).

6. Magee, 19.

7. R.W. Southern, *The Making of the Middle Ages* (New Haven, CT: Yale University Press, 1953), n.p.

8. *Stanford Encyclopedia of Philosophy*, s.v. "William of Ockham," <http://plato.stanford.edu/entries/ockham/> (accessed October 10, 2008).

9. As one historian wrote: "The whole process of simplification and arrangement was a revelation both of the powers of the mind, and of the orderliness which lay behind a bewildering complexity of apparently unrelated facts. The world of learning and the world of experience were, for the most part fragmentary and disjointed . . . Men who had learned that there were only fourteen (or was it nineteen) kinds of valid argument and only nine (or was it ten?) categories of experience, and that every possible statement could be classified on a simple system whose rules even a schoolboy could learn to apply, were ready to extend the same process of analysis to the deadly sins, the cardinal virtues, the gifts of the Holy Spirit, the Sacraments, and even to the Persons of the Trinity, to the substance and accidents of the Eucharist, and the Humanity and Divinity of Christ." Southern, 181.

10. Magee, 59.

Lesson 2.2: Part II: Aristotle Is Lost and Then Found

1. Louis Brandeis, *WorldofQuotes.com*, <http://www.worldofquotes.com/topic/Logic/1/index.html>.

2. Magee, 74-77.

3. Evidence of a backlash can be seen in the literature of the period. Here is an example from 1835: "Give a boy *Robinson Crusoe*. That is worth all the grammars of rhetoric and logic in the world . . . Whoever reasoned better for having been taught the difference between a syllogism and an enthymeme? Who ever composed with greater spirit and elegance because he could define an oxymoron or an aposiopesis? I am not joking but writing quite seriously when I say that I would much rather order a hundred copies of *Jack the Giant-Killer* for our school than a hundred copies of any grammar of rhetoric or logic that ever was written." Lord Macauley, quoted in Southern, 184.

4. Irving Copi, *Introduction to Logic*, 5th ed. (New York: Macmillan Publishing Co., 1978), 189.

5. Peter King and Stewart Shapiro, "The History of Logic," in *The Oxford Companion to Philosophy* (Oxford: Oxford University Press, 1995), 496-500. Specific information taken from <http://individual.utoronto.ca/pking/miscellaneous/history-of-logic.pdf>, 5.

6. The logic that many instructors wanted to emphasize was informal logic, often called "critical thinking." A real transformation occurred in the 1970s with the publication of Howard Kahane's *Logic and Contemporary Rhetoric*, which teaches the practical application of logic through the informal fallacies and the critique of examples from contemporary media. Numerous similar books have emerged over the last thirty years, and our *The Art of Argument* has been one of the first such books specifically created with secondary school students in mind.

Lesson 3.2: The Three Acts of the Mind

1. Lorraine Hansberry, *A Raisin in the Sun*, *The Quote Garden*, <http://www.quotegarden.com/thinking.html>.

Lesson 4.2: Categorical Form Introduced

1. Baltasar Gracian, *ThinkExist.com*, <http://thinkexist.com/quotation/don-t_take_the_wrong_side_of_an_argument_just/10365.html>.

5. Pojman, p. 8.

Lesson 4.3: Propositions

1. Dorothy Thompson, *ThinkExist.com*, <http://thinkexist.com/quotation/there_is_nothing_to_fear_except_the_persistent/338962.html>.

2. *Merriam-Webster Online Dictionary*, s.v. "Truth-value," <http://www.merriam-webster.com/dictionary/truth-value> (accessed March 11, 2008).

3. The exclamation "Ouch!" seems to have a truth value. Typically, when people say, "Ouch!" what they really mean is, "That hurts me!" which is a self-report. Since "Ouch!" is an opinion given by the receiver of the pain, it should not fall into the exclamations category. "Ouch!" is really a self-report in the form of an exclamation and is therefore a statement that exclaims that one is in pain.

Lesson 4.4: Translating Arguments Step 1: Finding the Propositions

1. Dave Barry, *ThinkExist.com*, <http://thinkexist.com/quotation/i_argue_very_well-ask_any_of_my_remaining_friends/202498.html>.

Lesson 4.5: Translating Arguments Step 2: Finding the Subject Term and the Predicate Term

1. David Hume, *QuotationsPage.com*, <http://www.quotationspage.com/quote/3615.html>.

2. John Stuart Mill, "On Liberty," in *The Internet Encyclopedia of Philosophy: An Overview of John Stuart Mill*, <http://www.iep.utm.edu/m/milljs.htm#SH2e>.

3. Karl Marx, "The Communist Manifesto," in *BrainyQuote.com*, <http://www.brainyquote.com/quotes/authors/k/karl_marx_3.html>.

4. Myrna R. Grant, *Poems for a Good and Happy Life* (New York: Random House, 1997), 110.

5. Ibid., 58.

6. William Shakespeare, "A Midsummer Night's Dream," OpenSourceShakespeare.org, <http://tinyurl.com/ozbmdj3>.

Lesson 4.6: Translating Arguments Step 3: Affirmo *and* Nego

1. Rufus Choate, *Book of Famous Quotes*, <http://www.famous-quotes.com/author.php?aid=1499>.

Lesson 4.7: Translating Arguments Step 4: Supply the Proper Quantifier

1. Oliver Goldsmith, *The Deserted Village*, taken from *WorldofQuotes.com*, <http://www.worldofquotes.com/author/Oliver-Goldsmith/1/index.html>.

Lesson 4.8: Translating Arguments Step 5: Propositions Translated into Categorical Form

1. Patricia Curd, ed., and Richard D. McKirahan, trans., *A Presocratic Reader* (Indianapolis: Hackett Publishing Company, Inc., 1995), n.p.

2. Alexander Hamilton, Harold Coffin Syrett, Jacob Ernest Cooke, *The Papers of Alexander Hamiton*, <http://tinyurl.com/qdzz42t> (accessed April 8, 2015).

3. William Pitt, "You Cannot Conquer America," *History Database Search*, <http://tinyurl.com/lguogmd>.

4. John Adams, "Be Yourselves, O Americans," *ProjectGutenberg.com* <http://www.gutenberg.org/ebooks/15391>.

5. Maximilien Robespierre, "Terror Is Nothing Else Than Justice," *Wikipedia*, <http://en.wikipedia.org/wiki/Maximilien_Robespierre>.

Lesson 5.2: The Square of Opposition

1. Spock, "I, Mudd," *Star Trek*, season 2, episode 8, via IMDB.com, <http://www.imdb.com/title/tt0708432/quotes>.

2. *Define.com*, s.v. "Infer," <http://define.com/infer> (accessed February 26, 2009).

3. *Define.com*, s.v. "Imply," <http://define.com/imply> (accessed February 26, 2009).

4. Sir Arthur Conan Doyle, "The Adventures of the Dancing Men," *The Return of Sherlock Holmes*, *LiteratureCollection.com*, <http://www.literaturecollection.com/a/doyle/sherlock-holmes2/3/>.

Lesson 5.3: Contradiction

1. Curd, *A Presocratic Reader*, n.p.

Lesson 5.4: Contrariety and Subcontrariety

1. Douglas Adams, Quotation #26280, *Quotations Page*, <http://www.quotationspage.com/quote/26280.html>.

Lesson 5.5: Subimplication and Superimplication

1. From *The Evangelical Outpost: Reflections on Culture, Politics and Religion from an Evangelical World*, <http://evangelicaloutpost.com/archives/2007/02/the-syllogisms-of-seinfeldthe-connections-between-logic-and-humor-2.html>.

2. Beth Henschen and Edward Sidlow, *America at Odds: The Essentials* (Florence, KY: Wadsworth, 2004), 357.

3. Ibid., 78.

4. Ibid., 83.

5. "Player Under Pressure," *Bones*, season 3, episode 11, first aired April 21, 2008.

Lesson 5.6: The Square of Opposition and Inference Analysis

1. Pojman, 35.

2. Ibid.

Lesson 6.2: Logical Equations

1. Cardinal de Retz, *ThinkExist.com*, <http://thinkexist.com/quotations/arguments/>.

Lesson 6.3: The Obverse Relationship

1. Dale Carnegie, *QuoteDB.com*, <http://www.quotedb.com/quotes/845>.

2. David Kelley, *The Art of Reasoning with Symbolic Logic* (New York and London: W.W. Norton and Company, 1990), 185.

Lesson 6.4: The Converse Relationship

1. Michel Eyquem De Montaigne, *Book of Famous Quotes*, <http://www.famous-quotes.com/topic.php?tid=70>.

2. *Online Etymology Dictionary*, s.v. "Imply," <http://www.etymonline.com/index.php?term=Imply> (accessed June 26, 2009).

3. Ibid.

Lesson 6.5: The Relationship of Contraposition

1. William G. McAdoo, *The Quotations Page*, <http://www.quotationspage.com/quote/23566.html>.

Lesson 7.2: Arranging the Syllogism

1. Sir Arthur Conan Doyle, *A Study in Scarlet*, *Wikiquote.com*, <http://en.wikiquote.org/wiki/Sherlock_Holmes#A_Study_in_Scarlet_.281888.29>.

Lesson 7.3: Categorical Syllogisms

1. "I Am Nobody" T-shirt, *Zazzle.com*, <http://www.zazzle.com/i_am_nobody_nobody_is_perfect_therefore_i_a_shirt-235163787612964834>.

2. Thomas Aquinas, "Question 4, Article 3. Whether comprehension is necessary for happiness?" *Summa Theologica*, *NewAdvent.com*, <http://www.newadvent.org/summa/2004.htm>.

3. Thomas Aquinas, *Summa Theologica*, "Question 5, Article 3. Whether one can be happy in this life?" <http://www.newadvent.org/summa/2005.htm>.

Lesson 7.4: Enthymemes

1. Jerry and Elaine, in "The Wink," from *Seinfeld*, in "The Syllogisms of Seinfeld: The Connections Between Logic and Humor," *The Evangelical Outpost: Reflections on Culture, Politics and Religion from an Evangelical Worldview*, <http://evangelicaloutpost.com/archives/2007/02/the-syllogisms-of-seinfeldthe-connections-between-logic-and-humor-2.html>.

2. Augustine, *City of God*, bk. 1, chap. 1, *NewAdvent.com*, <http://www.newadvent.org/fathers/120101.htm>.

3. Augustine, bk. 5, chap. 13, *NewAdvent.com*, <http://www.newadvent.org/fathers/120105.htm>.

4. Sir Arthur Conan Doyle, *The Adventure of the Empty House*, <http://www.gutenberg.org/files/108/108-h/108-h.htm#linkH2H_4_0001>.

5. Homer Simpson, *The Simpsons*, *ThinkExist.com*, <http://en.thinkexist.com/quotation/english-who_needs_that-i-m_never_going_to_england/338890.html>.

6. William Shakespeare, *Julius Caesar*, Act 3, Scene II, <http://shakespeare.mit.edu/julius_caesar/julius_caesar.3.2.html>.

Lesson 7.5: Moods and Figures

1. Winnie the Pooh, *ThinkExist.com*, <http://thinkexist.com/quotes/winnie_the_pooh/2.html>.

2. Martin Cothran, *Traditional Logic: Advanced Formal Logic* (Louisville, KY: Memoria Press, 2000), 10.

Lesson 8.1: Validity and the Counterexample Method

1. Dorothy L. Sayers, *Strong Poison* (New York: HarperCollins Publishers, 1930), n.p. Also available at <http://www.nonduality.com/hl1915.htm>.

2. You can learn about the most common types of inductive arguments in Classical Academic Press's book *The Argument Builder*. In addition, Classical Academic Press's book *The Art of Argument* teaches about thirty "informal" (and mostly inductive) fallacies.

Lesson 8.2: Evaluating Validity: Terminological Rules 1 and 2

1. J.K. Rowling, *Harry Potter and the Sorcerer's Stone*, "Treebeard's Stumper Answer," <http://www.rain.org/~mkummel/stumpers/17mar00a.html>.

2. The Declaration of Independence, *The Charters of Freedom: The Declaration*, <http://www.archives.gov/exhibits/charters/declaration_transcript.html>.

Lesson 8.3: Evaluating Validity: Terminological Rules 3 and 4

1. J.R.R. Tolkien, "J.R.R. Tolkien Quotes," *ThinkExist.com*, <http://thinkexist.com/quotes/j.r.r._tolkien>.

2. *Merriam-Webster Online Dictionary*, s.v. "Venn Diagram," <http://www.merriam-webster.com/dictionary/venn%20diagram> (accessed July 3, 2009).

Lesson 8.5: An Introduction to the Venn Diagramming Method of Establishing Validity

1. Charles Dickens, "Charles Dickens Quotes," *BrainyQuotes.com*, <http://www.brainyquote.com/quotes/authors/c/charles_dickens.html>.

Lesson 8.6: Combining the Skills

1. Agatha Christie, "Agatha Christie Quotes," *BrainyQuotes.com*, <http://www.brainyquote.com/quotes/authors/a/agatha_christie.html>.

Lesson 9.2: Types of Disagreements

1. William Shakespeare, "William Shakespeare Quotes," *BrainyQuotes.com*, <http://www.brainyquote.com/quotes/authors/w/william_shakespeare.html>.

2. *Dictionary.com*, s.v. "Pyrrhic victory," <http://dictionary.reference.com/browse/pyrrhic%20victory> (accessed July 27, 2009).

Lesson 9.3: Types of Definitions

1. J.R.R. Tolkien, "J.R.R. Tolkien Quotes," *ThinkExist.com*, <http://thinkexist.com/quotes/j.r.r._tolkien/2.html>.

2. Dorothy L. Sayers, "Dorothy L. Sayers Quotes," *ThinkExist.com*, <http://thinkexist.com/quotes/dorothy_l._sayers/2.html>.

3. *The Free Dictionary*, s.v. "Cheater," <http://www.thefreedictionary.com/Cheater> (accessed August 10, 2009).

4. *Merriam-Webster Online Dictionary*, s.v. "Woman," <http://www.merriam-webster.com/dictionary/woman> (accessed July 27, 2009).

5. *Dictionary.com*, s.v. "Table," <http://dictionary.reference.com/browse/chair> (accessed July 17, 2009).

Lesson 9.4: Extension vs. Intention

1. Dana Scully and Fox Mulder, "Quotes from *The X Files*," *PlanetClaire.com*, <http://www.planetclaire.org/xfiles/dana_scully.php>.

2. Roy Clouser, *The Myth of Religious Neutrality: An Essay on the Hidden Role of Religious Belief in Theories* (Notre Dame, IN: University of Notre Dame Press, 2005), n.p.

3. *WhatHappensNow.com*, s.v., "Burglary vs. Robbery," <http://www.whathappensnow.com/articles_show.cfm?id=194&cat=5&sub=1> (accessed August 10, 2009).

4. "The Lorelai's First Day at Yale," *Gilmore Girls*, season 4, episode 2, WB, September 30, 2003.

5. Richard McKeon, *The Basic Works of Aristotle*, from "Nichomachean Ethics," bk. 9, chap. 8 (New York: Random House, Inc., 1941), 1086-1087.

Lesson 9.5: Modes of Definition

1. Spock, "The Squire of Gothos," *Star Trek*, season 1, eposide 17, <http://www.imdb.com/title/tt0708478/quotes>.

2. In traditional Aristotelian logic, sometimes the term "comprehension" is used instead of intension.

3. In common, everyday language, the term "denotation" is often used to mean the objective meaning of a word, and "connotation" is used to mean the subjective or emotive meaning of a word. This is not precisely how logicians use these words, since logicians use the terms as synonyms for extension and intension. To avoid confusion between the conventional and logicians' use of these words, we will consistently use the terms "extension" and "intension."

4. *Thesaurus.com*, s.v. "Love," <http://thesaurus.reference.com/browse/love> (accessed August 10, 2009).

7. *Webster's Ninth New Collegiate Dictionary*, s.v. "Integrity," (Springfield, MA: Merriam-Webster, 1983).

8. *Thesaurus.com*, s.v. "Integrity," <http://thesaurus.reference.com/browse/integrity> (accessed July 31, 2009).

Lesson 9.6: Presuppositional Disputes

1. Aristotle, "Aristotle Quotes," *BrainyQuotes.com*, <http://www.brainyquotes.com/quotes/quotes/a/aristotle143026.html>.

2. Plato, *Euthyphro*, *The Internet Classics Archive*, <http://classics.mit.edu/Plato/euthyfro.html>.

Lesson 9.7: Pursuing Truth

1. G.K. Chesterton, *The Quotations Page*, <http://www.quotationspage.com/quotes/G._K._Chesterton/>.

2. This is a paraphrase of Plato's work. You can find a direct translation of Plato's *The Republic*, book 7, at <http://classics.mit.edu/Plato/republic.8.vii.html>.

3. Lewis Carroll, *Alice's Adventures in Wonderland*, *Answers.com*, <http://www.answers.com/topic/alice-s-adventures-in-wonderland-chapter-5>.

4. McKeon, 1086-1087.

GLOSSARY

Abstraction: The process of observing and then mentally categorizing something. **3.1**

Acts of the Mind: Different processes through which the mind proceeds in the act of reasoning. See also **judgment**, **inference**, and **simple apprehension**. **3.1**

Affirmo: Latin word meaning "I affirm." **4.6**

A priori: An idea or truth accepted as already true. **1.2**

Aquinas (AD 1224-1274): A medieval philosopher and theologian who wrote famous works, such as *Summa Theologica*. **1.3**

Argument: An activity in which people provide examples or rational reasons for or against an action with the intent to persuade. **3.1**

Aristotle (384-322 BC): A Greek philosopher and student of Plato who wrote famous works, such as *Nicomachean Ethics* and *Metaphysics*. **1.3**

Augustine (AD 354-430): A medieval philosopher and theologian who wrote famous works, such as *Confessions*, *City of God*, and *De Trinitas*. **1.3**

Axioms: Statements or propositions that are presented as true statements and from which an argument can be built. Also referred to as "postulates." **1.2**

Being Verb: The forms of the verb "to be," including *am*, *is*, *are*, *was*, *were*, *be*, *being*, and *been*. **1.3**

Borderline Cases: Cases in which it is unclear to which cases a certain term applies and which can be clarified by précising definitions. **9.4**

Categorical Form: The arrangement of the terms and words in a statement so that the statement either affirms (supports) or negates (denies) something about a specific topic. **4.2**

Categorical Logic: The branch of logic pioneered by Aristotle that deals primarily with categories of things. In a categorical argument, an argument can be represented with symbols, and each of those symbols represents a term, or a word or phrase, that describes a category of things. Categorical logic is always deductive logic, so only the structure or form of the argument is used to determine validity. Example: "All men are mortal" becomes *All S is P*. See also **term**. **1.3**

Categorical Proposition: A proposition that either confirms or denies something about a class of things. **4.6**

Categorical Syllogism: A syllogism in which the premises and the conclusions are written in standard categorical form, such as *S is P*. **1.3**

Category: A class of things represented by a term. **1.3**

Cause: Something that brings about a result or an effect. **3.1**

Certainty: The condition of knowing something absolutely. **8.5**

Clarity: One of the three principles of critical thinking in which language used in an argument is clear and not open to multiple interpretations. See also **presumption** and **relevance**. **3.1**

Class Inclusion: A state that occurs when one class of items is included in another class of items. **3.2**

Commands: Verbal statements that instruct someone to perform an action. **4.3**

Complement: The term that denotes everything not represented by a term; usually, this is represented by inserting the word "non" before the term. **6.3**

Complex Empirical Dispute: This is a dispute that concerns the facts in an argument for which an answer cannot be easily located in a book. Complex empirical disputes often involve many intertwining variables and factors and are often debated, even by experts in the matter. **9.2**

Conclusion: What a person believes based on evidence; the point of persuasion in a syllogism; that which the speaker is hoping his audience will be persuaded to do or believe; the last statement in an argument. **2.2**

Conclusion Indicators: Words or phrases, such as "therefore," "thus," "so," "it follows that," and "in conclusion," that indicate that the conclusion is about to follow. **4.4**

Connotation: See **intension**. **9.5**

Content: The ideas and information an argument contains. **1.1**

Contradiction: The relationship of opposition that exists between *A* and *O* propositions and *E* and *I* propositions. Contradictory statements cannot both be true or both be false at the same time. See also **contrariety**, **subcontrariety**, **subimplication**, and **superimplication**. **5.1**

Contraposition: This is a relationship of equivalence that occurs when you obvert a statement, then convert it, and then obvert it again. It exists only for *A* and *O* propositions. See also **conversion** and **obversion**. **6.1**

Contrariety: The relationship of opposition that exists between *A* and *E* propositions. *A* and *E* propositions cannot both be true at the same time, but they can both be false at the same time. See also **contradiction**, **subcontrariety**, **subimplication**, and **superimplication**. **5.1**

Conversion: The relationship of equivalence that occurs when you switch the subject and predicate of a proposition. It only works on *I* and *E* propositions. See also **contraposition** and **obversion**. **6.1**

Copula: The logic name for the being verb in a proposition. **4.5**

Counterexample Method: A method for determining the validity of syllogisms in which a person attempts to find a syllogism in the same schema that has true premises leading to a false conclusion. If a syllogism like this can be found, it proves that the syllogism schema is invalid. **8.1**

Deductive: Relating to reasoning that argues by inference from *a priori* truths. See also **deductive inference**, **deductive logic**, and **deductive reasoning**. **1.1**

Deductive Inference: A mental process through which a person arrives at new knowledge based on the truth of one or more given axioms or postulates. See also **axioms** and **postulates**. **3.1**

Deductive Logic: Logic that proceeds by inference from *a priori* propositions. **1.1**

Deductive Reasoning: A method of determining the validity of a "formal argument" (see **formal logic**) in which the conclusion must, necessarily, be true if the premises used to support it are true. Deductive arguments are said to be "black" or "white" and cannot be gray. **1.1**

Definitional Dispute: A dispute that centers around the definition or use of a word in an argument. See also **empirical dispute** and **presuppositional dispute**. **9.2**

Definition by Subclass: A definitional device that is a listing of various subclasses that fit into that class. See also **extensive definition**. **9.5**

Definition by Synonym: A method of definition that provides words similar or identical to the word being defined. **9.5**

Demonstrative Definition: See **ostensive definition**. **9.5**

Denotation: See **extension**. **9.5**

Dialectical: Pertaining to the language of debate or to the interchange of ideas between two people, as opposed to the logic of one man reasoning all by himself. **1.1**

Dilemmas: Situations in which one must choose between two unpleasant alternatives. **1.3**

Distributed (or Distribution): A quality that describes a term that is talking about all of the members represented by that class. **8.3**

E

Effect: A result or consequence that follows a cause or specific action. See also **cause**. **3.1**

Either-Or Scenarios: Scenarios in which one of two options is possible. **1.3**

Empirical Dispute: A dispute that centers around the facts in an argument. See also **definitional dispute** and **presuppositional dispute**. **9.2**

Enthymeme: An abbreviated form of a syllogism in which one of the premises is missing. See also **first-order enthymeme**, **second-order enthymeme**, and **third-order enthymeme**. **7.3**

Enumerative Definition: A definition device that lists items that illustrate a term. **9.5**

Equivocating Term: A term that occurs more than once in an argument that is presented as being used in the same way each time but is actually used in two different ways. **9.3**

Equivocation: A fallacy in which a term that is used in two different ways is presented as being used in only one way. See also **formal fallacies** and **fallacy of four terms**. **8.2**

Evidence: Facts used to support a conclusion or hypothesis. **1.2**

Exclamations: Verbal expressions, such as "Good grief!" and "Terrific!" which are indications of strong emotion, such as surprise, anger, or happiness. **4.3**

Explanation: A series of statements in which a cause is given for an effect. **3.1**

Extension: The quality of a term that describes all of the members belonging to, or denoted by, that term; the sum total of all of the members of a class. Also referred to as "denotation." See also **extensive definition**, **intension**, and **intensive definition**. **9.5**

Extensive Definition: A definition that indicates, in some manner, the members that belong to a category denoted by a term. See also **extension**, **intension**, and **intensive definition**. **9.5**

F

Fallacies: Poor arguments often created using false or invalid inferences. **1.1**

Fallacy of Four Terms: A formal fallacy that occurs when a syllogism contains four terms, or when a syllogism uses three terms, one of which is used in two different ways. **7.3**

Fallacy of the Undistributed Middle: A formal fallacy that occurs when the middle term of a syllogism is not distributed in at least one of the premises. **8.3**

Fallacy of Two Negative Premises: A formal fallacy that occurs when a syllogism has a conclusion following two negative premises. **8.4**

Figure: The way in which the middle term is arranged in a syllogism. See also **mood**. **7.4**

First-Order Enthymeme: A syllogism that has an implied first premise. **7.4**

Form: Pertains to the structure of a deductive argument. **1.1**

Formal Fallacies: Fallacies that pertain to errors in the structure and form of a syllogism. See also **equivocation** and **fallacy of four terms**. **8.1**

Formal Logic: One of the two branches in the study of logic (see also **informal logic**) centering on the form of an argument; it is reasoning in the abstract, focusing on deductive reasoning, where the validity of an argument is based solely on the structure (form) of the argument. **1.1**

G

Generalizations: Theories or hypotheses that are formed on the basis of perceived patterns in a variety of examples. **1.2**

Genus and Difference: A definitional device that indicates the larger category to which a term belongs and then the particular characteristics that distinguish it from other terms in that category. **9.5**

Givens (or Given Propositions): Basic conditions or assumptions. **1.2**

Greetings: Verbal expressions that communicate welcome or hospitality to a person or group of people. **4.3**

H

Hypotheticals: Possible scenarios. **1.3**

Hypothetical Syllogism: A syllogism that draws a conclusion from a cause-and-effect relationship between possible scenarios. **1.3**

I

Illegitimate Appeal to Authority: An informal fallacy in which someone draws a conclusion from the testimony of an authority whose expertise lies in a different field. **Appendix D**

Illicit Major: A formal fallacy that occurs when the major term of a syllogism is distributed in the conclusion but not in the premises. **8.3**

Illicit Minor: A formal fallacy that occurs when the minor term of a syllogism is distributed in the conclusion but not in the premises. **8.3**

Immediate Inferences: Another name for the relationships of equivalence, which tell us what equivalent statement a proposition immediately implies or to which it is identical. See also **relationships of equivalence**. **6.2**

Implied Conclusion: A conclusion that is not directly stated but can be inferred from the premises of a syllogism. **7.4**

Implied Premise: A premise that is not directly stated but that can be inferred from the other premise and the conclusion of a syllogism. **7.4**

Indefinite: The state of not being sure or certain. **4.8**

Inductive: Pertaining to reasoning that draws conclusions from generalizations. See also **inductive inference** and **inductive reasoning**. **1.1**

Inductive Inference: A reasoning process that occurs when someone arrives at a general conclusion or hypothesis based on observations of patterns in a group of examples. See also **generalizations**. **3.1**

Inductive Reasoning: A method of determining the validity of an informal argument that tends to start with evidence that can be observed and compiled and works toward generalizations that are reasonably accurate with more or less probability. Inductive arguments are said to be either "strong" or "weak." **1.2**

Inference: A reasoning process through which a person arrives at new information through the implications of other axioms, postulates, or observed examples. See also **acts of the mind**, **judgment**, and **simple apprehension**. 3.1

Informal Logic: One of the two branches in the study of logic (see also **formal logic**). Informal logic deals with ordinary-language arguments that tend to emphasize "inductive," rather than "deductive," reasoning. The structure or form of an argument is less the issue than the weight of the evidence, and the arguments are generally determined to be reasonably accurate with more or less probability. 1.1

Intension: The sum total of qualities that identify which entities are members of that class. Also referred to as "connotation." See also **extension**, **extensive definition**, and **intensive definition**. 9.5

Intensive Definition: A definition that indentifies which entities are members of that class. See also **extension**, **extensive definition**, and **intension**. 9.5

Invalid: Refers to an argument that has a conclusion that is not supported by its premises. It describes a deductive argument that is structured incorrectly. See also **valid**. 1.1

Judgment: A thinking process that occurs when a person expresses a relationship between two terms; a mental process by which we recognize and name an object. See also **acts of the mind**, **inference**, and **simple apprehension**. 3.1

Key Terms: In a statement or proposition, these are the subject and the predicate. 4.4

Lexical Definition: A definition for a word found in the dictionary. 9.4

Logic: The art and science of reasoning. Most often broken up into formal and informal logic. See also **formal logic** and **informal logic**. 1.1

Logical Operators: Words, such as "and" and "or," which connect parts of propositions. 1.3

Major Premise: The first premise in a properly structured syllogism; contains the major term. See also **major term**, **minor premise**, and **minor term**. 7.2

Major Term: The predicate of the conclusion, and the term that appears in the major premise. See also **major premise**, **middle term**, **minor premise**, and **minor term**. 7.1

Middle Term: The term that appears twice in the premises of a syllogism but not in the conclusion. It links the major and minor terms. See also **major term** and **minor term**. 7.1

Minor Premise: The second premise in a properly structured syllogism; contains the minor term. See also **major premise**, **major term**, and **minor term**. 7.2

Minor Term: The subject of the conclusion of a syllogism. It appears in the minor premise. See also **major premise** and **major term**. 7.1

Mnemonic: A device used to assist in memorizing a series of facts, words, dates. 7.5

Mood: The manner in which a syllogism's propositions are arranged according to quality. See also **figure** and **quality**. 7.4

Nego: Latin word meaning "I deny." 4.6

Nonsense Sentences: Sentences that are incomprehensible or whose key terms do not correspond to reality. 4.3

Obversion: A relationship of equivalence that occurs when the quality of the subject of a proposition is changed and then the predicate is negated. It can be performed on all propositions. See also **contraposition** and **conversion**. 6.1

Operative Definition: A definition that gives a set of procedures (or "operations") that can affirm if a term has the necessary qualities to fit into a given class. 9.5

Ordinary-Language Arguments: Arguments that are stated in the language people use when they are having an informal conversation. These arguments are not stated in categorical form and must be translated for use in deductive logic. Sometimes referred to as "everyday-language" or "everyday-English" arguments. 1.1

Ostensive Definition: A method of definition in which an example of a term is pointed at or indicated in some way in order to serve as an illustration of the term. Also referred to as a "demonstrative definition." 9.5

Particular Affirmative: A proposition that affirms something about some of the members of a category represented by a term. See also **particular negative**, **universal affirmative**, and **universal negative**. 4.6

Particular Negative: A proposition that denies something about some of the members of a category represented by a term. See also **particular affirmative**, **universal affirmative**, and **universal negative**. 4.6

Particular Proposition: A proposition that affirms or denies something about some of the members of a category represented by a term. 4.6

Persuasive Definition: A definition that is worded in such a way as to convince people of a certain view of that term. 9.3

Plato (428-347 BC): A Greek philosopher who wrote famous works, such as the *Republic*, *Euthyphro*, the *Apology*, and the *Crito*. 1.3

Postulates: Statements or rules considered to be true and through which further truths can be discovered. See also **axioms**. 1.2

Précising Definition: A definition that reduces vagueness and ambiguity and indicates in which circumstances the term under consideration is to be used. 9.4

Predicate Term: The term in a proposition that follows the verb and renames or describes the subject. 4.4

Premise: A reason given that leads to the arguer's conclusion. 2.2

Premise Indicators: Words or phrases, such as "since," "because," "for these reasons," and "it follows from" that indicate that the premises are about to follow. 4.4

Presumption: One of the three principles of critical thinking in which language used in an argument presents data fairly and does not make unnecessary assumptions. See also **clarity** and **relevance**. 3.1

Presupposition: A certain view or opinion held about the world. 9.6

Presuppositional Dispute: A dispute that centers around people's opinions or views of the world. See also **definitional dispute** and **empirical dispute**. 9.2

Probability: The likelihood or general reliability that something is right, true, or accurate. 1.2

Process of Inference: The steps through which a person proceeds in deductive or inductive inference. See also **deductive inference** and **deductive reasoning**. 3.1

Proposition: A single declaration or report of facts or opinions. This term is often used interchangeably with the term "statement." See also **statement**. 1.1

Propositional Logic: A type of logic that deals with statements and their relationship to each other. 1.3

Qualitative Rules: Syllogistic rules that pertain to whether or not the propositions in a syllogism are positive or negative. See also **terminological rules**. 8.2

Quality: The aspect of a proposition describing whether or not it supports or denies something. 4.3

Quantifier: A word in a proposition, such as "all," "no," "some," and "some not," which signals the amount of a class that a proposition discusses. 4.3

Quantity: The aspect of a proposition describing whether or not the proposition discusses all or some things. 4.3

Questions: Sentences that raise issues and ideas by inquiring or asking another's perspective; they do not report facts or relationships of equivalence, which are the relationships that demonstrate which propositions are identical to other propositions. 4.3

Relationships of Equivalence: The relationships that demonstrate what can be inferred from propositions that are equivalent to each other. These relationships are used as a tool to change propositions into equivalent propositions. See also **contrapostion**, **conversion**, and **obversion**. 5.2

Relationships of Opposition: The relationships that demonstrate what can be inferred from propositions in opposition to each other in quality and quantity. See also **quality** and **quantity**. 5.2

Relevance: One of the three principles of critical thinking in which the premises of an argument provide some support for the conclusion. See also **clarity** and **presumption**. 3.1

Schema: The mood and figure of a syllogism. 7.5

Second-Order Enthymeme: A syllogism that omits the minor premise. 7.4

Self-Reports: Expressions of feeling or belief. 4.3

Simple Apprehension: The recognition and naming or classification of an object or concept. See also **acts of the mind**, **inference**, and **judgment**. 3.1

Sound Syllogism: A syllogism that is both true and valid. 8.1

Square of Opposition: A diagram that illustrates the relationships of opposition. See also **relationships of opposition**. 5.1

Standard-Form Syllogism: A syllogism written in categorical form with two premises and a conclusion. Each of the three propositions contained in a standard-form syllogism has a subject, verb, and a *copula*. See also *copula*. 7.2

Statement: A single declaration or report of facts or opinions. This term is used interchangeably with the term **proposition**. 1.1

Stipulative Definition: A definition for a word that is created *ad hoc* (on the spot) in order to add more clarity or to provide common ground in a discussion. 9.4

Stoics: A Greek school of philosophy founded in the third century BC. They studied logical problems, such as the liar's paradox, which transcended the boundaries of Aristotelian logic. 2.1

Straw Man Fallacy: A fallacy that occurs when a person draws a conclusion from a caricatured or otherwise distorted version of his opponent's argument. 9.6

Structural: A characteristic of formal logic that pertains to its investigation of the process through which an individual proceeds in order to reason from one statement or proposition to another. 3.1

Subcontrariety: A relationship of opposition that exists between *I* and *O* propositions. Subcontrary statements cannot both be false, but they can both be true. See also **contradiction**, **contrariety**, **subimplication**, and **superimplication**. 5.1

Subimplication: A relationship that exists between *A* and *I* propositions and *E* and *O* propositions. The truth of the universal implies the truth of the particular. Also referred to as "subalternation." See also **contradiction**, **contrariety**, **subcontrariety**, and **superimplication**. 5.1

Subject Term: The term in a proposition about which the proposition is written. It is the first noun term in the proposition. 4.4

Superimplication: The relationship of opposition that exists between *I* and *A* propositions and *O* and *E* propositions. The falsity of the particular implies the falsity of the universal. Also referred to as "superalternation." See also **contradiction**, **contrariety**, **subcontrariety**, and **subimplication**. 5.1

Syllogism: A deductive formal argument consisting of two premises followed by a conclusion. 3.1

Symbols: A sign or figure used to represent a word or concept. 1.1

T

Term: A word or phrase that represents a class of related things. 1.3

Terminological Rules: Syllogistic rules that apply to the terms in a syllogism. See also **qualitative rules**. 8.2

Theoretical Definition: A definition built upon a certain philosophical view of a word. 9.4

Thesis: The main idea or proposition of an argument. 3.1

Third-Order Enthymeme: A syllogism that omits the conclusion. 7.4

Translate: The act of putting an ordinary, everyday argument into categorical form. 4.1

True Syllogism: A syllogism that is factually accurate and correct. 8.1

Truth: A right understanding of reality. 1.1

Truth-Value: The truth or falsity of a proposition or statement . 4.3

U

Undistributed: A term is undistributed when only *some* of a class is referenced in a proposition. 8.3

Universal Affirmative: A proposition that affirms something about all of a category. See also **particular affirmative**, **particular negative**, and **universal negative**. 4.6

Universal Negative: A proposition that denies something about all of a category. See also **particular affirmative**, **particular negative**, and **universal affirmative**. 4.6

Universal Proposition: A statement that affirms or denies something about all of a category represented by a term. 4.6

Using the Complement: Providing the complement of a word in a proposition. See also **complement**. 6.3

V

Valid (or Validity): An adjective describing a deductive argument that is structured properly, or uses right reasoning form. Inductive arguments are considered "strong" or "weak," whereas deductive arguments are considered "valid" or "invalid." See also **invalid**. 1.1

Valid Syllogism: A syllogism that is structured correctly. 8.1

Venn Diagram: A diagram consisting of interlocking circles that illustrates the relationships between the three premises of a syllogism. 8.3

Verb of Being: Also known as "being verbs." Verbs such as *am*, *is*, *are*, *was*, *were*, *be*, *being*, and *been*, which serve as the *copula* of a proposition. See also *copula*. 4.5

BIBLIOGRAPHY

Adams, Douglas. Quotation #26280. *Quotations Page*. <http://www.quotationspage.com/quote/26280. html>.

Adams, John. "Be Yourselves, O Americans." *ProjectGutenberg.com*. <http://www.gutenberg.org/ ebooks/15391>.

Aquinas, Thomas. "Question 4, Article 3. Whether comprehension is necessary for happiness?" *Summa Theologica*. *NewAdvent.com*. <http://www.newadvent.org/summa/2004.htm>.

————."Question 5, Article 3. Whether one can be happy in this life?" *Summa Theologica*. <http:// www.newadvent.org/summa/2005.htm>.

Aristotle. "Aristotle Quotes." *BrainyQuotes.com*. <http://www.brainyquotes.com/quotes/quotes/a/ aristotle143026.html>.

Augustine. *City of God*. bk. 1, chap. 1. *NewAdvent.com*. <http://www.newadvent.org/fathers/120101.htm>.

————. *City of God*. bk. 5, chap. 13. *NewAdvent.com*. <http://www.newadvent.org/fathers/120105.htm>.

Barry, Dave. *ThinkExist.com*. <http://thinkexist.com/quotation/i_argue_very_well-ask_any_of_my_ remaining_friends/202498.html>.

Berry, Wendell. "Compromise, Hell!" in *The Way of Ignorance and Essays*, n.p. Berkeley, CA: Shoemaker and Hoard, 2005.

Brandeis, Louis. *WorldofQuotes.com*. <http://www.worldofquotes.com/topic/Logic/1/index.html>.

Carnegie, Andrew. "Famous Andrew Carnegie Quotes." <http://www.quotes.net/quote/3069>.

Carnegie, Dale. *QuoteDB.com*. <http://www.quotedb.com/quotes/845>.

Chesterton, G.K. *The Quotations Page*. <http://www.quotationspage.com/quotes/G._K._Chesterton/>.

Choate, Rufus. *Book of Famous Quotes*. <http://www.famous-quotes.com/author.php?aid=1499>.

Christie, Agatha. "Agatha Christie Quotes." *BrainyQuotes.com*. <http://www.brainyquotes.com/quotes/ authors/a/agatha_christie.html>.

Clouser, Roy. *The Myth of Religious Neutrality: An Essay on the Hidden Role of Religious Belief in Theories*. Notre Dame, IN: University of Notre Dame Press, 2005.

"Connections Between Logic and Humor, The." *The Evangelical Outpost: Reflections on Culture, Politics and Religion from an Evangelical Worldview*. <http://evangelicaloutpost.com/archives/2007/02/the-syllogisms-of-seinfeldthe-connections-between-logic-and-humor-2.html>.

Copi, Irving. *Introduction to Logic*. 5th ed. New York: Macmillan Publishing Co., 1978.

Cothran, Martin. *Traditional Logic: Advanced Formal Logic*. Louisville, KY: Memoria Press, 2000.

Curd, Patricia, ed., and Richard D. McKirahan, trans. *A Presocratic Reader*. Indianapolis: Hackett Publishing Company, Inc., 1995.

Declaration of Independence, The. *The Charters of Freedom: The Declaration*. <http://www.archives.gov/exhibits/charters/declaration_transcript.html>.

Define.com. <http://define.com/>.

Dickens, Charles. "Charles Dickens Quotes." *BrainyQuotes.com*. <http://www.brainyquotes.com/quotes/authors/c/charles_dickens.html>.

Doyle, Sir Arthur Conan. *The Adventure of the Empty House*. Project Gutenberg. <http://www.gutenberg.org/files/108/108-h/108-h.htm#linkH2H_4_0001>.

———. *A Study in Scarlet*. *Wikiquote.com*. <http://en.wikiquote.org/wiki/Sherlock_Holmes#A_Study_in_Scarlet_.281888.29>.

Evangelical Outpost: Reflections on Culture, Politics and Religion from an Evangelical World, The. <http://evangelicaloutpost.com/>.

Feinberg, Joel, and Russ Shafer-Landau. *Reason and Responsibility: Readings in Some Basic Problems of Philosophy*. Belmont, CA: Thompson Wadsworth, 2008.

Free Dictionary, The. <http://www.thefreedictionary.com/>.

Goldsmith, Oliver. *The Deserted Village*. Taken from *WorldofQuotes.com*. <http://www.worldofquotes.com/author/Oliver-Goldsmith/1/index.html>.

Gracian, Baltasar. *ThinkExist.com*. <http://thinkexist.com/quotation/don-t_take_the_wrong_side_of_an_argument_just/10365.html>.

Grant, Myrna R. *Poems for a Good and Happy Life*. New York: Random House, 1997.

Hamblin, C.L. *Fallacies*. London: Methuen, 1970.

Hamilton, Alexander, Harold Coffin Syrett, and Jacob Ernest Cooke. *The Papers of Alexander Hamiton*, <http://tinyurl.com/qdzz42t>. Accessed April 8, 2015.

Hansberry, Lorraine. *A Raisin in the Sun*. *TheQuoteGarden.com*. <http://www.quotegarden.com/thinking.html>.

Henschen, Beth, and Edward Sidlow. *America at Odds: The Essentials*. Florence, KY: Wadsworth, 2004.

Hooker, Richard. "Ancient Greece: Sparta." <http://matrix.msu.edu/hst/guide/history140r/unit6/mod/sparta.html>.

Hume, David. *QuotationsPage.com*. <http://www.quotationspage.com/quote/3615.html>.

"I Am Nobody" T-shirt. *Zazzle.com*. <http://www.zazzle.com/i_am_nobody_nobody_is_perfect_therefore_i_a_shirt-235163787612964834>.

Kelley, David. *The Art of Reasoning with Symbolic Logic*. New York: W.W. Norton and Company, 1990.

Kissell, Joe. "Zeno's Paradoxes: Proof That Motion Unexists." *Interesting Thing of the Day*. <http://itotd.com/articles/529/zenos-paradoxes/>.

King, Peter, and Stewart Shapiro. "The History of Logic." In *The Oxford Companion to Philosophy*. Oxford: Oxford University Press, 1995.

Kreeft, Peter. *Socratic Logic: A Logic Text Using Socratic Method, Platonic Question, and Aristotelian Principles*. 3rd ed. Sound Bend, IN: St. Augustine's Press, 2008.

Locke, John. "Quotes from John Locke." *ThinkExist.com*. <http://thinkexist.com/quotation/logic_is_the_anatomy_of/170278.html>.

"Lorelai's First Day at Yale, The." *Gilmore Girls.* Season 4, episode 2, WB. September 30, 2003.

Magee, Bryan. *The Story of Philosophy.* New York: Dorling Kinserly, 2001.

Marx, Karl. "The Communist Manifesto." *BrainyQuotes.com.* <http://www.brainyquotes.com/quotes/authors/k/karl_marx_3.html>.

McAdoo, William G. *The Quotations Page.* <http://www.quotationspage.com/quote/23566.html>.

McKeon, Richard. *The Basic Works of Aristotle.* From "Nichomachean Ethics." Bk 9, chap. 8. New York: Random House, Inc., 1941.

Merriam-Webster Online Dictionary. <http://www.merriam-webster.com/>.

Metaphysics Research Lab, The. *Stanford Encyclopedia of Philosophy.* <http://plato.stanford.edu/>.

Mill, John Stuart. "On Liberty." In *The Internet Encyclopedia of Philosophy: An Overview of John Stuart Mill.* <http://www.iep.utm.edu/m/milljs.htm#SH2e>.

Moncur, Michael. "Michael Moncur's (Cynical) Quotes." Quotation #1152. Aristotle. <http://www.quotationspage.com/quote/1152.html>.

Montaigne, Michel Eyquem De. *Book of Famous Quotes.* <http://www.famous-quotes.com/topic.php?tid=70>.

Monty Python and the Holy Grail. "She's a Witch." Transcript. From <http://www.youtube.com/watch?v=zrzMhU_4m-g>.

Online Etymology Dictionary. <http://www.etymonline.com/index.php>.

Pitt, William. "You Cannot Conquer America." *History Database Search.* <http://tinyurl.com/lguogmd>.

Plato. *Euthyphro. The Internet Classics Archive.* <http://classics.mit.edu/Plato/euthyfro.html>.

"Player Under Pressure." *Bones.* Season 3, episode 11. First aired April 21, 2008.

Pojman, Louis P. *Classics of Philosophy.* Vol. I, *Ancient and Medieval,* Plato, the *Apology.* New York: Oxford University Press, 1998.

Pooh, Winnie the. *ThinkExist.com.* <http://thinkexist.com/quotes/winnie_the_pooh/2.html>.

Retz, Cardinal de. *ThinkExist.com.* <http://thinkexist.com/quotations/arguments/>.

Robespierre, Maximilien. "Terror Is Nothing Else Than Justice." *Wikipedia.* <http://en.wikipedia.org/wiki/Maximilien_Robespierre>.

Rowling, J.K. *Harry Potter and the Sorcerer's Stone.* "Treebeard's Stumper Answer." <http://www.rain.org/~mkummel/stumpers/17mar00a.html>.

Sayers, Dorothy L. "Dorothy L. Sayers Quotes." *ThinkExist.com.* <http://thinkexist.com/quotes/dorothy_l._sayers/2.html>.

———. *Strong Poison.* New York: HarperCollins Publishers, 1930. Also available at <http://www.nonduality.com/hl1915.htm>.

Schagrin, Morton L. "Logic." In *World Book Encyclopedia.* New York: Scott Fetzer Company, 1992.

Scully, Dana, and Fox Mulder. "Quotes from *The X Files.*" *PlanetClaire.com.* <http://www.planetclaire.org/xfiles/dana_scully.php>.

Seinfeld, Jerry, and Elaine in "The Wink." In "The Syllogisms of Seinfeld: The Connections Between Logic and Humor," *The Evangelical Outpost: Reflections on Culture, Politics and Religion from an*

Evangelical Worldview. <http://evangelicaloutpost.com/archives/2007/02/the-syllogisms-of-seinfeldthe-connections-between-logic-and-humor-2.html>.

Shakespeare, William. *Julius Caesar*. Act 3, scene 2. <http://shakespeare.mit.edu/julius_caesar/julius_caesar.3.2.html>.

———. "A Midsummer Night's Dream." OpenSourceShakespeare.org. <http://tinyurl.com/ozbmdj3>.

———. "William Shakespeare Quotes." *BrainyQuotes.com*. <http://www.brainyquotes.com/quotes/authors/w/william_shakespeare.html>.

Simpson, Homer. *The Simpsons*. *ThinkExist.com*. <http://en.thinkexist.com/quotation/english-who_needs_that-i-m_never_going_to_england/338890.html>.

Southern, R.W. *The Making of the Middle Ages*. New Haven, CT: Yale University Press, 1953.

Spock. "I, Mudd." *Star Trek*, season 2, episode 8. Via IMDB.com. <http://www.imdb.com/title/tt0708432/quotes>.

———. "The Squire of Gothos." *Star Trek*, season 1, eposide 17. <http://www.imdb.com/title/tt0708478/quotes>.

Stanford Encyclopedia of Philosophy. <http://plato.stanford.edu/>.

Thompson, Dorothy. *ThinkExist.com*. <http://thinkexist.com/quotation/there_is_nothing_to_fear_except_the_persistent/338962.html>.

Tolkien, J.R.R. "J.R.R. Tolkien Quotes." *ThinkExist.com*. <http://thinkexist.com/quotes/j.r.r._tolkien>.

———. "J.R.R. Tolkien Quotes." *ThinkExist.com*. <http://thinkexist.com/quotes/j.r.r._tolkien/2.html>.

Thesaurus.com. <http://thesaurus.reference.com/>.

Webster's Ninth New Collegiate Dictionary. Springfield, MA: Merriam-Webster, 1983.

WhatHappensNow.com. <http://www.whathappensnow.com/articles_show.cfm?id=194&cat=5&sub=1>.

WordNetWeb, Princeton University. <http://wordnetweb.princeton.edu/perl/webwn?s=friend>.

Notes

Notes

Notes

Notes

Classical Subjects...

RHETORIC Alive!

...Creatively Taught

TEACHER'S EDITION

by Alyssan Barnes, PhD

BOOK 1:
PRINCIPLES OF PERSUASION

Rhetoric Alive! Book 1 explores the principles of winsome speech as developed in the foremost text on persuasion: Aristotle's *Rhetoric*. The 15 chapters of *Rhetoric Alive! Book 1* step through the essential components of persuasion—the 3 appeals, the 3 types of speech, and the 5 canons. Each chapter includes an exemplary classic text for analysis and discussion, spanning from Pericles's "Funeral Oration" to Martin Luther King, Jr.'s "Letter from Birmingham Jail."

THREE APPEALS
Ethos (speaker's credibility)
Pathos (audience's emotion)
Logos (argument's reasoning)

FIVE CANONS
Invention • Organization • Style
Memory • Delivery

THREE PARTS OF SPEECH
Deliberative (exhort or dissuade)
Ceremonial (praise or blame)
Judicial (accuse or defend)

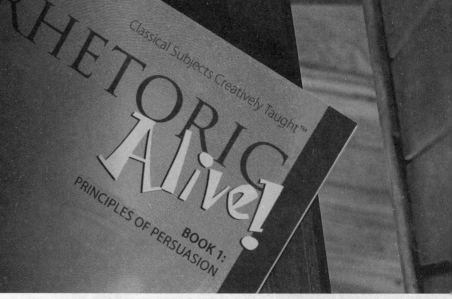

"This text has the potential to shake up English studies at the secondary level. It is a formidable and appealing innovation that is wonderfully old-fashioned and yet as fresh as anything I've seen in a long time."
—John Briggs, PhD, Director, University Writing Program, UC Riverside

www.ClassicalAcademicPress.com

WALKING TO WISDOM

LITERATURE GUIDE SERIES

LEWIS TOLKIEN SAYERS

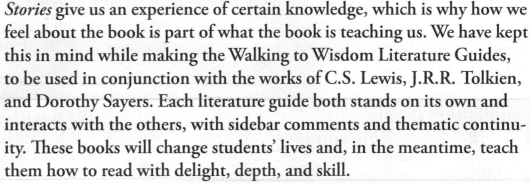

Stories give us an experience of certain knowledge, which is why how we feel about the book is part of what the book is teaching us. We have kept this in mind while making the Walking to Wisdom Literature Guides, to be used in conjunction with the works of C.S. Lewis, J.R.R. Tolkien, and Dorothy Sayers. Each literature guide both stands on its own and interacts with the others, with sidebar comments and thematic continuity. These books will change students' lives and, in the meantime, teach them how to read with delight, depth, and skill.

Our literature guides thoughtfully instill students with the following habits:
- taking notes in their books
- answering reading questions and creating their own questions
- keeping notes book-wide on themes and motifs
- answering discussion questions about thematic material
- memorizing important quotations
- preparing, while reading, to write
- participating in creative enrichment activities related to the books

"I believe that a large part of the value of reading great books is wrestling with the ideas and stories, and this series seems to be one of the best I've ever seen for accomplishing this." —Cathy Duffy